Casper Hauser

By

Jacob Wassermann

Table of Contents

1. The Strange Youth 4
2. Caspar Hauser's Story Recorded by Daumer 13
3. An Official of High Rank Looks Behind the Scenes 20
4. The Mirror Speaks 31
5. Caspar Dreams 46
6. Religion, Homeopathy and Visitors From Many Places 57
7. Daumer Puts Metaphysics To The Test 74
8. A Disguised Person Make His Appearance 89
9. The Heart Of The Blackbird 106
10. A Message From Far Away 118
11. The English Earl 132
12. The Secret Mission And What Prevented Its Execution 144
13. A Conversation Between one Who Remains Masked and One Who Discloses Himself 163
14. Night Will Come 182
15. A Chapter In Letters 189
16. Worship Of The Sun 211
17. Some Points About Herr Quandt As Well As About A Lady As Yet Unknown 223
18. Joseph And His Brethren 239
19. Castle Falkenhaus 247
20. Quandt Treads On Delicate Ground 260

21.	A Voice Calls	269
22.	A Journey Is Decided Upon	284
23.	The Journey Is Undertaken	299
24.	Schildknecht	309
25.	An Interrupted Performance	321
26.	Quandt Undertakes A Last Assault Upon The Mystery	333
27.	Aenigma Sui Temporis	346

1. The Strange Youth

In the early summer of the year 1828, there were curious rumors in Nurnberg concerning a person who was kept in custody in the Vestner tower of the castle, and who gave daily food for wonderment to the authorities and the townspeople.

He was a boy of about seventeen years. No one knew whence he came. He himself was not able to give any information, for he could not speak more than a two year old child. Few were the words he could pronounce clearly and he repeated these constantly, sometimes plaintively, then again cheerfully, as though there were no meaning to back them, and as though there were merely tokens of an anxiety or a pleasure which he did not understand. His walk, too, was that of a child which had just learned to take his first steps. He did not place his heel on the ground first but would put his whole foot awkwardly and cautiously.

The citizens of Nurnberg are and inquisitive lot. Every day hundreds of them would climb the Castle Hill and ascend the ninety-two steps of the grim old tower to behold the stranger. It was forbidden to enter the half-dark cell where the prisoner was kept, and so in great crowds they started from the threshold and at the remarkable human being that cowered in the farthest corner of the room, generally playing with a small white horse. He had seen it accidently in the possession of the children of the warden, and, touched by his helpless stammering way of asking for it, they gave it to him. His eyes did not seem able to comprehend light; and when he lifted his groping hand it seemed as if the air offered a mysterious resistance.

What a pitiful object, people said. Many thought that a new species had been discovered, perhaps some kind of cave dweller, and among the curious reports not the least strange was that the boy rejected with horror any form of nourishment except bread and water.

Gradually the circumstances surrounding the boy's sudden appearance became public knowledge. On Whit-Monday about five o' clock in the afternoon he has suddenly appeared, standing on the Unschlitt Square not far from the New gate; he had looked about for a while in a disturbed fashion and then he tottered into the arms of the shoemaker, Weikmann, who happened to come along at the moment. His trembling finger pointed to a letter bearing the address of Calvary Captain Wessenig, and, with help of several other people along the road, was dragged with great difficulty to the Captain's house. There he fell exhausted on the steps, blood trickling through his torn shoes.

The captain did not come home until twilight and his wife then told him of the starving creature, hardly a human being, who was sleeping on the straw in the stable. She also gave him the letter. The captain, after breaking the seal, read it through several times with the greatest astonishment; the communication facetious in some ways, was savagely explicit in others. He went to the stable and had the stranger wakened, which was accomplished with great effort. The military precision of the officer's questions elicited no replies from the boy, just meaningless sounds. Herr von Wessenig quickly decided to send the strange fellow to the police station.

This undertaking was difficult, for the stranger could now scarcely walk. Blood prints marked his path; he had to be dragged through the streets like a balky calf, and the holidaymakers returning from their outings enjoyed the spectacle. "What's the matter?" asked those who were not so near the unusual hubbub. "Oh, they are just helping a drunk peasant walk," was the answer

At the police station the clerk tried in vain to examine the prisoner. He constantly stammered the same half-idiotic words, and abuse and threats were of no avail. When one of the soldiers struck a light a curious incident occurred. With his body, the boy made jumping gestures like a dancing bear, his legs not joining in the motion, and snatched at the candle flame with his hands, but when he felt the burn he began to cry so bitterly that the observers shuddered to their very marrow.

Finally, the clerk had the idea of offering him a piece of paper and a pencil and the strange boy snatched at them, and with big childish letters slowly formed the words 'Caspar Hauser'. After this he staggered to a corner, dropped heavily on the floor and fell into a deep sleep.

Because Caspar Hauser—for so the stranger was called from now on—on his arrival had been dressed in peasant-fashion in an old frock coat from with the skirts had been cut, a red tie and high leather boots, it was at first thought that he must have been the son of a nearby peasant who had been neglected in some fashion, or stunted in his development. The first one who emphatically contradicted this assumption was the warden of the prisoner tower. "No peasant looks like that," said he, pointing to the wavy light brown hair of his charge, which had the inexpressible sheen and luster of the fur of animals that lived in the dark. "And such fine white hands, such velvety skin, and these delicate temples and the blue veins showing in the neck, he really looks more like a young lady of aristocratic birth than a peasant."

"Not badly observed," said the municipal court doctor, who in his deposition, duly entered on the blotter, stressed not only these points, but also the peculiar formation of the knee and the absence of callous skin on the soles of the feet. "One thing is evident," his testimony concludes, "we are dealing with a person who has no conception of his fellow men, does not eat, does not drink, does not feel, does not speak like others, does not know anything of yesterday or tomorrow, does not grasp time, does not know he is alive."

The worthy police magistrates did not permit this judgement to swerve them from the prescribed formalities in examinations of this kind. They suspected that the police court doctor had been influenced and misled by his friend, Professor Daumer, a teacher in the gymnasium, to the of indulging in such vagaries. The prison warden, whose name was Hill, was ordered to watch the stranger without arousing his suspicion. He often peeked through a hidden hole in the door when the boy had every reason to think he was alone, but he always beheld a sober sadness in his features, now impassive and indifferent, now contracted and distorted with some invisible fear. It was also in vain that the warden slipped into the boy's bed at night, when he has asleep, and knelt to listen to his breathing or wait for words betraying the sleeper's inner thoughts.

For people who harbor evil thoughts frequently speak in their sleep, also they prefer to sleep by day rather than by night when they can work out their schemes and plots. But this boy fell asleep as soon as the sun set and woke up when the first rays of morning came through the closed shutters. It might seem suspicious that he startled every time the door to his prison was opened, but probably this resulted not from a bad conscience, but from an unusual irritability in his senses, which suffered from the approach of any noise from the outside.

"Our friends at city hall will have to waste a lot more paper if they want to get anywhere along these lines," said good old Hill one morning—it was the third day of Caspar Houser's imprisonment—to Professor Daumer who came to visit the boy. "I know all the tricks of the rogues, but if this boy is a pretender you may hang me."

Hill unlocked the cell and Professor Daumer walked in. As usual the prisoner was frightened, but when his visitor was once in the room Caspar Hauser no longer seemed aware of his presence and sat in a dull, unknowing torpor staring straight ahead.

Then it happened that, when Hill had opened the shutters of the windows, the boy, perhaps for the first time in his life, raised his fettered eyes and turning from the silent continuous fear which seemed to dwell in his breast, he gazed out into the sunny open space where row upon row of brightly red-tiled roofs rose against the background of hazy blue fields and woods. He stretched out his hand, and expression of surprise and joyless astonishment overspread his face. Hesitatingly he stretched his arm out into the glowing picture, as if he wanted to seize this array of brilliancy with his fingers, but when he had convinced himself that it was nothing—something distant and intangible and deceptive—his face darkened and he turned away annoyed and disappointed.

The same afternoon Mayor Binder came to Daumer's house and, discussing the strange waif's case, told Daumer that the city magistrates were inclined to be hostile and skeptical rather than kindly toward the young man.

"Skeptical?" replied Daumer, puzzled. "Skeptical in regards to what?"

"Well, they're inclined to think that the boy is hoodwinking us," rejoined the Mayor.

Daumer shook his head. "What human being with a sense or ability would consent to live on bread and water for the pleasure of deceiving others, and to reject with disgust everything that is pleasing to the palate?' he asked. "And for what advantage?"

"Nevertheless," replied Binder hesitatingly, "it seems a complicated story. Since no one can guess what he is driving at, it is all the more necessary to be careful for careless gullibility on our part will expose us to ridicule."

"That almost sounds as though only those who doubt and deny could be called capable of judging," remarked Daumer, wrinkling his forehead. "Of that ilk we have, unfortunately, plenty."

The mayor shrugged his shoulders and looked at the young teacher with the gentle irony that is the armor of the experienced in dealing with enthusiasts. "We have decided upon a fresh examination by the court doctor," he continued. "Magistrate Behold, Baron Tucher and you, my dear Daumer, are to attend the examination as a commission. The minutes will then be sent to the District Government along with the police reports which already have."

"I understand: reports, reports, reports," said Daumer, smiling sarcastically.

The Mayor placed his hand on the young man's shoulder and said good-naturedly: "Don't be superior, my worthy friend, our world does taste of ink, and certainly you bookworms are not without responsibility in the matter. Moreover," he put his hand in his breast pocket and took out a folded piece of paper, "as a member of the commission you are duly requested to consider an important document. This is the letter which our prisoner gave Captain Wessenig. Read it."

The unsigned letter reads as follows: "I am sending you a boy, Captain, who wishes to become a soldier and serve his king faithfully. The boy was brought to me in 1815; one winter night he was suddenly found lying at my door. I have children myself, am poor, I can hardly make both ends meet; he's a foundling and I have not been able to ascertain his mother. I have never let him stir out of the house, no one knows about him; he does not know the name of my house, nor does he know the village. You may ask him but he won't be able to talk decently. If he had parents—which he hasn't—he might have entered a decent calling; you need only show him anything and he will able to do it at once. I took him out of the house in the middle of the night and he has no money about him, so if you don't want to keep him you will have to kill him and hang him down the chimney."

When Daumer had read the paper he returned it to the Mayor, and walked up and down with a serious look.

"Well, what do you make of it?" inquired Binder. "Some of the gentleman thinks the stranger might have written the letter himself."

Daumer stopped his walk with a sudden halt, wrung his hands and exclaimed, "Why, in heaven's name?"

"Of course, there's no reason," hastily added the Mayor. "It is evident that the writing of the letter was dictated by some cunning plan to mislead, and to obstruct any investigation. There is a cynical indifference about the letter which has lead me from the beginning to suspect that the boy is the blameless victim of a crime."

The Mayor's daring surprise found district support in an incident which occurred shortly after the members of the commission entered Casper Hauser's cell the next morning. While he warden was undressing the boy, a peasant band suddenly began to play below on one of the Castle Hill alleys, blaring loudly as the players passed along the wall. Caspar's body trembled in a horrible way. His face, even his hands burst into perspiration, his eyes rolled, every fiber of his body became tense from fright, then he uttered an animal cry and fell to the ground, where he lay shaking and sobbing.

The men turned white and stared at one another helplessly. After a while Daumer walked up to the unfortunate boy, laid his hand on his head and spoke to him consolingly. This had a soothing effect and he became quiet. Nevertheless, the tremendous impression of the sounds he had heard seemed to have wounded his body externally and internally; for days he continued to show evidences of the shock he had experienced; he lay in a fever on his sack of straw, his skin of a citron hue. Kindly questioning gained his deep sympathy, and he would try to find words to show his appreciation, which caused his usually bright eyes to grow dark and troubled. Particularly towards Professor Daumer, who came to see him two or three times a day, he showed a touching gratitude, now silent, now fumbling for words.

On one of these visits when Daumer was left alone with the boy for the first time; the warden at his request had locked the door downstairs. He sat close to the prisoner, talking, questioning, and probing. It was a vain expenditure of affection, patience and ingenuity. Finally he contented himself with a close observation of the boy's behavior and bearing. Suddenly Caspar emitted the usual confused sounds; he appeared to be asking for something and peered searchingly around. Daumer soon guessed, and handed him the pitcher filled with water which Hill had placed on the bench by the stove. Caspar too the pitcher, put it to his lips and drank. He drank in long gulps, with complete surrender, his eyes shining with ecstasy, as though forgetting for the brief moment of pleasure that his demoniacal pursuers were pressing in upon him from all sides.

Daumer fell into a state of unusual excitement. When he reached home he walked up and down his study for half an hour with long strides. Towards eight o'clock there was a knock on the door; his sister came in and called him to supper.

"What do you think, Anna," he called to her eagerly and with significance, "twice two makes four, doesn't it?"

"It appears to," replied the young girl, laughing with surprise, "everyone says so. Have you discovered it to be otherwise? It would be just like you, subversive wretch!"

"Not just that, but something of the sort," said Daumer gayly, placing his arm on his sister's shoulder. "I am going to lead our good Philistines a merry dance; yes, I'll have them dancing with astonishment."

"It has something to do with the foundling? Are you planning anything with him? Be careful, Friedrich, don't get into trouble. You're not as popular as it is."

"Certainly," said he, quickly discouraged, "the multiplication table might come to harm."

"Does one still know nothing about the rare bird?" asked Daumer's mother, a gentle old lady at dinner.

Daumer shook his head. "For the present, one can only conjecture; soon we shall know," he replied, with his gaze fixed on the ceiling.

The next day the *Morgenpost* had an article called "Who is Caspar Hauser?" Although there was no reader who could answer this question, the crowd of persons moved by curiosity became so great that the Mayor was obligated to issue strict regulations for visiting hours. At times people stood packed close together in front of the open door, and on every face appeared the same questions.

"What is the matter with him? What kind of person is he? Why can ne not understand the words yet speak? How can he fail to recognize objects and yet be able to see? He has hardly stopped crying before he begins to laugh; he seems guileless and yet he's so secretive. And perhaps there is some misdeed and disgrace behind those innocent bright eyes."

The prisoner was no doubt painfully aware of the prudent curiosity with the people started at him and perhaps it was a desire to satisfy them which produced the first glimmer of the mental dawn that slowly restored his own past within him, so that he sought in his uneasy heart for what he had been. Seeking for the past, he perhaps first felt it and it connected it with the present, and filled with the deepest horror, he learned to measure time and the change it had wrought in him; he tried to relate what he saw to what he had seen. He grasped the demand in the question and beheld the way in which he could satisfy the inquiring faces.

With hungry senses he sought the releasing word. His supplicating glance dragged words from the mouths of men capable of speech.

Here Daumer was in his element. He was able ultimately to do what doctor, warden, mayor, and especially the clerks, had entirely failed to accomplish for it required care and systematic patience. He became so occupied with the foundling that he forgot his studies and his private obligations; he almost neglected his duties; he seemed like a man whom fate has presented with an experience destined for him alone, and offered a happy corroboration of his whole life and thought. Among his notes on Caspar Hauser there was one which read as follows:

"This trembling figure, helpless in a strange world, this torpid glance, this expression stamped with fear, this noble forehead, combined with a somewhat underdeveloped chin and mouth, from which peace and purity radiate, are for me evidences of an indomitable power of understanding. If the conjectures which suggest to me prove to be correct, if I can dig up the roots of his being and make his branches bloom, I shall show the jaded world a mirror of untainted humanity; then people will see that there are valid proofs for the existence of the soul which all the idolaters of today deny with base vehemence."

The eager pedagogue had a difficult road to travel. In the stage at which he was obligated to begin his labors, human speech was a shadowy unreal thing; word after word had first to have meaning attached to it; memory has to be awakened; cause and effect had to be shown in their relations. Between one question and the next there lay worlds of understanding; a yes or a no, often interpolated helplessly, was of no avail where every conception had first to be evolved out of darkness, and understanding halted from word to word. And yet light, as if from a far distant past, seemed to give the boy's spirit wings, so that he progressed far more rapidly than even the hopeful Daumer himself had dared to expect. It was astonishing with what ease and force he retained what had once been said, and how he produced from a chaos of lifeless sounds, as if by magic, what had living and plastic importance for him. It seemed to Daumer as though he were merely observing a slowly resurrecting memory. He seemed to hold the boy's body, while his spirit returned to the regions from which it had come, bringing tidings which no ear had ever heard.

2. Caspar Hauser's Story Recorded by Daumer

So far as Caspar could remember he had always been in the same dark space, never anywhere else, always in the same space. Never had he seen a man, never had he heard his step, never had he heard his voice, never the song of a bird, never the cry of an animal; he had never seen the rays of the sun, nor the gleam of moonlight. He had never been aware of anything except himself, and yet he had known nothing of himself, never becoming conscious of loneliness.

The room must have been very narrow, for he thought that he had once touched the opposite walls with his outstretched arms. Before this, it had seemed immeasurably large; chained to his bed of straw without seeing his chain, Caspar had never left the spot of ground on which he slept and waked dreamlessly. Twilight and darkness were indifferentiated, therefore he must have known day and night. He did not know their names, but he did see darkness, for when he woke up in the night the walls had disappeared.

He had no measure of time. He could not say when this unfathomable loneliness had begun, and there was no time at which he thought it might ever end. He did not feel any change in his body, he did not wish that anything might be different from what it was, nothing casual frightened him, no hope of anything to come drew him on, and the past had no words. The regulated hours of this scarcely conscious life passed silently, and his inner being was as silent as the air which surrounded him.

When he awoke in the morning he found fresh bread near his bed and the water pitcher filled. At times the water did not taste the same; when he had drunk it, he lost his liveliness and fell asleep. Then, when he woke up, he had to take the pitcher in his hand very often, he held it for a long time to his mouth, but no water came out any more. He constantly put it down and waited to see whether the water would not come soon, because he did not know that someone had to fetch it, for he had no conception that anyone existed besides himself. On the days he found clean straw on his bed, a fresh shirt on his body, his nails cut, his hair shorter and his skin clean. All this had happened while he was asleep, without his having noticed it, and it left no after thoughts to disturb his mind.

Caspar Hauser was not entirely alone; he had a comrade. He possessed a little white wooden horse, a nameless motionless thing which at the same time was something in which his own being was darkly mirrored. Since he dimly conceived that it was a living form, he regarded it as his equal, and all the light of its outer world was centered in the dull glance of its artificial pearl eyes. He did not play with it, he did not even converse silently with it, and although it stood on a little board with wheels he never thought of pushing it about. But before he ate his bread he passed every bite to the horse before putting it into his own mouth, and before he fell asleep he stroked it with a caressing hand.

This was his sole occupation, for many days and for many years.

Then it happened that once while he was awake the wall opened and, from the never seen outside, there appeared a huge figure, the first other person who uttered the word "thee" and whom Caspar therefore called the Thee. The ceiling of the room rested upon his shoulders, there was something incomprehensibly buoyant and lithe in the movements of his limbs, there was a noise about him which filled the ear, sound after sound flowed rapidly from his lips; the light in his eyes compelled breathless listening, and about his clothes there was the overwhelming smell of the beyond.

Of the many words which came out of the mouth of the Thee, Caspar at first understood not a one, but though excited attention he gradually comprehended that this extraordinary giant wanted to take him away, that the thing which had shared his solitude was called a horse, and that he should have other horses and that he should learn.

"Learn," repeated the Thee constantly, "learn, learn." And in order to make clear to Caspar what this meant, he placed a bench with four round feet in front of him, put a piece of paper on it and wrote the name "Caspar Hauser" twice, and then directed Caspar's hand in rewriting it. This pleased Caspar, for it was black and white.

Then the Thee placed a book on the stool and, pointing to the tiny signs, he spoke the words. Caspar could repeat them all without having in the least understood them. He also babbled after him some other words and expressions which the man told him; for example: "I should like to become a horseman like my father."

The Thee seemed satisfied. In any case, as a reward he showed him that the wooden horse could be pushed along the floor, and Caspar amused himself with this when he awoke the next morning. He pushed the little horse up and down in front of his bed and this made a noise which hurt his ears; he therefore ceased and began to talk to the horse, repeating the incomprehensible sounds which he had heard out of the mouth of the Thee. It was a wonderful pleasure for him to hear himself, and he lifted up his arms and filled the room with his joyous babble.

Probably this irritated and disturbed his jailer, who no doubt wished to silence him. Suddenly Caspar saw a stick swing over his shoulder and simultaneously felt such a severe pain in his arm that he fell forward from fright. In the midst of his anxiety he made the astonishing discovery that he was no longer chained to his bed. For a while he remained quite still, then he tried to slide forwards, but the touch of his bare feet on the cold earth made him shudder. With difficulty he reached his bed and fell asleep at once.

Night and day returned three times before the Thee returned and tried to see whether Caspar could write his name and read the words out of his book. He did not conceal his astonishment when the boy was able to do this with ease. He pointed to objects in the room and pronounced their names; he spoke slowly to Caspar, looking him steadily in the eye, and holding him by the shoulder; by means of his glances, his gestures and the expression of his features Caspar understood, what he said and he shuddered while obeying the man, with a stammering tongue.

During the following night he was roused from his sleep. He felt the attempts to wake him long and painfully, but he could not quite wake up. When he finally opened his eyes the wall was open and a purple-red light flooded the room. The Thee was bending over him and speaking gently, perhaps in order to calm his fears. He sat him up, dressed him in trousers, a shirt and boots, then stood on his feet, leaned him against the wall and turned his back upon him. He seized his legs, picked him up and Caspar clasped his arms around his neck, and then they went up what seemed to Caspar a steep hill; actually it was probably the steps of an underground prison. The breathing of the man resounded frighteningly, something cool and damp struck Caspar in the face and settled in his hair which began to move on its own accord and stuck to his skin.

Suddenly the darkness gave away; it rushed to the ground, everything became broad and soft and yet remained dark; in the distant depths great strange things rose up, from above a blue beam broke and was lost again; the slippery damp blew the folds off their clothes and penetrating smells surrounded them. Caspar began to cry and fell asleep on the man's back.

On waking up he lay on the ground, his face turned towards the earth, and from beneath him the cold streamed into his body. The Thee sat him up. The air burned curiously and an unbearable bright light fitted before his eyes. The Thee made him understand that he must learn to walk, and holding him under his arms from behind, he struck his head against his breast, thus ordering him to look on the ground. Caspar obeyed, swayed and trembling, the air and the brightness burned his eyelids, the smells made him dizzy and he lost his senses.

Again he slept, for how long he did not know; nor did he know how often he had tried to walk before it again became dark. At times he thought night had come on again, whereas they were only in the woods. He did not take in the road; he did not know whether they went up or down hill. Whether there were trees or meadows or houses, he did not know. At times everything seemed steeped in a red glow, but when softness and darkness came to earth and air stretched ahead blue and green. Whether people passed he was not pouring water on him; he pointed to the air and said: "Rain, rain."

How long had he been thus under way he did not know. It seemed to him every time he lay down exhausted from walking, a day had passed. Fear drove him on and mastered his fatigue; it stretched his muscles and kept his head up, whereas his eyes constantly moved over the ground. The Thee gave him the same bread that he had eaten in his prison and let him drink water out of a bottle. He sought to conquer Caspar's exhaustion and his anxiety when the wind howled through the bushes, or when an animal screamed, or when the grass rustled under his feet, by the promise of beautiful horses, and when Caspar was able to make continuous effort at walking, he said they would now soon be there. He pointed into the distance with his arm and said: "Big City."

Caspar did not see anything; he staggered on. After a time the Thee tugged him by the arm as a sign to stand still, gave him a letter and said, with his mouth close to Caspar's ear: "Get someone to show you where the letter goes."

Caspar walked on a few steps and when he looked around the Thee had disappeared. Suddenly he felt stones under his feet, he groped in every direction for a support, he saw stone walls which glowed in the sunlight, but horror first seized him when he became aware of people; first one person, then two, then many. They came frightfully near to him, they surrounded him, they shouted at him, one took hold of him and dragged him forward, all about him was noise and confusion. He wanted to sleep, they did not understand him; he spoke of his father, of his horses: they laughed and did not understand him. He slept in the Captain's stable, then other figures appeared again, only to disappear with unaccountable dispatch. The air was heavy and he could scarcely breathe; the monstrous things, for such the houses seemed to him, pressed upon him, and in the police station the wild countenances and gestures of the people frightened him so that he took refuge in tears.

Again he slept for a long time, after which he was taken to the tower. The man who led him up the big staircase spoke to him in a loud voice and opened the door which echoed strangely. Scarcely had he lain down on a bag of straw, when the tower clock began to strike, which filled him with boundless astonishment. He listened tensely, but little by little the sounds ceased, his alertness abated and he felt only the burning of his feet. His eyes did not pain him, for it was dark. He sat up, waiting to reach for the little pitcher in order to quench his thirst. He saw no water and no bread; instead he saw a floor quite different from the one where he had been previously. Now he wanted to reach for his little horse in order to play with it, but it was not there, and he said: "I should like to become a rider like my father."

This was intended to mean: "Where are the water, and the bread, and the little horse?"

He noticed the bag of straw on which he lay and observed it with astonishment, and did not know what it was. Striking it with his finger he heard the same sound that had always come from the straw in his bed. This quieted him so that he fell asleep again and did not wake up until he was awakened in the middle of the night by the repeated pealing of the great bell. He listened for a long time, and when the sounds had died away he saw the stove, which was green in color and had luster—for Caspar was able to differentiate colors even in the profoundest darkness. He regarded it very intently and murmured again, "I should like to become a rider like my father."

This meant: "What is that thing and where am I?" It also expressed his desire for the shining object.

In the morning the warden opened the shutters of the windows and the bright daylight hurt Caspar's' eyes; he began to cry and said, "Tell me where the letter belongs," by which he meant to say "Why do my eyes hurt? Tale away what's burning me and give me back the little horse and don't bother me." For in his mind he conversed with the Thee from whom he thought he might obtain aid. He heard the clock strike again and this took away half his pain; and while he was listening a man came and asked him all sorts of questions, but Caspar did not answer because his attention was fixed upon the last reverberations of the sound. The man took him by the chin, raised his head and spoke in a loud voice. Now Caspar heard him and repeated all the words he learned, but the man did not understand him. He let go his head, sat down next to Caspar, and continued to question him. When the clock struck again Caspar said, "I should like to become a rider like my father."

This was intended to mean: "Give me the thing that sounds so beautifully."

The man did not understand him and continued to talk, and Caspar began to cry and said, "Give the horse," which meant that the man was to please stop bothering him.

He sat alone for a long time. From a great distance came the sound of a trumpet from the royal stables, and when another man came in Caspar repeated the formula about the letter, which meant: "Don't you know what that is?" The man brought the water pitcher and let Caspar drink; this put him in good spirits and he said, "I want to become a rider like my father," This meant: "Now water you must not go away any more." Soon the trumpet blew again, and Caspar listened joyously. He thought that when his little horse came he would tell him what he had heard.

But on this day the tormenting he was to endure from so many persons began.

3. An Official of High Rank Looks Behind the Scenes

Of course it took Professor Daumer many weeks to obtain such complete insight into the boy's past. To bring these facts to light, to make them clear and tangible, had much resembled the work of digging a well. What had at first seemed like a delirious dream, now assumed traits of reality.

Daumer did not fail to present the situation to the authorities in a conscientiously prepared paper. The result was that this magistrate decided to give up the resort to formal interviews and to begin a course of intimate association with the unfortunate boy. The striking peculiarities of his personality were to be examined once again, was the suggestion recorded in one of the legal comments. Hence the doctors, scholars, police officials, shrewd lawyers, in short, countless persons who had interest themselves in his fate of their own accord, were sent to see him at the tower. There was an endless snooping and discussion, incredulity and astonishment, but the various explanations all led to one conclusion, and the naked eye could do no better than confirm Daumer's report.

A few days later, early in July, the Mayor published a proclamation which roused great astonishment and uneasiness all over the country. After describing Caspar Hauser's appearance, and after repeating with great detail the boy's own story, the writer described him himself. He spoke of the gentleness and goodness of the boy which charmed all who came in contact with him; how at first he had thought affectionately of his oppressor and always been moved to tears, and now was conscious only of being released, and of how touching was his devotion to those who frequently came near him, of his undoubted readiness for the right conduct, associated with some conception of evil; and further, of his extraordinary desire for knowledge.

"All of these circumstances," continued the eloquent decree, "in the same measure that they corroborate the boy's memories, convince us that he is endowed with splendid qualities of heart and mind, and justify the suspicion that some great crime is connected with his former incarceration, which deprived him of parents, freedom, fortune, perhaps even of the advantages of high birth; in any case, of the greatest pleasures of childhood and the chief blessings of life."

This was a bold and pregnant hypothesis, which did more honor to the Lord Mayor's kind heart and romantic spirit than to the circumspection normally characteristic of his high office.

"There are many indications," the decree continued, "that the crime was committed at a time when the boy has already acquired the power of speech and the rudiments of a distinguished education, which shines in his character like a beacon of light in the darkness. The most earnest appeal is therefore made to all legal, police, civil and military authorities, and to everyone who has a human heart in his breast, to make known to the authorities even the slightest traces and grounds of suspicion. And this not for the purpose of getting rid of Caspar Hauser; for the municipality which has taken him in loves him, and regards him as a gage of love sent by Providence, and would not give him up to anyone without excellent evidence, but rather wishes to discover the crime, and to punish the criminal and those allied with him."

Probably the authors hoped a great deal from this manifesto, but the matter took quite an unexpected turn and created some embarrassment for the gentleman of Nurnberg. At first a lot of silly and libelous accusations were received concerning more than one noble family, and the intimate lives of the aristocracy were exposed. Murders of children, kidnappings and substitutions of children, were, according to the populace, crimes which people in high positions indulged in daily for their pleasure.

What was worse, the Mayor's official notice came to the ears of the Supreme Court of the Rezat District unofficially. Some angry judge of this court at once wrote in great heat to the court in Ansbach that, in the first place, the proclamation of the Mayor of Nurnberg was against the law; secondly it was characterized as quixotic and furthermore, he complained bitterly that the premature publication of these important facts would make a criminal investigation, if not vain, at least very much more difficult. The angry judge, therefore, urged the authorities to hold the Mayor strictly to account and to send on the police records regarding the case to him at once.

The authorities did not need a second admonition. They addressed a rescript to the commissioner of the city of Nurnberg to say that the story of the life history of the foundling was so grossly improbable that one could not help suspecting some gross deception. At the same time the copies of the *Intelligenzblatt* and of the *Friedens und Kriegs-Kurier* which were still available, were confiscated. This was reported to the appellate court in due course and the question raised whether legal proceedings should be resorted to against the prisoner.

The city authorities were struck dumb with fear. In great haste they packed up the papers regarding the boy and sent them to Ansbach by the express post. Perhaps they thought the matter was now adjusted, but the angry judge raised his voice again. "The examination of the prisoner and of the witnesses, according to the records submitted, is not above reproach," he stormed. "By no means all of the persons who first came into contact with the boy have been examined by the police. Furthermore, in order to provide a proper legal basis for the publication of the government's findings, the records of Professor Daumer's conversations with the foundlings should have been included among the papers."

The government, as its final admonition, warned the Mayor against one-sided proceedings. Whereupon the Mayor, in an attack of indignant rage, retorted that the measures which they demanded involved a danger of retarding the progress of the disclosures, and this complaint the high authorities denied with hot emphasis. Make good your omissions, they demanded; register examinations and send documents, documents, nothing but documents.

Professor Daumer had followed the proceedings with concealed rage. He denounced the proceedings of the Ansbach authorities as disgusting bureaucratic pettifogging, and thought seriously of expressing his disgust in a defiant letter to the government. His friends restrained him with difficulty from doing this. "But something must be done!" he answered them, horrified.

"They are in the best way to commit legal murder and shall I sit with my hands idle?"

"The wisest thing to do," replied Freiherr von Tucher, "would be to appeal personally to Staatsrat Feuerbach."

"That would mean go to Ansbach?"

"Certainly."

"Do you think that he, as president of the appellate court, is already familiar with the doings of his subordinates and perhaps disapproves of them?"

"However that may be, I think something would come of a discussion face to face. I know Herr von Feuerbach, he is the last person to close his ear to the demands of justice."

The trip was agreed upon. The next day already found Daumer and Herr van Tucher in Ansbach. Unfortunately, President Feuerbach was off on a trip of inspection in the district, but was expected back in five days, so that the two men, in order to carry out their purpose, had to prolong their stay in the old provincial capital beyond their expectations.

In the meantime the foundling had a bad time of it. The tower in which he was imprisoned was the goal of all the idlers and curiosity seekers in town. People hurried there as to exhibition of some strange amusing object, for the Mayor's proclamation had made the boy public property. Those who had protected him up to now became a little more reserved, for no one knew how the thing would end, and whether some all-knowing appellate court would not dare to interfere with the general amusement of the populace; the Mayor himself had rescinded his former regulations, because it seemed worthwhile for as many people as possible to see the stranger. He was often sorry for the helpless boy, but on the other hand his vanity was flattered at being the master of such a prodigy though whom, moreover, quite the number of pennies found their way into the public coffers.

When morning came and Caspar Hauser got up from his bed curiously tired, with his eyes avoiding light, he would sit sadly and silently in a corner while Hill shook up a bag of straw and brought water and bread. Even at this early hour the first visitors began to appear, those whose occupations made them perforce rise betimes, street sweepers, servant girls, bakers' boys, mechanics on their way to work, boys who wished to punctuate pleasantly their hard road to school; and even the disreputable sight of the shabby gentlemen who had spent the night in the gutter of in a barn was not lacking.

As the day progressed the company became more refined; whole families came: the accountant with his wife and child, the major, Schneidermeister Bugelfleiss, Graf Rotstrumpf with his ladies, Herr von Uebel and Herr von Struebel, who interrupted their morning walks for the purpose of gazing at this curiosity.

It was a gay affair; they conversed, they whispered, they laughed, they joked and exchanged opinions. They were generous and brought the boy all kinds of presents, which he looked at just as a dog, who has not yet learned to fetch and carry, looks at the stick which his master has thrown for him. They put food in front of him to tempt his appetite; for example, the wife of Kanzleirat Zahnlos—teeth-less—brought a whole leg of ham, which it is true disappeared before the next day: no one knew whither, although certain important deductions were made.

Above all the cry was "Show us the wonder, show us the wonder which has caused so much talk." But when the silent, gentle boy did not do any of the things which their eager expectations had led them to imagine, they began either to scold—as though they had paid an entrance fee and had been cheated—or they committed the most astonishing stupidities. By worrying him constantly with questions as to where he came from, what his name was, how old he was, and so forth, they induced in themselves a superior feeling of cleverness and sophistication. His supplicating shake of his head, his senseless yes or no, which sounded simultaneously timid and merry, as from the mouth of a child, his stammering and his credulous attentiveness, all contributed to their sense of well-being. Some brought their faces very close to his, and were very much amused when he was obviously frightened at their strange gaze. They felt his hair and his hands and his feet, forced him to walk about the room, showed him pictures which they wanted him to explain and acted with simulated affection towards him, whereat they winked slyly at one another.

But these adventurous spirits soon became bored with the pointlessness of these pranks. They wanted to make sure that it was really true that the prisoner rejected all nourishment but bread and water: they held meat or sausage, honey or bread, milk or wine, in front of his face, and were vastly amused when the boy went quite beside himself with disgust. "What an actor!" they screeched; 'he behaves as though he disdained our delicacies; probably got indigestion in the kitchen of some distinguished gentleman."

Especially amusing was the incident when two young master goldsmiths brought some liquor and determined to force Hauser to take it. One held him; the other wanted to pour the full glass into his mouth. But they were unable to carry out their plan, for the very smell of the stuff in the glass made their victim faint. They were somewhat taken aback and did not know what to do with the unconscious boy; fortunately they saw him breathe and had no further anxiety.

"Don't believe his trick," said a foppishly dressed young gentleman who had been standing by somewhat bored. "I will bring him to all right." Immediately he smilingly pulled out a golden snuff-box and stuck a large pinch of snuff under the nose of the supposed pretender, upon which Caspar's face twitched convulsively, whereupon all three burst out laughing. When the jailer came and took them severely to task, they withdrew with much reviling and made way for a fat old gentleman who poker Caspar—who was slowly returning to life—on all sides, placed his finger on the boy's forehead, cleared his throat, shook his head, addressed him first in French, then in Spanish, then in English, whispered to the jailer; in brief, almost bursting with self-importance. Caspar, however, only looked at him and said, in pitiful tones, "Show me the way home."

"Why do you not play with your horse?" asked the jailer as soon as this important personage had left. One still communicated with Caspar more by means of gestures than by words, and what words could not say, he would read from eyes and hands.

He looked a long time at Hill and said, "Direct me home."

"Direct me home,' replied the warden, divided between irritation and pity, "where then, where is home? Where is your home, you poor wretch? In that hole underground? Do you call that being at home?"

"I want the Thee to come," said Caspar clearly, and distinctly, and slowly.

"I'd like to see him try it," replied Hill, smiling threateningly.

"The Thee is coming, the Thee is coming soon," insisted Caspar, and he looked with fervent intensity into the evening sky, as though he were convinced that the Thee could walk through the air. Then he got up in his painful fashion, took his toy horse and tried to carry it, for all the presents which he had received this was the only one he wanted to take with him when the Thee came.

Hill understood his action. "No, Caspar," he said, "now you have to stay in the world. That you may not like it, I understand well. I don't like it either, but remain you must."

Caspar, although he could not follow the words entirely, nevertheless understood the adamant will of fate which lay behind them. He began to tremble all over and threw himself on the floor, crying bitterly, and even later when the dismayed Hill had succeeded in consoling him it seemed as though he were eating his heart out with sorrow. The sadness of his spirit clouded the chill-like face as though with a dark veil, and the next morning his eyelids were clotted with tears he had shed in his sleep.

For the first time he no longer wanted to play with his horse, and he crouched for hours in the same spot without moving. He shook at every creak of the steps and shuddered when again and again new faces appeared on the threshold. Tremblingly he looked at these people, the smell of their breath was painful to him, and to be touched by them unbearable. He was most afraid of their hands. First he looked at these hands and noticed their various shapes and colors, and before he felt them on his skin he was already afraid of them. They seemed to him independent creatures, crawling, sticky, dangerous animals whose behavior from moment to moment one could not foretell.

Only Daumer's hand, the only one whose touch was pleasing to him, had disappeared. Why thought Caspar, why was all this going on? Why this strange noise from morning till night? Where did these strange figures come from? Why so many, and why were their mouths and eyes so wicked?

The fresh water no longer tasted good and he no longer enjoyed the salted bread. In his fatigue he thought in the middle of the day that night had come, and those hot shinning things which he had been told were the rays of the sun changed to purple dusk before his tired eyes. He was afraid of the rustling of the wind, for he mistook it for the voices of people. He longed for the loneliness of his prison. To return home was his only thought.

An Official Of High Rank Looks Behind The Scenes | 27

It was Sunday. Late in the afternoon Daumer and Herr von Tucher had returned from Ansbach, and Staatsrat von Feuerbach was with them. He had determined to visit the foundling himself, and if possible to clarify the fruitless muddle of decrees and documents. After he had taken lodgings in the Lamm Hotel, the President had the two gentlemen conduct him at once to the tower in the Castle. Nine o'clock had already struck when they arrived. Great was their astonishment to find Caspar's room empty. The wife of the warden explained with embarrassment that her husband had gone with Caspar to the Krokodil Inn; Rittmeiser Wessenig had wanted to show the foundling to some friends from out of town and had sent up to have Caspar brought down.

Daumer turned pale; sensing evil he stared darkly at the floor. Herr von Tucher was scarcely able to control his irritation, and a half-mocking, half-contemptuous smile played about the beardless lips of the President. His commanding bearing reminded on of a prince offended by an omission of duty as he said sternly to the two men: "take me to the inn."

Darkness had come; the moon shone wan over the city hall. Silently the three men walked down the hill, and scarcely had they left the maze of narrow streets when Daumer stood still and whispered in excited tones: "There he is."

Then they saw Caspar, like one deathly sick, swaying on Hill's arm as they left the gate of the Krokodil Inn. The President and Herr von Tucher both stood still and now they noticed that the boy suddenly stopped, shrank back, and stared at the ground in astonishment, his eyes wide with terror. The three men hurried up to him to find out what was wrong: they saw nothing except the shadow of the boy and his companion on the sidewalk.

Caspar did not dare to move any further because he saw every movement of his body copied by this incomprehensible thing. His lips were parted for a scream, his face snow white, and his knees trembled. It was as if all the horrible and mysterious quality of the world into which chance had thrown him had congealed itself into this curious figure wriggling on the ground.

Daumer, Herr von Tucher and the warden tried to help him; the President stood by silently. Daumer, when he looked up, observing him secretly and intently, saw his stern face unaffectedly moved.

Hill, who was the first to encounter the President's anger, came near being discharged that very night; only the courageous intervention of Herr von Tucher saved him and directed the wrath of the old jurist against more responsible persons, for the neglect which the boy had suffered was all too evident. With his usual impetuosity the President at once sought out Mayor Binder and reproached him hotly. Herr Binder could not but agree pusillanimously with the President; the decision with which the latter took up the matter made a deep impression upon him, and he had to admit having committed an almost irreparable fault. He had only been tepid about the matter, the difficulties with the government had annoyed him; now suddenly, when this powerful man raised his voice in behalf of the foundling, he became conscious of his willingness to do everything to help Caspar Hauser, and at once declared himself willing when Herr von Feuerbach asked that he should be removed from his present circumstances at once. "He must have regular care," said the President. "Professor Daumer has offered of his own accord to take him into his house, and I wish these steps taken without the slightest delay."

Binder bowed. "I shall take the necessary measures early tomorrow," he answered.

"Not before I have spoken to the boy myself," the President hastily replied. "I shall be at the tower at ten o'clock and I should like to be alone for an hour with the prisoner."

Daumer, too, had returned home rather excited. After days of absence he rarely had tie for proper meetings with his mother and sister, "the fine ladies and gentlemen must have carried on high," he growled, walking continually up and down; "the boy is quite beside himself; that's what I call being human, that's what I call having a consideration. They are barbarians and murderers, and it's among such people that I am compelled to live."

"Why don't you tell them so yourself?" remarked Anna Daumer dryly. "Scolding behind four walls is useless."

"Tell me, Friedrich," the old lady now addressed her son, "are you really convinced that you are not throwing your heart away upon a false idol?"

"From your question it is evident that you have not seen him," replied Daumer almost pityingly.

"That's certain; there was too much of a crowd."

"Well, then. One can't exaggerate in speaking to him, because language is too poor to express his personality. It is like a very old legend, this appearance of a fairy-like creature; out of a dark nowhere, we suddenly hear the pure voice of nature, a myth becomes a reality. His soul resembles some precious jewel which no covetous hand has yet touched; I shall seize it, for I am justified by a high purpose. Or am I unworthy? Do you think that I am not worthy?"

"Your enthusiasm is running away with you," said Anna, after a long pause, almost unwillingly.

Daumer shrugged his shoulders and smiled. Then he walked up to the table and said, in a voice whose gentleness seemed intended to defeat some already foreseen resistance: "Caspar is moving into our house tomorrow. I have appealed to Excellency Feuerbach and he has granted my request. I hope, mother, that you won't have any objection and that you believe me when I assure you that it is a matter of great importance to me. I am on track of important discoveries."

Mother and daughter looked at one another, frightened, and remained silent.

Next day at ten o'clock, Daumer, the Mayor, the city commissioner, the municipal doctor and several other persons met in the court in front of the prison tower and waited an hour and a half for the President, who was inside with the foundling. Daumer, who wanted to avoid talking to the others, stood almost continually at the outer wall and looked out at the picturesque maze of streets and roofs.

When the President finally appeared, those who had been waiting pressed eagerly about him to hear the opinion of so famous and redoubted a man. But the face of the President was so dark and serious that no one ventured to disturb him by addressing him. His powerful eye was burning inwardly, his lips were tightly pressed together, his forehead was furrowed with thought. His silence was interrupted by the Mayor, who asked whether his Excellency would not deign to take lunch with him. Feuerbach thanked him: important business forced him to return immediately to Ansbach, he said. Thereupon he turned to Daumer, shook hands with him and said: "See that Hauser is moved at once, the poor soul needs rest and care badly. You will hear from me soon. Good afternoon, gentlemen."

Then he walked away with small, loud, rapid steps, hurried down the hill and disappeared at once in the direction of the Church of St. Sebald. Since all were convinced of the boundless perspicacity of this man, and that no eye but his could see through the darkness which hung over crime and sin, they were dismayed by his silence, which seemed to them studied and purposeful.

That same evening Caspar found himself in Daumer's house.

4. The Mirror Speaks

Daumer's house adjoined the so-called Annengartlein on the Island of Schutt. It was an old building with many nooks and corners and half-dark rooms, but Caspar was given a fairly large, well-furnished room overlooking the river.

He had to be put to bed at once. The consequences of his recent experiences suddenly became apparent. He was again speechless and at times appeared to have no sensation of life. He tossed feverishly about on his unaccustomed pillow. How pitiful it was to see him shudder every time a board creaked; and the patter of the rain on the windows brought a state of terrified commotion. He heard the steps which resounded on a wide square in front of the distant forge. The sound of a voice produced a symptom of pain on his withered skin, and his features changed constantly from an expression of exhaustion to painful alertness.

For three days Daumer scarcely left his bed. This sacrifice and devotion aroused the admiration of his family. "I must get him to live," said he, and Caspar began to live. From the third day on his condition improved steadily and quickly. When he awoke in the morning a pensive smile played about his lips. Daumer was triumphant. "You behave as if you had escaped the prison yourself," remarked his sister, who could not help sharing in his pleasure. "Yes, and I have received the world as a gift," he answered eagerly; "just look at him! He's the springtime of his youth."

The next day Caspar was allowed to leave his bed. Daumer led him into the garden. To prevent the bright daylight from hurting his eyes he tied a green paper shield around his forehead. Later he selected twilight, or times when the sky was cloudy, for these outings.

They were indeed momentous journeys and there was nothing uneventful or commonplace about them. What pains he took to make him see and to find names for what he saw! He had to learn to acquire confidence in objects, and before he had learned to take their reality for granted, he became dismayed by their unexpected nearness. When he finally realized how high the sky was and the distance on the ground from the path to path, his steps became lighter and his bearing more confident. It was all a question of courage, everything lay in strengthening the self-confidence in him.

"That is air, Caspar; you cannot touch it, but there it is, when it moves it becomes wind, but you need not fear the wind. What lies behind the night is yesterday, what is beyond the next night is tomorrow. From yesterday to tomorrow time passes, hours pass; hours are divided time. This is a tree, this is a bush, here is grass and here stones; there are sand and leaves, there blossoms and fruit."

Out of hollow sounds the word arose. A form came to have a meaning because of the unforgettable word. Caspar rolls a word on his tongue, it taste bitter or sweet, it contents him or it leaves him dissatisfied. Then too, many words had faces, or they sounded like the chimes of a bell out of the night, or they stood out like flames in the mist.

It was a far cry from thing to word. The word was elusive and you had to run after it, and when it was finally caught it was nothing and made you sad. Nevertheless the same road brought one to persons; indeed it was as if one stood behind a fence of words which made people's features strange and formidable. If, however, one broke down or got behind this barrier then they were beautiful.

If it has seemed unaccustomed in the morning to say "the flower," by moon it was already familiar, by evening it was already old. "This heart and mind, destined to fruitfulness after long waiting, like arid soil which has finally been watered, now produces buds and blossoms and fruit in one night," noted the industrious Daumer. "What the glance wearied by custom cannot perceive appears to this eye as though fresh from the hand of God. And where the world is an unsolvable riddle, where its secrets begin, he stands curiously pondering, and asks confidently why and wherefore. Every sound and every sight calls forth this doubting, wondering, hungry, irreverent questioning."

It cannot be denied that Daumer was often frightened by the feeling of his own inadequacy. "Is this pedagogy?" he pondered; "can this still be called gardening when the wild plant escapes, when the great organism runs riot and knows no barriers? How will all this end? Undoubtedly I am on the trail of an unusual phenomenon, and my precious contemporaries will be forced to admit some belief in miracles."

Caspar still loved to imagine that someday he would be allowed to return home. "First I'll learn, then I'll go home," he would say with an expression of indomitable resolution. "But you are at home, you're at home here with us," Daumer would impose. But Caspar shook his head.

At times he would stand by the fence and look over into the adjoining garden, where children were playing. He would study their ways with amusing astonishment. "Such little people," he remarked to Daumer, who one surprised him at this occupation. "Such little people." His voice sounded sad and greatly puzzled.

Daumer suppressed a smile and as they walked into the house he tried to explain to the youth that everyone had once been so small including Caspar himself. But Caspar did not wish to concede this. "Oh, no, no," he exclaimed, "not Caspar; Caspar always like now, Caspar never had such short arms and legs, oh, no!"

Nevertheless this was so, Daumer assured him not only was he once small, but he was still growing daily, changing constantly, quite different now already from the Caspar Hauser of the tower, and after many years he would grow old, his hair would turn white, his skin be filled with wrinkles.

At this Caspar turned pale with fear. He began to sob and stammered that this was impossible; he did not want it so and implored Daumer to see that it did not come to pass.

Daumer whispered something to his sister, who went into the garden and soon brought back a rosebud, a full blown rose, and a faded flower. Caspar reached for the full blown rose, but at once turned away with disgust, for, much as he preferred red above all colors, the strong smell of the flower was distasteful to him. When Daumer tried to explain to him the difference in age between the bud and full bloom, Caspar said, "But you have made it yourself. It's a dead thing, with no eyes and no legs."

"I didn't make it myself," his teacher replied, "it is alive, it grew, every living thing has grown."

"Every living thing has grown," repeated Caspar almost breathlessly, pausing after every word. Here there was an obvious danger of mental disturbance.

The trees in the garden were also alive, he was told, and he did not dare to approach them, for the rustling in the tree tops disturbed him. He continued dubious and asked who had cut out all these leaves and why, why so many?

"These, too, have grown," was the answer.

But out on the lawn there was an old sandstone statue and this was declared by Daumer to be dead, although it looked like a human being. Caspar could not turn his eyes away from it for hours. Bewilderment mad him dumb. "Why has it a face?" he finally asked, "why is it so white and dirty? Why does it always stand and not get tired?"

When he had conquered his fear, he went to it and ventured to touch the figure, for, without touching things he did not believe the evidence of his eyes. He wished mightily to be allowed to take the thing apart in order to know what was in it. How much there was always onside of things, how much there was always back of things.

An apple fell from the branch and rolled for some distance down the steep path. Daumer picked it up and Caspar asked whether the apple was tired for having run so quickly. He turned away with a shudder when Daumer took the knife and cut the fruit in two. Then a worm could be seen wriggling its thin body against the light.

"It was confined in darkness up to now, as you were in prison," said Daumer.

The word "prison" made Caspar thoughtful; thoughtful and distrustful. How many things of which he knew nothing were imprisoned. Every inside was a prison. And in a singular state of confusion the memory of the blow which he had once received, after his Thee had taught him how one could move the little horse freely, attached itself to these thoughts. An impending blow lay hidden in all strange things; danger lurked in everything unknown. In spite of a peculiar radiant cheerfulness which little by little began to pour from

Caspar's being, to the delight of all about him, he was never free from the foreboding and apprehension of fear.

Once, after several hours of rain, on stepping out of the gate with Daumer, Caspar perceived a rainbow in the sky. He was struck motionless with joy. "Who made it?' he finally stammered. The sun. How did the sun do it? Why! The sun is not a person! Daumer found the material explanations of natural phenomena inadequate and was obliged to attribute them to God. "God is the Creator of living and inanimate matter,' he said.

Caspar remained silent. The name of God had a strangely gloomy sound to him. The image of God which he sought was similar to his Thee, resembling it at the time when the ceiling of the prison weighed down on his shoulders. It was enveloped in uncanny mystery, like the Thee when it dealt Caspar a blow for having spoken too loudly.

How mysterious was everything which took place between morning and evening! The bustle and murmur of the universe, the water flowing in the river, the movements of the airy-faint objects high up in the air, which were called clouds, the passage of inexplicable events which did not recur, the fugitive movements of humans, their pained gestures, their loud speech and their curious laughter. How much there was to find out about, to learn!

Daumer's heart contracted whenever he saw the boy buried in profound thought. During these periods he seemed numb, he cowered down with clenched fist and no longer heard of felt what was going on about him.

Caspar, at these times, was really sunk in complete darkness. Only after a sufficient period had been spent thus inanimately, something like a spark leaped out of the depths and out of his heart an indistinct murmuring voice began to speak. When the spark died again, the outer world would reassert itself, but the melancholy discontent had settled upon the boy.

"We must go out to the country with him sometime," said Anna Daumer one day, when she and her brother had been discussing the situation. "He needs diversion."

"He does need diversion," Daumer smilingly admitted. "He is too introspective, the whole universe still weighs upon his heart."

"Since it will be his first walk, it will be wise to undertake it as quietly as possible, otherwise all the curious will be at hand," said old Frau Daumer. "They gossip enough about him and us, as it is."

Daumer nodded. He wanted no one but Herr von Tucher to be of the party.

On the first Sunday in September the excursion took place. It was already five o'clock in the afternoon when they left the house, and as they had to be considerate of Caspar's slow gait, it was late when they got into the country. The people they met stopped in order to stare at them and one often heard the surprised and sarcastic remark: "There's Caspar Hauser, look at the foundling; how high and mighty he acts, how grand!' For Caspar wore a new little blue swallow-tail coat, a fashionable vest, his legs were clad in white silk stockings and his shoes had silver buckles.

He walked between two women and observed the road carefully, although it was no longer swayed up and down before his eyes. The men walked a certain distance behind. Suddenly Daumer raised his right arm forward and Caspar immediately stood still and gazed about questioningly.

Delighted, Daumer called to him, with a tone of affection, to go on. A few hundred feet further on, he lifted his arm again, and Caspar immediately stood still and turned towards him.

"What's that; what does this mean?" asked Herr von Tucher, astonished.

"There is no explanation," answered Daumer, full of silent triumph. "If you like I can show you something much more remarkable."

"Witchcraft will be resorted to, I hope," remarked Herr von Tucher, a little ironically.

"Witchcraft?" no but as Hamlet says: There are more things in heaven and earth than—"

"So you have already reached the end of human understanding?" Herr von Tucher interrupted, still ironically. "I for my part side with the skeptics. Well we shall see."

"We shall see," Daumer repeated, cheerfully.

After frequent short rest they stopped at the edge of a field and all lay down on the grass. Caspar fell asleep at once. Anna spread a cloth over his face, and then unpacked a small basket of food which they had brought along. In silence they all four began to eat. I was not a natural silence; the lovely day sinking to rest, the beautiful bloom of summer should rather have conducted to merry talk, but a spell lay about the sleeping boy. Everyone felt his presence more strongly now than before, but only a few indifferent words which sounded softer than his breathing were spoken. Far and wide there was not a soul to be seen, for they had purposely chosen a rarely frequented road.

The sun was sinking when Caspar awoke and, sitting up, looked grateful and somewhat shamefacedly at each of his friends in turn. "Look over there, Caspar, at that red ball of fire," said Daumer, "have you ever seen the sun so big?"

Caspar looked. It was a beautiful sight. The purple disk was descending as though it were cutting its way into the earth along the border of the sky; a great trail of scarlet streamed behind it, the whole air was aglow; there was a profusion of red arteries to mark a forest in the distance, and pink shadows slowly descended over the plains. Only a few minutes more, and the dusk flushed through the soft carmine mist in which the distant landscape was bathed; for a moment the earth quivered, then the crystal green bundles of rays shot over the western sky, converging on the setting sun.

A ghostlike smile played over the faces of both men and both women, as they saw Caspar with a gesture of mute fear stretch his hand towards the horizon. Daumer approached and seized his hand, which had become ice-cold. Caspar turned his face towards him, trembling, full of questions and fear, and finally his lips moved and he murmured shyly, "Where does the sun go? Does it go away entirely?"

Daumer was unable to answer at once. So may Adam, he thought, have trembled as his first night broke in Paradise, and it was not without a shudder of awe, not without a curious uncertainty, that he consoled the boy and assured him that the sun would return.

"Is God there?" asked Caspar in a whisper, "is the sun God?"

Daumer pointed in general to the entire surrounding scene and answered, "Everything is God."

This dictum of the pantheistic philosophy was, however, a little too complicated for the boy's powers of comprehension. He shook his head skeptically and then with an expression of profoundly idolatrous veneration, "Caspar loves the sun."

On the way home he was quite silent; so were the others, even Anna, who was always in good humor; they were curiously depressed, as though they had never before strolled through an evening late in the summer, or as though they already had a premonition of a scene which would make these hours in which they had been together unforgettable.

Just in front of the city gate Anna stood still and called the attention of all to the glorious starlit sky. Caspar, too, looked up and was endlessly surprised. Short, swift, incoherent sounds of passionate delight came from his mouth. "Stars, stars," he stammered, taking the word he had heard from Anna's lips. He pressed his hands against his breast and an indescribably happy smile beautified his features. He could not look his fill and repeatedly resumed his gazing at the splendor, and from his feeble and inarticulate words they could understand that he could distinguish groups of stars in the firmament and the single stars that were particularly bright. In a voice that showed him to be almost beside himself he asked who had put so many beautiful light up there and who it was that lighted and extinguished them?

Daumer answered that they shone all the time, but could not always be seen, whereupon he asked who had first put them up there to make them burn all the time.

Suddenly he fell into deep thought. He stood a while with bent head and saw and heard nothing. When he had recovered himself again, his pleasure had turned into depression, he fell down on the grass and broke into deep sobs, which they could not quiet.

It was long after nine o'clock when they finally reached home. While Caspar went upstairs with the women, Herr von Tucher said good-bye to Daumer at the garden gate. "I wonder what was going on in his mind," he pondered. And as Daumer said nothing in reply, Herr von Tucher went on thoughtfully: "Perhaps he already feels the irrevocable passage of time, perhaps the past already shows him her true features."

"Undoubtedly it was painful to him to look up into the shining vault of heaven," answered Daumer, "he has never been able before to lift his eyes to the sky at night. Nature does not show him a friendly face and he has experienced little of her so-called kindness."

For a time they were silent, then Daumer said: "I have invited a few friends and acquaintances to my house tomorrow afternoon. I want to tell them about my series of highly interesting experiments and observations which I have made with Caspar. I should be delighted if you would come, too."

Herr von Tucher promised to come. To his surprise when he arrived somewhat late the next day, he was led into a completely darkened room. It seemed like a séance already in progress. From one corner he heard the monotonous voice of Caspar reading. "It's a page of the Bible which the City Librarian has turned to at random," Daumer whispered to Herr von Tucher. The darkness was so great that the listeners could not see one another; nevertheless, Caspar read without hesitating, as if his eyes were themselves a source of light.

Everyone was amazed. The astonishment increased when Caspar was able, still in total darkness, to differentiate various objects, which first one and then another—in order to eliminate any suspicion of preparation or collusion—held up for him at a distance of five or six feet.

"I am now going to try him with wine," said Daumer, as he opened the blinds. Caspar pressed his hands to his eyes and it was a long time before he could stand the light. Someone brought wine in an opaque glass and Caspar not only smelled it at once, but showed obvious symptoms of a slight intoxication. His eyes rolled and his mouth showed a wry distortion. Was all this being produced by honest means? Was such sensitiveness possible or conceivable? They repeated the experiment a second and a third time, and behold, the effect became stronger. For the fourth experiment water was put into the glass, outside the room, and now Caspar said he felt nothing.

But it was far more remarkable to observe his reaction toward metals. While Caspar was out of the room a gentleman concealed a piece of copper. Caspar was called back and all eagerly watched how he seemed literally drawn to the hiding place; it looked as though a dog were detecting the presence of a piece of meat. He found it and they all applauded. No one paid any attention to the fact that he was white and covered with cold sweat. Only Herr von Tucher observed it and disapproved of the whole business.

Of course, this one experiment was not permitted to be the last. The thing was quickly noised about, and the house was turned into a museum. Everyone of any position or influence in the city appeared, and Caspar had to be ready all the time, had to do what he was bidden. When he was tired he was allowed to sleep, but they examined whether his sleep was profound and Daumer was overcome with joy when Dr. Rehbein stated that he would never have believed in the possibility of such petrified slumber.

Even pathological conditions of the boy's body gave Daumer an opportunity for demonstration, or at least for study. He tried to influence him by hypnotic contacts and mesmeric caresses, for he was an ardent advocate of the then new theories which manipulated the soul of man as an alchemist manipulates the contents of his test-tube. Or, when these means failed, he would try the healing properties of remedies of a certain type. He experimented with arnica, aconite and nux-vomica. He was always eager, constantly filled with his mission, always taking notes and affording evidence of an almost pathetic solicitude.

What a serious trifling all this! What eagerness there was about proving and interpreting and making what was clear as day obscure, muddling what was simple. The public honestly tried to believe, the apparent witchcraft was heralded in all directions, but not to the advantage of Caspar nor for his welfare, as was soon made apparent. For, unfortunately, the world is full of contemptible creatures whose skepticism cannot be destroyed by any amount of proof. Perhaps they expected to be shown something sensational each time and placed their expectations too high. At any rate they said that the wonder man only excelled in the tricks he had studied for public exhibition and in these—according to them—he had something of the readiness of a little trained monkey.

The program became, in a word, a little monotonous; only newcomers could find pleasure in it. The others regarded Daumer somewhat as one regards a circus director, or an author who bores his friends by constantly re-reading a mediocre poem, whereas they still found enough opportunity to amuse them in Caspar himself.

Was it not amusing when, for example, he criticized the dust on the coat collar of an officer of high rank or touched the hair of a director of the Chamber of Commerce, saying with pitying astonishment: "White hair, white hair"? Or when, in the presence of some distinguished person in the city, on observing him twiddling his cane with his fingers, he wanted to do the same thing, or expressed his aversion for Magistrate Behold's black beard, or refused to kiss a lady's hand because, as he said, it wasn't necessary to bite it?

The skeptics of Nurnberg felt themselves recompensed by such little incidents. If they could laugh all was well. On the other hand, these occurrences angered Daumer, who tried to explain to Caspar the amenities of polite society.

"You always forget to greet newcomers," said Daumer. As a matter of fact, Caspar, when engrossed in a book or a game, did not look up until he was called. When he perceived a face which he knew or had come to love, he would smile bewitchingly and impishly, and then begin to chat and ask questions without any introduction. No matter how important the people who were present, he never left his place without carefully putting away all the things with which he had been occupied and carefully brushing from the table, with his little broom, all of the pieces of paper and the bread crumbs. They had to wait until he was through.

He had no shyness. To him all people seemed good; he considered them almost all beautiful. It seemed to him a matter of course when some gentleman would place himself before him and read to him an endless number of names and figures from a slip of paper that had been previously prepared. His memory never forsook him and he could repeat name after name, number after number even if there were a hundred, all in the proper order. He noticed, of course, from the surprise of the audience, that he had done an astonishing thing, but not a glimmer of vanity ever appeared on his face; he only looked a little sad if the thing was repeated time and time again, if they never seemed satisfied.

He could not understand that what was so natural to him might be wonderful for them. But no one cared about things that to him were wonderful. And he was not able to formulate these things, for they lay rooted in his deepest feelings. It was a scarcely felt question; in the morning, perhaps when he awoke, it was a steady, silent, desperate seeking for which there existed no designation. It lay way back; it was bound up with him, but he did not possess it. Something had happened to him, sometime, somewhere, and he did not know it. He felt of his body, but he scarcely found himself. He said "Caspar" to himself, but that something in the distance did not answer to this name. Therefore his expectations attached themselves to something external. When the clock in the next room struck, what a curious surprise in each new stroke! It was as if a wall were to dissolve and to disappear into space. The past night had been full of imperceptible events. Had anyone knocked at the window? No. Had anyone been there, had anyone spoken, called or threatened? No. Something had occurred, but Caspar had not had anything to do with it.

An inscrutable sense of care. He must learn; perhaps then it would be clear. He must learn of what things consisted, learn what was hidden in the night, when one was not alive and nevertheless felt things. He must learn the unknown, seize what was in the distance, know what was dark and hidden, learn to question people. He became passionately devoted to the reading of books. He began to show impatience when he found himself disturbed by strange visitors continuously and much to his annoyance, for now people already came from beyond Nurnberg, since Caspar Hauser was being spoken of and written of all over the country. Daumer, too, could scarcely meet all the demands which were made upon him. He was often weary and out of humor, and regretted that he had exposed Caspar Hauser to the world.

There were times, when he was alone with the boy, when his nobler nature reasserted itself and he became more profoundly attached to this lad whom he so curiously possessed, body and soul, than was required by his original purpose. There came an hour when Daumer saw a picture reminding him of paradise: Caspar was seated on a bench in the garden with a book in his hand, swallows circled about him and doves pecked about his feet, a butterfly rested on his shoulder and the house-cat purred on his arm. In him we see mankind free from sin, said Daumer to himself while observing this picture, and what more is there to do than to maintain such a condition? What need to decipher or forecast anything more?

Another day there suddenly arose a loud noise in the neighbor's garden. A vicious dog had broken his chain and cavorted in savage leaps, foaming at the mouth. He knocked over a child, bit a servant who was chasing him, and sprang against the fence of the Daumer garden. A board gave way, the animal slipped through and stared wildly with his bloodshot eyes at the little group seated under the lime trees—Daumer, his mother, Mayor Binder and Caspar. They all jumped up frightened, Binder lifted his stick, the animal jumped about, suddenly stood still, sniffed, trotted over to Caspar, who sat white and still, and licked the boy's hand, which depended from the arm of his seat. Then he looked at him with an uncertain glowing eye, full of humility almost, expecting a caress, beseeching forgiveness. It was as if he were begging pardon for his offense. Caspar's eyes showed the same uncertain and humble expression; he was sorry for the dog and did not know why.

It was said that after this scene Daumer had wept.

Two days later, it was a rainy October evening, Daumer was sitting with his mother and Caspar in the living-room. Anna had gone to an entertainment in the assembly hall, the old lady sat knitting in an easy chair by the open window, for in spite of the fact that autumn was well under way, the air was warm and full of the damp smell of decaying plants. There was a knock at the door and the glazier brought in a large mirror for the wall, which the maid had broken the week before. Mrs. Daumer told him to lean the mirror against the wall, which the man did before he left the apartment.

He had scarcely gone when Daumer asked with astonishment why she had not had it hung in its place and thus have been saved the work the next day. The old lady answered with an embarrassed smile that one should not hang a mirror at night; that meant bad luck.

Daumer did not have humor enough for these half-serious crotchets. He reproached his mother with being superstitious, she contradicted him and he grew angry, which means that he spoke in his gentlest tones through tightly closed teeth.

Caspar, who could not bear to see Daumer with an unfriendly expression on his face, laid his arm on his shoulder and sought to soothe him with childlike coaxing. Daumer cast his eyes down, was silent a while, and then thoroughly ashamed said, "Go over to my mother, Caspar, and tell her that I am in the wrong."

Caspar nodded and without much thought stepped over to Mrs. Daumer and said, "I am in the wrong." Thereupon Daumer laughed, "Not you, Caspar, I," he said and pointed to himself. "When Caspar is in the wrong he should say 'I'. I address you as 'you' but you say 'I' to yourself. Understand?" Caspar's eyes became big and thoughtful. The little word "I" suddenly penetrated through him like some strange tasting drink. Hundreds of figures suddenly approached him, a whole city full of people, full of men, women and children, suddenly surrounded him. The animals on the earth, the birds in the air, the flowers, the stones and the very sun itself all came up to him and all together addressed him as "you." He, however, replied timidly "I."

He spread his hands flat on his breast and then let them slip down over his hips: his body was a wall between inside and outside, between *I* and you. At the same moment his own picture stood forth from the mirror standing over across the room. "Ah," thought he a little troubled, "who is that?"

Naturally he had often walked by the mirror before, but his glances, dazzled by the many sights of his own world, had passed by without lingering, without thinking, and he had become as accustomed to his mirrored reflection as to his shadow on the ground. So casual an observation, affording no impediment to his acts at the moment, could not secure admission to his more serious consideration.

Now his eye had become mature enough for this appearance. He looked into the mirror; "Caspar," he murmured. Inside of him the answer was "I." There were Caspar's mouth and cheeks and the brown hair curling over his forehead and ears. Approaching he looked back of the mirror along the wall with playful and doubting curiosity; there was nothing there. Then he placed himself before the mirror again and it seemed to him as if behind his picture the light divided itself and a long, long road ran backwards and in the far distance there stood another Caspar, another *I*, with closed eyes, who looked as if he knew something which the Caspar who was here in the room did not know.

Daumer, who was in the habit of watching the boy's behavior, was observing him with intense interest. Suddenly, an unusual sound: something whirled through the air and fell on the floor near the table. It was a piece of paper which had flown in from outside. Frau Daumer picked it up. It was folded together like a letter. Uncertainly she turned it about and then handed it to her son.

He tore it open and read the following words written in a large hand: "This is to warn the house; this is to warn the master of the house, this is to warn the stranger."

Frau Daumer got up and was reading over his raised arm; a shiver passed over her. Daumer, as he stared silently at the note, felt as if the blade of a sword had grown out of the ground in front of his feet, its point menacingly uppermost.

Caspar had not been aware of anything that had happened. He left his place in front of the mirror and walked absentmindedly past both of them to the window. There he stood sunk in contemplation, then he insensibly leaned out farther and farther, entirely unconscious of himself, filled with the will to seek, until his breast rested on the window-sill and his brow protruded into the surrounding darkness.

5. Caspar Dreams

The next morning Daumer turned over the mysterious missive to the police. Investigations were set on foot, but naturally resulted in nothing. The incident was also officially reported to the Appellate Court and after a while Regierungsrat Hermann, who was a friend of Baron Tucher, wrote him a personal letter, in which among other things he expressed it as his opinion that Caspar Hauser should continue to be observed and questioned closely. It was possible that deep-rooted fear forced him to keep quiet about a number of things concerning which he would otherwise speak freely.

Herr von Tucher sought out Daumer and read him this part of the letter. Daumer could not suppress a satirical smile. "I am quite aware," said he, somewhat unwillingly, "that some mystery, woven by the hand of man, lies back of everything connected with Caspar, quite aside from the fact that President Feuerbach recently wrote me about the matter, and in most peculiar terms, at that, which lead me to infer the presence of some unusual condition. But what do they mean by 'questioning' him, or 'observing' him? Has not the utmost already been tried? Both medical prudence and human feeling require that I take the greatest care of him. I hardly dare to make the change from the simple food to which he is accustomed, to the diet he now requires by reason of the conditions in which he is now living."

"Why do you not dare?" asked Herr von Tucher, quite surprised. "We had agreed to accustom him to the use of meat, or at least of other cooked dishes."

Daumer hesitated to answer. "He already can stand milk and rice and warm soup quite nicely," he then said, "but I don't want to encourage him to eat meat."

"Why not?"

"I am afraid I may destroy forces which are perhaps connected with the purity of his blood."

"Destroy forces? What forces could be as important for him as the strength of his body and the freshness of his mind? Would it not be far more advisable to lead him away from what is unusual, from what must sooner or later be disastrous to him? Is it well to apply a different yardstick to him from the one used in any natural education? What, indeed, do you want, what are you planning to do with him? Caspar is a child; we must not forget that."

"He is a miracle," retorted Daumer hastily, much moved. Then in half-bitter, half-didactic tones which necessarily sounded offensive to a man of the world like Tucher, he continued: "Unfortunately we live in a time in which it is an offense to gross common sense to call attention to anything that is unfathomable. Otherwise Everyone would be obliged to see and feel that in this boy we are surrounded on all sides by the secret forces of nature in which our whole being rests."

Herr von Tucher remained silent for a time; then his face assumed an expression of defensive pride as he said: "It is better to seize reality completely, fully, and to satisfy its demands completely, than to wander about fruitlessly in the mist of the supersensual."

"Does not reality, upon which I can call to bear me out, justify me?" interposed Daumer, whose voice became lower and more caressing as he grew hotter over the conversation. "Must I remind you of single instances? Are not the air and the earth and the water still inhabited for this boy with evil spirits with which he has living contacts?"

Baron Tucher's face became gloomy. "The whole business seems to me to be only the consequence of a harmful over-sensitiveness," said he briefly and sharply. "Those are not the sources from which life springs; a useful human being cannot be developed from such conditions."

Daumer bowed his head and in his eye there was impatience and contempt, but he answered in yielding and friendly tones. "Who knows, Baron? The sources of life are unfathomable. My hopes aspire very high and I expect things of our Caspar which will certainly alter your opinion. Genius is made of such stuff."

"One always wrongs a person when one attaches expectations to his future," said Herr von Tucher with a sad smile.

"Maybe, maybe, nevertheless I put my faith in the future. What lies back of him is not my affair and what I know of his past shall serve me only to free him from it. That is the wonderful and hopeful thing: we have here for once a being without a past, the untrammeled creature without previous responsibility, fresh from the first day of creation, all soul and all instinct, endowed with glorious possibilities, not yet seduced by the serpent of knowledge, a proof of the presence of hidden forces whose study is the task of the centuries that are to come. It is possible that I am mistaken; then, however, I shall have been mistaken in mankind and shall have to declare my ideals to be lies."

"Heaven save you from that," answered Herr von Tucher and quickly took his departure.

On the same day Daumer's mother drew his attention to the fact that Caspar's sleep was no longer as quiet as usual. When Caspar came to the table somewhat tired the next morning, Daumer asked him whether he had slept badly.

"No, I didn't sleep badly," replied Caspar, "but I woke up once and then I was frightened."

"What were you afraid of?" his teacher wanted to know.

"Of the dark," answered Caspar, and thoughtfully he added: "During the night the dark sits on the lamp and howls."

The next morning he came out of his bedroom into Daumer's room half-dressed and told him anxiously that a man had been there. At first Daumer was frightened, then it became evident to him that Caspar had dreamed. He asked what manner of a man it had been and Caspar replied it had been a big, handsome man with a white cloak. Had the man spoken to him? Caspar said no; he had not spoken; he had carried a wreath, which he had laid on the table and when Caspar had reached for it, the wreath had begun to shine.

"You dreamed," said Daumer.

Caspar wanted to know what that meant. "When the body rests," his teacher explained, "the soul stays awake and during sleep makes a picture of what the body has felt or experienced during the day. This picture we call a dream."

Then Caspar wanted to know what the soul was. Daumer said, "The soul gives life to your body. Body and soul are mingled together. Each alone is what it is, but they are as completely mingled as water and wine when one pours them one into the other."

"Like water and wine," asked Caspar with distaste. "But that spoils the water."

Daumer laughed and explained that he had only been making use of a comparison. Later he perceived that Caspar's dreams were of a peculiar, unique type. Ordinarily dreams are attached to some accidental incident, he said to himself. They play, regardless of any law, with foreboding, wish and fear, but in him they resemble a man lost in a dark wood, feeling about, looking for the road. Something is not right in his case; I must get to the bottom of it.

The striking part was that certain images gradually condensed into a single dream which from night to night became more complete, assumed more definite form, and regularly returned with constantly increasing distinctness. At first Caspar could only tell it in parts, piecemeal, as the images appeared to him. Then one day just as the painter draws aside the curtain that covers a finished picture, he was able to give his guardian a detailed description.

He had slept longer than usual, and Daumer for this reason had gone to his room. He had scarcely stepped up to the bed when Caspar opened his eyes. His face was glowing, his glance reflected an internal preoccupation, and his mouth was impatient to speak. In a slow voice, full of emotion, he began.

He was in a big house and was asleep. A woman came in and woke him up. He notices that the bed is so small that he does not know how he has found it large enough to lie in. The woman dresses him and leads him into a room, all around the walls of which are mirrors in golden frames. Back of glass walls silver dishes are shining and on a white table there are fine white, delicately painted porcelain cups. He wants to remain and look about, but the woman pulls him on. There is a room with many books and from the middle of the curved ceiling a chandelier is suspended. Caspar wants to look at the books but the lights of the chandelier slowly go out, one after the other, and the woman draws him on. She conducts him through a long corridor and down an immense staircase; they walk through a gallery in the interior of the house. He sees paintings on the walls, men in helmets, and women with golden jewelry. He looks through the arch of the wall from the hall into the court, where a fountain is splashing. The column of water is silver white at the bottom and at the top red with the sun. They come to a second staircase, the steps of which mount upwards like golden clouds. An iron man is standing by the stairs, a sword in his right hand, but his face is black, no, he has no face at all. Caspar is afraid of him and does not want to pass him, whereupon the woman bends over and whispers something into his ear. He goes by him and walks up to an immense door, where the woman knocks. The door is not opened. She calls and no one hears. She tries to open the door, but the door is locked. It seems to Caspar that something important is taking place behind the door; he himself begins to call, but at that moment he wakes up.

Curious, thought Daumer, these are things which he can never have seen before, like the man in armor without a face. Curious! and his search for words, his helpless circumlocutions and at the same time such distinct power of observation. Very odd.

'Who was the woman?" asked Caspar.

"It was a dream lady," replied Daumer soothingly.

"And the books and the fountain and the door?" Caspar insisted. "Were they dream books? Was it a dream door? Why did they not open the dream door?"

Daumer sighed and forgot to make reply. What was it that was gaining power over his Caspar, his soul in a test-tube? This dream was closely bound up with temporal and material things.

Caspar dressed slowly. Suddenly he raised his head and asked whether everyone had a mother. And when Daumer replied in the affirmative, he wanted to know whether everyone had a father? This question had also to be answered affirmatively.

"Where is your father?" asked Caspar.

"He is dead," answered Daumer.

"Dead," Caspar whispered after him.

A breath of fright passed over his features. He relapsed into a deep brooding; then he began again. "But where's my father?"

Daumer was silent. "Is it he with whom I was; the Thee?" insisted Caspar.

"I don't know," answered Daumer, knowing that he was displaying but little skill and superiority.

"Why not? You know everything? And have I a mother, too?"

"Certainly."

"Where is she then? Why does she not come?"

"Perhaps she is also dead?"

"Really? Can mothers die, too?"

"Ah, Caspar," exclaimed Daumer painfully.

"My mother is not dead," said Caspar with remarkable decision. Suddenly his face was aflame and he asked with emotion, "Perhaps my mother was back of the door?"

"Back of what door, Caspar?"

"There! In the dream!"

"In the dream? Why, that's not real," Daumer replied, timidly, resorting to his teaching manner.

"But you said that the soul is real and makes the dream? Yes, she was back of the door, I know it. The next time I shall open it."

Daumer hoped that this dream world would gradually fade away, but this was not the case. This one dream, Caspar called it the dream of the big house, expanded constantly, until it was interlaced and overgrown with all kinds of blossoms and clinging branches, like a plant of fable. Caspar always walked along a certain course, and the course always ended in front of a high door which was never opened. Once the earth trembled from steps which were inside, the door seemed to swell like a garment, flames appeared through a crack on the threshold, then he awoke and was unable to forget the distress of the dream, which stayed with him through all the subsequent hours of the day.

The persons changed. Sometimes it was a man that came instead of the woman, a man who led him through the arched hall. And as they were about to mount the steps there came another man who, with a stern expression, handed him something glittering, which was long and narrow and which dissolved in his hand like rays of the sun when Caspar tried to seize it.

To this main dream there were attached peculiar little dreams, dreams of unknown words which he had never heard when awake and which, when the dream was over, he vainly sought to lay hold of. They had mostly a soft sound, but he felt that they never referred to him but to what went on behind the closed door.

Dream messengers they were, like birds of the sea which tirelessly carry objects from a half-sunken ship to the distant coast.

One night Daumer lay sleepless, when he heard a noise of rather long duration in Caspar's room. He got up, slipped on his dressing gown, and went to the boy's room. Caspar, in his shirt, sat at the table, a sheet of paper in front of him, and seemed to have been writing something. Pale moonlight filled the room. Caspar fixed upon him a glance that was profound to the point of self-intoxication and answered in low tones: "I was in the big house. The woman led me to the fountain m the court; she had me look up at a window; up there stood the man in the cloak, very handsome to look at, and he said something; then I got up and wrote it down."

Daumer made a light, took the paper, read it, threw it down, took Caspar by both hands and exclaimed, half with dismay, half with irritation: "Why, Caspar, that's perfectly incomprehensible stuff."

Caspar stared at the paper, spelled murmuringly to himself, and said, "In the dream I understood it."

Among these meaningless tokens, resembling the words of an artificial language, there appeared at the end the word "Dukatus." Caspar pointed to the word and whispered: "That's what woke me up because it sounded so beautiful." Daumer felt himself bound to inform the Mayor of these distresses of Caspar's, as he called them. What he feared happened. Herr Binder attached great importance to the incident. "First it is imperative to write President Feuerbach as detailed an account as possible, for some definite conclusions can certainly be drawn from these dreams," he said. "Then I suggest that some time you go up to the Castle with Caspar."

"To the Castle, why?"

"Well, it's just an idea of mine. Since he constantly dreams of castles, perhaps the sight of a real castle will rouse him, and give us more definite clews."

"Do you really think then that these dreams have a meaning?"

"Most certainly. I am convinced that he really lived up to his third or fourth year in surroundings of that sort and that, with his new awakening to life and to consciousness, the memories of his earlier existence are now returning to him in the form and content of his dreams."

"A very obvious and matter-of-fact explanation," remarked Daumer, bitterly. "So the background of his destiny is nothing more than a plain wild west story."

"A wild west story? I don't mind if you wish to call it so. I don't know why you object to the word. Must we believe that the boy has fallen out of the moon? Do you not want to explain him as subject to the conditions of our planet?"

"Oh, certainly, certainly," sighed Daumer. Then he continued: "I had deluded myself with other hopes. I wanted to save Caspar from this delving and seeking in the past. It was his freedom, the fact that he was untrammeled and without destiny, which moved me so strongly about him. Unusual circumstances have endowed this boy with gifts such as no other mortal can boast of, and all this is now to be spoiled, to be directed into the channel of events which may in themselves be tragic enough, but certainly are by no means without a parallel."

"I understand you don't want to disturb his mystic halo," interrupted the mayor with somewhat pedantic contempt. "But we have graver duties towards our fellow-men than towards the unique phenomenon of Caspar Hauser. Let me tell you that very seriously, my dear Professor. There are no longer any angels in our days, and where wrong has taken place there must be expiation."

Daumer shrugged his shoulders. "Do you think that you are thus doing anything for Caspar's welfare?" he asked, in a tone of fanaticism which seemed ridiculous to the Mayor. "You are only burdening him and defiling him by contact with the world and the world's vulgarity. Already there is so much bickering going on about him that I am becoming annoyed with having anything to do with his affairs. It's an ugly story we shall be dealing with."

"But they should be unveiled; if they only do come out, 1 replied Binder eagerly. "I say, let each man do his part.

The next morning the Mayor appeared at Daumer's house and they went with Caspar to the castle. Herr Binder knocked at the porter's lodge and the porter appeared with a big bunch of keys and led them to the entrance gate.

When they stood in front of the huge gate with its double door, it was as though a veil suddenly dropped from Caspar's face. He drew himself up, then bent forward and stammered: "A door like that, just like that."

"What do you mean, Caspar? What's on your mind?" asked the Mayor affectionately.

Caspar did not reply. With his eyes on the floor and the slowness of a sleep-walker, he walked through the hall. The two men let him go ahead. After a few steps he would always stop, reflecting.

His agitation increased as he walked up the broad stone steps. At the top he looked around and sighed; his face was pale; his shoulders shook. Daumer was sorry for him and wanted to break through this absorption, but when he began to speak, Caspar with a far-away look murmured, "Dukatus, Dukatus," and listened as if to suck a secret meaning from the word.

He looked at the long row of pictures of the Burggraves on the walls, he looked through the long suite of open rooms, he stood in the gallery and closed his eyes, and finally, in reply to a murmured question from the Mayor, he turned around and said in a stifled voice that it seemed to him as if he had once had such a house, and he did not know what he should think of it. The

Mayor looked at Daumer in silence.

In the afternoon they went to see Herr von Tucher, and together with him they drew up their report to President Feuerbach. The final draft was sent by mail the same day.

Strangely enough there was no answer, nor any sign at all that the President had received the communication. The letter must have gone astray or have been stolen. Baron Tucher inquired in secret and personally of Herr von Feuerbach, and it was found that Feuerbach knew of nothing. The three men were disturbed and dismayed. "Is there an invisible arm at work here, as with the note that was thrown in through the window?" Daumer wondered apprehensively. Inquiries at the post-office were without result and so the report was written a second time and handed to the President personally by a reliable messenger.

Feuerbach answered in his categorical fashion that he would bear the thing in mind and for obvious reasons refrain from sending a written expression of opinion. "I judge from the medical certificate of the municipal doctor, which mentions Caspar's paleness in spite of an otherwise satisfactory physical condition, that he is in need of regular exercise in the open air," he wrote. "This must be remedied. Let him ride. Von Rumpler has been recommended to me as a riding master. Let Hauser take a riding lesson from him three times a week, the expense to be charged to the City Commissioner."

Perhaps it was the dreams which made Caspar white. Almost every night he found himself in the big house. The arched walls were flooded with a silver light. He stood before a closed door and waited and waited. Finally one night the dim rooms of the big house stretched out silent and empty and from the lowest passage a swaying figure appeared. Caspar thought at first it was the man in the white coat; but as the figure came nearer he perceived that it was a woman. She was covered with white veils which hung from her shoulders and blew about her in the breath of an inaudible wind. Caspar stood as though rooted to the spot. His heart hurt him as though a fist had snatched at it and seized it, for the countenance of the woman showed an expression of anxiety such as he had never noticed on a human countenance before. The nearer she came, the tighter his heart contracted; she walked by him, very serious; her lips uttered his name, it was not the name of Caspar, and yet he knew that it was his name, or at least that it was intended for him alone. She did not cease to utter the same name, and when she was already in the distance and the veils blew like white wings from her shoulders, he still heard the name. Then he knew that the woman was his mother.

He woke up bathed in tears, and when Daumer came he rushed to him, crying: "I have seen her; I have seen my mother. It was she; she has spoken to me."

Daumer sat down at the table and rested his head in his hand. "Look here, Caspar," he said after a while. "You must not give way credulously to such delusions. Honestly, it worries me and has for some time. It is as if someone were allowed to wander for pleasure in a flower garden and instead of giving himself up to pleasurable enjoyment, digs up the roots and burrows holes in the ground. Understand me clearly, Caspar, I don't want you to give up the right to discover everything which relates to your past and to the crime which has been committed against you. But remember that men of great experience like President Feuerbach and Herr Binder are at work on the problem. You, Caspar, must look forward, live in the light and not in darkness. Your existence is in the realm of light; there is happiness. Every man of good sense can do what he wishes to. Do, for the love of me, turn away from your dreams. Not for nothing do we say 'Dreams foam' "

Caspar was dumfounded. This was the first time that the idea had been suggested to him that his dreams might not be true. But, for the first time also, his own conviction was stronger on a subject than the opinion of his teacher. The sensation, however, gave him regret rather than satisfaction.

6. Religion, Homeopathy and Visitors From Many Places

Thus December came, and one morning the first snow of the belated winter began to fall.

Caspar never tired of watching the silent falling of the snowflakes. He thought they were little winged animals until he stretched his hand out of the window and they melted on his warm skin. Gardens and streets, roofs and window ledges glistened, and through the mass of snowflakes a light mist glided like the breath pouring from a breathing mouth.

"What do you say to this, Caspar?" Frau Daumer called to him. "Do you remember that you did not want to believe me when I told you about the winter? Do you see how white everything is?"

Caspar nodded without shifting his gaze from outside. "White is age," he murmured; "white is old and cold."

"Your riding lesson is at eleven, Caspar, don't forget it," Daumer, who was on his way to school, warned him.

A superfluous worry; Caspar did not forget his riding. He had become too fond of it in the short time since he had begun.

He loved horses, for their shape was very familiar to him. Sometimes evening shadows rushed by in the form of black horses, halting at the edge of the sky and looking back at him to invite him to follow them into the unknown distance. Horses, too, rushed through the wind, and the clouds, too, were horses, and in the rhythm of music he heard the measured beat of trotting hoofs, and when in some happy mood he thought of anything that was noble and perfect, he would first behold the image of a proud steed.

At his riding lessons he had from the very beginning shown an aptness which had aroused the greatest astonishment on the part of his teacher. "You ought to see how that boy sits and holds his reins and understands the animal," said Herr von Rumpler. "I'll burn a hundred years in hell if this thing has come about without foul play." And all who had any expertness in the matter spoke in the same tone.

How happy Caspar was, trotting and galloping! This pulling and flying, this sensation of being lightly carried onward and forward, this gentle motion up and down; this being alive on something alive, how it all delighted him!

If only people weren't so bothersome. The first time he went out with the riding master they were followed by a large rabble, and even sedate citizens stood still and laughed bitterly. "Ah, he knows his business," they mocked; "he has feathered his nest; that's the way to begin to make yourself comfortable."

Today, too, there was another such unpleasant scene. The sky had cleared and the sun shone as they rode through Engelhardt Street. A crowd of boys followed them, and on all sides windows were thrown up. The riding master spurred on his horse and urged Caspar's horse with a whip. "By heaven, it makes you feel like a circus rider," he exclaimed angrily.

They cantered to the Jacob Gate. "Wo, whoa," called a voice, and Herr von Wessenig rode down a side street, also on horseback. Rumpler greeted the officer, who joined Caspar. "Wonderful, wonderful, my dear Hauser," he exclaimed with exaggerated astonishment. "You ride like a young Indian chief. And all this you have learned among the good citizens of Nurnberg. It's incredible."

Caspar did not hear the incredulous undertone of suspicion in this speech. He felt flattered and glanced gratefully at the officer.

"Only guess, Caspar, what I have received today," continued the officer, for he was itching to tease Caspar. "I have received something today which greatly concerns you." Caspar looked at him questioningly. Perhaps it was the noble calm in the expression of his features which made the officer hesitate. "Yes, I have received something," he repeated obstinately. "I have received a little letter." He spoke in the ingenuous tones which adults assume when they joke with children, and the watchful expression of his eyes said, "We'll see whether he will be scared."

"A little letter," said Caspar. "What is in it?"

"Yes, I suppose you'd like to know, wouldn't you?" said the officer, as he laughed loudly. "There are important things in it, important things."

"From whom is it, then?" asked Caspar, whose heart began to beat expectantly. Herr von Wessenig showed his teeth and stood up in his stirrups with pleasure. "Now guess," said he; "we'll see whether you can guess. From whom can the letter be?" He winked knowingly at Herr von Rumpler while Caspar's head sank.

Caspar's senses were suddenly bathed in the air of dreams, and a hope caressed him and cast out the wretched claims of the day that was. The distressed lady of his dreams rose out of her veils and floated on before the three horses. Abruptly he looked up and said, hesitatingly: "Is the letter perhaps from my mother?"

The officer frowned a little, doubting whether it were wise to carry the joke so far, but quickly dismissed this serious mood, slapped Caspar on the shoulder and exclaimed, "You've guessed it, you devil, you've guessed it. More I won't say, my friend, otherwise I'll get into trouble." And with these words he settled himself in his saddle and rode off.

A quarter of an hour later Caspar came home breathless. They looked at the boy eagerly and Anna unconsciously got up when Caspar, his forehead drenched with perspiration, walked up to her brother's chair and exclaimed in a broken, jubilant voice, "Herr Wessenig has received a letter from my mother."

Daumer shook his head. He tried to make Caspar understand that there must be some mistake or deception; his mother and sister supported him as best they could. It was in vain. Caspar folded his hands entreatingly, and begged Daumer to go with him to Herr von Wessenig. Daumer refused with decision, but as Caspar's excitement grew he declared himself ready to go to Herr von Wessenig alone. He ate his lunch quickly, took his coat and hat and went out.

Caspar ran to the window and looked after him. He did not want to sit down at the table until Daumer returned. He twisted his handkerchief in his hand, and breathing hard he looked up at the sky and thought: "Oh, sun, if I am to love you, do make this come true." Thus the time passed; one o'clock came and Daumer returned. He had expostulated with the officer and they had had a heated discussion. Herr von Wessenig had at first taken the thing humorously, but this attitude had roused Daumer, who was already angry enough at the unpleasant remarks which were daily reported to him. Only the day before he had been told that at a party given by Mayor Binder's wife, a much respected aristocrat had made fun of him, calling him a master of somnambulism, of magnetism and occult science, who was weaving a magic carpet for Caspar Hauser to fly with, but instead of disappearing into the void, as Everyone had been led to expect, the good Caspar sat tight where he was and enjoyed the good things of life.

These things rankled with Daumer, and he had told the officer to his face that the sneering gossip of the idle world was indifferent to him. "Even though I was more prepared for help and approval than for justification and defense, I know quite well that your frozen heart and the hearts of your ilk will not beat more humanly for any consideration!" he exclaimed. "But I have a right to demand that the boy who is under my protection, as well as under that of the Herr Staatsrat, shall at least be spared malevolent jokes."

He spoke and went, but he did not leave a friend behind him.

When he reached home, seeing Caspar's silent pleading, he said with a composure which he found it difficult to assume: "He made a fool of you, Caspar. Of course there wasn't a word of truth in it. You must not believe such people."

"Oh!" exclaimed Caspar full of pain; then he was silent. Not until Daumer was leaving for school after the noon rest did Caspar break through his silence to say, in a lifeless and changed voice: "So Herr von Wessenig did not tell the truth?"

"No, he lied," replied Daumer briefly.

"That's wrong of him, very wrong," said Caspar.

He was astonished in the first place at the fact of the lie, and still more surprised that such a distinguished gentleman should be guilty of lying to him. "Why did he tell me that about the letter?" he pondered. He spent hours in repeating the officer's words to himself, again and again, and in recalling the appearance of the face in which, unknown to him, the lie had dwelt.

Something was not right. He thought and thought and reached no conclusion. To distract his thoughts he opened his arithmetic and did his daily task. When this did not help him he turned to his musical glasses, which a lady from Bamberg had given him, and practiced for half an hour the simple melodies which he had learned to play upon them.

Suddenly he got up and stepped in front of a mirror. He gazed steadily at his own face to see whether a lie dwelt in it. In spite of the uneasiness which it caused him, he was tempted to lie once just to see how his face would look afterwards. Anxiously he looked around, then looked again into the mirror, and said softly, "It's snowing." He thought this was a lie, because the sun was shining.

There was no change in his face; one could therefore lie without anyone's noticing it. He had thought that the sun would grow dark or would hide, but it simply continued to shine.

That evening Daumer came home with a fresh cause for irritation. When his mother asked what was wrong again, he drew a small newspaper out of his pocket and threw it on the table. It was the Katholischer Wochenschatz. On the first page there was an article about Caspar Hauser, which began with the question, printed in large type: "Why does the foundling of Nurnberg not enjoy the blessings of religion?"

"Yes, indeed, why not?" said Anna, sarcastically. "And one dares to print that in a Protestant city," remarked Daumer with an angry face, "if these gentlemen only knew how dreadfully afraid the boy is of their priests. While he was still in the tower four appeared there simultaneously. Do you think perhaps that they addressed themselves to his heart or attempted to awaken a religious spirit? Far from it. They chattered about the anger of God, and of retribution for sin, and as he looked increasingly frightened they began to storm and to threaten as though the poor boy was to be led to the gallows the next day. Accidentally I came in and politely asked them to spare their pains."

As Caspar entered the room just then, the conversation was cut short.

But the cry raised by the Katholischer Wochensc hat z did not die down unheard. "You can't fool with religion," said the gentlemen of the magistracy, and one of them even expressed a doubt as to whether the boy had ever been christened. This was debated pro and contra for some time, but finally the question was allowed to drop, since one was living among Christians in a Christian land and the boy could not very well have come from Tartary.

The question of the Catholic or Protestant denomination was not so easily decided. Although the priests had little power in the city, the unprotected soul had nevertheless to be snatched from the hungry jaws of Rome; on the other hand, they were too timid for a bold seizure, because sooner or later some person of importance might produce claims of a different nature.

The Mayor appealed to Daumer, requesting that Caspar should have religious instruction; he would leave it to Daumer to find a reliable man. "What about Kandidat Regulein?" asked Binder.

"I have no objection," replied Daumer indifferently. The probationer lived on the ground floor of Daumer's house and had the reputation of being a respectable and industrious man.

"Although I am not of a pious turn of mind." said the Mayor, "yet the agnosticism which is so much the fashion now is very distasteful to me, and I should not like our Caspar to grow up in frivolous worldliness. And I am sure you can have no such desire either!"

"Aha, a dig for me," thought Daumer with silent anger. "I am again being insulted and suspected; I make them uncomfortable; very lovely, gentlemen; very lovely of you." Aloud, he merely said: "Certainly not. In my own way I have not failed to influence him. And my method, whatever else you may say of it, is no worse than any other. Unfortunately all sorts of people have constantly interfered in a way that was quite uncalled for. In the beginning I had finally succeeded after a lot of trouble in breaking his obstinate attitude and imparting to him some idea of the mighty urge to growth which pervades all nature. Then one day, while Caspar was sitting in front of a flower-pot, watching with innocent astonishment the sprouts which had blossomed during the night, some woman or other comes along. 'Well, Caspar,' she asks foolishly, 'who is it that has caused all this to grow? 'It has grown of its own accord," he answered proudly. 'Why, Caspar!' she exclaims, 'there must be someone who has caused it to grow.' He did not deign to reply, but the well-meaning woman rushed about and told Everyone Caspar was being made into an atheist. This makes matters very difficult."

"It's a question in the last analysis of giving him some idea of a higher obligation," said Binder.

"He has that, he has that, but his intelligence does not recognize any limitation and wants to be entirely satisfied," Daumer went on passionately. "Yesterday he was visited by two Protestant clergymen, one from Fiirth, the other from Farnbach; one fat and one thin, both as eager as miniature Pauls of Tarsus. First they sung all sorts of praise in my honor. I let them see Caspar and before you could count three they began a theological discussion with him. Oh, it was funny, it was very funny. First they talked about the creation of the world, and the fat one from Fiirth said that God had created the world out of the void. And when Caspar wanted to know how that had been done, they cheated him out of his explanation by both of them wringing their hands and talking to him as though he were an atheist worshiping an idol. Finally they calmed down, and then my good Caspar said, confidingly, if one wanted to make something one had to have something out of which to make it, would they please tell him how anything else was possible in the case of God. They were silent for a while, then they whispered to one another, and finally the thin one answered that with God everything was possible, because He was a spirit and not a man. Then Caspar smiled at me, for he thought that they were making fun of him, and pretended to believe them, as the best way of getting rid of them."

The Mayor shook his head disapprovingly. He was entirely displeased with Daumer's sarcasm. "Don't forget that there is another view of God than the one which can be so readily made fun of," he replied quietly.

"A different view, certainly. Only don't forget that it entirely contradicts the common one. And if I try to make him accept it I expose myself to reproaches and to being misunderstood. Next year he is to go to public school, a sufficiently difficult thing, under the best of circumstances, for a boy of at least eighteen years, then my teachings would be destroyed and the result for him would be confusion. I am already beginning to be cowardly and to give him answers of expedience rather than of truth. Recently, because of a weakness of his eyes, he could not work, and he asked me whether he might ask God for something and whether he would get it. I said that he could ask, but he must realize that it depended upon the wisdom of God whether He would grant his request or not. He replied that he wanted to ask God to cure his eyes and God could not object to this, for he needed the use of his eyes in order not to waste his time in idle gossip and play. Whereupon I said that God had at times inscrutable reasons for denying us something which we believed to be good for us; He wished, perhaps, to test us through suffering, to give us practice in patience and submission. Then he hung his head sadly. Certainly he thought I was no better than the pious people whose reasoning seemed mere quibbling to him."

"But what can be done?" asked the Mayor with a worried expression. "Doubting and denying will of necessity stunt his capacity for virtue."

"It's scarcely doubting and denial," replied Daumer unwillingly. "God does not dwell in heaven; he lives only in our breasts. The rich spirit senses him in a wide range of feelings; the poorer soul becomes aware of him through the hardships of life and calls this faith, he might also call it fear. The true God assumes his form in beauty and joy, in creating. What you call doubt and denial is the honest hesitation of a soul not yet certain of itself. If one gives a plant as much sun as it needs, it possesses a God."

"That is philosophy," replied Binder, "and, moreover, philosophy which must sound frivolous to an everyday man like myself. Every peasant must reckon with storm and bad weather for his harvest, and it can only occur to a very conceited man that he amounts to anything by himself. But enough of this. Have you ever actually taken Caspar to church?"

"No, I have avoided it up to now."

"To-morrow is Sunday. Have you any objection to my taking him with me to service in the Frauenkirche?"

"Not the slightest."

"Fine, I'll call for him at nine o'clock."

If Herr Binder had expected some unusual effect from this visit he was very much disappointed. When Caspar entered the church and heard the loud voice of the preacher, he asked what the man was scolding about. The crucifix made him shudder painfully, because he took the pictures of Christ nailed on the cross to be living creatures suffering torment. He looked everywhere and he marveled endlessly; the playing of the organ and the singing of the choir deafened his sensitive ear to such an extent that he did not perceive the harmony of the sounds, and the exhalations of the crowd of people almost made him faint.

The Mayor saw his mistake, but he did not give up, insisting upon regular attendance at church, although Caspar struggled obstinately against it each time. When Kandidat Regulein complained of his difficulties to Mayor Binder, the latter replied, "Be patient, habit will force him to become reverent." "I don't think so," replied the licentiate with discouragement. "He behaves as if he were going to his death when I suggest going to church." "No difference; it's your calling to break his resistance," he was told.

Poor, good-natured, helpless Kandidat Regulein. A little young man who had never been young, whose religious knowledge was of as thin a consistency as his legs. He trembled secretly at the lessons which he was obliged to give Caspar, and whenever a question put him in a dilemma, which happened not infrequently, he postponed the answer until the next lesson, promising himself to look up the answer in certain books so as not to offend against theology. Caspar waited innocently, but the following lesson brought little or nothing. The Kandidat, who secretly hoped his pupil had forgotten, became frightened and avoided the issue. This did not help. The merciless questions of Caspar drove him from one entrenchment into another until in desperation the argument was brought forth that it was wrong to attempt to explore the mysterious questions of faith.

Caspar hurried to Daumer and complained that he was not getting any explanations. Daumer asked what he had wanted to know. He had asked why God no longer came down to man as in olden times in order to instruct people about the many things which were incomprehensible to them.

"Yes, but look here, Caspar," said Daumer, "There are secrets which cannot be understood with the best will in the world. In such cases one must have faith that someday God will enlighten us about such matters. We all of us do not know where you come from and who you are, nevertheless we hope that the justice and wisdom of God will someday vouchsafe us an explanation."

"But certainly God had nothing to do with my having been in prison," replied Caspar gently; "man did that." And in perplexity he added, "It just is like that. One time the licentiate says God gives people free will, the next time he says that He punishes them for their evil deeds. It all makes me feel like a fool."

This discussion took place on a stormy afternoon toward the end of March and put Daumer into such a sad mood that he was unable to finish some writing which he had begun. They are robbing me of him, they are breaking him to pieces, he thought. Full of sadness, he took up a large copy book which contained his notes on Caspar, and turned the pages. He started with fright when his sister entered somewhat brusquely with her coat and fur cap still on, just as she had come in from the street. Her face betrayed excitement and she turned to Daumer and exclaimed rapidly and excitedly: "Do you know what is being said in the city?"

"Well?"

"People are saying that Caspar Hauser is of royal descent, a prince who has been put out of the way."

Daumer gave a forced laugh. "That is the last straw," said he disdainfully. "What more will there be?"

"You don't believe it. I thought so at once. But where would such rumors come from? There must be something back of them."

"There need not be anything back of them. They are gossiping. Let them talk."

Half an hour later Herr Wurm, the director of archives from Ansbach, called on Daumer. He was a small man, somewhat crippled, who never smiled. It was said of him that he was very intimate with Herr von Feuerbach, and the right hand of Herr Mieg, the President of the Board of Governors. He brought Daumer greetings from the former and said that the President was soon coming to Nurnberg, and he was going into the Caspar Hauser affair very thoroughly.

After a little brief and unimportant conversation, the director suddenly put his hand in his coat pocket, produced a small paper-bound book and silently handed it to Daumer. The latter took it and read the title, "Casper Hauser, Not Improbably a Swindler," by Polizeirat Merker in Berlin.

Daumer looked at the book with hostile eyes and said wearily: "That's plain enough. What does the man want? What's itching him?"

"It's a nasty pamphlet, but sounds very plausible," answered the Director. "He has carefully and diligently collected all grounds for suspecting the foundling, which have been smoldering in skeptical spirits for some time. He examines all of Caspar's statements most suspiciously, and offers illustrations from the past, in which similarly manufactured lies have later been exposed. You, dear professor, and your friends here don't get off any too well."

"Naturally, I can imagine that," murmured Daumer, and, striking with his open hand upon the book, he exclaimed, "not improbably an impostor, some slick smart man who sits in Berlin and dares, dares!— Why, it cries to heaven. Someone ought to confront him with this probable impostor, he should be compelled to confront his angelic expression; oh, it's shameful. The only consolation is that no one will read the trash."

"You are mistaken," replied the director quietly. "The pamphlet has a tremendous sale."

"Well, then I shall read it," said Daumer. "I shall take it to Pfisterle, the editor of the *Morgenpost*. He's the right person to reply to this distinguished policeman."

The Director measured Daumer's excitement with a quick and indifferent glance. "I should not approve offhand of such a measure," he remarked diplomatically. "I think I may speak in accordance with Herr von Feuerbach's wishes in advising you against such a step. What good would it do? One must act, and act with care and silence, that's the best way."

"With care and silence? What do you mean to say?" asked Daumer anxiously and distrustfully.

The Director shrugged his shoulders and looked at the floor. Then he got up, said he would return on the afternoon of the following day to see Caspar, and shook hands with Daumer. When he was already on the steps Daumer hurried after him and asked whether it would disturb him to meet strangers in the house on the following day, some ladies and gentlemen who said that they would call. The Director said he would not mind.

It was one of Daumer's peculiarities that when he had once made up his mind to a thing he persisted in it, going to the length of openly harming himself. In spite of the cautious Herr Wurm's admonition, he had scarcely read the book—which took less than an hour—before he went, full of bitterness, to the editor of the *Morgenpost*. The editor, Herr Pfisterle, was a hot-headed man. He seized the opportunity, like a vulture snatching at carrion, to let loose the spleen and anger which he always had on tap. He wanted to have material, and Daumer arranged to have Pfisterle come to his house at noon on the following day.

That evening a curiously oppressive atmosphere dominated the Daumers' house. During supper there was little conversation, and Caspar, who had no conception of what was going on, was astonished at the scrutinizing glances, or the mournful silence which followed some light-hearted question on his part. He was accustomed to taking up a book and reading before going to bed. He did this today, too, and it happened that when he opened the book his glance fell on a passage which caused him to applaud with delight and to laugh in his hearty way. Daumer asked what was the matter. Caspar pointed with his finger to the page and said, "Just look, Professor." For some time he had stopped addressing Daumer as "Du" and quite of his own accord, curiously enough almost on the same day on which he had eaten meat for the first time and been sick afterwards.

Daumer looked at the book. The words which Caspar had seized upon were, "The sun will bring it to daylight."

"What is so surprising in that?" asked Anna, who was looking at the page over her brother's shoulder. "How beautiful, how beautiful!" exclaimed Caspar, "the sun will bring it to light, that's very beautiful!"

The three others gazed at one another full of curious feelings.

"It's always beautiful when one reads the word sun," Caspar continued; "it sounds so lovely."

When he had said good-night, Frau Daumer said: "One really has to love him. It does one good to watch how nicely he occupies himself. He is like some little insect spinning quietly. He is never bored, never a burden because of caprices or whims."

Pfisterle came the next day, as agreed upon, shortly after lunch, but remained immoderately long and would not understand the impatient hints of Daumer, who would gladly have gotten rid of him before the arrival of the expected guests. When these arrived at three o'clock, he was still sitting in the same place and he remained. Probably Daumer had roused his curiosity by telling him the name of one of the three guests, who was a popular author from the North of the Empire. The others were a Holstein baroness and a professor from Leipzig, who were traveling to Rome, an undertaking which at that time, at least in Nurnberg, gave a man the reputation of being a bold explorer.

Daumer greeted his guests very graciously, and after he had sent for Caspar he lit the lamps, in spite of the early hour, for the fog lay like heavy wool in front of the windows. The Leipzig professor engaged Caspar in conversation, but he spoke to him with an immense superiority. He kept his gaze fastened upon him, and at times the yellow eyes back of the round spectacles glittered unkindly. Meantime Herr von Tucher and the director came in, and

Religion, Homeopathy and Visitors From Many Places | 69

after they had allowed themselves to be introduced, they sat down on the sofa.

"So your prison was always dark?" asked the traveler to Rome, slowly stroking his beard.

Caspar answered patiently, "Dark, very dark." The author laughed, whereupon the professor nodded at him significantly.

"Have you heard this nonsense about his royal birth which is being talked about here in the city?" the Holstein baroness was heard to say in a voice which sounded as if it had come from the cellar.

The professor nodded: "Really, great demands are made here on the credulity of the public."

For a time they remained silent, as if frightened by a revolver shot. Finally Daumer, in a husky voice, with the politeness of a bad actor, asked,

"What leads you to question my honor?" "What leads me?" shouted the choleric gentleman. "These tricks are the reason. The fact that the whole country is being deluged with nonsensical fairy stories. Must the good German people always be the victim of adventures a la Cagliostro? It is a disgrace."

Herr von Tucher had arisen and was looking at the excited man with such unfeigned contempt that the latter suddenly became silent.

"We are naturally convinced, Professor," interrupted the author, a lean, thin gentleman, with a bald head, who was trying to act as mediator, "that you are acting in all good faith. You are a victim like the rest of us."

Now Pfisterle, who was simply bursting with rage, could no longer control himself. With clenched fists he jumped up from his chair and exclaimed, "Why in the devil's name shall we put up with this? You come here, no one has asked you, you come here in order to be able to say you have been here, in order to be able to talk with the rest; you have known better than we all along, and if you are as blind as moles and can't see, you proudly clap on your chests and say: we don't see anything, therefore there is nothing. Why should it be nonsense, Madame, that people are talking about his birth? Why, please? Do you perhaps deny that behind the walls where live the great, there happen things which people don't want brought to daylight? Do you deny that the ties of blood are set at naught and the rights of man trampled underfoot if it is to the advantage of one single person? Shall I present you with a few facts? You can't deny them. With us, at any rate, the few dozen men have not been forgotten who carried their brave banner of freedom through the land and with burning torches illuminated the dark nest of lies in palaces."

"Enough, enough," the professor interrupted the rabid newspaper man. "Moderate yourself, sir!"

"A demagogue," said the baroness and got up with frightened eyes. The director fastened a cold and reproachful gaze upon Daumer, who had sunk his head and obstinately closed his lips. When he looked up his eyes rested on Caspar, who stood there simply and guilelessly, letting his clear smiling glance travel from one to the other, not as though he were being talked about or participated in what was going on, but as if it gave him pleasure merely to observe their expressions and gestures. Actually he scarcely understood what was being said.

The Leipzig professor had taken up his hat, and turned once more talking to Daumer, ignoring Pfisterle. "What is proven by these assumptions of stupid brains?" he asked shrilly. "Nothing is proven. The only fact is that some clod of a peasant from some God-forsaken village in the Frankish woods has strayed into the city, that he can't speak properly, that all culture is unknown to him, that the new is new, and the unfamiliar appears strange. And a lot of honest but short-sighted men go out of their heads over this and take the crude fabrications of this slick vagabond for something genuine. It's too queer for me."

"Just like Polizeirat Merker," the Director could not refrain from speaking. Pfisterle, too, wanted to interfere, but was induced to keep silent by an energetic shake of the head on the part of Herr von Tucher.

Suddenly the wheels of a carriage were heard outside in the street. Director Wurm went to the window and as the carriage stopped in front of the house he said, "The Staatsrat is coming."

"What?" said Daumer quickly, "Herr von Feuerbach?"

"Yes, Herr von Feuerbach." In his amazement Daumer forgot his duties as a host, and when he had recovered sufficiently to receive the President, the latter was already on the threshold. With his imperial glance he quickly took in all the faces in the room, and when he perceived the Director of Archives, he exclaimed, "How lucky to find you, dear Wurm. I have something to say to you."

He was dressed like a simple civilian and wore no decorations except the little cross of an order near his collar. The extraordinarily proud bearing of his broad massive body and the stiff, upright commanding military poise of his head, which he carried thrown back always, aroused respect and awe. His face, which at the first glance resembled that of an irritable old coachman, was ennobled by the dark glowing eyes, in which lay the restlessness of intellectual passions, and by the tightly closed, boldly arched lips.

He did not make the impression of a man who had much time. In spite of the dignity imparted to him by his position, and which his personal qualities did not diminish, his manner was somewhat vehement and his mode of greeting those in the room was formal and stern. All those present were therefore frightened when Caspar walked up to him without nervousness and of his own accord stretched out his hand to him, which Feuerbach took and even held for a time in his own.

Caspar had felt wonderfully at ease since the President had entered. He had often thought of him since he had spoken to him in the prison tower, and since his first handclasp he particularly loved the President's hand. It was a warm, hard, dry hand which closed tightly when he greeted you, as if it made trustworthy promises, and his own hand rested in it as safely as his tired body rested in bed at night.

Daumer conducted the President and Director Wurm into his study, and then returned. The strange guests started to leave; the arrival of Feuerbach had caused them to lose some of their superiority. Caspar wanted to help the lady into her coat, but she made a gesture of protest and quickly followed her companion. Herr von Tucher and Pfisterle also left.

Caspar took his copybook out of the drawer and sat down by the lamp to finish his Latin exercise, as the President and Director Wurm came into the room again. Feuerbach went up to Caspar and, laying his hand on his head, he gently bent it backward so that the light of the lamp fell full upon Caspar's face. For a remarkably long time he looked with penetrating attention into Caspar's face, who met his glance steadily, and finally murmured, turning towards

Wurm and breathing deeply. "There's no mistake; they are the same features."

The Director nodded silently.

"That and the dreams; two important proofs," said the President in the same tone of preoccupation. He walked to the window with his hands on his back, and looked out for a time. Then he turned to Daumer and asked suddenly how matters stood with Caspar's food.

Daumer replied that he had recently tried to accustom him to meat. "At first he protested strongly against it, and it does not look as if this altered diet agreed with him very well. I am even afraid that it essentially weakens his inner strength. He is getting perceptibly duller."

Feuerbach frowned and pointed at Caspar. Daumer understood the hint and suggested that Caspar join the ladies. He did not wait until the boy had left the room, but continued with timid zeal: "On the same day on which Caspar ate meat for the first time, our neighbors dog, who had been devoted to him up to then, snapped at him and barked angrily at him. That was a wonderful lesson to me."

The President replied somberly, "Perhaps that may be; but I disapprove of the numberless experiments that you are trying with the young man. What is the point of it all? Why magnetism and other cures? I am informed that you are using homeopathic remedies for certain sick conditions. Why? That can only irritate such a delicate organism. It is youth which heals illness."

"I am surprised that Your Excellency objects to this," replied Daumer, coldly and humbly. "The human body is often seized with temporary ailments which are best reached by homeopathic remedies. Only last Monday a small dose of silicon dioxide worked wonders, I can assure you. Does Your Excellency not know the beautiful old proverb:

"The wise physician's antidote is taken whence the ill: Salinity is cured with salt, and fire with flames we kill. So take ye, Nature's children, of all the arts a tittle, Make little out of much to come, and much again of little."

Religion, Homeopathy and Visitors From Many Places | 73

Feuerbach could not refrain from smiling. "Maybe, maybe," he grumbled, "but that proves nothing, or if it did it is beside the point."

"But my case does not rest on that."

"So much the better. Do not forget that a right has to be enforced here, the right of a life. Is it necessary to be clearer? I scarcely think so. Very soon I hope the darkness which hangs over this perplexing person will be lifted and the thanks which I and others, my dear Daumer, already owe you will not be lessened by the disapproval which must be connected with your perhaps harmful mistakes." There was a solemn ring in these words.

"I am being lectured like a schoolboy," thought Daumer bitterly when the President and Director Wurm had made their adieux. "Why did it enter my head to take up the cause of the homeless foundling? If I had only remained at my work, in my solitude!"

"All these fabrications about his destiny are no business of mine," he continued his vexatious meditations; "however, the tone of the President leads one to infer some peculiar condition. I wonder whether the talk about Caspar's birth has any real foundation. Be that as it may, why should it concern me? Of what importance is it whether he be the son of a peasant or of a prince? Of course, when some high-standing gentleman crosses one's path one acts like an attentive servant; acknowledged rank and noble birth demand the respect of the bourgeois. But life is one thing and ideas are another, and it is one thing to humor the mighty because it is useless to oppose them and another thing to forget them, shut away, and proof against them, in the golden halls of philosophy. Between these two lies the path which separates the man made of dust only, from him who has a soul. Has my optimism carried me too far in seeing in Caspar the being with a soul? It may be doubted still."

These thoughts were not free from ominous sadness.

7. Daumer Puts Metaphysics To The Test

President von Feuerbach remained in the city more than a week. During this time he either came to Daumer's house to talk to Caspar, or he had the boy summoned to his hotel. Feuerbach did not like to have anyone present when he was with Caspar. Since one of the first days when he had walked through the streets with him—when the prematurely aged man, with his imperious bearing unchanged, however, walking next to the delicate slightly bowed boy, had aroused much attention—and suddenly at one of the corners which they were obliged to pass, a suspicious looking man, who seemed to have grown out of the earth, slunk along by their side, the President had ceased to show himself in public with his protégé.

His conversations with Caspar, although at times planned very cleverly to appear quite irrelevant, naturally pursued a certain aim. Caspar, who noticed little of this, spoke to his protector without shyness. Feuerbach's heart was often strangely moved by his innocent chatter, so that he who had the gift of words and language in unusual degree found himself not infrequently condemned to silence. And he even lost some of his security of manner: "Caspar's glance is like the pure morning sky before the sun has risen," he wrote to an old and trusted friend. "Sometimes I feel when he gazes at me as though the rushing onslaught of the wheels of fate were pausing for the first time. The whole past rises before me, wrongs suffered and laws circumvented, humiliations inflicted by envy and many an act whose fruits lie rotting and hideous along one's path. Moreover, in regard to his past I am on the trace of something which is leading me, I very much fear, towards a dangerous abyss, where one must trust to the gods, for it is a domain in which human beings are no longer subject to any rules."

On the last day of Feuerbach's visit Caspar was preparing to go out rather early, as the President had asked him to come to see him. He went into the living room to say that he was going, and found Anna Daumer alone. She was sitting at the window reading the pamphlet of Polizeirat Merker: no sooner had Caspar opened the door than she hid the book quickly, frightened, under her apron. "What are you reading and why are you hiding it?" asked Caspar, smiling.

Anna blushed and stammered something. Then she looked up with damp eyes and said: "Ah, Caspar, people are really too wicked!"

He did not reply, but continued to smile. This seemed striking to Anna, but Caspar thought nothing further of it. It was one of his peculiarities that he could never make up his mind to take any feminine person quite seriously. "Women can't do anything except sit still and sew or knit a little," he used to say; "they eat and drink continuously without any sensible plan, and that is why they are always sick. They abuse other women, but when they are together they act affectionately and well behaved." Once when he was talking thus Frau Daumer complained of his unfairness, but he answered: "You are not like a woman, you are a mother." Once it chanced that there was a parade of tight-rope walkers, and the gay decorations and skillful riding of one of the girls having aroused his attention, he followed her through a few streets, and was very angry at himself, for he felt that he had now run after a woman, as he had heard other men sometimes did.

He said that he would be home for supper, but Anna replied that this would be too late, her mother had spoken of spending the evening with Caspar at Magistrate Behold's; the Magistrate's wife had already asked them several times; she was an influential person; and if Daumer did not want to make an enemy of her he must go.

"The President comes first," said Caspar with annoyance and left. It was mild weather, the snow had long since disappeared and white clouds blew over the pointed gables of the roofs. When Caspar entered the room occupied by the President, he was sitting at his desk, with his body thrown back, gazing darkly into space. It was some time before he turned to Caspar and addressed him, speaking from out of his dark thoughts without any greeting. "I am returning to Ansbach to-morrow, as you know, Caspar," he began, covering his eyes with his hands. "You will not see me for some weeks, perhaps not for some months. I should like to have news of you now and then, from you yourself, but I do not want to ask you to write to me regularly, for I do not wish it to be an irksome task for you. Now I thought I should like to give you an opportunity to express yourself, which would make you rely more on yourself than on other people. You are not being ordered to give an account of yourself, but record here what you would entrust to a friend, or to your mother."

Then he handed Caspar a copybook bound in blue. Caspar took it mechanically and read on a white, heart-shaped label the words: "Diary: Book of Hours for Caspar Hauser." He opened it and perceived that a steel portrait of Feuerbach was pasted on the front page and in the President's handwriting the words: "Who loves the hours as they pass loves God; the corrupt soul flees from itself."

Caspar looked at the President fearfully with big eyes. He repeated to himself silently, with a visible motion of his lips, the written words and then what the President had said to him; everything melted into mist and then, because of the solemnity of Feuerbach's voice, into some perception of danger.

There was a knock at the door and upon the President's "Come in," a messenger brought a letter marked "Urgent." Feuerbach had scarcely seen the seal when, without opening the letter, he rang the bell and ordered the servant who answered it to have his horses harnessed at once. "I must be off to-night," he said to Caspar.

Caspar remained waiting, as he stood, his ears intently avid for more words. The postillion in the courtyard cracked his whip. A breath of distant air seemed to fan Caspar; he suddenly felt something of the bigness of the world, and the clouds in the sky seemed like arms stretched out to lift him up. When the President put out his hand to say good-by, he said coaxingly, with a smile of entreaty: "I should like to go with you."

"What, Caspar!" exclaimed the President with feigned surprise, and suddenly he returned to his former habit of addressing him with the word "Du." "Dost thou wish to leave Nurnberg? Hast thou forgotten what thou owest thy good foster-father? What would Herr Daumer say if thou wouldst forsake him so thanklessly, and many other good men who have taken an interest in thee? Thou surprisest me, Caspar. Art thou not glad to be here?"

Caspar remained silent and lowered his eyes. It is everywhere the same, he thought. He longed to be away from here; he reflected that he might be able to depart some time at night; one had only to open the door and could go without knowing the road. Perhaps then someone would come and ask, "Where are you going, Caspar?" And he would lead him to a castle in front of which many people are assembled and inside a voice calling Caspar's name; the people make way for him, and many arms point to the gate towards which he walks.

"Speak!" said the President brusquely.

"They are all good to me," whispered Caspar with quivering lips.

"Well, then!"

"It is only—"

"What, what is it? Come, let's have the words."

Caspar slowly raised his eyes, then with his arm he made a sweeping gesture as if to include the whole of the globe in the one word, and then he said, "My mother."

Feuerbach turned away, walked to the window and stood in silence.

A quarter of an hour later Caspar walked through the narrow streets near the City Hall and into the EgydienPlatz, which was deserted. It was already dark; in front of the church an oil lamp was burning, and as he was turning to the left where the low bushes hemmed in a little garden toward Laufer Street, he saw a man standing quietly, with lowered head, and looking at him. Caspar went a little more slowly, suddenly he saw the man lift his arm and motion to him with his finger.

Caspar's heart beat loudly. Something or other compelled him to follow the silent invitation of the unknown man. The latter continued to motion with his finger, and as if suffering some outward compulsion Caspar took a few steps towards him. Hereupon the man went farther into the grove but did not cease beckoning. Caspar could not see his face; it was hidden by his hat, which was placed low over his forehead.

He followed the man, although every fiber in his body resisted; with horror he felt himself drawn on step by step, his eyes were wide open, his face showed astonishment and fright and his hands were stretched out before him with taut fingers.

He was already so close to the stranger that he could see his yellow teeth glisten between his lips, and who knows what might have happened had not at that moment a group of drunken boys been heard on the other side of the bushes. The man emitted a low cooing growl and at once disappeared under cover of the bushes.

Caspar, too, turned around and ran towards the church; he ran right into the group of revelers, who tried to stop him, and thus a new terror was added to the old. It was only with difficulty that he tore himself away; some of the boys followed him, yelling; he redoubled his haste, his hat fell from his head, he let it lie and ran as fast as he could through the Judengasse and straight on, and not until he found himself on the bridge leading to the Island of Schiitt did he go more slowly.

Daumer had already become uneasy and was waiting in front of the door of the house. He listened with concern to Caspar's hasty and muddled account of what had happened, and after some reflection on the adventure, he said he scarcely believed it. "Your ever lively fancy has played you some foolish prank," he said with unusual severity. "No, it's really true," Caspar assured him. Then he complained that he had lost his hat, and finally, suddenly becoming quite cheerful, he showed him the note-book which the President had given him, and which he had held tightly clasped in his hand during the whole incident.

Distractedly, Daumer looked at it. "Didn't Anna tell you that we are going to see the Magistrate's wife?" he asked irritably. "It's high time. Go at once and put on your Sunday suit."

Caspar gave him a side-long glance and went into the house reluctantly. Daumer, who was already in evening clothes, strolled twice to the banks of the Pegnitz and back again; half an hour passed, and Caspar's staying away so long finally made him impatient. He hurried up the steps and entered Caspar's room, where a candle was burning. He perceived with anger that Caspar was lying, dressed, asleep on the bed. He shook him by the shoulder, suddenly stopped, walked several times through the room without overcoming his sense of irritation; then suddenly he exclaimed in anger, "What's the use? Let the curious be cheated of their amusement."

He walked through the dark corridor into his sister's room, where he found her sitting at the piano, playing. He put the case before her and Anna at once agreed with him that he should let Caspar stay at home. "Then someone must go to the Councilor's wife and present our excuses for not coming," said Daumer in a tone which implied that otherwise their staying might be misinterpreted, and he feared unpleasant consequences. Anna replied that the maid was not at home, and after a moment's thought she said she would carry the message herself.

When she had gone, Daumer sat down to his books, adjusted the lamp and read. But his conscience was not clear and he started at every sound. After a considerable time he heard steps; Anna walked up to his chair and said hastily that the Magistrate's wife had come with her to fetch Caspar. "That would be carrying things too far," he murmured indignantly. Anna put her hand over his mouth, for the lady was already standing in the doorway, richly dressed in a silk coat with a costly lace shawl on her head. She was a very stately woman, no longer very young, uncommonly tall, with an unusually small head. There was a not altogether fortunate mixture of the fashionable French and the provincial Nurnberg in her manner, and when she wished to display the former, the latter protruded like the train of a badly concealed shabby garment under a tunic of velvet.

She rustled up to Daumer with the majesty of a billow rolling on the beach, and the good man, awed by so much splendor, forgot his resentment, and raised to his lips the hand which she extended. "Must I myself remind you of your promise?" she exclaimed in a deep sonorous voice. "What does this mean, Professor? What has happened! Why this refusal? You see I have forsaken my guests to make you redeem a promise which you are breaking so lightly. No excuses, dear Daumer; Caspar must come with me. Where is he?"

"He's asleep," Daumer timidly replied.

"He's sleeping, nom de Dieu! To think of such a thing! We will wake him. Hurry, lead the way."

Daumer did not have the courage to refuse: her manner brushed all possible objections aside. He took up the lamp and led the way. Anna, who remained behind, made an indignant exclamation which in no way disturbed Frau Behold, who merely shrugged her shoulders disdainfully.

Daumer stood by Caspar's bed so lost in thought that he forgot to set down the lamp. Actually it would be hard to find anything more beautiful than the angelic peace, the rosy bloom which radiated from the sleeper's face. Frau Behold involuntarily clasped her hands, and in the gesture there was sincerity and feeling.

"Do you still insist upon waking him?" asked Daumer, with the voice of a judge pronouncing the law; "sleep is sacred; the holy spirits will take their flight as soon as our hand touches him."

Frau Behold opened and shut her eyelids as if to disperse her trace of feeling, as one drives out flies with a feather duster. "Nicely put," she jested, and her voice hummed like the tiny wheel of a spindle. "But I insist upon my agreement. I will give the boy a present for coming, and so far as those sacred spirits of yours are concerned, they will return again; there are nights enough for sleeping.

While Daumer lifted the sleeping boy by his shoulders and sought with affectionate words to calm rather himself than Caspar, Frau Behold's little face showed remarkable excitement. Her eyes blinked, her lower lip relaxed and showed a firm row of determined teeth, like a rodent's. "Pauvre diable" she murmured, "poor child," and she seized Caspar's hand.

This woke Caspar fully; he snatched away his hand and shook himself. His dazed and tired look inquired what was wanted of him, and Daumer explained, poured out a glass of water and gave it to him to drink, took his best coat, which was already at hand, and held it out for him to put on.

Caspar looked steadily and darkly at Frau Behold, and said obstinately, "I don't want to go to that woman's house,"

"What, Caspar?" exclaimed Daumer, astonished and hurt. For the first time he heard this, "I don't want to"; for the first time Caspar's will was opposed to his. Caspar was frightened himself, and his glance was already submissive when Daumer continued in a serious tone: "But I want you to. I also want you to beg the lady's pardon. It is not right that you should let a mood get the better of you. If we were all relieved of being considerate towards one another, we should all be as helpless as you were on the first day."

With eyes cast down, Caspar did as he was told. Frau Behold took the incident lightly. She patted Caspar's cheek and thought the Professor rather amusing.

Half an hour later they were in Frau Behold's festively lighted rooms. Caspar, surrounded by people, was overwhelmed with the usual flood of questions. Frau Behold did not quit his side;

she laughed at almost everything he said, and he gradually became confused and uneasy. He felt fear at their words; it seemed to him dangerous to speak, as if words had a double meaning: one open, the other concealed; and the people, too, like the words, seemed to have a double meaning. Involuntarily his glance sought in each person a second person concealed behind the first, and winking at him with fingers of seduction.

He could not understand what they wished of him; their clothes, their gestures, their nodding and laughing and sociability, were all incomprehensible to him, and he himself began to be equally incomprehensible to himself.

Meantime Daumer was having a bad hour of it. Frau Behold, who was proud to be able to make her house a gathering place for distinguished strangers, today had as one of her guests a gentleman who was said to be traveling under an assumed name, on an important diplomatic mission to a small capital in the eastern part of the country. It was also whispered about that the important stranger took great interest in the foundling Hauser, and that he had expressed himself, in the presence of many persons of note, contemptuously and disapprovingly on the nonsensical stories of Caspar's origin. And it must be admitted that these influential persons by no means closed their minds to the weight of such an opinion, but the behavior of the distinguished man gave rise to some suspicion, and Editor Pfisterle, grumbling as usual, even asserted that in his opinion the diplomatic gentleman was nothing other than a secret spy.

However that might be, Daumer in his obliviousness of the world's doings had heard nothing of all these new developments. The stranger joined him after a short time, a conversation ensued between them, and it was easy for the visitor to arrange that they should sit apart from the rest of the guests. Daumer was intimidated by the manners and the delicate ease of the imposing gentleman, whose breast was covered with orders, and at first could scarcely answer more than yes or no, like a schoolboy. Gradually he became freer and told his listener much about Caspar, and happened to mention his timid nature, and related, as he strove to illustrate the boy's behavior, how he had that very evening come home in flight from an imaginary, doubtless an imaginary, pursuer.

The stranger listened attentively. "Perhaps he was not mistaken," he replied in careful tones; "it may be that certain things are going on under cover. I believe that you yourself, dear Professor, received some sort of warning some time ago. You must not be surprised if certain threats develop into more serious incidents."

Daumer was startled, but the stranger continued to chat with apparent harmlessness, and evincing a most gratifying candor. "You ought to accustom yourself to the idea that there are forces at work which would not shrink from anything in order to carry out their designs with vigor. These disturbing rumors no doubt give rise to misgivings on our part, perhaps they have something up their sleeves and wish to avoid publicity. It may be that for the time being the power which is working behind the scenes desires to set matters right with as little fuss as possible, but it might also play an open game, it might quite calmly tie the hands of the printed page, and that they will not fail to inflict punishment themselves by the pulling the wires behind the stage."

Daumer was startled again; the words of the man who sat facing him seemed to be pointing a definite allusion, but the stranger did not give him any opportunity to consider this; he continued in a clear, almost familiar tone: "I believe that they fear worse than anything else the dissemination of all this stupid gossip by the easy and obvious means of the printed page, and that they will not fail to punish any such step. People in high places do not like to expose themselves, still less do they like to be exposed; and even less to have their most intimate concerns made public; one can understand that. The private citizen has liberty enough, let him disport himself as he likes in his own domain; when he rises above that he will find himself restricted,"

What was that? Daumer thought he understood what the stranger was driving at. He resolved to obey this veiled command; in fact, he had already of his own accord anticipated what was being urged.

"May I permit myself a question, dear Professor," the stranger resumed, "are you really convinced that this stray boy—in whom after my fashion, I admit, I take a certain detached interest—deserves and justifies this uninterrupted attention of serious men? Is it worthwhile to occupy the whole world with the doubtful question of his status? What remains for the important concerns of the nation, for science, for art, for religion, for life as a whole, if a man like you will waste the best powers of his mind on a strange sentimental freak of natural forces? People praise the foundling's unusual gifts. I have tried in vain to discover such gifts; I make so bold as to maintain that in doing this I am only faintly approximating your own uncertainty. Let us allow a little time to pass, and we shall no doubt attain distressing certainty on this point. In our human society there are hundreds of thousands of beings born with equally great or greater qualities, who nevertheless have met with immeasurably worse fates. Genuine human feeling would require that we take up the cudgels in their defense also, for in theory there can be no limit to our compassion with human distress in all its forms. But where would the man end who would tear his heart into shreds and fritter it away on all those deserving of his attention? He would stand emptyhanded when a really great object should demand a worthy sacrifice of him. Think of what Caspar will be ten or twelve years from now, when the supposed wonder will be exposed to its very foundations and will have nothing more to give you than the humiliating every-day matter of a perfectly simple fact. At best there will remain a curiosity with which to season the conversation over our dinners; a curiosity and a little mystery, which seems so exciting to immature intellects."

Daumer's face reflected a contradiction and a resistance; his glance traveled in search of Caspar, but the only thing he was able to say was: "It is not by words that the soul can bear witness of itself."

The stranger smiled bitterly. "The soul, the soul," he remarked sarcastically, "it cannot prove anything by words, for it is only a word like any other. The eye sees, the finger feels, every little hair lives in its own way, the blood runs through its veins, every sense fills space with life and makes death a thing which one feels; why do you scholars embellish and furbish up an unreality into a special entity, by speaking of the soul, as if a soul were an article of jewelry which a vain woman shuts up in a casket and occasionally wears upon her breast, in order to shine at a ball. Everyone is provided with a general stock of strength, and his surplus is not a privilege, but merely a hope. Or may the eagle alone lay claim to the possession of a soul, merely because he flies better than the gander? The soul! You gentlemen insult the Creator, whether you deny the soul or write books to prove its existence."

There was a pause. He speaks like Satan, thought Daumer, but as he was starting to reply the stranger took up the conversation with polite intensity. "I know that you love Caspar," he said in an altered voice, speaking seriously and warmly. "You love him as a brother, and this instinct does not spring from pity, but from the beautiful desire to seek out constantly the God who lives in another's breast, seeking only to recognize itself in his likeness. But you are seeking an excuse for your affection, that's it! Need I tell you that there are no deeper wounds than the disappointments which spring from such conflicts? I advise you to fly from the face and the society of one who will afford you nothing other than disappointments."

"Are we then too weak to retain our attitude towards an experience which we thought we had when we were seeking it?" exclaimed Daumer in despair.

The folds of experience in the stranger's face expressed a grimace of regret. A slight gesture showed that the conversation was for him at an end, and they joined the other guests. Daumer, who was completely disconcerted, wanted nothing so much as to leave the noisy group. He sought Caspar and noticed him silent and pale among shining gowns and brown and gray coats. Frau Behold sat on a low stool, almost at his feet, and her face was hard and gloomy.

The goodbyes were profuse. After they had walked silently for some distance, Daumer threw his arm over Caspar's shoulder and exclaimed: "Oh, Caspar, Caspar." It sounded like an entreaty.

Caspar, who was hungry for knowledge, and whose heart was full of questions to the point of overflowing, sighed and then smiled up into his teacher's face with renewed confidence. Whether it was the glance and the smile which penetrated into some portion of Daumer's being, where he felt uncertain and guilty, or whether it was the night, the loneliness, the painful doubts, or the remarkable conversation which he had just had which kindled his spirit to exaggerated warmth, he stood suddenly still, clasped Caspar more warmly and exclaimed with uplifted eyes: "Oh, man, man!"

The word penetrated to Caspar's very marrow. It was as if suddenly it had become clear to him what this creature man meant. He saw a being tied down and chained, looking up from depths far beneath him; strange, strange even to himself, strange to the other who called the word "man" to him and to whom he could answer nothing but this pregnant word: man.

His ear retained the sound, which because of Daumer's emotion had acquired a measure of solemnity for him. The next morning he took up his diary and the first entry which he made was the three words, "Man, oh, man!"—in anyone else's eyes of course a meaningless hieroglyph, but for him a token pregnant with meaning, almost a secret revealed, a motto and a magic word for avoiding danger. It was characteristic of his childlike nature that from that hour on he regarded the diary as something sacred to which he turned only in times of meditation and self-communion, and in one of those sad yearning moods which often overcame him, he made the curious and momentous decision that no other being but his mother should ever look into this book or should ever read what he would set down in it. He was quite capable of clinging with the greatest tenacity to decisions of this kind.

A few days later, when the Princesses of Kurland, friends of Feuerbach, who took the greatest interest in Caspar, came to Daumer's house, it happened in the course of the conversation that the gift which the President had made to his protégé was mentioned. Daumer said that the diary contained an excellent steel engraving of Feuerbach, and the ladies wanted to see it. To the astonishment of Everyone, Caspar refused to show it. Daumer, who was frightened, reproached him for his rudeness, but he remained obstinate. The ladies did not insist further, indeed they even turned the conversation tactfully to other matters; but when they had left Daumer took the boy to task and asked him the reason for his refusal. Caspar remained silent. "And if I asked you, would you refuse to show me the book?" asked Daumer. Caspar looked at him with big eyes and answered innocently, "I am sure you won't ask it, please."

Daumer, very much hurt, walked away in silence.

Towards evening Herr von Tucher came, and asked to speak to Daumer alone, whereupon he said without further ceremony: "Unfortunately, I must tell you that I have caught Caspar lying twice."

Daumer silently clasped his hands. That was more than he could stand, he thought.

Lying, caught lying twice! Good heavens! How did that happen?

The thing had transpired in the following manner: On Sunday he had gone into Caspar's room with the Mayor, Herr von Tucher explained, and had asked the boy to accompany him to his house. Hereupon Caspar, who was sitting at his books, replied that he could not go, Daumer had forbidden him to leave the house. This had at once seemed suspicious to the Mayor, particularly as Caspar had scarcely dared look at him, and he had quietly asked Daumer, as Daumer would doubtless recall, and found his suspicions justified. The next day they had both, Herr Binder and Herr von Tucher, while Daumer was away, visited Caspar and upbraided him with his untruthfulness. Turning red and then pale, he had confessed his fault, but like a frightened rabbit driven into a corner, and seeking the first way out, he had stupidly invented a tale of a lady who had visited him and promised him a present and for whom he had stayed at home.

"We were more dismayed than severe in our questions, and after some persuasion he admitted that he was guilty of this lie also," continued Herr von Tucher with great earnestness. "He admitted that he only wanted to be let alone to study and that he had thought of no other way of getting rid of these annoying disturbances. He begged us earnestly not to tell you of his offense, he would never resort to it again. I have considered the matter and reached the conclusion that it is better that you should know all. There is perhaps still time to fight the evil successfully. We can't look into his heart, but I still believe in his fundamental innocence, although I am convinced that only the greatest care and the sternest measures will save us from serious disappointments."

Daumer looked completely annihilated. "And this from a person on whose sacred love of truth I would have taken an oath," he murmured. "If it were not you who had told me this I should have laughed. Up to an hour ago I should have regarded as a knave anyone who said that Caspar was capable of lying."

"It has touched me closely, too," replied Herr von Tucher, "but we must be patient. Observe him, keep your eyes open, wait until you have a clear case to deal with, and then take him in hand, and firmly, too!"

A lie; no, two at once! Poor Daumer, he did not know what to think. He sat down and considered the matter. Herr von Tucher takes the whole thing too seriously, he said to himself. He is a very just man, but certainly a man of many prejudices, which lead him to add to a little lie all the incriminating circumstances of depravity. Herr von Tucher does not know every-day life, which teaches us to differentiate between lies that are wrong and what the force of circumstances demands of even the most righteous, ordinary white lies, you might call them. But what have I to do with Herr von Tucher? My concern is with Caspar Hauser. I thought once that I could ask of him what one cannot demand of anyone. Was it mere madness, was it presumptuous on my part? We shall see: I must now find out whether his will is still capable of responding to the call of a voice which men cannot hear. If his ear is already closed to the breath and sound of that spirit, then his lie is a lie like any other, but if I can still rouse the supersensual powers of understanding in him, then I shall scorn the Philistines who are only too eager to resort to the schoolmaster's rod.

It took Daumer a whole sleepless night before he matured his plan, which involved a sort of ordeal of God. Caspar's refusal to show his diary gave the final impetus. I want to force him to show me the book of his own accord, Daumer calculated. I will establish something like a metaphysical communication between him and me; without speaking a word, I shall strive to infuse him with my spiritual longing, and I will fix an hour within which he is to carry out my unsaid wish. If he can obey me all is well; if not, then farewell to my faith in miracles, and the glib-tongued materialist who sought to argue away the soul will have things his own way.

The next morning, toward nine o'clock, Anna came to her brother and said she did not like Caspar's condition at all; he had gotten up as early as five o'clock and was restless in a way he had never been before; at breakfast he had constantly looked anxiously around and not eaten a bite.

Daumer smiled. Does he already sense what I am planning to do with him, he wondered, and his mood became gentle and confident.

A suitable excuse was easily found to get the women out of the house. Frau Daumer was obliged to go to market and Anna was persuaded to make some calls. At eleven o'clock, Caspar settled down to his lessons, Daumer went into the adjoining room, but left the door open. He seated himself on a little chair, slightly back of the threshold, his face turned to where Caspar was sitting, and he at once succeeded in concentrating all his thoughts with astonishing energy on his one goal, in making them converge on one point. The house was very still, no sound disturbed his curious undertaking.

He sat there white and strained and observed that Caspar frequently got up and walked to the window. Once he would open the window, only to shut it again the next moment. Then he walked to the door and seemed to consider whether he should go out. His eye was unsteady and his mouth painfully contracted. Aha, he's feeling it, rejoiced Daumer; and every time that Caspar approached the little closet in which the blue copy book probably lay, the heart of the unhappy sorcerer beat high with expectation.

How far removed was Caspar from even an inkling of what was going on in Daumer, of suspecting that at this moment his character and destiny were being placed on trial!

He was immensely afraid today. He was so afraid that several times he had the distinct foreboding that some disaster would overtake him. He could not free himself from the feeling that someone who would harm him was approaching. The air in the room was stifling; the clouds in the sky hung threateningly, the swallow flying along the eaves in front of the window looked like a black hand shooting through the air with the swiftness of an arrow;; the ceiling pressed in upon him, and there was an uncanny creaking behind the panels of the wall.

Caspar could endure this no longer. His glance fell, a cold shower of fear ran through his veins, his chest contracted, and something drove him forth, out—suddenly he left the room, a youth fleeing from harm.

Daumer remained quietly sitting, gazing ahead like one waking from a dream. He was ashamed both of his mistaken attempt and of his defeat, for he was an intelligent man and was sensible enough to realize that the plan which had just miscarried was not a serious scientific test, but a gambling with destiny.

Nevertheless, he was seized with a fit of the most gloomy indifference. Any thought of the hopes which until recently were attached to Caspar's person left a bad taste in his mouth. He firmly determined that in the future he would dedicate his life as heretofore to his profession, to solitude, to study, and to sacrifice the faculties of his mind only where every gift is visibly repaid by the pleasures of knowledge and the search for knowledge.

8. A Disguised Person Make His Appearance

Caspar had gone into the garden. He ran across the damp grass as far as the fence and looked across towards the river. A leaden mist hung over the towers and the confusion of the city's roofs, and only the gayly colored tiles of the roof of the Lorenzkirche shone brightly; but the whole scene was more like a picture mirrored in water than a tangible reality.

Caspar shivered although it was warm. He turned toward the house. Opening the little gate, he paused in dismay at the empty vestibule. A broad streak of sunlight which ran along the stone flagging and trembled up the white steps of the winding stairway strengthened the impression of loneliness. From behind one of the doors of the corridor where Kandidat Regulein lived, there came the sounds of a violin; the Kandidat was practicing. With one foot already on the steps, Caspar stood still and listened.

There, there it was! There he came! First a shadow, then a form, then a voice. What did the voice say, that deep voice?

A loud voice back of him uttered these words: "Caspar, you must die."

Die! Thought Caspar astonished, and his arms stiffened like sticks of wood.

He saw a man standing before him, his face partly covered by a long black silk cloth which was moving slightly in the wind. He wore brown shoes, brown stockings and a brown suit. There were gloves on his hands, and in his right hand there shone something bright, a metallic brightness that flashed quickly and died away. He struck the boy with the object. As Caspar forced his paralyzed glance to look upward he felt a terrific pain in his head.

Suddenly Kandidat Regulein ceased to play the violin. Steps were heard, which died away again, but probably the disguised man had been made to hesitate and was prevented by fright from striking a second time. When Caspar opened his eyes, something wet and burning was running down from the middle of his forehead; the man had disappeared.

Oh, if only he had not worn gloves, I should have recognized his hand among a thousand, thought Caspar as he reeled over sideways. He found nothing to hold on to on the narrow side of the vestibule. He tried to clamber up the steps, but the streak of sunlight was like an impeding barrier of fire. He slipped back again and clung to the stone newel-post, sitting there silently for half a minute until he was seized by the fear that the disguised man might return. With might and main he clung to his fast-receding consciousness, sat up and stumbled forward, feeling his way along the wall as if to find a hole into which he could creep.

When he reached the cellar door, which was standing ajar, it gave way before the pressure of his hand so that he almost fell down headlong. Scarcely able to see, and without reflection, he felt his way down the dark steps as quickly as possible, for he thought he heard the steps of the masked man behind him. When he got down to the cellar, water spurted up from under his footsteps; it was rain-water which formed puddles down here in bad weather. Finally he found a dry corner, and as he was lying down, collapsing into a shapeless ball with fright and horror, the tower clock struck twelve; after that he saw and felt nothing more.

At quarter past twelve Frau Daumer and Anna returned. Anna, who preceded her mother into the hall, perceived the big pool of blood and screamed. At the same moment Kandidat Regulein came out of his rooms and exclaimed: "Well, what's the matter now?" The old woman, who had no idea of anything wrong, said that probably someone had had a nose-bleed. Anna, however, more and more concerned, pointed to the bloody finger marks which were visible as far as the cellar door. She sprang forward: Caspar was her first thought, she looked into all the rooms and said to her brother, "Downstairs everything is covered with blood." Daumer rose from his desk with an exclamation of anxiety and hurried down.

Meantime Regulein had followed the bloody tracks down into the cellar. In a hoarse voice he called for light and added in shriller tones, "He's down here, Hauser's lying down here. Help, help, quickly!"

The Daumers, all three of them, rushed to the cellar. Anna came panting up again to get a candle; the others tried to raise

Caspar's cowering body, and then the three carried him upstairs. "The doctor, get the doctor," Frau Daumer screamed to Anna, who was running towards her. Anna put out the light, threw the candle on the floor and rushed away.

When Caspar was finally gotten to bed they washed the clotted blood from his face, revealing a serious cut in the middle of his forehead. Daumer walked up and down wringing his hands and moaning continually, "That this should happen in my house! I've always said it, I've always known it."

The square in front of the house was already filled with people when Anna returned with the doctor. Policemen and city officials were in the hallway. A few minutes later the municipal-court doctor appeared. Both physicians assured them that the wound was not dangerous, but whether the boy's mind had received a dangerous shock or not, they would not undertake to say.

An official report could not be made, for Caspar was only conscious during far intervals; he then stammered a few words which, to be sure, revealed as in a sudden flash of lightning what had happened to him. He spoke of the disguised man, of his shining boots and yellow gloves, but then relapsed into vague hallucinations and a delirious fever. On examining the premises, it was discovered how the unknown man had entered; underneath the steps, there was a little door communicating with Baumann's garden and the padlock on this door had been forced.

To cross-question Daumer was useless: emotion made it impossible for him to speak. Towards evening Herr von Tucher arrived and told him that an express messenger had been sent to President Feuerbach.

The Mayor had at once set elaborate investigations on foot. The guards at all of the major and minor gates of the city were ordered to be particularly vigilant. The inns and hotels, where people of the lower orders generally stopped, were carefully searched and the police forces in the neighboring counties were ordered to be exceptionally alert. An official notice was posted on the bulletin board of the City Hall, and two clerks and half of the police force were entrusted with the pursuit of the criminal.

The crime occurred on Monday; his duties in connection with a case he was trying unfortunately kept the President from coming to Nurnberg at once; not until Thursday did he reach the city by an express diligence. He went at once to the City Hall. He had the chief magistrate inform him of the measures that the police had taken, as well as the results of these measures, but he showed such dissatisfaction with everything, and was so enraged when told of several ineffectual efforts, that all of the officials lost their heads. He made sarcastic remarks about the reports and the testimony of the witnesses: the wife of a watchman had seen a well-dressed man on the Schiessgraben washing his hands in a basin in front of the principal hospital; there was an old woman selling fruit who had met a stranger in Saint John's who had asked her who had charge of inspections at the Tiergartner Gate and whether one could get into the city without being stopped; suspicious journeymen and homeless vagrants had been arrested; someone had observed two fellows who had met on the Fleischbrucke and made signs to one another.

"Too late, too late," grumbled the President. "Why did you not check up all the registers of all the inns for names of strangers arriving and leaving?" he thundered at the trembling clerk. "The clews would lead in many directions," the unfortunate man replied timidly.

"Certainly, incompetence has many excuses," remarked the President bitingly. "By God, man, listen: the criminal we are pursuing does not wash his hands in the street, he does not converse with fruit vendors, and does not need to fear the sentry at the Gate. You sought too low, much too low."

He took a secretary with him, to make a personal inspection of Daumer's house once more. Magistrate Behold accompanied him and made himself obnoxious by his incessant babbling. Among other things Behold said that he had heard that Professor Daumer did not want to keep Caspar any more, and he offered to take the boy into his house. Feuerbach took this for mere conversation and got rid of the man by sending him to Herr von Tucher with a message.

But when he talked to Daumer, the latter's perturbation surprised him. In order not to disturb him further, Feuerbach conducted the hearing so that it seemed more like a friendly conversation. Daumer remembered the secret meeting that Caspar had had in front of the Egydien Church and told the story.

"And of this we now hear for the first time?" exclaimed the President. "And was there no direct sequel to the affair? Did you not observe anything suspicious?"

"No," stammered Daumer, frightened by the Presidents glance which penetrated him like an edge of steel. "That is to say, something does occur to me. That same evening at Frau Behold's I met a gentleman who gave me the most curious hints or warnings, I cannot make out which!"

"What kind of a man? What was his name?"

"He was said to be a diplomat who was traveling; I don't remember his name. Oh, yes, but I do: Herr von Schlotheim-Lavancourt; but he was said to be here under an assumed name."

"What did he look like?"

"Fat, big, slightly pock-marked, well on in the fifties."

"Describe your conversation with him."

Daumer repeated as well as he could the contents of the conversation. Feuerbach sank into deep thought, then he made some notes in his little note book. "Let us go to Caspar," he said, getting up.

Caspar's forehead was still bound up, his face was almost as white as the bandage, and he received the President with a wan smile. He had already suffered three examinations; at the first one he had told everything worth telling: this did not prevent the worthy officials from going over the ground again in strange circumlocutions, in an endeavor to catch their victim in some contradiction. One can work with contradictions; if a person always says the same thing the matter becomes hopeless for the police. The President refrained from questions. He found Caspar a changed person; there was an air of anxiety about him, his glance was less unconstrained, it was no longer so profoundly radiant and free from guile, it was more closely fettered to mundane things.

While the women were declaring themselves satisfied with Caspar's condition, the doctor came and readily confirmed their impression that the boy was now entirely out of danger. In a tone that expressed a command rather than a mere wish, the President said that he hoped that all strange visitors should be kept out for the next few days, without exception. Daumer replied that this would, of course, be done. Only this morning he had turned away a lackey in uniform, who had asked to let his master see the young man.

"He was the servant of a distinguished Englishman who is living in the Hotel Adler," added Frau Daumer, "moreover, he returned in an hour in order to inquire in detail about Caspar's condition."

There was a knock at the door, Herr von Tucher came in and after a little while made an astonishing communication: the same Englishman, apparently a rich count or lord, had called on the Mayor and given him one hundred ducats as a reward for the person who should succeed in discovering the criminal who had attacked Caspar.

There was a surprised silence which the President interrupted by asking whether anyone knew what the stranger was doing in Nurnberg. Herr von Tucher replied in the negative. "We only know that he arrived night before last," he replied, "a wheel of his carriage broke near Burgfarrnbach and he is waiting here for the damage to be repaired." The President frowned, distrust clouded his glance; thus the hunting dog becomes suspicious when a new track crosses the confusing mass of footprints. "What's the man's name?" he asked with apparent indifference.

"The name has escaped me," replied Baron Tucher, "but he is said actually to be a gentleman of high rank; Mayor Binder praises his affability most highly."

"Distinguished gentlemen are called affable if they tread on your foot and then apologize politely," Anna, who was sitting by Caspar's bed, was heard to remark pertly. Daumer threw her a reproachful look, but the President broke out into a loud laugh which infected all the others; for several minutes he kept chuckling to himself and his eyes twinkling with pleasure.

Caspar alone did not join in this merry little episode; his glance looked reflectively into the open; he wanted to see the man who had come from far away and given so much money that the person who had struck him might be found. From far away! It was this that appealed to him. Only from far away could that for which Caspar was yearning come, from the distant sea, from unknown lands. The President, too, had come from far away, but not so far that his brow was colored with the radiance of the unknown, that a sweet smelling wind still clung to his clothes, or that his eyes were like stars, free from reproach and without their perpetual questions. He who would come from a distance, perhaps arrayed in shining silver, and with many horses, would not need to question, he would know everything without needing to ask; the others, all those who were near, who were always present, who constantly went in and out, they never looked as if they came fresh from their foaming steeds, their breath was as acrid as the air in a cellar, their hands fatigued, like a horseman's hand. Their countenances were masked, not masked in black like the face of the man who had struck him and who had been closer to him than anyone else, but vaguely veiled: that was why they spoke in indistinct voices, in simulated tones, and that was why Caspar was now obliged to dissemble, unable to look them straight in the eye or say what he might have said. He found it more cozy and sadder to remain silent than to speak, particularly when they were expecting him to speak. Yes, he liked to be somewhat sad, to have many secret dreams and thoughts, and to bring those about him to the realization that they could not approach him after all.

Daumer was too preoccupied with himself and too much oppressed by the idea of soon carrying out the unalterable decision he had made, namely, to observe whether Caspar responded to him in the same open childlike way as heretofore. Herr von Tucher was the first who pointed out certain peculiarities in Caspar's behavior and dropped some hints on the subject to the President as they left Daumer's house together.

The President shrugged his shoulders and remained silent. He asked the Baron to accompany him to the Adler Inn; there they inquired whether the English gentleman was at home, but found that His Grace Lord Stanhope—so the waiter expressed himself—had left just an hour before. The President was disagreeably surprised and asked whether they knew in what direction his coach had gone They did not know exactly, was the answer, but since it had left by Jacob's Gate it was to be assumed that it had gone south, perhaps toward München.

"Too late, everywhere too late," murmured the President, "I should have been glad to know what moved His Grace to bring so many ducats to the City Hall." Feuerbach's face was so lined with thought and care, so strained with constant vigilance, as well as with the ardor of a consuming temperament, that it resembled that of a sick man, or one possessed.

And thus it had been for months. The clerks under him were afraid of him, the smallest neglect of duty, even the slightest contradiction, made him rave. His outbreaks of temper had always been things to be feared, and now they trembled the more before them since the slightest provocation would call forth such a storm. Then his voice would resound through the halls and corridors of the appellate court, and the peasants below in the market place would stand still and say with solicitous regret, "His Excellency has been crossed again," and from the Regierungsrat down to the lowest clerk they all sat on their chairs pale and dutiful.

Perhaps they would have borne this yoke the more willingly if they had known what pain it caused the man himself, how much, when conquered by his anger, he suffered from shame and remorse, and how as if to redeem himself by some outward action he would toss a coin to the first beggar he met on the street. They had, of course, no idea that these ugly vapors of ill-humor screened a sharp struggle between duty and honor and that this man's great intellect was busily at work, seeking, in the midst of outward bustle and restlessness to piece together a marvelous bit of mental construction and, with the true penetration of a seer, to see his way clear through a veritable inferno of wickedness and crime.

With a magician's hand he had succeeded in constructing a connected web out of the dark threads which attached Caspar's fate to an unknown past, and suddenly there stood revealed in letters of flame the thing that time, as well as a curious combination of circumstances, had hidden in darkness.

He faced his own creation, terrified, for the foundations of his existence were trembling under him. For him there was no longer any doubt. But did he dare to come forth with the frightful truth and to brush aside the considerations which his position and the confidence of his king demanded of him? Would it not be better to continue to play the part of a spy in secret in order finally, with crafty cunning, to attack these treacherous forces from behind at the right opportunity? There was nothing to gain, not even gratitude, but there was everything to lose.

Oh, what a torture! he often thought during a sleepless night, what a rare torture, to be obliged to watch this godless behavior with a powerless hand, to measure great crimes and small sins by the standards of inadequate laws, to adhere blindly to the letter while life runs on in its accustomed way, producing and destroying one form after another, and never to be a master of real deeds, always to be the bloodhound of the evildoers themselves, and never to know what things to nip in the bud and what things to prosper.

He would not have been the man that he was if he had not found a middle path between public action and cowardly silence which sufficed for his self-respect. He drew up a detailed memorandum to the king, wherein he presented in a neat logical enumeration all the features of the case, frankly and boldly, from beginning to end; every sentence was a hammer-stroke.

The document began with the declaration that Caspar Hauser must be a legitimate, and not an illegitimate, child.

If he had been an illegitimate child, it went on to say, less dangerous and cruel methods would have been used to cover up his antecedents than the monstrous crime of keeping him imprisoned many years and then finally turning him loose The more distinguished either of his parents was, the more easily could the child be gotten away, and people of slight position and no great means would have had even less cause to resort to such expensive and unsafe measures; the bread and water which Caspar was obliged to eat in secrecy would in such a case be offered to him openly, without any secrecy. If one assumes Caspar to be an illegitimate child, whether of high or low standing, whether rich or poor, the means used would in none of these cases be commensurate with the purpose pursued. And who would, without some real reason, undertake the burden of so serious a crime, especially when it imposes upon the criminal the frightful torment of having to repeat his crime day after day for an unending period? From all this it seems evident, the merciless prosecutor continued, that very powerful and very wealthy persons are participants in the crime, persons who can easily surmount common obstacles, and who, either through fear, or through the extraordinary advantages and brilliant hopes which they have to offer, can find willing tools; they are persons who can leash tongues and padlock more than one mouth with gold. Could one explain in any other way how Caspar could be exposed in a city like Nurnberg, in broad daylight, while the perpetrator disappears without a trace, and why the tireless zeal of months of investigation has discovered no circumstances that can be properly connected with the affair, which might point to a definite place or a definite person, why even great rewards have not led to one satisfactory piece of intelligence?

Therefore Caspar must be a person of such importance that widely ramified interests are connected with the matter of his life or death, continued Feuerbach. Neither revenge nor hate could have been the motives of his incarceration, but he was gotten out of the way in order to insure to others advantages that belonged to him alone. It was necessary for him to disappear that others might take his place, that others might assume his estate. He must be of high birth; certain remarkable dreams which he has had show this, dreams which are nothing but reawakened memories of early youth; the whole course of his imprisonment and the inferences to be drawn from it indicate his lofty origin. Of course, he was kept in prison and sparsely nourished, but there are examples of persons who are incarcerated with a friendly rather than a hostile purpose, not in order to destroy them, but to protect them from those who are seeking their lives. Perhaps his mere existence made it possible to bring pressure to bear on someone who had participated in the affair with a hesitating conscience, and yet had not dared protest. Caspar had been treated kindly and with care. Why? Why had not this mysterious person killed him? Why did he not put one more drop of opium into the water which was used at times to daze his senses? The dungeon-keep designed for the living prisoner would have been twice as safe for the dead one.

Now if, in any family of high station or only of distinction, or let us say even only of respectable standing, a child who is now Caspar had ever disappeared, without anything being known about its life, or death, or how it had disappeared, the family in which this misfortune had occurred must long ago have become known. Since Caspar's fate has been for years a much discussed event, and been disregarded, and not the slightest thing has been said about such a family incident, Caspar must be sought among the dead. That is to say, a child has been declared to be dead, and is still regarded as dead, while in fact it is alive in the person of Caspar. This means that a child who was the nearest heir or the last surviving male of his family was put out of the way, never to appear again. Perhaps this child happened to be sick and a dying or dead child was put in its place, which substituted child was exhibited in its coffin and duly buried, and Caspar thus enumerated with the dead. If the doctor was in the game, and had been ordered to kill the child, and from motives either of kindness or wisdom had pretended to obey but actually spared the child, the pious deception could the more easily be carried out. Here everyone was acting on instructions from above, but where was the mouth that had ordered the deed? Where was the master mind which was ready to assume such a burden of responsibility to the end of time? In what dynasty had this unheard-of crime occurred?

At this passage in his report, the President's hand faltered—for days, for weeks. Not out of weakness and indecision, but with the painful hesitation of a general who is certain of ruin and disaster, however the battle may go. To snatch a crown from the head of a prince, and to point with the finger of scorn at a tarnished diadem, was not this to offend against the majesty of even his own king and ruler? Did this not mean trampling sacred traditions under foot, and rousing the opposition of immature and irresponsible demagogy? Yet, he felt, as he had never felt before, the convincing force of words and how truth springs from truth and urges action.

He gave the name of the dynasty. He pointed out that the old line had suddenly and most unaccountably, against all human probability, become extinct in the male line, yielding place to a younger branch, the issue of a morganatic marriage. This extinction had not resulted from a childless marriage, but had fallen upon a union blessed with many children, and it was only the sons that died; the daughters lived on. The mother had been a true Niobe; yet though Apollo's mortal dart had stricken sons and daughters alike; here, the angel of death had spared the daughters, slaying only the sons. And it was not merely a striking fact, but one that was almost a miracle, that the angel appeared while the boys were still babes in their cradles, snatching them away from a surrounding bevy of blooming sisters. How shall we explain, asked Feuerbach, a mother's bearing the same husband three healthy daughters and no sons that were fit to live? There is not mere accident in this, he courageously insisted, there is a method in it, otherwise one would have to believe that Providence had for once interfered with the usual course of nature, and performed an extraordinary feat in order to carry out a political coup. Not long after Caspar's appearance in Nurnberg the report had spread that he was a prince of that family who had been considered dead, and these dark rumors had continued to arise repeatedly; there was even a report of an alleged appearance of a ghost which, as was declared in the public prints, had ventured to assert that the present rulers had usurped the throne while a rightful prince was still alive. Rumors, of course, are merely rumors, but they often spring from proper sources. In the case of secret crimes they often arise from the fact that one of the accomplices may gossip or make too free with his confidences, or perhaps from some carelessness, or someone may wish to ease his conscience, or undertake to avenge some disappointed hope, or someone may even have sought to bring about the discovery of the truth without being obliged to play the role of the betrayer.

The President did not merely mention the dynasty by name, and the land which was their inheritance; he named the prince whose sudden death more than ten years ago had aroused suspicion, he named the princess of high rank, who grieved in the solitude she had chosen over her inscrutable fate. He named those who had thus passed to the throne over corpses, and next to the picture of a weak, but ambitious man, there appeared the figure of a woman, a diabolical figure, the master mind of the frightful enterprise.

There was something of the bitterness of a personal experience in the unembellished reasoning of the President. For he knew the courtly world, where malice and cunning are steeped in sweet smelling incense and duplicity dazes its victim with hypocritical favors. He had breathed that air, and later from those tables he had absorbed their poison, he had wasted his life and strength in their service, and his purest devotion had been rewarded with scorn and persecution. He knew their creatures and their minions, he knew the men for whom history meant nothing more than the enumeration of an ancestral tree, religion the songs of a priest, philosophy a disgusting Jacobinism, politics a blind man's bluff of documents and reports, the budget an arithmetical problem that does not need to check up, the rights of human beings a game of forfeits, the monarch a mirror of their own greatness, their country a tenure of land, and freedom the criminal folly of audacious madmen. The years which were gone forever sounded loudly through his written words, the disdain he had endured, which had darkened his life. He did not wish to think of himself, but his words revealed his sorrow, though not for the eye of the king, who was only to read what was written.

The report was sent off and the most meticulous care was used to prevent its falling into any other hands than the rulers, but the President waited week after week for a reply, for some decision or sign of life. Then came the news of the attempted murder of

Caspar. Feuerbach went to Nurnberg; his own investigations were as fruitless as those of the police. On the tenth day of his stay he received a letter from the King's Private Chancellory. His communication was acknowledged and received with due thanks, and his perfectly astonishing cleverness in unraveling a complicated situation was appropriately admired, but in all essentials the letter showed an inflexible reserve; one would investigate, one would consider, one would wait and see; important considerations had to be taken into account; personal relations that would be readily grasped might impose unsavory obligations. The nature of this incredible story, according to the missive, was rather an invitation to astonishment and horror than to precipitate action; still one would promise, yes, one would promise. But above all silence was recommended, complete silence; it would mean the loss of all the royal favor if such material should reach the outside world as the authentic utterance of a high official of state; on this point discretion and submission were expected.

    The effect of this secret communication, simultaneously a menace and a caress, which resembled a kindly outstretched hand in which a sharp dagger gleamed, was all the stronger for having been long surmised and dreaded. Feuerbach foamed at the mouth. He crushed the epistle under his heels, his breast heaving, he strode about the room ceaselessly, his fists clenched against his temples; then he sank upon the bed; the beating of his pulses frightened him, and he relieved himself with mad peals of a laughter that was full of anger and rage.

    Then he lay still for hours, unable to think of anything but the single word: silence, silence, silence.

    That same afternoon Mayor Binder had come to the hotel several times and had wanted to speak to the President. The waiter had always returned with the information that he had knocked in vain; the President was either asleep or did not wish to be disturbed. Towards evening, Binder came again, and was finally admitted. He found the President absorbed in some documents and his apologies were brushed aside with the brusque, humiliating request that he come to the point.

    The Mayor was offended; stepping back, he stated with dignity that he was not aware that he had given any cause for His Excellency's displeasure, but, however that might be, he must decline to submit to such treatment. Then Feuerbach rose and replied, "For heaven's sake, man, drop that tone! When one is being burned at the stake, one has some ground to neglect the rules of politeness."

Binder dropped his head and was silent with astonishment. Then he explained the purpose of his visit. The President was probably aware that Daumer did not intend to keep Caspar in his house any longer. Since the boy had recovered so far, Daumer had decided not to wait any longer, but to send him as soon as possible to the Beholds, who would be very glad to have him. All this had been thoroughly gone over and it was desired only to inform the President and ask his approval.

"Yes, I know that Daumer is tired of this business," said the President irritably, "I don't blame him. No one wants his house to be the cynosure of murderers' eyes, although precautions can and will be taken to prevent repetitions of this incident. From today on Caspar shall be placed under strict police surveillance; the city is responsible to me for him. But why is Daumer in such a hurry? And why is Caspar to go to the Behold family? Why not to Herr von Tucher, or to you?"

"Herr von Tucher is obliged to be away on business for some months, in Augsburg, and I,—" the Mayor hesitated and his face grew pale for a moment, "as for me there is no peace in my home."

The President looked up quickly, then he walked over to Binder and silently shook him by the hand

"And what about these Beholds? What kind of people are they?" he asked, changing the conversation

"Oh, they are good people," answered the Mayor somewhat uncertainly. "The man is certainly a respectable merchant. As to the lady there are differences of opinion. She spends a lot on her clothes and things, in fact, she squanders a lot of money. One can't say anything bad of her. Since, as we have agreed, it will now be for Caspar's good to send him to a public school, mere supervision among decent people will suffice for him."

"Have they any children?"

"A girl of thirteen." The Mayor, who knew as well as everyone else that Frau Behold treated this child badly, wanted to add something in order to ease his conscience, but at this moment Magistrate Behold and Daumer were announced. The President had them shown in. The grinning, friendly face of the councilor appeared at once; his aggressive black beard was an amusing contrast to the hair on his head, which was already gray and hung in moist strands, redolent of pomade, over his forehead.

Bowing profusely, he advanced toward Feuerbach, who only vouchsafed him a brief greeting and at once turned to Daumer. The latter scarcely dared to meet Feuerbach's penetrating eyes, and when asked whether one could subject Caspar to the mental and physical strain of such a revolutionary change, he replied by an embarrassed silence. When Herr Behold joined in the conversation and assured them that Caspar would be treated in his house as if he were his own son, the Mayor interrupted him with words pronounced almost against his will, to the effect that that meant nothing, as one could see by the example of Caspar himself how some people could neglect their own children.

The councilor looked embarrassed; he rubbed his thin finger along the edge of the chair and stammered that he could say nothing more, he would do his best.

The President, who had been made suspicious by the implications of these remarks, looked at the two men in turn. Then he went close up to Daumer, placed his hand on his shoulder and said earnestly, "Must it really be?"

Daumer sighed and replied with emotion: "Excellency, God knows how hard my decision is."

"God may know," answered the President grumblingly, and his short heavy figure seemed suddenly to grow and threaten, "But will He therefore approve? If one rubs stone and flint together one gets sparks; beware, however, when only dirt and crumbs fly from the stone. Then there is no permanence or soundness in all the realm of nature."

He is dismissing me again like a schoolboy, thought Daumer, and a blush of irritation rose to his face. "I have done all I could," he said hastily and obstinately. "I am not closing my house to Caspar; and certainly not my heart. But, in the first place, I can no longer guarantee his safety and I believe that no one can. How can anyone sow in a field under which a pernicious fire smolders, consuming every seed that is sown? And furthermore I am disappointed, I admit that I am disappointed. I shall never forget what Caspar has been to me, who indeed could forget it? But the bloom has left the peach; time has destroyed it."

"Over, yes, over," murmured Feuerbach gloomily. "Sooner or later the word had to be spoken. Our eyes become dulled from gazing into the light. Our sons are cast forth when they demand an over-measure of our affection. But we give the beggar the soup he begs for. My worthy gentlemen," he continued loudly and formally, "in any case remember that you are responsible to me for Caspar's welfare."

When Daumer got out into the street he was still angry at the President's tone and words. At the same time he could not hide the fact that he was dissatisfied with himself. In one of the deserted streets near the castle he met Rittmeister Wessenig. Daumer was glad to have someone to talk to, and accompanied the man to the barracks. From the beginning, Herr Wessenig turned the conversation upon Caspar and Daumer did not notice, or did not want to notice, that the Captain's loquacity was flavored with scorn.

"A curious affair, this business with the marked man," said Wessenig, suddenly becoming more open. "Does anyone really believe it? In clear daylight a fellow, some chap with gloves on, if you please, enters an inhabited house, hangs a veil over his face and takes an ax out of his pocket? Or is he supposed to have carried the ax through the open streets? And with gloves. By holy St. Thomas, that's a bold tale of adventure."

As Daumer did not reply, Captain Wessenig continued eagerly, "Let us suppose that the funny man with the mask really intended to kill the boy? Why, then, this slight wound? He would only have had to strike a little harder and everything would have been at an end, the mouth which would betray him would have been silenced. One really has to believe that the gloved murderer wanted merely to fondle his victim a bit for the time being. Well, in truth, it's a ticklish story. All of my acquaintances, parole d'honneur, my dear professor, are amazed at the spirit of credulity which can be deceived by such childish clap-trap."

Daumer felt it beneath his honor to show either anger or indignation. He pretended that he was not disinclined to agree with the Captain, and, as if to seek information, asked what one was to think of the whole affair. Hen* Wessenig shrugged his shoulders significantly. He had probably expected a heated denial and a sharp reprimand, and since this did not come he put aside his restrained hostility, retaining astuteness enough, however, to express himself in general terms only. "Perhaps our good Caspar was drunk and fell down the steps and then cooked up this tale of an assassin in order to make himself interesting. That would still be a comparatively innocent matter. Others have a much blacker version: they think the scamp wanted to make trouble for his protector by a neatly devised escapade."

Daumer was no longer able to contain himself. He stood still and stretched his hands out as if the remarks of his companion were besetting him like so many venomous insects, and without a word of good-by he hurried away.

So that is the world, those are its voices, he thought with dismay; it's possible to think such a thing and any mouth may utter it. And you, poor Caspar, are to be swallowed up in this welter of folly and malice. Even if you are not the messenger from heaven for whom I took you, you nevertheless soar above them as an eagle over a race of pygmies. Of course, they will clip your wings. In vain will your innocence radiate from your soul, they will not see it. You will laugh or cry before them in vain; you will seize their hands and shudder with cold, you will look at them and they will remain dumb. Your soul will anxiously seek a path to theirs and treachery will guide you along the most dangerous path of all. . . .

One is a prophet and one has a heart that feels pity; one knows people; one knows that fire burns, that a needle pricks and that the hare, when it is shot, falls into the grass and dies; one knows the consequences of the things one does, doesn't one, Herr Daumer? But is this a reason for opposing the course of things, which is an enemy with sword already raised, and to intercept the arm that impels the descending blow? No, it is no reason. Or is it a reason for changing one's mind about a little resolution once made? No, it's no reason. In this respect the idealists and students of the soul are in no way superior to thieves and usurers.

One goes home, one walks home philosophizing and goes to bed, and the next morning the world looks far more acceptable than on the previous evening, which had much to make it a depressing one.

9. The Heart Of The Blackbird

Twenty-four hours later a carriage stops in front of Daumer's house and Frau Behold comes to fetch Caspar herself. Really Frau Behold has not been a niggard: she sports a shining black coach and a pair of horses and a servant with gold buttons on the box.

Caspar is accompanied to the door by Daumer and the two women, and Kandidat Regulein, too, leaves his bachelor cell to see him off. Anna cannot hold back her tears; Daumer gazes darkly ahead of him; Frau Behold makes a sign to the coachman; the horses snort; the wheels whirl round; and those left behind stare silently into the darkness which swallows up the carriage.

This was his farewell, and it seemed to Caspar as if he were going far away. But he was really going only from a house on the Schutt to a house on the Market Place. It was a tall, narrow house, so tucked in between two others that it looked as if it could not draw a breath. It had a tinned gable which slanted steeply like the shoulders of a hungry chancery clerk; the windows did not have a frank and open look, but seemed to be blinking; the front door seemed to be hiding, and inside, a dark staircase wound deviously through the various stories as if pursuing evasive courses; the old treads creaked and groaned at every step, and whenever the doors were opened, only a dim light shone from the rooms.

Caspar lived in a room overlooking the square court inside the structure; outside the windows there ran a wooden gallery with an ornamented balustrade, at each side there were glass doors with green hangings, and down in the yard stood an iron fountain that yielded no water.

The curious part of it was that there was the Market Square outside, where many persons talked loudly, where the tradespeople had their little shops and tents, filled from morning till night with chattering women, screaming children, neighing horses, cackling chickens, and yet one had only to close the door behind one in order to be as quiet as in a tomb.

This amused Caspar at first. It resembled a game of hide and seek and he found fun in hiding, sometimes taking it upon himself to assume a different face from the one corresponding with his mood, or to say other things than were expected of him. On one of the first days Frau Behold lost a little silver chain; Caspar said that he had seen it outside the house, although he had not seen it.

He was forbidden to leave the house without permission. He asked who had given the order and was told it was Frau Behold, but when he inquired of her she said that the magistrate had forbidden it; however, when he applied to him he was told that the President had forbidden it. Such was the extent to which everything in this house was complicated and mysterious!

Once Frau Behold tried to enter his room. She found it locked and bolted from the inside. "Why do you lock yourself in, in broad daylight?" she asked, poking about on the table where his books and school work lay. "Are you perhaps afraid?" she went on loquaciously, "in my house you need not be afraid, there aren't any masked rogues." He admitted that he was afraid and this flattered Frau Behold; she assumed a fierce air of protection, and smiled provocatively.

Every morning when he returned from school—he now went for two hours a day into the third class of the gymnasium—Frau Behold asked him how things had gone. He would answer sadly, "Things went badly" and actually he got little pleasure out of it. The teachers complained that his presence made the other pupils inattentive; the fact that a policeman constantly followed him in the street and that the police watched the house in which he lived day and night, seemed extraordinarily exciting to the boys and they] tormented him with the silliest questions. His silence was of course misinterpreted, and if he began to address them frankly in his way, they either drew back shyly or made fun of him, for he was in their eyes nothing but a great big fool who was twice as old as they and not yet beyond the merest rudiments of knowledge. It often happened that during the lesson he would get up and ask one of his childlike questions, and then the whole class would burst out laughing and the teacher would laugh, too. Once during a tremendous windstorm which howled outside, he left his seat and took refuge in a corner near the stove; the amusement of the boys knew no bounds, and when the fat teacher pulled him out and shoved him to his seat on the bench they accompanied the process with veritable cat calls.

The most curious thing of all was to observe him on the way home walking amid a crowd of boys, reserved and worried among the noisy carefree groups, a man among half grown children, and constantly at his side the minion of the law.

Very frequently Daumer asked his colleagues for information about Caspar. "Ah," they said, "of course he has the best intentions but only middling intelligence. He shows that he's clever, but he does not retain very much. We can't complain of him, but neither can we praise him."

Daumer was hurt. You can't complain of him, yet you do complain, he thought; it is easy to damn with faint praise, particularly when you praise the person you complain of as he deserves. He appealed to the Magistrate and tried to persuade him to speak well of Caspar, but Herr Behold was no lover of candid opinions. He was a man who led a one-sided life, spending his days in a gloomy office on the Zwinger and anyone who wanted an opinion of him generally met with the reply, "You must ask my wife about that."

Daumer now seemed almost like an unsuccessful lover in the way in which he followed the doings of his former protégé with care and anxiety, at the same time gladly avoiding a meeting or a conversation with Caspar. He secretly followed the doings of Frau Behold with the greatest distrust, racking his brain as to why she had been so eager to get the boy to her house.

"What are you puzzled about?" said Anna, who had as much excellent common sense as her brother fantastic pessimism, "it's quite clear that she wants a toy doll, an amusement for her salon."

"A toy, why, she has a child and she neglects even that, so people say."

"Of course! but there's nothing unusual in having a child like Everyone else. It must be something that's talked about, something interesting, something that gives one an opportunity to play the grand lady and occasionally read one's name in the newspapers. Then, too, one is called a benefactress, one's husband may get an important decoration, and above all one dispels one's boredom. I know the woman as I know myself. I pity Caspar."

    Frau Behold was always going about and was in fact only at home when she had company. She had to see people constantly, she liked well-dressed, genial people, men with titles and women of rank; she loved parties and jewelry and elaborate clothes. She might have been called gay if her ambition had not made her so restless. She would at times have appeared a complacent person, even friendly and agreeable, if she had not been a victim of a vain curiosity which penetrated into her very soul and did not leave her even during sleep. She had read a huge number of French novels, which made her irritable and eager for adventure, and the phlegmatic indolence which was a part of her temperament served to conceal these other qualities. The person who accepted her for what she appeared to be was deceived at the very outset.

    As regards Caspar, she at first took him humorously, particularly when he was sad and thoughtful. "What an amusing thing he has said again." was her perpetual remark. It often appeared as if she had taken a little court jester into her service. "Now, my dear little moon calf, do say something," she would ask him in the presence of her guests. When she would see him eagerly memorizing Latin words she would laugh aloud. "How scholarly, how scholarly," she would exclaim, running her hand through his wavy hair.

    "Let it go, let it go," she would say consolingly if he complained of a difficult problem in arithmetic, "you won't get anywhere with it; it is as if I should take up tight-rope dancing."

    Meantime he soon aroused a strange curiosity in her in another way. One morning she came in while he was standing in the kitchen, watching the butcher's boy take the raw meat, still bloody, out of the basket and place it on the sideboard. Caspar's face showed tremendous pity, he drew back trembling, unable to make a sound, and then fled in distress. Frau Behold was amazed and did not want to admit her emotion. What's that, she thought; he must be pretending; what is the blood of an animal to him?

    In order to please him she did more for him than her own sense of convenience would usually have permitted. Nevertheless he did not seem to feel at home in her house. "Botheration, what has crossed you again?" she flew at him at once, noticing his sad face. "If you don't get livelier I'll take you to the slaughter house and make you watch them cutting off the calves' heads," she once threatened him, and burst out laughing over the horror painted in his face.

No, Caspar did not feel in the least at home. Frau Behold was utterly incomprehensible to him; her glance, her speech, her manner, all repelled him greatly. It cost him much thought and artifice not to show his dislike, although he was sick and miserable when he had spent only an hour in her company. All interest in work forsook him and he stopped going to school altogether, which he hated anyway. The teachers complained to the Magistrate; Herr von Tucher, who was living in the city again and had legally been appointed Caspar's guardian, took him to task. Caspar did not want to speak, an attitude which Herr von Tucher interpreted as obstinacy and which caused him much anxiety.

And there was something else which made Caspar thoughtful. Sometimes on the steps, or in the hall, or in one of the remote rooms, he met Frau Behold's daughter, a half-grown girl with a white face. Her eyes rested upon him with hostility. When he tried to speak to her she ran away. Once when he was looking from the gallery into the courtyard he saw her standing by the well behind the iron pipe, upon which a board had been displaced, so that one could look into the bottom. The girl stood silently, gazing for at least a quarter of an hour into the black hole. Caspar silently left the gallery and slipped downstairs, but no sooner did he enter the court than the girl ran past him with an angry face. While Caspar was hesitatingly following her, he met the Magistrate and eagerly told him what he had seen. Herr Behold frowned and said soothingly, "Yes, yes, certainly the child is not well. Don't bother about her, Caspar, don't bother."

But Caspar did bother. He asked the maids what was the matter with the child, and one of them replied cuttingly: "She doesn't get anything to eat; the foundling eats all her food." Whereupon Caspar hurried post haste to Frau Behold and repeated what the maid had said and asked whether this was true. Frau Behold flew into a rage and dismissed the maid on the spot. When, however, Caspar nevertheless in his tactless and precocious way reprimanded her, saying that she should pay more attention to her daughter than to him, otherwise he would go away, she cut him short with the sharp reproof: "How can you go away? Where will you go? Where's your home if one may ask?"

Frau Behold now reached the conclusion that Caspar was in love with her daughter. She set to work to question him on the point. However, he answered her questions so childishly that she was almost ashamed of her suspicions. "Grand Dieu," she said aloud to herself, "it seems to me that the simpleton does not even know what love is." Indeed, more than this, she felt that he had never given the least thought to the matter. This was very curious to the good lady, for her own desires and passions always played about in the cloudy waters of semi-fictitious, semi-lubricous passions, however virtuous she was obliged to appear before her fellow citizens.

He certainly is made of flesh and blood, she reflected, and even though that foolish Daumer raves so about his angelic innocence, a grown-up man cannot fail to know what goes on between the rooster and his hens. He is pretending, he's fooling me; wait and see, boy; I'll make him smart.

On the market place to the right in front of the Beholds' house stood the so-called "Beautiful Fountain," a masterwork of medieval Nurnberg art. From time immemorial the children were told that the stork fetched the babies from the depths of the fountain. Frau Behold asked Caspar whether he had heard this, and when he said no, looked at him with a sly wink and wanted to know whether he believed this. "I don't see how the stork could fly down," he replied innocently; "it's all closed in with iron netting."

Frau Behold was astonished. "Oh, you simpleton!" she exclaimed; "look me straight in the face."

He looked at her. Then she was obliged to drop her eyes. And suddenly she got up, hurried to the sideboard, brusquely opened a drawer, poured herself out a glass of wine and emptied it at one gulp. Then she went to the window, folded her hands, and with a dull expression murmured: "Jesus Christ, save me from sin and lead me not into temptation."

One need hardly mention that she was otherwise a most advanced lady who was not seen in church once a year.

It was already the middle of August and very hot. One Sunday the Mayor organized a picnic in Schmausenbuk. Caspar had ridden that morning with Herr Rumpler and some boys as far as

Buch, and was so tired that he fell asleep in his room after lunch. Frau Behold wakened him herself and told him to get dressed as the carriage was waiting to take him to the picnic ground. To Caspar's question whether anyone else was going along, she replied that two boys were going to drive out with them, the sons of General Hartung. Caspar was disappointed and said that he wished Frau Behold would allow her daughter to go with them, for she would be disappointed if she had to stay at home. Frau Behold was startled and almost lost her temper, but she controlled herself. She leaned forward, seized a handful of Caspar's curls, and said maliciously, "I'll cut your hair off if you begin with that again."

Caspar pulled away. "Don't come so near," he begged with staring eyes, "and please don't cut it."

"I've got you," threatened Frau Behold with forced merriment. "Now I've got you, you timid little boy. Cross me once again and I'll get the scissors."

During the drive Caspar remained silent. The two boys, who were fourteen and fifteen years old, teased him and tried to get something out of him, for they had always heard him spoken of as a curious animal. Like typical schoolboys they began to speak boastfully, as if there were no cleverer or more sharp-sighted people alive than they. Some distance along the road one of them exclaimed that he already heard the music from the woods, whereupon Caspar, annoyed at the exhibition that they were making of themselves, said that surprised him, for he did not hear anything, but he did see a little flag flying on a high pole over the trees. "Oh, the flag," said the boy disparagingly; "we have seen that for a long time." This, too, surprised Caspar, for he had only just that moment perceived it, a narrow ribbon, visible only when the wind blew.

"Good," said he; "when it blows again I'll ask you whether you see it." He waited awhile and then, while the flag was at rest, asked the misleading question, "Well, is it blowing or not?"

"It's blowing," replied the boys in one voice, but Caspar replied quietly, "I now perceive that you don't see anything."

"Ah," cried they, "then you're lying."

"Then tell me," Caspar went on unconcerned, "what color it is.

The boys were silent and looked; then one of them said rather timidly, "Red"; the other somewhat more boldly, "Blue." Caspar shook his head and repeated, "I see that you don't see anything; it's white and green."

It was difficult to cavil about this, for a quarter of an hour later they could all convince themselves of the truth. But the boys gazed hatefully at Caspar; they would gladly have shone before Brau Behold, who had listened in silence to the whole affair.

Caspar's presence at the festival drew a crowd of gapers as usual; among them there were some acquaintances, young men who thought that they ought to pay some attention to him and who snatched him away from Frau Behold in spite of her protests. It was at first only a small group, which gradually grew, however, and as one spurred the other on, they indulged in wild antics. They knocked over tables and chairs, frightened the girls, bought out the shopkeepers' stalls, uttered deafening screams, and behaved in all this as if Caspar were their leader and responsible for all this turmoil. Their behavior became more and more unruly. When evening came they tore the Chinese lanterns from the trees and compelled a few musicians to precede them in order to accompany the racket with their trumpets. Two young salesmen lifted Caspar on their shoulders and he, who could scarcely see or hear any longer, crouched on his living throne with the unhappiest face in the world.

Amid laughter and songs the wild group reached the platform, where the dancing had begun; they could get no further; the assembled crowd kept them from going either forward or sideways. Suddenly Caspar saw quite close at hand the two boys who had driven out with him in Frau Behold's carriage; they stood on the steps leading to the platform where the dancing was going on and carried a long branch of a tree with a white piece of cardboard on the end of it, on which was painted in big letters the words: "Here one can see His Majesty, little Caspar, the King of Swindledom." They held the placard so that the inscription was turned toward Caspar, and all of the people standing about at once perceived it and Everyone burst out laughing. The trumpeters gave a toot and the whole train started past the inn toward the illuminated grove.

Caspar shouted to be let down, but no one paid any attention to him. Then he pulled the ear of one of the boys who was carrying him and the hair of the second. "What are you pinching me for?" screamed the one. "Why are you pulling at me?" yelled the other. Furious, they both stepped aside and Caspar slipped down. The two boys who carried the placard stood before him, smiling scornfully. "We have a little flag for you, too," said the other; "just see whether it waves or not." At that moment they started, for a commanding voice uttered their names threateningly. It was the father of the boys, the general, who, with another gentleman, was sitting not far away at a table to one side. They all arose, for the sky was covered with black clouds and the roll of thunder could already be heard.

Frau Behold received Caspar with the words, "What stupid pranks you are up to! Aren't you ashamed of yourself? Allons! We're going home." In a loud manner she bade the gentlemen good-by and hurried to the gate where she screamed for her coachman. "Sit down," she ordered Caspar when they had gotten the carriage. She herself got up on the box with the coachman and seized the reins. Now a mad drive began, first through the woods, then over the dust-whirling road. She drove the animals on so that they fairly galloped along, and sparks flew from their hoofs as they struck the stones. There was not a star in the sky; the landscape stretched out dark before them; there were frequent flashes of lightning, and the thunder sounded nearer.

In little more than half an hour they were in the city, and as the horses stopped on the Market Square, sweat steamed from their flanks. Frau Behold opened the door of the house and let Caspar go ahead. He felt his way in the darkness to the door of his room, but the woman snatched his arm, drew him along and took him into the so-called green drawing room, a big apartment whose windows were shut and the air of which was musty. Frau Behold lit a candle, threw her coat and hat upon the sofa, and sat down in a leather chair. She was humming gently to herself. Suddenly she ceased and said, continuing her singing, "Come here to me, you innocent sinner."

Caspar obeyed.

"Kneel down!" ordered the woman.

Hesitatingly he knelt down on the floor and looked at Frau Behold anxiously.

As she had done in the afternoon, she again put her face close to his. Her narrow long chin trembled a little, and her eyes laughed curiously.

"Why are you resisting?" she cooed as he bent his head backwards. "Ma foi, the boy does struggle! Haven't you ever smelled living flesh? Oh you rascal, who believes you? Why, you devil, are you really afraid? Haven't I had the most delicate food served to you? Didn't I give you a beautiful blackbird yesterday? I have a good heart. Caspar, there, listen to how it beats and pulses— "

With great force she pressed his head against her breast. He thought she was going to injure him and screamed, whereupon she pressed her lips upon his mouth. He turned cold with fear, his body collapsed as if the joints were dissolved from his bones, and when Frau Behold realized this sudden collapse she became frightened and jumped up. Her hair had become undone and a thick braid lay like a snake over her shoulder. Caspar crouched on the floor; his left hand clasped the back of the chair convulsively. Frau Behold bent over him once more and sniffed curiously, for she loved the smell of his body, which reminded her of honey. But no sooner did Caspar sense her repulsive proximity than he struggled up and flew to the other end of the room. He remained standing with his side pressed against the door, his head bent forward, and his arms half outstretched.

A remote perception of some monstrous thing began to dawn in him; no word that he had ever heard gave any hint, nevertheless he divined something as one concludes that there is a raging fire burning behind the hills from the redness of the sky. He was ashamed of himself, secretly he felt about, to see whether he was wearing clothes on his body, and then he looked at his hands to see whether they were dirty. He was ashamed, he was ashamed before the walls and the chairs, he was ashamed before the light of the candle, and he wished that the door might open of itself so that he might silently disappear.

A rosy blaze of lightning which shot through the room seemed like frightfully flashing eyes; the clap of thunder which followed seemed a tremendous scream. Caspar pressed his shoulders together and began to tremble.

Meantime, Frau Behold strode up and down like a man, and laughed harshly to herself several times; suddenly she seized the candle and walked up to Caspar: "You beast, you corrupted beast, what did you think?" she said bitterly. "Do you think that I care anything about you? Yes, as much as for a worn-out shoe! Get out of here, and if you dare to talk I'll murder you."

She laughed as though at bottom the incident were a joke, but to Caspar she seemed immense, her black shadow filled the whole room; beside himself with fear, he ran out, the woman behind him;

he rushed down the steps to the door and rattled at the knob, but the door was locked. He heard the rain on the pavement outside, at the same time he was aware of quick tripping steps; a key turned in the lock and the Magistrate appeared on the threshold. The constant flashes of lightning illuminated Caspar's quaking figure, and the roll of the thunder drowned out the surprised man's questions.

Up on the staircase stood Frau Behold, the proximity of the candlelight furrowed her face with wild gleams and her voice resounded above the thunder, as she called to her husband, "The fellow's drunk; they made him drunk at Schmausenbuk. Don't you show yourself again today. Be off and get to bed."

The Magistrate shut the door and closed his dripping umbrella. "Come, come," he said, "it's probably not as bad as that."

Frau Behold did not reply. She slammed a door and there was darkness and silence.

"Come with me, Caspar," said the councilor. "We'll make a light and see what's the matter. Give me your arm." He led Caspar to his room, made a light and repeatedly murmured short soothing phrases. Then he smelled Caspar's breath to see whether he had been drinking, shook his head and said with surprise, "Nothing of the sort. Frau Behold is mistaken. But forget it all, Caspar. Confide the matter to the Lord and it will all end well. Good-night."

When Caspar was alone his timid gaze wandered from flash to flash of lightning. Each time the lightning flamed he had a pain under his eyelids as if needles pricked him; at each thunder clap his whole body seemed to crumble. His hands and feet were as cold as ice. He did not dare to go to bed, but remained as if rooted where he stood. He remembered with horror the first storm he had experienced in the tower of the castle. He had crawled into a hole in the wall, and the wife of the jailer had come to comfort him. She said, "You mustn't go out, there is a big man outside who is scolding." Always when the thunder pealed he leaned quite over to the ground and the woman said, "Don't be afraid, Caspar, I'll stay with you."

Now, too, it seemed to him as if there were a big man outside scolding, but there was no one there to comfort him. The blackbird which sat in a cage near the window with drooping head at times made little piping sounds. He would have set it free long ago, for he pitied the animal, but he feared Frau Behold's scorn.

When the storm abated he quickly threw off his clothes, crept into bed and covered himself up to his forehead, in order not to need to see the lightning. In his hurry he even forgot to lock the door, and this circumstance had a curious sequel.

On the next morning when he woke up he noticed a penetrating smell. Yes, there was the smell of blood in the room. Shuddering, he looked about, and the first thing he noticed was that the bird cage by the window was empty. Caspar looked for the little animal and perceived that the blackbird lay dead on the table, its wings spread out in a pool of blood. And next to it on a white plate lay the little bleeding heart.

What could this mean? Caspar made a face and his mouth trembled like that of a child before it cries. He dressed to go to the kitchen to question the servants, but as he left the room he suddenly became frightened, for Frau Behold stood in the corridor next to the door. She had a broom in her hand and was decidedly untidy in appearance. Caspar looked at her sallow face and continued to look at her for a time, with almost the same dismay and feeling with which he had looked at the dead bird.

10.   A Message From Far Away

From this time on life with Frau Behold was unendurable. Probably the terrible mental trouble which was later to end her life so disastrously was already beginning to show traces in her at this time. Everyone avoided having anything to do with her. No sooner had she sat down than she jumped up again; at five o'clock in the morning she was already awake, moving noisily in the rooms and on the staircases, waking Caspar out of his sleep and making such a racket that he woke with an aching head and was not fit for work for an entire day. At the table he was not allowed to speak, and if he ever contradicted her she threatened to make him eat with the servants in the kitchen. If a stranger came and Caspar was called, she delivered herself of biting remarks. "I wonder whether you can get anything out of the dunce?" she would say. "No doubt you have been told that you will find him uniquely intelligent. Just convince yourself. See whether he says one sensible word." This embarrassed the guest, whoever he was, and Caspar stood there, not knowing where to look.

As formerly, people had to come to fill the rooms of the house; laughter must be made to echo along the dilapidated staircase and resounding steps brush away the dust of decades. But the days were as different from the nights, as an illuminated ballroom is changed when the guests have left, and the doorkeeper has turned out the lights, and mice flit over the spotted carpets. In such an existence guilt flourishes like a weed in a neglected field. A great guilt may have a cleansing effect through repentance or the suffering it engenders; but small omissions and nameless iniquities, extending over many hours and days, destroy the soul and consume the backbone of life.

Certainly Frau Behold was a very moral nature; she showed this in her inability to forgive the person who had jeopardized her virtue, if only for one sultry hour before a storm. But was it only that? Was it not rather that her whole world had been turned upside down by the unexpected image of innocence that the boy had presented? She could not bear to live in such a topsy-turvy world. She had been robbed and she demanded vengeance.

The change of conditions in the Beholds' house did not remain unknown to Caspar's friends. Mayor Binder was the first to declare emphatically that Caspar could not stay there any longer. Daumer emphatically supported this point of view, and Editor Pfisterle, hot-headed and troublesome as usual, reviled the Magistrate in his newspaper and expressed a suspicion that an attempt was being made to make the foundling harmless and to silence those voices which had tried to enforce the rights of his mysterious birth. "There the puzzling boy, on whose forehead glitters an invisible diadem, lives like a solitary beast, and only ventures a few shy leaps into the daylight, skipping across the field with odd motions of his head and tail which amuse his enemies, looking anxiously about only to creep back again into the first hole at hand."

Thus wrote the excited knight of the pen. Hereupon the city fathers, after some consultation, determined to set aside a sum, as they had done before, for the maintenance and education of the boy at the expense of the city, and as nobody seemed so well suited to offer the fatherless boy a home as Herr von Tucher, they laid the matter before him in the most moving terms, appealing to his generosity and to the extraordinary position of his family, whose name alone would be sufficient to protect the boy from any ordinary pursuers.

Herr von Tucher had some hesitation. The sudden attacks upon the Beholds annoyed him. "First you were glad to find a shelter for the young man, and suddenly you resort to Star Chamber proceedings." he said. "Why should I assume that matters will go better with me? I don't want to run the danger of having my private affairs pried into; I don't care to have every idle cock disturbing my peace by crowing in my front yard."

The family, too, raised objections, particularly Herr von Tucher's mother warned him against getting into such an adventure. It was even said that the old lady had made an unpleasant scene and had said that if he took Hauser into the house he would have to defray his expenses out of community funds; she would not contribute a penny.

But Herr von Tucher had a sense of duty. He thought it was his duty to take Caspar in. Since he regarded him as a half-lost soul, he thought that by taking him in he might be able to lead back the wandering boy to a proper attitude towards life. "Perhaps Caspar only needs a strong masculine hand," he said to himself; "the tomfoolery of the miraculous and the supernatural, this business of being constantly stared at and admired, was harmful to him; simplicity, order, well placed severity, in brief, the principles of wholesome training will cure him. Let's try it."

Herr von Tucher had set himself a task in this matter and that was all important. He said: "I am prepared to take charge of the foundling, on condition that I shall be allowed to do as I like in all things and that no one, no matter who, shall venture to interfere with my plans, or to come between Caspar and myself for any purpose whatsoever."

Naturally, this was agreed to and promised.

No sooner had Frau Behold heard what was going on behind her back than she resolved to steal a march on the course of events. She waited for an afternoon when Caspar was away from home, had all of his possessions, clothes, underwear, books and other objects thrown into a box without a lid and the box carried into the street. Then she locked the door herself, and smiling with satisfaction, sat down at a balcony window on the first floor to watch for Caspar's return, and to enjoy the amazement of the assembled crowd.

Caspar soon came; he was informed by his body guard of what had happened, and while the man hurried off to the City Hall to report what had occurred, as was his duty, Caspar leaned against his box, now and again looking up in amazement at Frau Behold. It took two full hours before they could decide at the City Hall what should be done, and before Herr von Tucher was notified. Meanwhile it began to rain, and if a good-natured market woman had not brought a bag with which she covered the box, all Caspar's possessions would have been wet through. Finally the policeman reappeared with one of Herr von Tucher's servants; they brought a little hand-cart and dragged the box along. . . . Thus they proceeded, and a silly crowd followed them, gossiping until they reached the Tucher House in the Hirschelgasse.

Now an entirely new life began again for Caspar. Above all, he ceased going to school, instead of which there came to the house twice a day a young teacher, a student named Schmidt. Then the door was locked to all uninvited strangers. Furthermore, he was no longer allowed to ride. "Such exercise is for the aristocracy and for wealthy people, but not for a person who has to be brought up to the bourgeois business of earning his bread, and will certainly sometime be dependent upon supporting himself by the work of his own hands," said Herr von Tucher.

From this it was obvious that he did not attribute the slightest importance to the talk about the boy's distinguished birth, which had in no way died down with time. 'Things are bad enough as they are," Herr von Tucher would reply when someone pointed to a possibility of this sort. "I am not in the least inclined to sacrifice my principles to such a phantom."

Severity seemed important to him; he showed a stern face to Caspar. His chief maxim was not to let himself be moved. This accomplished, it was easy to express appreciation of a duty properly performed. The hours from morning till night were apportioned in detail. In the morning there were lessons, then a walk under the supervision of a servant or policeman; during the afternoon Caspar occupied himself alone. Next to his room there was a small chamber which had been fitted up as a workshop, and when he had finished his lessons he did all kinds of joinery and cardboard work, in which he was very skillful. The taking apart and putting together of clocks also gave him pleasure. His behavior satisfied Herr von Tucher completely. He could not help admiring the iron industry of the boy, and his tremendous eagerness for learning and culture. There was no contradiction or resistance; Caspar never did less than was asked of him. "It is evident that I have been falsely informed," thought Herr von Tucher. "The people who have taken care of him up to now have not known how to handle him; for the first time he is experiencing the blessings of a systematic guidance."

Principles triumphed.

Being alone frequently and for a long time was at first agreeable to Caspar, but in the course of time he began to feel that there was compulsion in this, and he ceased to shun the opportunities which promised distraction and amusement. When there was a noise on the generally quiet Hirschelgasse, he tore the window open and leaned out over the sill until everything was quiet again. If two old women merely stood still to gossip, our friend Caspar was at once at his post listening. He knew at exactly what time in the morning the bakers' boys came from the Webersplatz, and he enjoyed their whistling. As soon as the postillion at the Laufertor blew his horn, Caspar stopped his work and his eyes shone. Every sound from the interior of the rambling house surprised him, and not infrequently he ran to the door, opened it ajar and listened excitedly when he heard an unknown voice. The servants began to notice this; they said that he was an eavesdropper and took it upon themselves to tell the baron so.

    For the house itself Caspar had a vague sort of respect; he walked along the halls almost on his toes, just as one speaks in low tones before some distinguished gentleman. The structure stood in proud exclusiveness apart from the bustle of life; anyone who sought to enter had to permit himself to be eyed and questioned by a long-bearded porter. The walls were sunk so deeply into the earth; facade, roof and gables were so majestically fashioned and wrought together that it seemed as if ancient vested rights had contributed more to their prestige than the art of the builder. Caspar liked to look at night at the turret in the courtyard, with its winding staircase, when the delicately sinuous forms were covered with a bluish light and seemed to leap into a confused animation of their own.

    At times he saw back of a closed window a parchment colored face with iron gray hair parted over the forehead. It was the old baroness, who never showed herself in any other fashion. He was told that she was delicate and timidly clung to her room. This remaining a stranger within adjoining walls made him thoughtful. Gradually it became clear to him that he was surrounded by strangers, eating the bread of charity. One person took him and fed him, then a carriage came and he was taken away. Another house; one fine day his things are thrown on the street; again he goes elsewhere.

    How could this happen? Other people lived constantly in one place; they slept in the same bed from childhood on; no one could snatch them away; they had rights. That was it: they had powerful established rights. There were poor people who worked for money, who lay at the feet of those who were called rich, but even these had their roots somewhere in the world; they did their work, they received pay for their work; and they could go and buy their own bread. The one made coats, another shoes, the third built houses, the fourth was a soldier, and thus one was a protection and a help to another, and they received food and drink from one another. Why could they not be torn away from the place where they lived?

Because they were the children of a father and mother: that was the reason, that was why. This held for Everyone. Father and mother brought one into the community, and showed one where one came from and what one was intended to be.

That was it. Caspar did not know where he came from. For some undiscovered reason he was all alone, fatherless and motherless. And he had to find out why. He must try to find out who his father and mother were, and above all he must go and make a place for himself from which he could not be driven away.

One winter evening Herr von Tucher entered Caspar's room and found him deeply absorbed in himself. Two or three times a week, after the day's work was over, Herr von Tucher was in the habit of visiting his protégé in order to talk to him a little. This was a part of his plan for the boy's education. His principles, however, demanded of Herr von Tucher that he remain dignified and distant; his principles demanded that he renounce the pleasures of natural intercourse. And although it was sometimes difficult for him to practice such self-control, either because of his own need of expressing himself, or because a silent searching look of Caspar's penetrated his heart, there must be no hesitation, he clung grimly to the principle of not overstepping the limits of reserve more than utility demanded, like a cruel old Mexican god.

When, however, he perceived Caspar sunk in deep thought, the sight did affect him, and against his will his voice became milder as he asked the boy what was the subject of his meditation.

Caspar considered whether he might reveal his thoughts. As always, when he was moved, the left side of his face twitched convulsively. Then, with a charming and inimitable gesture which was characteristic of him, he pushed back his hair from one of his cheeks, towards the ear, and asked in a tone of deepest emotion, "What am I to be in life?"

Herr von Tucher was at once reassured by these words. His face took on an expression which seemed to say: the plan is bearing fruit. He had already thought of that, he replied; Casper should tell him what he most wanted to do.

Caspar remained silent and gazed undecidedly ahead of him.

"What about gardening?" continued Herr von Tucher benevolently. "Or how would you like to become a carpenter or a bookbinder? Your cardboard work is most excellent and you could learn bookbinding very quickly."

"Could I read all the books which I had to bind?" asked Caspar, sunk in thought, who was sitting with his head so low that his chin touched the top of the table.

Herr von Tucher wrinkled his forehead. "That would mean neglecting your work," he replied.

"I might become a clockmaker, too," said Caspar, who at that moment had a fairly exalted conception of a clockmaker. He thought of him as a man who stood inside of high towers and ordered the bells to ring; a man who fitted gold wheels into one another, one who made time invisible by means of a magic spell and shut it up in a tiny little house. Indeed, such names of callings were difficult to him. It was not a question of will, but an inconceivably complicated picture of life. Herr von Tucher, suspecting that there was no real seriousness in Caspar's behavior, got up and said coldly that he would consider the matter.

The next evening Caspar was summoned into Herr von Tucher's room. "With regard to our conversation of yesterday I have come to the following conclusion," said the Baron: "During the spring and summer you are to remain in my house. If you are industrious, your education in the elementary branches can be completed by September; Herr Schmidt assures me of this. In order that the day may be entirely at your disposal, you will no longer lunch with me, but take all your meals in your room. I shall soon talk with some reputable master bookbinder, then we shall know where we are at. Does this satisfy you, Caspar? Or have you other wishes? Come, speak out frankly, you can still choose."

A brief shudder ran down Caspar's spine. He shook himself a little, sat down and was silent. Herr von Tucher did not want to urge him further; he wished to grant him time. He walked up and down for a while, then he sat down in front of the piano and played a slow movement from a sonata. This was not the result of a chance mood. On Tuesday and Friday from six to seven in the evening, Herr von

Tucher played the piano, and since the cuckoo of the Black Forest clock had just screeched six times, any omission would have been greatly against the rules.

It was rather melancholy music. For Caspar it was a torment. Much as he liked marches, waltzes and gay songs — Anna Daumer, she can play, he always said—he was always uncomfortable during such music as Tucher now played. When Herr von Tucher had finished the final chords and turned around on the stool and looked at Caspar questioningly, the latter thought he was asked to state how he had liked the music, and said: "That's nothing; I can be sad alone; I don't need music for that."

Herr von Tucher lifted his eyebrows with surprise.

"What are you assuming?" he asked calmly. "I did not ask for any musical opinion from you and haven't the ambition to cultivate your taste in this respect. Moreover, go to your room."

Caspar was very glad not to have to eat with the Baron any more. The stiffness of their bearing at table always seemed a dreadful nuisance to him. Much delighted him in this man, particularly his calm and deliberate speech, the exceeding cleanliness of his body, his porcelain white teeth, and above all the pink arched finger-nails of his long hands. He knew many people with white nails and was always distrustful of them; white nails always awoke a notion of jealousy and cruelty in him.

Nevertheless, Caspar always had the feeling that Herr von Tucher had in some way or other received bad reports of him and was being misled by them. He sometimes felt as if he should shout to him: "Why, none of all this is true!" But what, what was untrue? Caspar could not say.

In his loneliness he felt as if people were tired of him and were thinking of getting rid of him. He was full of forebodings, full of unrest. On nights when the moon was in the sky, he would extinguish the lamp earlier than usual, sit down at the window and follow the course of the stars with rigid eyes. When the moon was full he was frequently unwell, his whole body shivered, and only the sight of the moon itself relieved the pressure in his breast. He knew from which roof, or between what gables the clear orb would rise; he conjured it forth as if with his own hands from the depth of the sky, and when there were clouds he trembled lest they touch the moon, because he thought that the radiant disc would be sullied.

His ear at this time seemed sometimes bent upon catching sounds from a world of spirits. One morning he got up suddenly during his lessons, went to the window and leaned out. Herr Schmidt, the student, did not interfere with him, but when he stayed too long at the window he called him back. Caspar straightened up and closed the window; his face was so pale that his teacher asked with concern what was wrong with Caspar.

"It seemed to me as if someone were coming," replied Caspar.

"As if someone were coming? Why, who?"

"As if someone were calling to me from below."

This seemed remarkable to the young tutor. He thought it over for a while and would gladly have asked a question. There had again been much talk in the city of late about a curious story concerning Caspar, or suggesting a connection with Caspar, and which had been worn threadbare by all the newspapers all over the country. But as Herr von Tucher had strictly forbidden the tutor ever to talk of such matters with Caspar, he controlled himself and remained silent.

Now Caspar had for months been in the habit of reading through carefully all the newspapers he could get hold of, and some of which he secretly procured, for Herr von Tucher feared their effect upon him, and rightly so. It happened that he now and again saw some news or information about himself, and although he had never found anything of importance, his heart beat whenever he as much as saw his name in print. A short time after this little digression with his teacher, it happened that he got hold of a copy of the *Morgenpost*, which was already several days old, and on reading it he found the following curious story:

More than ten years ago a fisher near Breisach had found a bottle floating in the Rhine, and on pulling it out had found a sheet of paper on which were written the words, "I am buried in an underground prison. He who occupies my throne does not know of my prison. I am subjected to cruel supervision. No one knows me, no one misses me, no one rescues me, no one mentions me." Then came a name half illegible and half distorted, all of the distinguishable letters of which were also contained in the name Caspar Hauser.

All this had already been reported by several papers, but owing to the absence of any further clew had of course been again forgotten. Then, four weeks ago, some unknown busy-body had brought the occurrence to light again from some old number of the Magdeburger Zeitung. Other papers seized the opportunity and finally the thing had raised a great hubbub. Suddenly it was proved that a Piarist monk had been accused by a certain dynasty of having thrown the bottle into the Rhine. It was furthermore discovered that the same monk had suddenly disappeared, and one fine day he had been found murdered in Alsace in one of the Vosges forests. The murderer had never been discovered.

"If this track does not result in lifting the veil of mystery which surrounds the foundling" exclaimed the querulous contributor to the *Morgenpost*, after he had recounted the story in detail, "then I don't give a penny for our whole judicial system."

Caspar read and read. He spent two hours in reading the strange tale over again from the beginning, weighing almost every word. The student surprised him at this; he felt certain that it was the same matter about which Caspar had not wanted to speak the other day, and said hastily: "Oh, Caspar, what are you about? What do you think of it, anyway? Most people consider it rubbish; nevertheless it is an undeniable fact that the matter was printed in the Magdeburger Zeitung. What do you make of it, Caspar?"

Caspar scarcely heard him. When the man repeated his question, he lifted his head, cast a moist glance at heaven, and said gently, "I did not write that story about the prison."

"About the prison and the throne," added the student with a curious greedy smile. "That you did not write it, I readily believe; why, you never could write till you came to us."

"But who can have written it?"

"Who? That's just the question. Perhaps someone who wanted to help, perhaps some hidden friend."

"About the prison and the throne," murmured Caspar with involuntary lips. He went off into a corner by the stove, huddled down on a chair and sank into deep thought. Neither calls, warns or commands could rouse him, and his teacher, feeling guilty, remained seated for the whole hour, in order not to draw attention to himself, and then left silently.

That same evening there was a party at the Tuchers'; all of the friends of the family were invited and for half an hour the carriage wheels rumbled outside the house. When the first notes of the dance music resounded from the ballroom, Caspar went into the hallway and listened. He was no longer allowed to attend such parties.

While he was still standing, leaning against the banisters, his head bent forward, feeling himself much unwanted, a hand touched his shoulder. It was a butler bringing him some sweets on a silver tray. Caspar shook his head and said, "I don't care for sweets"; whereupon the servant looked at him sullenly and made ready to leave him.

Then there was a footfall on the second stairway, which was not illuminated, and unexpectedly the old baroness, in a gray silk dress and silk head-cloth, stood in front of them. Gazing with her blue eyes severely into the boy's, she said, with haughty displeasure, "You do not care for sweets? Why do you not care for sweets?"

She came from downstairs. Caspar could smell the odor of human bodies from her clothes. It was her habit to retire early. Every evening before she went to bed she went through the whole house to make sure that there was no fire and that no thief had found his way in.

Her severe words made Caspar bend his head. Probably his imagination was unusually active that evening. Suddenly he felt a paralyzing fear. Things went black before his eyes. It seemed to him as if he heard the voice of the disguised man, and stretching out his arms he called imploringly, "Don't strike, don't strike."

The old lady, who had not intended to be so harsh, looked at him with surprise and fright. Meantime Caspar's loud scream had attracted the attention of some of the guests, who were walking up and down in the corridor below. They appealed to Herr von Tucher, and the latter hurried up the stairs, followed by some of the gentlemen. A report that something had happened spread among the guests in the ballroom, and as it was known that Caspar was living in the house, Everyone thought of an occurrence similar to the one at Daumer's. There ensued a silence, the dance music ceased, many people hurried out; the young ladies were particularly excited; and a number of them mounted the stairs and remained standing and looking.

Herr von Tucher, to whom all this was most painful, as any unnecessary excitement was an abomination to him, proceeded to take Caspar to task, but was frightened by the boy's stony gaze, as well as taken aback by his own mother's dismay.

An immense experience was taking place in Caspar. It seemed to him as if he had already gone through the same thing once before. It was as if a tidal wave had carried him back and time seemed to hold its breath. There was the old woman regally dressed, majestic to behold; did she not resemble a woman who had entered into a room while he was in it and had not her presence struck Everyone dumb? Had there not been someone lying on the bed, his head buried in the pillows? There was a servant who held a silver tray in his hands; was that not the old experience, too? Had not someone stood there formerly, too, bringing presents or sweetmeats or valuables? There were imposingly dressed men who seemed to be waiting for an order, for someone to come; even more imposingly dressed than themselves, before whom they had to bow. And those slender white girls in white veils, whose glances had depths and apprehensions? And the twilight up here which gradually faded downward over countless white marble steps, into the light below? Caspar would have liked to shout with exultation, for he seemed strange to himself and at the same time worshiped by Everyone; they bent their heads and recognized the prince in him. Now he perceived who he was and whence he came; he felt what those words about the prison and the throne meant; a ghostlike smile played about his lips.

Herr von Tucher terminated the unpleasant incident with as little fuss as possible. He led Caspar to his room, told him to go to bed and waited until he did so, then put out the light himself and left, saying as he went, in sharp tones, that he would call him to account the next day for his unseemly behavior.

This did not disturb Caspar much. Nor was a great deal made of the threatened reckoning. Herr von Tucher realized that actually there had been but a slight infraction of his fundamental principles. His cook confided to him in hollow prophetic tones that Caspar was moon-struck and would certainly some time climb upon the roof and fall down. Herr von Tucher could not do away with the moon; since the boy was a victim of a pathological state, one could not very well hold him responsible for certain lapses. Whether Caspar was to become a carpenter or bookbinder was still undecided; President

Feuerbach's opinion on this subject had to be asked. Herr von Tucher resolved to go to Ansbach in April and to talk to him.

Caspar was full of expectation. He was waiting for someone that was to come, for one who somewhere went about among people seeking a way to him, and so profound was his belief in the coming of this person that every morning he thought: today, and every night he thought: to-morrow. He lived in a constant state of inward alertness and his foreboding of joy was like a dream state. But just as the peacock spreads his tail when he perceives his own ugly feet, so did his own voice and his own tread make him hesitate, and how much more was he disheartened by the sight of other people, who daily disappointed his expectations.

His whole behavior at this time was unusual, and the tense attention with which he listened into empty space had something of distraction about it. Naturally, when considered in the light of the course of events, the matter presented a different aspect and would have given a man like Daumer remarkable material for his ideas.

Much that was strange and hostile beset Caspar's paths, and cold shivers ran down his spine when on a cloudy day a drop of water would fall from a gutter-spout. Timid premonitions accompanied him even to his sleep, and because he often woke up and was troubled by the dark he asked to have an oil lamp put next to his bed. This was done.

One night, although he was still asleep, he felt a curious tugging at his face as if a cool breath were fanning him from above. Abruptly he sat up, looked about his bed and the wall, and perceived a large spider hanging by a thread near his head. Horrified, he sprang out of bed, and, unable to move, he watched the animal get down on his pillow and creep across the white sheet, trailing a shining thread behind it.

Caspar's whole body was covered as with a new, shivering, icy skin. He clasped his hands together and whispered anxiously and with a curious wheedling, "Spider, oh spider, what are you spinning?"

The spider ducked its yellow body. "What are you spinning, spider?" he repeated entreatingly.

The animal climbed over the bedpost and reached the wall.

"Where are you going now, spider?" whispered Caspar. "Why so fast? Are you looking for something? I won't hurt you."

The spider was already up on the ceiling. Caspar sat down on a chair where his clothes lay. "Spider, spider," he murmured tonelessly. Four o'clock struck, and he had not yet gone back to bed. Then, before he lay down, he eagerly wiped his pillow and the wall with a handkerchief.

He caught a cold during the hour that he had sat up undressed, which kept him in bed several days. He became sad; he was already tired of waiting. And then, even when there was no longer anything wrong with him, he had no desire to leave his room. Herr von Tucher took his condition for a temporary hypochondria, but when he had convinced himself that both his continued indifference as well as his kindly interest was fruitless and that the boy was a prey to real dejection of mind, he became anxious.

Now it happened that one day an unexpected messenger presented himself at the house who asked to see Caspar in order to deliver a letter to him. Herr von Tucher refused permission for this. After some hesitation the man gave him the letter and withdrew. Herr von Tucher considered himself justified in opening the letter. It was couched in enigmatical terms, and made even more puzzling by the fact that it contained a valuable diamond ring as a present for Caspar. Herr von Tucher was undecided as to what he ought to do. To hand over the letter and the ring to the police, or to President Feuerbach, seemed the wisest plan. But this somehow contradicted his ideas of right. A fleeting mood of softness towards Caspar made him forget this plan entirely; he hoped to bring the boy out of his state of low spirits, and this purpose he fulfilled completely. He produced the ring and the letter.

Caspar read: "You who rightfully are what many deny you to be, have trust in the friend who is working for you at a distance. He will soon stand before you; he will soon embrace you. Meantime take this ring as a token of his devotion and pray for his happiness as he entreats God for yours."

When Caspar had read this he pressed his face against his arm and wept. silently to himself. Herr von Tucher sat at the table and thoughtfully permitted the sunlight to play over the beautiful ring.

11. The English Earl

In the afternoon of a day late in April a handsome traveling coach drove up in front of the entrance to the Hotel "Wilder Mann." A tall gentleman got out and greeted the host most affably, who had rushed out to meet him, for he was unaccustomed to such guests, most of his patrons being tradesmen and traveling salesmen. The stranger ordered the best rooms, without inquiring the price, and walked through the gaping crowd into the wide-arched door. The valet and coachman carried the trunks, suit-case and the rest of the luggage into the hall. The stranger asked for the registry book of his own accord and soon Everyone could read with awe his boldly written entry: "Henry, Lord Stanhope, Earl of Chesterfield, Peer of England." The newspapers of Nurnberg at once recorded the arrival of an English peer.

The event created such excitement that late into the evening people stood in the streets staring up at the lighted windows of the rooms occupied by the distinguished gentleman. The next morning Lord Stanhope left his cards at the house of the Mayor, and at the residences of several of the distinguished men of the city, and a few hours later received visits from them. The first to call was Binder, who of course distinctly remembered Lord Stanhope's previous visit.

Without any circumlocution, during the rather long conversation between the two, Lord Stanhope admitted that his present visit, like his previous one, was connected with Caspar Hauser. He felt the greatest interest in the foundling, he said, and hinted to Binder that he was determined to take a decisive step in the young man's behalf.

The Mayor replied that he would give His Grace complete freedom as far as the regulations permitted.

"What regulations?" asked the lord quickly.

Binder replied that Herr von Tucher was the boy's guardian, that he had far-reaching rights and would not be friendly to the intervention of a stranger; furthermore they could not, without the knowledge of President Feuerbach, propose any change in Caspar Hauser's mode of life.

Lord Stanhope looked anxious. "Then I shall have my difficulties," he remarked. Then he inquired whether they had obtained any clew to the attack in Daumer's house and whether any recipient for the reward which he had offered at that time had been found. Binder was obliged to reply in the negative. He said that the sum which had been so generously offered still lay untouched at the City Hall, and that his lordship could have it back whenever he pleased, since any possibility of discovering the criminal was now a thing of the past.

The next few days were spent by Lord Stanhope exclusively in the fulfillment of his social obligations. At luncheon, at tea time and in the evening he was invited out, or gave small but distinguished dinner parties in his hotel, for which specific purpose he engaged a French cook. If it was his secret object to make friends and win admirers in this way there certainly remained nothing further to be wished. If his purpose was to become acquainted with these good people and their opinions it was not a particularly difficult task; they expressed themselves without reserve, for they felt themselves honored by his presence and they admired his very slightest action.

He seized every opportunity to talk about Caspar Hauser; he wanted to know, he wanted constantly to hear something new, he rejoiced in the touching details which they were able to give him, but he did not consider it necessary—an omission which was regarded as extraordinary—to call upon Professor Daumer, contenting himself with having Warden Hill come to see him, and asking him questions.

Hill, whose head was somewhat turned by being distinguished thus, pictured most movingly—and in a way that was most astonishing for a man who had grown gray among criminals—the charming and forlorn manner in which Caspar had carried himself in the tower and the moving way in which he had been prostrated. Finally, glowing with eagerness, he exclaimed that so far as he was concerned, he would bear witness to the boy's innocence, even if God himself maintained the contrary. Count Stanhope was visibly moved. He smiled and said there was no question of any guilt and sent the man away with a princely reward.

Now finally he resolved to meet Herr von Tucher, and also Caspar, face to face. When people had asked him in astonishment why he had delayed this so long he had replied that this step required his complete composure and strength of mind, for he was afraid of the moment when he would see Caspar for the first time, a happy fear, like that of a child on Christmas Eve.

Herr von Tucher was in his study when the Englishman's card was brought to him. As a matter of course, he was aware of Stanhope's presence in the city, and knew how Stanhope had been spending his time. Since, in any event, he regarded him as someone who would disturb his peace; he was not predisposed in the man's favor.

From all the descriptions, he had expected to find in him an agreeable and winning personality, nevertheless he was surprised when he saw his distinguished guest coming towards him, and the dislike raised by his own vague forebodings, as well as what he had heard about the man, at once disappeared.

There was certainly something dangerous about the man; Herr von Tucher felt this at the first glance; but his person also radiated a winning charm, a combination of worldliness and intellectual grace. His proud bearing prevented the delicacy of his slender figure from seeming effeminate; his features, which were all strikingly English, were finely chiseled and made one, forget the grayish tone of his skin. The changing fire of his transparent eyes reminded one first of a gentle gazelle, then of the repose of a tiger; in brief, Herr von Tucher was placed in a condition of pleasant expectation which was not in the least disturbed by the conversation, which was not slow to open.

Lord Stanhope's simple questions about Caspar's physical and mental condition showed him to be a man of keen insight and knowledge of life, and what he said readily obtained his listener's approval.

He began of his own accord to talk of his motives in being here. What he said was indeed quite vague. He was evidently a master in the art of veiling his real purposes, but it could not occur to Herr von Tucher to be suspicious. The name of Stanhope was a sufficient warranty. What could prevent a Lord Stanhope from speaking plainly? If it was not delicacy and inborn tact, then it was a silence which implied an obligation to clear up everything in the proper manner, and at the proper moment. Herr von Tucher found himself rather restrained than surprised by this silence; without waiting for Lord Stanhope to express a desire to that effect, he asked politely whether he would care to see Caspar. While he was smilingly awaiting an assurance of his guest's gratitude, he rang and gave the order to fetch the boy.

There was now a silence; Herr von Tucher stood, watching involuntarily, at the door, and Stanhope sat with crossed legs, his head resting on his gloved left hand, his face turned toward the open window. It was a sunny Sunday afternoon; the bright blue sky rested upon the red-tiled roofs and twittering swallows flew along the gray house-fronts. As Caspar entered the room Stanhope slowly changed the direction of his gaze and, without actually looking at the boy, he seemed to grasp the whole picture. While Caspar, informed by Herr von Tucher in a few brief words about the illustrious man, was walking towards the Count, the latter got up and said with surprising excitement, evidently much moved: "Caspar, at last, what a blessed hour!" Then he opened his arms to him, and Caspar surrendered himself to their clasp, as if entering into a gate which has been opened after long yearning and waiting; a radiant beaming pleasure suffused him, and he could neither speak nor move.

This was he who came from far away. From him had come the ring and the message. Already upstairs, when the carriage had stopped in front of the door, a numbness had seized Caspar's limbs and when the butler called him it was as if the morning sun had flooded the house. When he reached the threshold of the door Caspar saw only him, the stranger, the trusted stranger, and as if half of his heart had been lacking up to now, he suddenly felt himself grown whole and round and new; with damp eyes he saw himself, created for a purpose. Gently the clock struck the hour; and the light of the afternoon was like honey, and sweet to the taste.

Caspar's remarkable emotion apparently had a great effect upon Lord Stanhope. For several seconds his face showed profound emotion and his eyes became clouded with painful astonishment. He was undoubtedly upset, and his usual command of words forsook him so that, when he first addressed the boy affectionately, his usually soft and gentle voice sounded harsh. He stroked Caspar's hair with his hand, pressed the boy's face against his breast and an absorbed glance encountered Herr von Tucher, standing to one side and observing the unusual scene with astonishment. Stanhope then asked him, since the veiled scene demanded an explanation, whether he might take Caspar with him for a few hours, a request which Herr von Tucher could not deny.

Soon after, Caspar was sitting next to Lord Stanhope in the carriage; the policeman, of course, had to go along and sit outside. While the carriage rolled out of the gate toward the Maxfeld Gardens a conversation slowly began.

Caspar complained; for the first time he could complain. But the moment the evil which had occurred was recognized as such and understood, he was already reconciled. The world had seemed bad until this day; now the heavens opened and an arm of destiny had reached out for him.

But it was not so much a question of recent events; here was someone who must know. Casper asked. Boldly and passionately he asked: "Who am I, who was I; what am I to be? Where is my father, where my mother?" And the Count's answer? Embarrassment, an embrace. "Patience, Caspar, only be patient until to-morrow; that cannot be answered in one breath! there is too much to be said. Tell me, rather, how you have lived; tell me your dreams. I understand that you have had wonderful dreams; tell me!"

Caspar did not need much urging. The essential contents of the picture amazed the listener; he clasped Caspar more tightly and thus hid his face from him. When the boy described the appearance of his mother, Stanhope started as if from fright and then tried to divert the conversation; he wanted to hear details about Caspar's life at the Daumers and at the Beholds; these subjects were not dangerous. Stanhope found himself amused at Caspar's original and apt expressions, his curious use of proverbs and Nurnberg forms of speech. On the way back he asked Caspar where the ring was which he had sent him. "I did not dare to wear it on my finger," replied Caspar.

"Why not?"

"I don't know why."

"Wasn't it beautiful enough for you?"

"Oh no, quite the contrary. It was much too beautiful for me. My heart always beat when I looked at it."

"But now you'll wear it?"

"Yes, now I'll wear it. Now I know that it really belongs to me."

The carriage stopped in front of the gate. Stanhope took an affectionate farewell of Caspar and told him to come to his hotel the next morning. "Good-by, darling," he even called to him.

Caspar stood much oppressed. Now time hung heavily again. Every step took him further from the charmed circle of the man; his hand and his eye now rested on nothing but what was old and dead.

Already at ten o'clock the next morning he was at the "Wilder Mann." He simply ran away from his lessons. If anyone had attempted to stop him he would have climbed out of the window by a rope.

Lord Stanhope came to meet him in the upper hall; he kissed him on the forehead in full view of Everyone, and led him into the reception room where there were presents laid out for Caspar on the table; a gold watch, gold cuff links, silver shoe buckles and fine white linen. Caspar could not believe his eyes; the exuberance of his gratitude choked him; he could do nothing but hold the generous hand of the giver in his own.

Lord Stanhope accepted this silent gesture with an emotion which he did not utter. But after they had walked a few times through the room together, arm in arm, and Caspar was evidently struggling to express his gratitude, Stanhope gently suggested that he omit all expressions of thanks. "These things are only slight expressions of my affection for you." he said. "The real thing, the big thing which I want to do, remains for the future. Meantime remain just as you are, my Caspar, for so you are just right, not full of noisy words, but dependable in heart. Dependable and faithful to me you must remain, a son, a comrade, a friend."

Caspar sighed. This was too much happiness. He had never supposed that the mouth of man could speak so. He was incapable of making any professions, only his eyes expressed, his feelings in a look of ecstasy.

Stanhope opened the door and conducted the boy to a little breakfast table which was set just for two in the adjoining room. They sat down and he filled the glasses with wine and smiled peculiarly when Caspar declared that he never drank wine. "How will it be, Caspar, when we travel in the south together? There are vineyards glowing on all the hills and the air is full of it. Why do you look at me so? Don't you believe me?"

"Really? Shall we really travel together?" asked Caspar jubilantly.

"Certainly we shall. Do you think that I want to be separated from you? Or do you think that I shall leave you in this city, where so much evil has befallen you?"

"Away then, really away? Away, a great distance!" exclaimed Caspar, and, as if beside himself, he pressed his two hands in front of his mouth and pushed his shoulders up to his ears in joyful excitement. "But what will Herr von Tucher say, and the Mayor and President Feuerbach?" he added, babbling away in his haste, while his face expressed the dismay which he felt at the idea that these men might disapprove of the Count's plans, or prevent him from carrying them out.

"They will not prevent it; they will no longer have any power over you; your way will lead you up above them," answered Stanhope, earnestly, at the same time giving Caspar a sharp penetrating glance.

Caspar turned pale, overcome by immense emotion. While desire and doubt were struggling dimly within him, absorbing all the vigor of his soul, the picture of the woman of the dream castle rose more brilliantly than ever before his eyes. . . . With a touching gesture of entreaty he turned to Stanhope and asked: "Count, are you going to take me to my mother?"

Stanhope put down his knife and fork and leaned his head upon his hand. "There are dreadful secrets, Caspar," he murmured in hollow tones. "I shall and must speak, but you must remain silent; you must not trust anyone except myself. Give me your hand, Caspar, and your promise. Friend of my heart! You unfortunate, fortunate boy; yes, I shall take you to your mother. Providence has chosen me to assist you."

Caspar sank down! His legs could not support him any longer; his head fell on the Count's knee. His pulses throbbed, and sobs relieved the tremendous tension of his breast. "How shall I address thee?" he asked with bold exuberance, for the ordinary formulas of speech seemed odd to him; they were insufficient to express his grateful affection.

Lord Stanhope lifted him up gently and said affectionately: "Just so shall you address me; the thee of trust shall be used between us; you must call me Henry, as if you were my brother."

The waiter who came in to announce the Mayor and the City Commissioner found them in this intimate proximity. Through the open door Lord Stanhope asked them to come in. It looked as if he wished the two men to witness his affectionate treatment of Caspar. He seemed unable to part with him; when the visitors had greeted him respectfully, and seated themselves, he continued to walk up and down with his arm over Caspar's shoulder, talking to him in low tones, then he accompanied him to the stairway, hurried back, went to the window, leaned out, looked towards Caspar and waved to him with his handkerchief. Although he noticed the surprise of his guests, he did not moderate himself; on the contrary, he behaved like a lover who expresses his emotion without any embarrassment.

Lord Stanhope's presents were brought to the Tucher house a few hours later. Herr von Tucher's surprise at the sight of the valuable gifts was great. "I shall take these things and put them away for you," he said to Caspar after a little thought; "it is not suitable for a bookbinder's apprentice to indulge in such luxury."

Then one should have seen Caspar! "Oh, no," he exclaimed, "that belongs to me. That's mine and I want it, and no one shall take it away from me." His bearing became threatening. His eyes blazed.

Herr von Tucher's face became quite white; without one word of reply he left the room. So, he's an ingrate, he thought bitterly, an ingrate; one who selfishly makes use of his opportunities and denies one benefactor when another offers him more.

His fundamental principles no longer triumphed. They were crushed and retired in sack-cloth and ashes.

To give way in such a case would be an unworthy weakness, of which I should have to be ashamed, said Herr von Tucher to himself. But what shall I do? Shall I use force? Force is immoral. He appealed to Lord Stanhope and told him of the affair. The Count listened to him kindly; he took pains to explain Caspar's misdemeanor as childish restlessness and promised to induce him to entrust his guardian with the presents of his own accord.

Herr von Tucher was delighted with his lordship's affability, and left him full of confidence. But he waited in vain for the obedience promised on Caspar's behalf. Doubtless his lordship's trouble had been fruitless; doubtless Caspar knew how to get the better of the good man. No doubt this boy was a slippery customer, a cunning, underhanded character. Much too proud to let any other person know of his humiliating experiences, Herr von Tucher contented himself for the time being with quietly watching events with the indignation of a man who feels he has been deceived. That Caspar should not once feel impelled to speak of his relation to Lord Stanhope, or about the subject of their conversations, hurt him deeply; the last thing he would have expected was such a lack of confidence.

At first Lord Stanhope had limited himself to visiting Caspar at the Tucher house, or at most to taking him for a drive, after formally asking the Baron's permission. Gradually this changed, and he asked the boy to meet him at strange places, where Caspar's inevitable bodyguard was obliged to keep fifty feet away from him. Herr von Tucher complained to the Mayor; he insisted that his lordship was violating his own express promise. But what could Herr Binder do? Could he take the distinguished gentleman to task? He once ventured a mild hint. His lordship jestingly quieted him; in order not to appear to disclaim responsibility for their promise, it was easy to attribute the offense to Caspar's heedlessness.

Thus one saw the two striking figures often walking through the streets of an evening. They walked arm in arm, engrossed in eager speech, heedless of the glances which followed them. Mostly they walked across the Stadtgraben and then to the Castle; here Caspar could give vent to his sad memories. The dark tower concealed the greatest terrors of his life, and when he looked down upon the city, where twinkling lights illuminated the dark maze of the streets, it was with very altered feelings that he heard the striking of the clock; now time united and interwove the strokes together; they were no longer separated by great gulfs of horror.

Lord Stanhope was never tired of talking. He spoke of his travels. He knew how to picture events and things in simple words. Caspar heard of the Alps, and that there are mountains covered with perpetual snow, and happy valleys where free people live. He saw Italy—the word in itself was an ecstasy—jeweled churches, enormous palaces, gardens with wonderful statues, full of roses and laurel and orange trees, a marvelous azure sky and the most beautiful women. He saw the sea and ships with white sails upon the water.

His longing was so great that he sometimes suddenly burst out laughing. Really to be permitted to go to these lands of sun and of unknown fruits, to be allowed to be there, and soon at that, such hopes made his heart stand still! It was a joy which gave pain.

One rainy evening they were both at the hotel. His lordship opened a chest and showed some of the treasures which he had collected on his travels. There were rare coins and stones; copper engravings, statues, gems, cameos, pearls and antique jewelry, a rosary which had been blessed in the Holy Land, a silver goblet with artistically carved figures, a Bible with the most beautiful initials and illuminations; a Damascene blade with a handle of gold, a pope's seal ring, an Indian silk coat embroidered with stars, a Pompeian lamp and old French porcelain vases, and many other things. Everything was curious and unusual; it all suggested the great world and marvelous adventures.

"I got this from the Elector of Mainz." said Lord Stanhope; "this is a present from the Prince of Savoy; this beautiful miniature I bought from a dealer in Barcelona and this clay figure comes from Syracuse. That is a talisman which Sheik Abderrahman honored me with, and my aunt sent me these Oriental materials from Syria. She is a remarkable person; she travels around in the desert with Arabs and Bedouins, sleeps in tents and practices alchemy and astrology."

What sounds and what distances! It was evidently a pleasure to the count to kindle the fire of longing in Caspar. Perhaps he was serious in his promises, perhaps it merely gave him pleasure to arouse desires and wishes, perhaps it was merely a conversational trifling. Perhaps, however, it was the frightful pleasure of so often describing a flight through the golden atmosphere to the bird destined to be perpetually imprisoned in his cage, that finally a joyous song of freedom breaks from his throat.

How he could talk, and how he used his words! A smile played about his lips like a tricky little animal and his white teeth glistened. He was not uniformly cheerful. A cloud passed frequently over his face. At times he was in the habit of getting up and walking to the door like an eavesdropper. His demonstrations of affection were not infrequently full of melancholy, and at times he would sit in silence and his searching glance would mournfully avoid the boy. One day Caspar took courage and asked: "Arc you really happy, Henry?"

"Happy, Caspar? Oh, no. Happy, what are you talking about? Have you ever heard of Ahasver, the Wandering Jew, the perpetual wanderer? He is considered the unhappiest of human beings. Ah, I should like to unfold my life to you, for it is full of dark, sorrowful pages. But I may not and I cannot. Perhaps later on, when your own fate will have been settled, when you go home with me." "Is that possible? When will that be?"

Lord Stanhope suddenly shuddered; it was as if he were throwing off a cloak, or as if he were seeking to withdraw from some invisible pressure. A convulsive animation took possession of him; he began to speak of Caspar's future greatness, but as always in secretive terms, and with ceremonious warnings about keeping silent. He spoke of Caspar's domains, of his subjects, doing this for the first time, as if giving way to some compulsion, shuddering and trembling himself, constantly repeating his emphasis of Caspar's solemn promise of silence, as if carried away by a phantom and forgetful of all danger. "I will guide you; I will crush your enemies. You are worth ten thousand times more than any single one of them. We will first go south in order to mislead them, then we will fly to my home, lay an ambush at the place where we must meet our pursuers, where we can collect our forces for the decisive blow."

Again he went to the door, again he listened, again he looked for some listener in hiding. Then anxiously, in order to divert Caspar, the count drew a picture of his home, the peacefulness of an English country manor, the lordly independence of an inherited castle, its deep woods and clear streams, the balmy air, the sweetness pervading all things, spring, autumn, and winter spent in a round of innocent pleasures.

In these descriptions there was something of the sadness of a penitent conscience, and of the pain of one repudiated forever. There was, however, something also of that modish sensitiveness, which under certain circumstances permits even the most hardened conscience to indulge in vain dreams of calming its self-created restlessness on the bosom of nature. Then he even consented to speak of his life. He chose to represent himself as a man who, although much envied, and weighed down with honors and official appointments and the tangible evidences of good fortune, was nevertheless the victim of hostile powers. Fate appeared, romantically garbed to drive forth the son of an accursed house to wander aimlessly from land to land. His father and mother were dead, former friends had conspired against the noble scion of the house of Stanhope and he, a man of fifty, was homeless without wife or child! Ahasver!

Such confidences opened Caspar's heart to friendship as nothing else could have done. For here finally was someone who gave himself, who opened his heart, who threw away all disguise. It was a bitter-sweet pleasure to see the adored figure descended from the pedestal upon which it was enshrined for everyone else.

As for himself, Caspar had at that time the appearance of a man at peace, at peace externally and internally. He looked like a man who has cast off his chains; his glance and gesture were free, his bearing upright, his forehead clear and his lips constantly smiling.

He became aware of his youth. He began to expand and it seemed to him as if he were a tree and his hands like branches full of blossoms. It was as if his blood gave forth a sweet smell. The air called to him, the land called to him, everything was full of him and everything uttered his name.

He sometimes had the habit of speaking aloud to himself, and when he was found doing this he would laugh. People who came into contact with him were fascinated. They never ceased to eulogize his lovable personality, in which childhood and youth were so touchingly interwoven. Young women wrote him tender letters and Herr von Tucher was frequently importuned with the request to have his picture painted.

The evil talk about him suddenly seemed blown away. No one admitted ever having spoken badly of him, his inveterate antagonists bowed their heads, the whole city suddenly arose as his protector. Many persons declared, with increasing boldness and definiteness, that he must be protected from the intrigues of the English count. One day Stanhope was forced to realize to his dismay that he was being closely watched and observed on all sides. He had to decide to act.

12.   The Secret Mission And What Prevented Its Execution

For some time people at tavern tables had been saying that Lord Stanhope wanted to adopt Caspar Hauser as his son. Actually, in the middle of June, Stanhope made a formal request to the Town Council, to be allowed to take charge of the boy; he wanted to provide for his future. The Town Council, through the Mayor, replied that in the matter of taking charge of the boy he would have to hand in a regular application in due form; so far as providing for him was concerned he would have in the first place to furnish evidence of the possession of adequate means, so that the city would have a certain guarantee for the welfare of its protégé.

Stanhope accepted this answer very ungraciously. He went to the Mayor, showed him his decorations, the credentials of various courts, even confidential letters from princes of high rank. Herr Binder regretted that in spite of his respect for Lord Stanhope he could not act contrary to the unanimous decision of the council.

The count was careless enough to express his contempt at the pedantry and presumption of this middle class riff-raff at a party to which he was invited. This was noised about, and although he hastened to apologize for his behavior in a letter to the Board of Directors of the Town Council, attributing it to a pardonable irritation due to wine, the matter nevertheless made bad blood. Suspicion was aroused once and for all. It was asserted that he frequently received suspicious looking people in his hotel with whom he had lengthy interviews behind closed doors. And why, moreover, people wondered, did so supposedly wealthy and distinguished a gentleman reside in a second rate inn? Is it perhaps the real reason that he is afraid of being seen by his own compatriots, if he were to live like them at the "Adler" or at the "Bayrischer

Hof"? This seemed plausible, if one believed an untraceable rumor which someone one day spread abroad, according to which Lord Stanhope had formerly wandered about Saxony selling tracts in the service of the Jesuits.

Stanhope made haste to leave. He paid a farewell visit to the Mayor at his office and spoke of urgent business which called him away. On his return he would bring the evidences to establish the solvency of his fortune which were required. At the same time he deposited unimpeachable bank notes aggregating five hundred florins, which sum was to be spent exclusively for the minor needs and pleasures of his favorite. The Mayor interposed that as a matter of fact Herr von Tucher should assume the administration of this money, but Lord Stanhope shook his head and said that Herr von Tucher had too much of determined severity about him, that he acted according to an artificially devised ideal of virtue and that such a delicate plant could only be brought up with the most affectionate leniency. "Let us remember that fate must indemnify Caspar for a past crime and that it is unkind to attempt to prune and suppress constantly where nature herself has created such a magnificent product, even in spite of the ill will of mankind."

The seriousness of these words, and Lord Stanhope's imperious manner, made a great impression upon the Mayor. He again expressed his regret that the desires of the Count could not be realized at once and assured him that the city would always regard it as an honor to receive such a guest within its walls.

From here Lord Stanhope went at once to Herr von Tucher. He was told that the Baron had gone out hunting with some acquaintances, and that Caspar, too, had gone out, but that he must return soon; would he be kind enough to wait?

Impatiently he strode up and down the drawing room. He took out his dispatch case, counted his money, jotted down some figures on a piece of paper, at the same time gnashing his teeth, while his delicate white neck slowly became dark red, like that of a drunkard. He stamped on the ground, his face was consumed with rage and his eyes glittered: "God damned beasts," he murmured, and his narrow lips expressed unbridled contempt.

There was no longer about him anything of the reserve or dignity of a nobleman. Oh, Count, must the curtain of public appearances fall for only a quarter of an hour in order that the actor, tired of his well learnt role, shall transform his mask into the frightful reality? What a pity that no mirror hung in the room, for perhaps it would have brought his lordship back to his senses and to his guard, for it was necessary only for a door to open quickly, to have the play begin again. But did not this circumstance bear witness in favor of the count? Would not more self-control have been a proof of greater art? The real comedian plays his part before empty benches and makes spectators of the walls themselves. In this breast, however, there were still the voices of betrayal, in its depths there was still a storm; it yet harbored dark subterranean creatures, still had eyes to feel the blessed rays of changing life.

Apparently his lordship was a bad arithmetician, for the figures which he jotted down could not be made to yield the necessary sum, so that he constantly reexamined the correctness of the various items, frowning as he did so.

"Certainly too little for the purpose of popularity," he said sullenly. The thoughtlessness of the remark was tempered by its being made in English. Then some curious words followed, sinister to listen to—words which seemed to come not from a well-wrought play, but straight from melodrama. "If I catch sight of the old gray dog again I'll pull his leg; he's taken swag enough for it. Crowns are not every-day commodities; he's got to divide more fairly!"

Poor Lord Stanhope! Solitude, too, has its sounds. The wind penetrates through a badly closed window pane, and it resembles a human voice, or, the wood of some century old piece of furniture contracts, making a sound like the report of a pistol, or like a miniature thunder-storm. In such matters Lord Stanhope was superstitious. The crackling of the plaster under the wall paper reminded him of death; if he entered a room with his left foot foremost he became sick with fear and uncertainty. This had happened here again; he controlled himself and became silent, the more since he heard Caspar's clear voice from the hall below. He reassumed his role, his eyes regained their gazelle-like expression, he fetched a volume of Rousseau from a bookcase in the corner, sat down in an arm chair and began to read with an expression of thoughtfulness.

Nevertheless, when Caspar entered, when his face, beaming with pleasure, appeared through the twilight, the pain which Lord Stanhope felt spread over his features, and a sudden consternation robbed him of speech. He even became confused; he looked off sideways and only when Caspar, struck by this strange behavior, addressed him in low tones, did he break his silence. It was natural to attribute his depression to the trip he was about to undertake, but this condition of inner recoil and sudden vacillation at such moments was not unknown to his lordship, although he felt it more strongly than usual today. It seemed to him at such times as if the sight of the boy prostrated a decision which he had reached, as if plans forged by great toil were breaking down as if assailed by a hurricane, so that the work would have to be begun again from the beginning, when he was alone and had recovered himself. At such times he resembled Penelope who at night ripped into threads again the skillful handiwork she had fashioned during the day.

Caspar's sad lamenting at the unexpected news was not silenced by the information that his own welfare required this parting, nor by Stanhope's assurance that he would return as soon as possible, perhaps in the course of a month. Caspar shook his head and said in a stifled voice that the world was too big; he clung to his friend and implored to be taken with him, the count should dismiss his servant, Caspar would be his servant; he needed no bed and no wages; he would live again on bread and water. "Oh, please do it, Heinrich," he exclaimed with tears. "What am I to do here without you?"

Lord Stanhope got up and gently freed himself from the boy's arms. The consolation which he could give saved him from himself and gave his words greater weight. "That you should be so fainthearted, Caspar, proves that you have little confidence in me," he said. "How can you even think that God, who has finally united us, should tear us apart again? That would mean questioning his wisdom and goodness. The world is a structure full of great harmony and man finds his way to man by a very special law. Hold fast to your determination, and time and space will carry you to the goal, and whether I remain away an hour or several weeks is a matter of indifference in the face of certain fulfillment. Some people wait until death for their delivery, and do not become impatient. And you must learn to control yourself, Caspar. The sons of princes do not cry."

It had become dark during this conversation. Lord Stanhope led Caspar to the open window and said with emotion: "Look up at the sky, Caspar; see how the stars break through the sky! Let us take these as a symbol of our friendship."

Stanhope noticed with satisfaction that Caspar became thoughtful and solemn. He was ashamed of an unbridled despair which would not take into account any necessity for alteration, and would not exchange the happy present for any future. It was as if Caspar felt the higher fatality of life, which intensifies its vicissitudes and binds people secretly to one another; perhaps his amazed eyes, gazing about the world, awoke in this hour to understanding; perhaps the dam which had hemmed the tide of his yearnings was now transformed into a prop to his spirit; the conquering of his passion raised the boy to a man. "Princes' sons do not cry," a strong expression; the gentle breeze which swayed the curtains repeated it. Stanhope looked at his watch and explained that he was in a hurry; on account of the heat he would drive during the night. Downstairs, in front of the carriage, he said good-by and gave Caspar a little bag full of gold pieces; he told him to do with it as he liked, and not to brook any interference.

These thoughtless, or perhaps slyly calculated instructions, were the cause of a serious dispute between Caspar and his tutor. Herr von Tucher heard of the repeated presents of the Count and demanded that Caspar give up the gold to him. Caspar again refused. Herr von Tucher insisted with the whole weight of his authority and he would have used force if Caspar, rendered timid by threats as well as the feeling that his powerful friend was absent, had not yielded. However, he persisted in silent rebellion, and this drove Herr von Tucher beside himself. "I shall put you out of the house," he exclaimed, no longer able to control himself. "I shall expose your disgrace to the world. People shall finally learn to know you, you rascal."

Caspar, distressed and excited, thought that he should threaten in turn. "Oh, if the Count knew this how he would open his eyes," he said bitterly and with naive implication, as if it lay in the count's power to adjust all the ills of this world.

"The Count? Why, you are guilty of ingratitude to him, too," replied Herr von Tucher. "How often has he assured me that he has urged you to be obedient and loyal and has implored you by all that was holy not to give your benefactor any cause for complaint? But you disregard his commands and are entirely unworthy of his generous love."

Caspar was astonished. He knew of no such advice of the Count's, rather the contrary, and he therefore contradicted Lord Stanhope's ever having said anything of the sort. Hereupon Herr von Tucher called him a liar with calm contempt, from which one may see that his judiciously devised system of education did not have the power of checking outbreaks of angry passion and wounded self-esteem, even in its founder.

The fundamental principles had been put to ultimate flight. Herr von Tucher was tired of this unedifying struggle; although he had decided not to keep Caspar any longer, he put off the execution of this determination until the Count's return. In order that the sight of Caspar should not expose him to the constant pain of disappointment, Herr von Tucher accepted an invitation from a cousin to go to his country estate near Hersbruck for the rest of the summer. His mother had already been there for three months. Since it was vacation time, and the teacher moreover was no longer coming to the house, he did not need to make any arrangements for Caspar's instruction. He recommended to him to study diligently by himself, made arrangements for his daily needs, gave him four silver dollars for pocket money, and left him, after a cold farewell, to the care of the police and an old household servant.

Caspar counted the days and crossed out each one with red chalk on the calendar as it went by. The silent house and the deserted street with the sun brooding over it made him conscious always of his solitude. He had no society. Strangers, who still came in large numbers, all the more because the passionate sympathy of a Lord Chesterfield enveloped him as with a halo, were not admitted, and he had no desire to seek out his former acquaintances.

In the evening he sometimes took up his diary and wrote; then his friend seemed nearer to him; it was like a conversation with him across the distance which separated them. Without forgetting the promise of silence on what Stanhope had confided to him, its pages came in this way to be privy to these mysterious indications. But from his method of writing it was very evident that he could not adjust himself in the least to them. It was a fairy tale. He could not understand the construction, could not grasp the intertwined labyrinthine texture of human society. The castle with its wide halls was still a dream, brooding in its solemn mystery of unknown stars. To go home was his only wish; this word had meaning and force. Woe to the day when he would awake to comprehension. It is only when darkness has lifted that the lost wanderer can determine how far he has been driven off his course.

In the beginning of September Caspar received his first brief news of the Count, announcing also his impending return. His joy was great, but it was mingled with a foreboding of pain, as if his relation to his friend could not again become what it had been, as if time had altered its countenance. At every sound of a carriage, at every noise at the gate, his heart expanded, ready to burst. When the one longed-for finally appeared Caspar was not able to utter a sound; he swayed and stretched out his hand as if doubtful of the reality of his appearance. Stanhope changed his bearing and expression, he looked as if he were postponing for a later moment a calculated change of front; the expectancy of his glance yielded to the gentler impulse which the boy always aroused in him, perhaps the only person whom he was forced to admit to have power over his inner feelings and whose fate he at the same time dragged about with him as a hunter drags his slain victim.

He thought that Caspar looked ill, and asked him whether he had had enough to eat. The report about the quarrels with Herr von Tucher merely brought forth sarcasms, but he did not seem further irritated by it. "Did you think of me sometimes, Caspar?" he inquired, and Caspar answered with the expression of a faithful dog: "Much, constantly," then he added, "I even wrote to you, Heinrich!" "Wrote to me," repeated the lord with surprise, "you did not know where I was!"

Caspar clasped his hands and smiled. "I wrote it in my book," he said.

The Count became nervous, but he assumed a confidential attitude. "In what book? And what did you write? May I not read it?"

Caspar shook his head.

"Secrets then, Caspar?"

"No, no secrets, but I can't show it to you."

Stanhope broke off the conversation, but determined to get to the bottom of the matter.

He was living at the "Wilder Mann" again, but he lived differently from before. He ordered champagne and expensive wines at every meal, and spent money lavishly, as if he wished to show his wealth. He brought his own carriage with him, the wheels of which were gilded and the door resplendent with a crown and coat of arms. As servants he had a footman and two butlers, gold-braided employees who aroused the astonishment of the inhabitants of Nurnberg.

He did not fail to renew his request to have Caspar Hauser entrusted to him. As evidence of his favorable financial circumstances he referred, as if incidentally only, to the letter of credit which he had since his return deposited with Simon Merkel, the bank director. There was a gesture of boastfulness in this, as if such small sums were not worth mentioning; as a matter of fact the sums placed at his disposal by German banking houses in Frankfurt and Karlsruhe were quite considerable.

The magistrate saw himself robbed of every valid objection to his lordship's wishes. The question was raised in a meeting of the city fathers. What does he really want Hauser for? Hereupon Mayor Binder read with particular emphasis a part of the Count's letter wherein he said: "The undersigned feels himself all the more called upon to espouse the cause of the unfortunate foundling, since after long association with him he has found this childlike spirit so affectionately attached and grateful to him that it would be pleasing even to the heart of a father."

"Let us ask Caspar himself," they said, "he must know whether he wants to go with the Count."

Caspar was called before the council. With profound emotion he declared that he was convinced that the Count took the profoundest interest in his fate and said that he wished to go wherever the Count would take him.

In spite of all this the formal permission was delayed, at first on account of an intangible circumstance, which however gradually took on the proportions of a decided resistance, and finally grew into one single voice which no one dared to gainsay.

His lordship's undue haste in attempting to secure possession of Caspar's person again and again afforded a new lease of life to the mutterings of subterranean suspicion. His pompous appearance was displeasing to the bourgeois, who felt greater confidence in a more modest mode of life, even among those in high places, than in a mania for extravagance, which only served to stir up the evil

The Secret Mission And What Prevented Its Execution | 152

instincts of the crowd. People grew bitter when the Count drove by in his ostentatious carriage, and purposely choosing the most frequented streets, tossed copper coins right and left among the people, who then, devoid of any dignity, groveled in the mud before the stranger enthroned in indolent affability.

It was said that Stanhope had borrowed heavily on his letters of credit from bank president Merkel. Merkel, although he seemed secure, was warned to be careful; it was said that his lordship could not realize on the papers, or only up to a prescribed limit.

Meanwhile Herr von Tucher had returned from the country. He was familiar with the development of the situation; he wished for his part to bring the matter to a definite conclusion. He addressed a fairly circumstantial letter to Lord Stanhope in which he concluded by giving him the choice, either of taking entire care of the boy himself and thereby relieving him, the Baron, of all responsibility, or of paying a yearly sum which would make it possible to entrust Caspar entirely to some intelligent and cultivated person. In the latter case, however, his grace must have the goodness to give up all communications with Caspar, either verbal or written, for a period of several years; he, for his part, would obligate himself to give Lord Stanhope regular accounts of Caspar's progress and performances.

The rest of the letter was permeated with the appropriate respect. "I must express to your much respected grace my warmest thanks for the countless evidences of kindness with which you have showered me during the few weeks of your stay here," he wrote among other things. "From the bottom of my heart I wish to express the unfeigned admiration which I am compelled to feel for your kindness of heart and your unusual nobility of spirit. From these feelings there arises the duty of that confidence which you have so often urged upon me, and so, your noble lordship, I must now state my position openly and frankly, trusting that you will listen to my words with well-disposed ears. Caspar is not the person for whom you appear to take him. How indeed could you become fully acquainted with this remarkable hybrid who, in his intercourse with you, to whom he owes everything and from whom he expects everything which his heart desires, is called upon by every circumstance to appear in his best light? Your grace, you showed him such friendship as one offers only to one's equals. In view of the measureless vanity with which nature has disfigured his soul—along with the other rich gifts with which she has endowed him—and which silly people here have cultivated, you have innocently added to his already sick character a poison which no doctor of souls, even the most expert, will ever be able to eliminate. There is nothing from which I am further removed than any wish to reproach you with this and I beg you most earnestly not to regard what I have said in this light. You are free from all blame. But I must assert that during the entire time that Caspar was in my house there was no reason for being dissatisfied with him, whereas—since your stay here, I say this with reluctance and a bleeding heart, and with the affection and the respect due to so superior a man—the boy has been like one transformed and perverted." Such language must flatter even the most pampered ear.

Nevertheless, Lord Stanhope assumed the appearance of being provoked and offended by the Baron's letter and spoke about it in society everywhere. In a petition to the district court in Ansbach, which was found to be necessary, and wherein he declared his willingness to assume responsibility for the care of Caspar Hauser, not only during his lifetime, but also to provide for the boy in the case of his — Stanhope's—own death, he mentioned that matters had taken place between him and Herr von Tucher which made any association between them impossible for the present and the future; it was therefore important that Caspar should be placed in other surroundings at the earliest possible opportunity.

Hofrat Hofmann in Ansbach hastened to inform Herr von Tucher of Lord Stanhope's veiled accusation. Herr von Tucher was beside himself. He informed the municipal authorities verbally of the letter he had written Stanhope, painted again in dark colors the unfavorable influence which the Count had had upon Caspar's character and demanded his speedy discharge from a guardianship which, as he expressed it, had been a care, an annoyance and a burden, and had finally brought him ingratitude and a misunderstanding of his honorable intentions. Since the authorities of Ansbach had asked an opinion concerning Lord Stanhope he wrote back that he had come to regard the count as an unusual man with extraordinary qualities. The report was that he was very rich; Stanhope himself stated that he had a yearly income of twenty thousand pounds sterling, that is three hundred thousand florins, which income, however, since he was an earl and an hereditary

British peer, by no means placed him among the wealthy nobility of his country. "Presuming that the very estimable board of guardians receives sufficient guarantees [he closed his long letter] and explanations regarding certain suspicious conjunctures in England, I, as the tutor of Caspar Hauser, have no objection, particularly on the financial side, to Lord Stanhope's adopting him."

A circumstantial procedure, an endless series of appeals! Stanhope tossed about with anger and impatience. Nevertheless, in spite of all the busy gossip and the clash of opinions on the subject, every obstacle seemed overcome and he saw himself near the goal which he had from the beginning aimed at with slow persistence, when suddenly everything was again overturned. For President Feuerbach forbade Caspar's removal from Nurnberg. He sent a private courier to Mayor Binder, informing him that he had just returned from his cure in Karlsbad, and that all these doings were entirely new to him. He forbade any decision before he should have examined the case, which seemed to him involved and suspicious, and before he should have approved the necessary steps.

The Mayor felt himself bound to inform Lord Stanhope at once of this new state of affairs. Stanhope received and read Binder's note in his hotel while he was being shaved. He pushed the barber aside, jumped up, and ran excitedly about the room with the soap suds still on his face. It took considerable time before he remembered his toilet; he tore the note which Binder had sent him into a hundred little pieces and again sat in the chair with a face so full of hatred and rage that the barber began to tremble and, having finished his work, hurried, in short order, out of the room.

Too late the Count recollected that he had forgotten himself. But how severe must have been the blow which struck him, if it could shake the inflexible calm and reserve of a person so adamant in the pursuit of his purpose.

He quickly wrote a few lines, folded and sealed the letter, sent for his footman, told him to saddle a horse, and ordered him to deliver the communication to the address in the course of forty-eight hours, let it cost what it might.

The man went away in silence. He knew his master. He knew that his master did not occupy himself with trifles, love affairs and paltry intrigues. He was familiar with this expression on his lordship's face, this tension as if faced with a frightful decision, this look of straining in a race, this convulsive control of the gambler. He had often undertaken similar rides by day and by night; one had to keep one's mouth shut in order to be able to keep the unpleasant elements of such a task hidden from a curious world, for it not infrequently looked as if one were the mediator of shady transactions. Speed was always ordered; he did always get there on time, but the words "let it cost what it may" were partly mere swank. He did not always get his wages and often had to wait for weeks and secretly snatch at crumbs which fell from his lordship's table. His excellency did not have funds at the moment, he was expecting money from England and France, or, sometimes the messenger was even sent to some distinguished gentleman, and it was striking that the Count's request did not meet with an altogether eager response. The speech of the distinguished gentleman savored rather of contempt than of respect for his lordship.

 What was the reason of all this? How was it that the threads of this man's destiny, raised so high above the crowd, attached themselves somewhere to common want? Why was the noble scion of a noble house spending his days wretchedly in low taverns, why was one of the proudest names of a proud kingdom dependent on the greasy friendliness of an innkeeper, condemned to trample the essence and marrow of his life into the mud with his own feet, to sacrifice the austere memory of inviolable ancestors? What was the reason for all this?

 Every hour of the present was a ruin of the past, every day the sad vestige of golden days gone by, of days when the name of Stanhope still played a role in the capitals of Europe which seemed to its bearer today a mere legend of the past, when the youthful lord was the delight of the salons of Paris and Vienna, when he had been rich and had used his riches to satisfy his insatiable youth and to offer to his peers the spectacle of an unparalleled extravagance. His festivals and dinners had been famous. He had traveled from country to country with a staff of cooks, secretaries, butlers, mechanics and entertainers. In a pergola in Madrid he had had twenty-five thousand pounds' worth of flowers distributed among the women. During the Congress of Vienna he had entertained kings and princes, had organized horse races which in themselves had consumed a fortune, and had had oratorios and operas given at his own cost. His luxurious whims had held society breathless; he gave villas and estates to his friends and pearl necklaces to his mistresses. He had been for years the Timon of the continent, surrounded by an army of eager parasites, all of whom made profit at his expense, and satisfied their debauched instincts to his cost. His generosity and kindliness had become proverbial, his manner of constantly distributing handfuls of gold about him, regardless of whether it fell into the gutter or on elegant carpets, seemed like a mania or a mad test of human covetousness.

Then the crash: the failure and suicide of a banker hastened the inevitable collapse. One evening in the Palais Bourbon, there had been playing for high stakes; Stanhope lost many thousands but his easy chatter and the fire and grace of his spirit had been all the more attractive. The ambassador, Lord Castlereigh, walked up to him and whispered some hasty news. He was seen to grow pale, a peculiarly melancholy smile froze on his delicate features, and the next day he left. He thought that at home he could lead the life of a retired country gentleman, but in this he was unsuccessful. The estates were in debt, creditors pressed from all sides, besides which he dreaded the loneliness and hated a depopulated countryside. He fled. He was obliged to borrow on the splendor of past days for a ragged existence which gradually was undermined from within by anxiety for his daily bread. Things had become silent about him; his wanderings were a pursuit of former friends and companions, but suddenly there was none who had not known everything beforehand and predicted ruin from his safe entrenchment, had "told him so," as it were. Exhausted, in despair, entirely hopeless in a hotel in Rome, he took strychnine. A young Sicilian girl nursed him back to life. The poison which left his body seemed to seize upon his soul. He struggled with the demon that had bowled him over; he became wild and cold. His contempt for mankind, which bordered on the sublime, made it the easier for him to make use of the weaknesses of those surrounding him. He became the employee of gentlemen of rank, and studied the filthy mysteries of their antechambers and back stairs. He became the emissary of the pope and the paid agent of Metternich. Soon his name was stricken from the list of the blameless and immaculate, and placed among those adventurers who play the dreaded role of marauders on the fringes of society.

His extraordinary talents made no task difficult, his constant compulsion to act and the diversity of his relations smothered the reproaches of his conscience and the sense of deep dishonor. Outlawed in the upper circles, he was avoided in spite of his usefulness, but among the lower classes he was still a distinguished man. He became a practiced hunter of men and ensnarer of souls. At first a result of the pressure of misfortune, this practice now became a trade with him; his irresistible gentle smile, his noble manners and chivalrous carriage, his winning conversation and remarkable culture, all was now his stock in trade; every movement of his eyelashes, every bow was trade—everything had consequences, everything reasons—a careless word might mean the failure of a task, and yet how full of privations was such a life, how pitiful the recompense! And all the time he was thus descending lower and lower into smaller circumstances, as if the chain he was dragging of its own accord, and without loosening, was dropping link after link in order to dash him into an abyss.

One day, "Caspar Hauser" became his slogan. The order was clear, its source was evident, the circumstances sinister beyond all precedent. It said: "You are the right man; the undertaking is difficult, but remunerative; it seems of slight importance, but big things hang in the balance." The transactions were not conducted face to face, everything was hidden, every messenger brought commands from a nameless person. This game of specters appealed to his fantasy, the abyss began to beckon. The working out of the plan was in some ways pleasurable; the strange bird had to be stalked in masterly fashion.

Yes, the command was clear; there was substance to it. You must remove the foundling from the territory in which he is beginning to be a menace to us—ran the order.—Take him with you, take him to a country where no one knows anything about him, let him disappear. Throw him into the sea or into a precipice or hire the knife of a ruffian, or if you know anything of quackery, let him become ill with some fatal malady, but do the job thoroughly, otherwise it will be of no use to us. You are assured of our gratitude, we quote it at such and such a sum deposited with the firm of Israel Blaustein, in X.

What was there to consider? All his distress might now be over. Mere hesitation alone made him an accomplice. For these people it was a necessity that they rid themselves of one who knew and remained inactive; there was no choice. The beginning of the undertaking lay far back; when the murderer had been sent into Daumer's house Stanhope had already had orders to intervene, in case the attack, in which he himself was not involved, should be unsuccessful. The rudeness and infamy of the means employed had frightened him, had offended his good taste and roused his better feelings. He fled and concealed himself. Misery and threatening hunger ensnared him again and so he came "from a great distance" in order to delude his victim.

But even their first meeting and the time they spent together was extraordinary. What a voice, what an eye! What was it that unstrung the undoer and charmed him so? This bird could sing; the ensnarer had not thought of that. Suddenly he saw himself loved; not as women love, that he had experienced, that can be appreciated and forgotten, too; it is a part of the flow of life; accident and instinct have an equal share in this.—He saw himself loved not as men love, or parents or brothers and sisters, or the way a child loves; law and propinquity, necessity and will bind the creature to his fellow-creatures, but in the profound depths of all these there is rivalry, struggle and hostility. This, however, was different, in an unconceived of and wonderful manner the beauty of a soul touched this inaccessible heart.

There is a legend of a land where no dew and no rain fell and therefore there was dryness in the land, and a dearth of water, because there was only one well which contained water in its lowest depths. When the people began to perish of thirst a youth came to the well who played a lute and produced such sweet melodies that the water rose to the surface of the well and overflowed the land.

With Lord Stanhope it was as with the well, when the boy Caspar was near him and played the sweet melodies of his nature. His spirit rose from the depths, a despairing glance flew back into time, shame kindled his throbbing soul, it seemed easy to make evil undone again, he found himself again, he saw the picture of his own unspotted youth in the boy's face, and saw himself as he might have been, accepted, trusted, glorified, all that might have been if fate had not crushed all that was noblest in him. And so truly, so richly, so unfathomably generous was the boy that the most atrocious miser and scoundrel would have ransacked his chests for treasures in order to free himself from any burden of guilt towards him.

But he gave—nothing. He could not give himself, for his person was already underwritten: his life was paid for by those whom he served; his nights and days were paid for, his regrets, his dissatisfaction and his evil conscience. He was planning the execution of a deed which marked every lineament of his countenance with a lie, but at times he really thought of fleeing together with Caspar. But whither should they go? Where was there a resting place for the outlaw of a continent? When he spent these quiet hours with Caspar and the boy's face—in which the pure radiance of human nature shone—inclined towards his, he felt that he, too, was still a human being and grieved over himself with measureless melancholy. Then he forgot his purpose and mission and revenged himself upon those whose guilty victim he was by exposing what he knew of their secrets and committing a double act of treason. He filled Caspar with expectations of power and greatness; this was his return, the gift of the miser. It was fortunate for him that the charm lost its strength when he was away from the boy, and he no longer felt the questioning glance resting upon him which made him feel as if a messenger of God were near him. In the midst of these sinister considerations and while following out these frightful plans he nevertheless wrote short passionate notes to his ensnared victim, such as: "In the first week when I came to know you I became your slave. If you ever feel for a woman what you feel for me I shall be lost"; or, "If you should ever notice that I am cold, do not attribute it to heartlessness but to an expression of the pain which I must conceal within me unto my grave. My past is a graveyard, when I found you I had half lost my God, it was you who tolled the bell that meant eternity to me." These expressions were in the taste of the time, influenced by the fashionable poets of the hour, but they nevertheless showed the perplexity of a profoundly disturbed mind.

So, torn in two directions, Stanhope himself impeded the progress of his undertaking. He let matters proceed as they would, and surrendered to the impact of events, for they were stronger than his resolutions. He knew that he would be obliged to carry out his shameful task and that he would do so, but he temporized and his procrastination gave him time to pity his own fate. He tried to find an excuse for himself before heaven, by prayer, and before the judge in his own breast, by making a fatality of his existence. He suppressed his consciousness of the fact that his very existence depended on enjoyment and good living, by means of the sophism that necessity was greater than love and pity, and he conjured away the image of the inevitable end with the cheap notion: it won't be so bad after all!

Meanwhile, his situation, after his hasty dispatching of the footman, became constantly more precarious, the expense of his stay constantly increased, his letters of credit were of little use; they were, for the present, mere decoys; necessity compelled him to act, and he decided to go to Ansbach and deal in person with President Feuerbach.

One Saturday towards the end of November he ordered his traveling carriage to be made ready quickly and sent word to the Tucher house that Caspar should come to him at once. However, after he had given an order to have Caspar wait until his return, he took a road on which there was no danger of meeting the boy, to the Baron's house, had himself conducted to Caspar's room under the pretext of wanting to wait for him, and when he was alone he rummaged in great haste through the boy's drawers, books and papers. He wanted to find a letter which he had himself written Caspar a few weeks before, in which extremely indiscreet remarks about Caspar's future had escaped him, and which he wished to destroy at all costs, for he had already been warned; the dark figures behind the curtain had already threatened.

His search was fruitless.

Suddenly a door opened and Herr von Tucher stood upon the threshold. In his timid haste his lordship had not heard the approaching footsteps. Herr von Tucher looked immensely big, for his forehead touched the upper beam of the door; his bearing showed a pained astonishment and after a long pause he remarked in hoarse tones: "Count, it cannot be that you are acting the part of a spy?"

Stanhope winced. "An insinuation of this nature you will allow me to pass over in silence," he replied with calm pride.

"But what does this mean," continued Herr von Tucher, "how shall I interpret what I have seen? It seems to me, Count, an inner voice tells me, that not everything is quite right here."

Lord Stanhope grew disturbed. He pressed one hand to his forehead and said in tones of entreaty: "I need more pity and clemency than you think, Baron." He pulled a handkerchief out of his pocket, pressed it before his eyes, and began suddenly to weep real unfeigned tears. Herr von Tucher was speechless. His first impulse was one of dark mistrust and the suspicion that all the nebulous hidden gossip about Caspar's fate must really have some serious foundation.

Stanhope, as if he suspected what was going on in the mind of his clear-eyed adversary, quickly mastered himself and said: "Do have pity on my vacillating heart. I am fumbling in the dark. Yes, it must be put into words: I doubt Caspar! I cannot exonerate him from deceitful acts and a certain lack of truthfulness."

"So you, too!" Herr von Tucher could not keep from exclaiming.

"And I am searching for evidence."

"And you seek this evidence in bureau-drawers and closets?"

"It is a question of secret writings which he conceals from me.

"What secret writings? I know nothing of any such things."

"Nevertheless they exist."

"Perhaps all that you mean is the diary which he received from the President."

Stanhope snatched with pleasure at this thought which half-way saved him from an unpleasant situation. "Yes, just that, unquestionably the same," he quickly declared, remembering at the same time certain compromising hints of Caspar's about the diary.

"I don't know where he keeps it," said Herr von Tucher, "and I should object to giving it to you in his absence. Moreover, I happen to know accidentally that some time ago he cut out the picture of the President which was on the first page and substituted yours, Count." Whereupon Herr von Tucher reached after a writing pad which lay upon the desk, pulled out its contents and handed it to Stanhope. It was the steel engraving of Feuerbach.

Lord Stanhope looked at it for a time, and as he gazed at these Jove-like features, a fear which he had never known before seized him. "So that is the famous man," he murmured. "I am on my way to seek him out. I expect a great deal from his incorruptible insight." But everything which he planned, the journey thither, the necessity of meeting the tremendous gaze of these eyes roused in him a state of nervousness which he was unable to master.

"His excellency will doubtless be delighted to make your acquaintance," said Baron Tucher politely, and as Stanhope started to go he asked him to convey to the President his respectful greetings.

Two hours later his lordship's carriage was speeding along the road. There was a bad storm. The dust rose in waves and spirals, Lord Stanhope wrapped in rugs crouched in a corner of the carriage and gazed incessantly upon the gloomy autumn landscape. But the sickly brilliance of his eye took in neither fields nor woods, but seemed rather to search the plain for hidden dangers. It was the eye of one possessed, or fleeing from danger. When, just before reaching the little city of Heilsbronn, the whining melody of a barrelorgan became audible, he pressed his hands to his ears and turned away, and, burying himself in the silken pillow, groaned at the lonely torment to which he was condemned. After this he sat up again, cold and hard as steel, a sorcerer's smile on his thin lips.

13. A Conversation Between one Who Remains Masked and One Who Discloses Himself

It was raining in torrents when late at night Lord Stanhope's coach thundered over the Ansbach Schlossplatz. Moreover, the horses shied suddenly at a dog trotting across the road and the Alsatian coachman cursed so loudly, in his abominable dialect, that a few white night caps showed themselves behind the dark window panes of the hostelry. The rooms in the inn "Zum Stern" were already ordered, the hotel keeper was dancing up and down in front of the gate with an umbrella, and greeted the stranger with countless profound bows, scrapings and polite assurances.

Stanhope walked by him to the steps, when suddenly a gentleman in the uniform of a police officer, his coat dripping with the rain, stepped toward him and introduced himself as Police-Lieutenant Hickel, who had had the honor of meeting his lordship a few weeks before, "all too briefly," at Rittmeister Wessenig's in Nurnberg. He took the liberty to offer his services to his lordship in this strange city, and begged his pardon for accosting him in a manner which seemed almost an incursion, but he assumed that his lordship would have little time and much to attend to, wherefore he wished to inquire at the first moment.

Stanhope looked at the man with surprise and considerable superciliousness. He saw a fresh round face with curiously impertinent and at the same time affectionately humble eyes. Starting back involuntarily, Stanhope felt that here was a person offering himself as instrument for any purpose, whatever it might be. There was nothing new to him about the covetous importunity of such glances. He thought he already knew his man inside out. But how did the officious fellow know of anything; who had given him the scent? He might at any rate be credited with a keen nose. Lord Stanhope thanked him briefly, and asked him to call at a certain time, whereupon the lieutenant gave a military salute and hurried out into the rain as quickly as he had come.

Stanhope occupied the whole first floor of the hotel; he had candles lighted everywhere at once, for he hated dark rooms. While the butler was preparing tea he took a little morocco bound book of devotions out of his traveling bag and began to read it. Or rather he made a pretense of reading; actually he was preoccupied with a hundred different thoughts. The quiet of the little country town was more dismal to him than the quiet of a cemetery. After he had taken some refreshment, he sent for the landlord and asked him this and that about conditions in the town, about the local aristocracy and bureaucracy. The landlord showed himself thoroughly disgusted with the new tendencies. He had lived during the happy period of the margrave, and on the day when courtiers and court ladies had taken flight from their pretty little rococo palaces, on account of the approaching wars, which had ended all the splendor of the world, it had become a stinking rats' nest, a second rate storehouse of documents, with the high-sounding name of appellate court, a miserable ink-stained den of legal scribes.

Ah, formerly, in those days people had known how to trifle. How gayly they had lived! People chatted and played and danced. And the fat man began before Lord Stanhope's eyes to execute some grave minuet poses, and pas de deux, at the same time trilling a long forgotten melody and jestingly lifting the tails of his coat with two fingers of each hand.

His lordship remained perfectly serious. He asked casually whether Herr von Feuerbach were in the city; but at these words the fat man made a sour face. "His excellency," he grumbled. "Yes, he is here. It would be better for us if he weren't. He watches us like a grumpy old bear and snarls at us if we whistle a tune. He meddles with everything, whether the streets are clean or whether the milk is watered, he is back of everything, but he has no gallantry in his soul. There is only one thing that he thoroughly understands, he is keen about food and for mercy's sake, your lordship, if you have anything to do with him you must praise everything which appears on his table."

Stanhope dismissed the gossip affably, then he showed the valet what clothes to prepare for the next morning and went to bed. The next day he arose late and sent the servant to Feuerbach's residence to ask for an interview. The man returned with the message that Feuerbach could not conveniently receive his lordship today or for several days to come; he requested him therefore to communicate his desires to him in writing. Stanhope was furious. He realized that he had overreached himself and drove at once to Hofrat Hofmann, to whom he had an introduction.

Meantime the news of his presence had spread, and at the end of twenty-four hours a veritable cycle of legends was already twined about his person. It was said that half a dozen sacks of gold guineas had been strapped onto the stranger's traveling carriage, that he intended to buy the margrave's castle; that he traveled about with a bed made of swan's down and embroidered linen; that he was the cousin of the King of England and Caspar Hauser his natural son. Stanhope, profoundly cool, saw that he had become the center of small-town gossip and was satisfied.

The Hofrat had been unable to give him any explanation for the President's behavior. In order to obtain official advice they sought out the archive director, Herr Wurm, who enjoyed Feuerbach's confidence. Stanhope felt that the matter was being approached with considerable circumspection; these official gentlemen could not boast of any free intercourse with a man whose hand rested upon them with the weight of iron.

That evening Stanhope accepted an invitation to a family party. Here, when he turned the conversation upon the President, a series of anecdotes was told, some of which were ridiculous, while others were bizarre. Or people, as if to hide their lack of affection and real understanding, told of circumstances which demanded pity, of the misfortune which Feuerbach had experienced with his sons, of a shattered marriage, of the solitude and hatred of mankind in which the old man dwelt and which was also looked upon as a secret expiation. "He is a fanatic," said a bald-headed office superintendent, "like Horatius he would deliver his own children to the hangman."

"He never forgives an enemy," said another complainingly, "and that does not betoken a Christian spirit."

"All that would not be so bad if he did not see a kind of criminal in every man," said the hostess, "and at every little harmless act set the whole of the punitive law in action. The other day at twilight I went walking with my daughter along the Triesdorf Road, and we were thoughtless enough to pick a few apples from the trees; suddenly his excellency appears before us, swings his stick in the air and screams at us in a frightful screeching voice: 'Oho, my lady, that is stealing from the city property.' Now I ask you, stealing! What does it mean?"

"But you must say, too, Mama," added the daughter, "that he smiled slyly and could hardly keep from laughing when we, trembling with fright, threw the apples into the ditch."

The very name of the man was like a stone boulder in a stream, impeding the flow of the water and causing it to rebound in spurts. Stanhope made no secret of his admiration for the President. He delivered quotations from his writings, seemed to know even his dryest legal works, and praised the abolition of the torture as a deed which would stand through the centuries. It was simply one of his ways of dazzling men's minds.

In all the streets and all the drawing rooms there was thereupon only one subject of conversation and that was Lord Stanhope. Lord Stanhope the hero, the asylum of persecuted innocence, Lord Stanhope the height of elegance, Lord Stanhope the freethinker, Lord Stanhope the favorite of fortune and fashion, Lord Stanhope the melancholy, the strictly religious. So many days, so many faces; today Lord Stanhope is cold; to-morrow he is passionate; if here he appears to be gay and free, elsewhere he will be profound and deferential; scholarship and idle trifling, the voice of feeling as well as the imperative of morality—it is only a question of what register the skillful organist requires. How interesting is his superstition, when at a gathering at Frau von Imhoffs he admits his fear of ghosts and describes that he was present when a compatriot went to hell in the crater of Vesuvius. How enchanting the irony with which on other occasions he could recite the godless poems of Byron!

The elements are mixed; one scarcely knows how. It is a pleasure to beat the waves into foam, to glide through the little provincial bog in a gilded boat.

On the fifth day the butler returned. He brought increased powers which Stanhope had partly anticipated by his trip to Ansbach; something like fear of Feuerbach's regulations was clearly evident. He was ordered in any case to submit to the President, since resistance would have aroused suspicion. The utmost was to be attempted, but he was to submit and dig new pits if the old had become useless. A dangerous document was mentioned which in the meantime must be gotten rid of, or rendered harmless, a copy of which was to be made in any case, however.

The present communication was to be destroyed and burned in the presence of the butler. This was done. Above all the boy brought money, wonderful, real money. Stanhope heaved a sigh of relief.

The next evening he invited some of the most distinguished families of the city to a sociable party in the rooms of the casino. It was whispered about that he had had the dishes prepared according to special recipes and had himself gone through the music with the director of the orchestra. At the beginning of the dance each lady received a favor, as ingenious as it was costly, a little gold shield on which was embossed the motto "Dieu et le cœur." After that Lord Stanhope took his glass and requested his guests to join him in drinking the health of a person who was so dear to him that he could not pronounce his name before so many people, although Everyone knew whom he meant: that wonderful creature who seemed placed by fate as if on an observatory of time. "Dieu et le coeur," this referred to him, the motherless boy whom mothers who had borne children should think of, as well as virgins dedicated to love.

People were touched; people were extraordinarily moved. Some white handkerchiefs fluttered in delicate hands and a bass voice murmured with emotion: "remarkable man." The remarkable man, as if he could not master his emotion otherwise, went out upon the adjoining balcony and looked thoughtfully down upon the people, some of whom stood in respectful whispering groups, others walking up and down in the darkness. Many had pressed against the opposite wall listening to the music, and a whole row of sallow faces gleamed in the light shining out of the window.

Then Stanhope suddenly perceived the man in uniform who had introduced himself on his arrival in the city. Stanhope had completely forgotten him; the man had been in the hotel at the appointed hour, but Stanhope had not kept the appointment and the visitor had merely left his card. Now he stood a few steps away under the lamp post and his face looked strikingly angry.

A feeling of discomfort seized upon Stanhope. He bowed politely in the direction where the man stood motionless. The latter had only waited for this; he came nearer, close to the balcony, so that his face was on a level with Stanhope's chest.

"Police officer Hickel, if I am not mistaken." said Stanhope, stretching out his hand: "I had the misfortune to miss your visit, please excuse me."

The policeman beamed with devotion and fastened deferential eyes on Lord Stanhope's mouth. "A pity," he replied, "otherwise I should certainly have enjoyed the advantage of spending the present evening in your lordship's society. My insignificant person is reckoned among the upper ten thousand; ha, ha!"

Stanhope moved his head scarcely perceptibly. What an unpleasant creature, he thought.

"Was your grace already at Staatsrat Feuerbach's?" continued the lieutenant. "I mean today. His excellency was obstinate until now and wanted to deal with your grace in writing only. I have finally succeeded in bringing the obstinate man to a different point of view."

All this was expressed in the most straightforward manner, but Stanhope showed an unconvinced face. "What do you mean?" he asked with hesitancy.

"Well, I can accomplish some things with the good President which other people might break their teeth upon in vain," replied Hickel with an amused and complacent expression. "Such hot-heads can be wound about one's finger if one only knows how to take them. Ha, ha, that's amusing, hot-heads wound about one's finger, ha, ha!"

Stanhope remained icy. He felt a dislike for the man, bordering on disgust. The police-lieutenant did not permit himself to be led astray. "Your lordship should in no case hesitate long," said he, "even though the matter may not be particularly pressing at the moment; you will find the Staatsrat in a condition of indecision, it seems to me, which should be made use of. And in regard to the dangerous document," he hesitated and paused.

Stanhope felt that he turned pale to his throat. "The document, what document are you talking about?" he murmured hastily.

"You will understand me fully, your Lordship, if you will only give me half an hour's hearing," replied Hickel with a subservience which bordered almost upon mockery. "What we have to say to one another is not unimportant, but need in no case be said today. I am at your convenience at any time that you like."

In spite of his uneasiness Stanhope thought that he ought to show indifference. Although a cue had been given which he could not overlook, he entrenched himself in haughty reserve. "I shall certainly appeal to you if I need you, sir," he said briefly and turned away frowning.

Hickel bit his lips and stared with some astonishment at the Count, who had disappeared through the open hall door, and then walked along the street whistling gently. Suddenly he turned around, bowed sarcastically, and said with affected courtesy, as if Stanhope were still standing in front of him. "Your Grace is in error, even Your Grace must cook with water."

When Stanhope returned again to his guests he drew the General Commissioner von Stichaner into conversation. In the course of their talk he said that he had decided to call upon the President the next day, and that, if Feuerbach should still insist on remaining so strangely obdurate, he would regard it as an intentional affront and would leave town. He said this in such a loud voice that some ladies and gentlemen standing next to them could not help hearing him. Among these was Frau von Imhoff, who was an intimate friend of Feuerbach. Obviously Stanhope had wished to address himself to her. Frau von Imhoff had become attentive; she looked over and said with some surprise: "If I am not mistaken, my lord, his excellency has called upon you. I met him late this afternoon in his garden just as he was about to start for the 'Stern.' You were probably not at home."

"I left my hotel at eight o'clock." replied Stanhope. An hour later many of the guests started to leave. Lord Stanhope offered to take Frau Imhoff, whose husband was away, home in his carriage. Since they were passing the "Stern," Stanhope ordered the carriage to stop and inquired whether anyone had called in his absence. As a matter of fact, Feuerbach had left his card.

The next morning at eleven o'clock the Count's carriage stopped in Heiligenkreuz Street in front of Feuerbach's garden. With aristocratic restrained steps, his elastic figure stretched to its full height, Stanhope approached the building, which looked like a country seat, keeping accurately to the middle of the lane of leafless trees. His suit showed the most painstaking care, in the button hole of his brown morning-coat shone the red ribbon of an order, his cravat was held in place by a diamond pin and a tired smile played about his clean shaven lips like an intellectual jewel. When he had gone about two-thirds of the way he heard a voice screaming from the house and simultaneously a cat ran over the gravel in front of him. A bad omen, he thought; he turned white, remained standing and looked back unconsciously. It was so foggy that he could no longer see his carriage.

He pulled the bell of the gate and waited a considerable time without its being opened; meantime the screaming inside continued; it was a man's voice in a wild rage. Stanhope finally turned the handle of the door, found the door unlocked and entered the hall. He saw no one and hesitated to go further. Suddenly a door was torn open, a woman rushed out, apparently a maid, and behind her a thick-set figure with a tremendous head, in which Stanhope at once recognized the President. But he was so frightened at the face, convulsed with anger, the disarranged hair, and the penetrating voice, that he remained as if rooted to the floor.

What had happened? Had some accident occurred, some crime been brought to light? Not any of these. A vile odor had merely passed along the corridor because a pan of milk had overflowed in the kitchen. The woman had remained gossiping when she had gone to fetch the water, and it was most undignified to see how the frantic old man thrashed about with his arms, and raved anew every time the berated woman ventured a whine in reply, how he gnashed his teeth, stamped with his feet and yelled with impetuous rage.

A funny little man, thought Stanhope, full of contempt, and it is for this little provincial tyrant and police philistine that I have trembled!

Clearing his throat discreetly, he walked up the three steps which separated him from this absurd theater of war when Feuerbach turned around with the speed of lightning. His lordship bowed deeply, gave his name and, smiling indulgently, asked to be excused if his visit was inopportune.

A quick flash spread over Feuerbach's face. He cast a rapid, almost biting, glance upon the Count, then a convulsive movement spread over his mouth and nose, and suddenly he burst into a laugh which contained embarrassment, self-irony and some sort of pleasant assurance; in brief, it had a relaxing, beneficent and Olympic sound.

With a wave of his hand he asked his guest to enter; they went into a large, well-kept room which showed extraordinary neatness in every detail. Feuerbach began at once to speak of his attitude towards Lord Stanhope up to the present, and, without assigning any reason, he said that the necessity which had determined him was stronger than any social duty. At the same time he had realized that he could not offend a man of such rank and reputation, also esteemed friends had told him so many pleasant things concerning His Lordship that he had finally decided to call on His Lordship yesterday.

Stanhope bowed again, regretted that he had not been able to receive His Excellency, and added modestly that he must regard this hour as one of the greatest of his life, since it afforded him the acquaintance of a man whose name and fame were unique, and had penetrated through the barriers of speech and of nationality.

Again that quick, sharp glance of the President's, an embarrassed satirical smile on the weather-beaten face, and back of it an almost touching beam of naive gratitude and pleasure. Lord Stanhope for his part represented completely a man of the world, embarrassed for perhaps the first time.

They seated themselves, the President indulging in his professional habit of turning his back to the window in order to have the light on his guest. He said that one of his reasons for wishing to speak to Stanhope was that a letter had arrived yesterday from Herr von Tucher, urging him to take Caspar into his house. This sudden change of mind had seemed remarkable to him, since he knew that Herr von Tucher had been favorably inclined toward the Count's desires; he had lost the thread of the matter, the whole story had gotten tangled up; now he wanted to see and to hear.

In tones of the greatest surprise Stanhope replied that he could not in the least understand Herr von Tucher's behavior. "One need only to turn one's back upon people and they change their faces," said he contemptuously.

"That is true," replied the President dryly. "Moreover, I don't want to keep you in suspense, Count, as I have already informed Mayor Binder that in no case can Caspar Hauser be entrusted to you. I must refuse entirely to consider such a request."

Stanhope remained silent. His features showed careless annoyance. He looked fixedly at the President's face and, as if it required some self-mastery on his part to speak at all, he finally said: "Let me explain to Your Excellency that Caspar's position in Nurnberg is untenable. There is extraordinary hostility to him and he is not understood by one of those who call themselves his protectors. He is burdened with a debt of gratitude, which fate itself is responsible for, and which he will never be able to discharge, otherwise every day and every experience would be a usurious tax, and he, young growing boy that he is, must waste his life away, exposed and defenseless. In addition to this the city, as I was expressly assured, will only provide for him until next summer and then apprentice him to some master tradesman to learn a trade. That, Excellency, seems to me a pity." Here Lord Stanhope raised his voice a little and his face with its downcast eyes took on an expression of suppressed arrogance. "It would seem to me a pity to allow that rare flower to be set out in a field tramped over by Tom, Dick and Harry."

The President had listened attentively. "Certainly, I know all that," he replied. "A rare plant, certainly. His first appearance was such that one thought one beheld an inhabitant of another planet straying about this world by a miracle, or the man mentioned in Plato, who had grown up in regions under the earth and had not ascended to the upper world and the light of heaven until his maturity."

Stanhope nodded. "My attachment to him, which has been universally condemned as exaggerated, developed when I first heard about him. There is, too, a certain atavistic justification for it in the history of my family," he continued in cool conversational tones. "One of my ancestors was proscribed under Cromwell and fled into the vault of a tomb. His own daughter kept him hidden and fed him with stolen bits of food until he succeeded in fleeing with difficulty. Since then, perhaps, a certain pleasure in the grave hovers about his descendants. I am the last of my race. I am childless. Only a dream, or, if you prefer, a fixed idea, attaches me to life."

Feuerbach threw his head back. His mouth shot into a straight line like a bow when its string is broken. Suddenly there was greatness in his gesture. "An inner responsibility prevents me from complying with your wishes, Count," he said. "Here such tremendous things are at stake that any token of favor or sacrifice of affection cannot, in comparison, even be taken into account. Here justice has to be snatched from demons of evil lurking in the background, and some evidence, if not trophy, given to the anxious eyes of the world that there is such a thing as retribution, even where crimes are covered over with a purple mantle."

His lordship bowed again, but quite mechanically. Inwardly he had grown numb. For he had become embarrassed in the presence of the elemental strength which addressed him from the breast of this man, and which subordinated even the rhetorical flourishes which had at first made him uncomfortable and put him in an ironic mood. He felt that to struggle against this will, which broke forth like a storm, would be a fruitless task, and though it was a higher power which had absorbed him, almost without his cooperation, into a labyrinth of dark intrigues, it seemed suddenly important to him to save an appearance of honor and virtue from the chaos of his internal being. He bent forward and asked gently: "And is the justice which you wish to snatch from these persons worth the suffering of him who has to bear it?"

"Yes, even though it should mean his death."

"And what if he perish without your reaching your goal?"

"Retribution will issue forth from his grave."

A Conversation Between One Who Remains Masked And One Who Discloses Himself

"I warn you to be careful for your own sake, Your Excellency," whispered Stanhope, while his glance slowly traveled from the window to the door.

Feuerbach looked surprised. There was something of betrayal in this expression, betrayal in some sense or other. But his lordship's blue eyes looked as transparent as sapphires, and there was a feminine sorrow in the bowed narrow head. The President felt himself drawn to the man and unconsciously his voice became mild, almost affectionate, as he said: "You, too, you speak of caution? My speech sounds bold to you; it is. I am tired of serving on a ship which founders disgracefully through the madness of its own officers; but I can imagine that it is incomprehensible to a citizen of free England that a man must give up his peace and the security of his existence in order to awaken the conscience of the state to the most primitive requirements of society. It is superfluous to warn me to be careful, my lord. I would say this in the hearing even of one who would admit to being willing to betray my confidence. I fear nothing, because I have nothing to hope."

Stanhope let a few seconds pass before he collectedly replied: "My cry of warning will astonish you less if I admit that I am not uninitiated in the circumstances you are alluding to. I am not the tool of chance. I did not seek out the foundling without an external impulse. It is as the messenger of a woman, the most unhappy of all women, that I regard myself."

The President jumped up as if lightning had struck the room. "Count," he exclaimed beside himself, "so you know."

"I know," replied Stanhope quietly. After he had observed with a gloomy expression how the President had convulsively seized the arms of his chair so that his arms visibly trembled, and how the big face was convulsed and furrowed with emotion, he continued in a monotonous voice and with a wan and curiously sweet smile: "You will ask: why the circumlocutions: what do I want the boy for? My answer is: I want to conduct him to safety; I want to take him to another country; I want to hide him; I want to remove him from the weapon which is suspended over him all the time. Can one be clearer? Do you want more? Excellency, I know of things which freeze my blood, even when I wake up at night and think of them in an interval of waking* as one thinks in a fever. Spare me from going into details. Considerations more binding than oaths paralyze my tongue. You, too, seem, I am puzzled to know how, to have gathered some insight into this horrible abyss of shame, murder and suffering, therefore I may say to you, that I, who have looked carefully and close at hand at the kings and lords of creation, have never seen a face on which birth and intelligence have bestowed such aristocracy, and pain a more touching power, than the face of that woman. I became her slave in the first moment, when the image of this tragic figure visited my spirit. It became the idea of my life to serve her and to assuage the wounds which fate had dealt her. I will remain silent as to how I obtained certainty about the condition of this martyred soul, wasting away upon the edge of death, and how slowly one layer after another of this web of suffering was uncovered, which had been slowly spun for decades about an unfortunate and unprotected person. The head of Medusa cannot be more horrible. Enough that I had to suppress my true nature and pretend to be stupid. I had to lie, to flatter, to sneak, to meet intrigue with intrigue; I have disguised myself and undertaken deceitful tasks. In doing so, anger burned into my very marrow and I asked myself how it was possible to continue to live with such knowledge in one's breast. But that is just it, one goes on living, one eats, one drinks, one sleeps, one goes to the tailor, one goes walking, one has one's haircut and day after day goes by as if nothing had happened. And it is just the same with those people of whom one thinks that their evil consciences must destroy their senses and corrode their arteries: they eat, drink, sleep, laugh and amuse themselves, and their deeds run off them like water off of a duck's back."

"Very true, that's it, that's how it is," exclaimed Feuerbach, moved to passion. He hurried several times up and down the room, then he remained standing in front of Stanhope and asked sternly: "And does the woman know everything—? Does she know about him? What does she know? What does she expect and what does she hope?"

"I can't tell you anything from personal observation," replied Lord Stanhope in that same sad, tired voice as before. Recently it was said at Countess Bodmer's that she had cried out loud when the name of Caspar Hauser was mentioned to her. Maybe the report is not entirely trustworthy; on the other hand I know of another incident which seems to indicate an almost super sensual relationship. One morning two years ago the princess was alone in the chapel of the castle and was saying her prayers; as she. was finishing, and was about to get up, she suddenly saw above the altar the picture of a beautiful boy whose face expressed endless sorrow. She called out 'Stephan,' the name of her son, her first born; then she fell in a faint. Later she recounted her vision to a lady whom she trusted and the latter, who had seen Caspar himself in Nurnberg, was deeply moved by the resemblance. And the remarkable thing was that the apparition appeared on the very day and at the very hour of the murderous attack in Daumer's house. One thing is clear, that on both sides there is a secret yearning for a reunion. Furthermore it is evident, Your Excellency, that every delay means danger, and the trivial wasting of a good opportunity. I am calling to you in direst distress. It may be that we shall be called to give an account of our omissions before a chair of judgment where no repentance will make up for what has happened."

His lordship got up and walked to the window. His eyelids had become red and his glance somber. Whom did he really betray? To whom was he lying? The people in whose service he was? The boy whom he had attached to himself? The President; himself? He did not know. He was profoundly moved by his own words, for they seemed true to him. How remarkable; all this seemed really true to him as if he were a helper in need. He loved himself for these few minutes and nursed his finer feelings. Dark forgetfulness came over him, and so far as he was able to recognize fatigue and disgust, they referred only to the bodiless phantom which had sat in his place, acted and talked in his place. He wiped twenty years of the past from the tablets of his memory, and stood there cleansed through a hallucination of kindness and pity.

Feuerbach had seated himself in front of his desk. His head resting in his hand, he looked thoughtfully into space. "We are the servants of our deeds, my lord," he began after a long pause and the ordinarily obstreperous or shrill voice had a soft and solemn sound. "To tremble before a bad ending would mean to give up every battle before it was waged. Frankness for frankness, Count. Think, I am here in a lost corner of the country. My life was intended for something different than to be terminated in the obscurity of a small provincial town, at least once I thought so. I was able to perform services for my king which were appreciated and which have perhaps contributed to lend the proud attribute of 'the just' to his name. I wanted to serve him further, to elevate his people, to make the crown a symbol of humanity. This having failed, I was pushed aside. Of course, I was rewarded, but not otherwise than servants are rewarded."

He stopped, rubbed his chin with the back of his hand and ground his teeth. Then he continued: "From my earliest youth I have devoted myself to the law. I have scorned the letter in order to honor the spirit. The human being was more important to me than the paragraph. My attempt was to find the rule which separates instinct from responsibility. I have studied vice the way a botanist studies a plant. The criminal was for me an object of solicitous attention. I calculated which of the sins of his sick mind resulted from the mistakes of the state and of society. I made myself a pupil of the masters of law and the apostles of humanity. I wanted to snatch this age from an outlived barbarism and construct paths for the future. It is superfluous to assert; my writings, my books, my proclamations, my whole past, that is to say, a chain of fretful days and nights of work, are witnesses.

I did not live for myself; I scarcely lived for my family. I have foregone the pleasures of sociability, of friendship and of love. I derived no profit from the favor I had won; no success gave me peace of mind or any manifest advantage; I was poor, poor I remained, tolerated by those above me and slandered by those below, ill used by the strong, outwitted by the weak. My opponents were stronger, their opinions were more convenient and their methods unscrupulous; they were numerous, I was alone. I was hunted about like a mangy cur. Slanderers and back-biters dragged my good cause in the mud. There was a time when I could not go through the streets of the capital without having to fear the grossest insults of the mob. When I was forced by the most disgusting intrigues and hostilities to give up my professorship in Landshut, and when the riff-raff of the students had been so incited against me that I fled to my home city, deserting wife and child, paid stool pigeons sought my life. It was the time of the great war; all order was destroyed; the Austrian party gave out that I was in league with the

French party, which was paving the way for Emperor Napoleon to build an occidental empire and to depose the reigning princes. The French, on the other hand, threw suspicion on my relations with Austria. There was a man, a professional and departmental associate of mine, a scholar, renowned and respected,—oh, a shameless coward; in time his name will be one of the stains on the escutcheon of this century—who had the effrontery to openly report me as a spy and who made my Protestant faith a pretext to render me suspicious in the eyes of the king. I did not succumb. There came an end to these troubles. My prince took me back again into grace, of course, only into grace. A new ruler ascended the throne; I remained in favor. Today I am an old man; I sit here in tranquility, still in favor; my enemies, too, are pacified, or pretend to be; they also enjoy the royal favor; but what it means to see a life dedicated to big purposes and the general welfare destroyed before the last fiber of the intellect which bore it and supported it has been consumed, this they do not feel; I alone know that."

  Feuerbach stood up and breathed deeply. After that he seized his snuff-box, took a pinch of snuff, and under the rough eyebrows there gleamed a touchingly anxious and grateful glance as he said: "Count, I am not quite clear what it is that moves me to speak to you so. I am astonished myself. You are the first who have heard what so desperately resembles the complaint of one who has suffered the insolence of office, but it is only intended as an explanation for an inimitable resolution. I am not concerned, in Caspar's predicament, with the specific facts or persons of the case, and the personality involved is not the factor that strengthens my resolve. I am impelled by the direst stress with which a man of gray hair can be faced, and am forced to ask of fate whether all the sacrifice and labor has been in vain, whether the only result it has shown to me and to others laboring in the same domain, is weakness here and indifference there. I must make the test, I must see it through, come what will; I must know whether I have talked for the empty air and written in the sand; I must know whether the promises with which the bitterness of my exile was sweetened were only cheap pretenses. I must and will know whether I and my cause are taken seriously. I have proof", Count; there is frightful evidence before me; I can strike; I hold the thunderbolt and can call forth the lightings; I have set down the whole business and formulated it in a special document. They know about it; matters will not be pushed to the limit; for I am determined to go to any length in order to preserve that precious possession whose guardian I have been appointed to be before God and man. Nevertheless I shall wait; great things require much patience. But Caspar may not be removed. He is the living weapon and the living proof which I need and he must be constantly accessible. If I lost him the foundation of my last work would be gone—for it is my last work, I feel that clearly—and every claim to a serious hearing would be without foundation. And you, noble sir, what would you lose? Do you wish to perform a deed of kindness or of love and not consider justice? That would be to discard gold for chaff."

Stanhope's face had gradually turned as pale as if no blood were flowing under the skin. He had seated himself, and bent over as if he wished to creep into a hole. Several times glances like wild animals that have destroyed their cages had flashed from his eyes, then he had called them back again, and nursed them within himself; he held his breath; he sat huddled with his fingers on the chain of his lorgnette, and when the President had finished he stood up with a passionate gesture. He had difficulty in recovering himself; it was hard to find words; his mouth was convulsed with rapid movements as though he wished to laugh or to suppress some bodily pain, and when he seized the President's hand he turned ice cold; his second self-stood by his side, this shadowy personification of his life, his commissions and omissions; it whispered the word of treason into his ear, but his eyes were damp when he said: "I understand; all that I can reply, Your Excellency, is, take me as your friend; regard me as your helper; your confidence seems to me a message from above. But what guarantee have you, what evidence that you have not opened your heart to someone who is unworthy, who only knows how to pretend better than all the rest? I could have abducted Caspar; I could still do so—"

"If this face with which you are standing before me lies, my lord, I for my part will declare it a chimera to seek truth upon this earth," Feuerbach interrupted with animation. "Abduct, abduct Caspar," he continued smiling genially. "You are joking; I for my part would advise anyone against it who still attaches value to walking in the sun." Stanhope sank for a while into motionless thought, then he asked hastily: "What is to happen? It is our duty to act quickly. Where is Caspar to go?"

"He is to come here to Ansbach," replied Feuerbach categorically.

"Here, to you?"

"To me, no. That is unfortunately impossible; impossible for many reasons. I must be alone a great deal; I have much work to do; I am away on trips a great deal; my health is broken, my character badly adapted for the role which I should have to play, and moreover the situation forbids me to form too strong a personal tie."

Stanhope breathed a sigh of relief. "Where will he go then?" he insisted.

"I shall inquire about for a family where he will have good care, and intellectual as well as moral support," said the President. "I shall talk to Frau von Imhoff this very day. She knows the people here. Be assured of this, my lord, that I shall watch over the boy as over my own child. The Nurnberg horseplay will not be repeated. That I give you complete freedom of intercourse with Caspar need scarcely be mentioned. Count, my house is yours. Believe me: under the cover of the official and the judge there beats a heart that is susceptible to friendship. In this country of petty spirits one is not pampered by much association with men."

After they had briefly discussed what reports were to be sent to Herr von Tucher and the Nurnberg City Council, Stanhope took his departure.

The President walked up and down for a long time, sunk in deep thought. From minute to minute his face became darker and more restless. A curious gnawing distrust, which was not to be waved aside, rose in his breast. With the flight of time after the Count's leaving the room, this painful sensation grew apace. He was too skilled in his knowledge of men to pass over certain indications which roused his suspicions. Suddenly he struck his head with his hand, went to his desk and wrote three letters in great haste: one to Paris to a friend in high position, another to the Bavarian Minister in London, a third to the Minister of Justice, Dr. von Kleinschrodt, in Munchen. In the first two letters he asked for accurate information about Lord Stanhope's person, in the third he announced that he would soon arrive in the capital and asked for a furlough for the purpose of traveling.

    He had all three letters sent off at once by express post.

14. Night Will Come

Stanhope had ordered the coachman to drive on ahead. He walked through the deserted streets in which his steps resounded as in a church. He was disturbed and broken, and unable to come to any sensible decision. When he reached the hotel he shut himself in and practiced fencing for half an hour with his small sword.

He did not stop until he heard a voice outside arguing with the butler, who had orders not to admit anyone. Stanhope listened, he recognized the voice, nodded indifferently, and with the sword still in his hand opened the door. It was Hickel, who at once entered and greeted the Count, who looked at him in silence, with some embarrassment.

When asked what he wanted, he cleared his throat and stammered a few disconnected flowery phrases from which it was evident that he knew of Stanhope's visit to Feuerbach. His behavior, in spite of something which affected one like cringing, betrayed an intangible, impertinent familiarity.

Stanhope looked steadily at the excited man in the handsome uniform. "What is the real meaning of your offering me your assistance in bringing about a meeting with the President?" he asked icily.

"But your lordship permitted me to be of assistance," replied Hickel. "Who knows whether the President would have been accessible without me; he knows how to make himself inaccessible. Your lordship will not condescend to recognize that. Ah, well," he added, shrugging his shoulders, "great men will have their moods."

"How do you come to offer yourself as an intermediary at all?"

"Intermediary? Your lordship attaches too much importance to my innocent offer of help."

"You have made it important yourself. You preferred to express yourself unclearly. You permitted yourself several expressions about which I politely request to be enlightened." Stanhope continued to conceal under an exterior of frigid dignity the insecurity which he felt with this man.

"I am entirely at your lordship's service," replied Hickel. May I, for my part, inquire how far your lordship intends to disclose himself?"

"To disclose myself? To disclose myself to whom? To you? I have nothing to disclose."

"Your lordship may regard me as a man of complete discretion."

"What does that mean?" exclaimed Stanhope with irritation. "Are you presenting me with charades to solve?"

"Before your lordship's arrival they were looking for a responsible person," said Hickel suddenly, with icy calm. "My many years of association with his excellency, the President, recommended me more than some of my modest capabilities."

Stanhope grew pale and looked at the floor. "So you have direct orders?" he murmured.

The policeman bowed. "Orders, no," he replied hesitatingly. "They made sure of my good will, and I was told to place myself at your lordship's service."

It seemed to Stanhope as if he had already once that day died a death of penitence and had arisen to life again, and were now finally and definitely handed over to his destiny.

He wanted to appear at five o'clock at tea at Frau von Imhoff's and asked the lieutenant whether he cared to drive a part of the way with him. Although from the sound of the question the desire for a refusal was evident, Hickel, who wanted to be seen in public together with Lord Stanhope, accepted gratefully.

The streets were somewhat more alive than at the noon hour; old civil servants and pensioners took their daily walk along the promenade at this hour. Many remained standing and bowed toward the interior of the distinguished carriage.

Now it happened that at one of the street corners the man on the box suddenly broke into his usual loud jabbering, for there stood on the corner a dreamy, sky-gazing gentleman who seemed to take no notice of the approaching ducal carriage. Greatly frightened, this man jumped when the Alsatian coachman began to swear, but not so quickly but that his clothes were spattered with the mud which splashed from the hoofs of the horses and the wheels of the carriage.

Hickel leaned his head out of the window and grinned, for the bespattered creature stood with a disconcerted and unhappy expression, holding his arms out from his body and looking at the mess he was in.

"Who is the awkward wretch?" asked Stanhope, annoyed at the policeman's gloating mien.

"He? That's the teacher, Quandt, my lord."

A curious coincidence. Half an hour later the same name was mentioned at Frau von Imhoff's. The President and his friend, after long consultation, had agreed to put Caspar under the care of Quandt.

"He is an enlightened and cultivated man and enjoys general respect, both as a citizen and as a man," said Frau von Imhoff.

"And is he inclined to accept so responsible an undertaking?" asked Stanhope absent-mindedly. But Frau von Imhoff was not able to give any reply.

The next morning, when Stanhope had himself announced at the President's, he met Herr Quandt himself there. Evidently they had already reached an agreement, for Feuerbach seemed very cheerful, and when Lord Stanhope apologized to Quandt for the incident of the day before with the carriage, the President was amused at the teacher's embarrassment, which he even increased by harmless jests about absentminded thinkers and so forth. His laughter produced anxious perspiration on Quandt's forehead, he bowed before Stanhope like a Mussulman before the Kalif and it looked as if he must feel flattered that the mud of the count's carriage had felt his unimportant person worthy of any notice.

"Now Quandt, don't put on such airs," the President warned him jovially. "I bet your wife scolded you thoroughly, and took a lot of trouble to get your jacket clean again."

"It was only my overcoat, Your Excellency," replied Quandt smiling and blissful over all this generous affability. Stanhope remained dignified. This time they were in the President's state reception room and three high windows looked out on the garden. The room was comfortably furnished and here, too, everything was extremely orderly. In a kind of deep niche there hung a good oil painting of Napoleon Bonaparte in his coronation robes. Stanhope studied it with pretended interest; actually he was carefully observing the personality and demeanor of the teacher.

Quandt was of medium size and lean. Over his high forehead his hair, of the yellow of tobacco, was brushed back to a ridiculous sleekness with the help of pomade. His eyes were shy, almost sorrowful, and blinked at times, his hooked nose protruded a little boastfully, his mouth hidden under an humble and stubby beard, had a bitter expression which betrayed the professional habit of much nagging.

Stanhope did not seem dissatisfied with the result of his observation. He asked the President whether the negotiations had been successfully concluded, and when the latter replied in the affirmative he turned to Quandt and stretched out his right hand to him in silent gratitude and said that he would call upon him in the afternoon. Stupefied at so much graciousness the teacher again bowed deeply, bowed low to the President, and left.

Stanhope, too, went away soon, as Feuerbach was obliged to attend a session of his court. On arriving back at the hotel, Stanhope spent two hours in writing a letter, and when it was finished sent the butler off with it. At half past one the police lieutenant arrived by appointment; they lunched together and then went to call on Quandt.

The teacher's little house, which was near the upper gate at Kronacher Buck, had been polished spick and span. Frau Quandt, a fresh, pleasing young woman dressed in a brown silk dress, as if for a wedding, stood curtseying at the entrance; in the best room a table was laden with pastry baker's cakes and the fine porcelain service gleamed invitingly on the snow-white table-cloth.

His lordship was paternally friendly toward the teacher's wife. She was pregnant and he accordingly congratulated her, a pressure of his hand strengthened his warm expression of interest. He asked whether it was the first time; the young woman turned scarlet, shook her head and said that she had already a three-year-old boy. When the coffee was served Quandt gave her a hint and she quietly left the room, leaving the three men alone.

Stanhope said that he could not yet reconcile himself with the idea of a separation from Caspar, but that he was enchanted with this peaceful and orderly domesticity and was much relieved to know his favorite would be taken care of here. So one might at least hope that the unfortunate boy who had been exposed to so many bungling hands and had suffered in body and soul had at last reached a harbor of safety.

Quandt placed his hand over his breast to indicate his pledge.

"Yes," interrupted Hickel, swallowing his last bite of cake and wiping his beard and lips with the back of his hand, "that's so, and now at last we shall have light on this child of darkness."

His lordship frowned, a sign of displeasure which Hickel did not fail to perceive; he smiled vacantly, however, and assumed a threatening mien.

"Unfortunately there is cause for suspicion," continued Stanhope, and his voice was toneless and cold. "Wherever one turns and however one looks at it, everywhere there is suspicion and doubt. So it is no wonder that one's original affection is steeped in bitterness. Though I feel ready to yield to my affectionate impulses, voices nevertheless make themselves heard, whose judgment or weight it would be senseless to suspect and the slumbering spark of suspicion has not been extinguished."

"So, then," Hickel broke in again, "I am right after all. We must make a clean sweep of things. The deceitful fellow must finally be made to behave himself. His tricks must finally be driven out of him."

Stanhope turned white; gazing past Hickel he said cuttingly: "Lieutenant, I must protest against such a tone. Whatever evidence there may be against the boy, he can only be regarded as the misguided victim of an unknown criminal."

Hickel bent his head and again a vacant smile passed over his face. "Excuse me, your lordship," he replied quickly, considerably frightened, "but that is the opinion of the whole world, at least of the enlightened and intelligent public. Only yesterday I was present when Baron von Lang and Pastor Fuhrmann gave their opinion about the foundling and the nonsense of the Nurnbergers. Your lordship should have heard that. We also know here, it has become known through judicial channels, what Herr von Tucher has written to you about the foundling's ingratitude and moral corruption. Just show Herr Quandt the Baron's letter and he will be convinced himself that I have only said what every decent and unprejudiced man thinks about the matter." And Hickel gazed curiously and penetratingly at the Count.

"That is not quite true," replied Stanhope curtly, mechanically sipping his coffee. "Herr von Tucher in his letter only speaks of some bad habits of Caspar's. I have eyes, too. A loving heart is never blind; even though one does not know how to measure, one does possess the gift of perception. Moreover, let us not anticipate our worthy host. It will be his task to judge. What has grown crooked he can straighten out, and if he cleans the ugly spots from my treasure I shall thank him royally."

Hickel drew a wry face and remained silent. Quandt had followed the conversation with intense attention. Why such a discussion, he thought, as if it weren't the easiest thing in the world to recognize whether he is a rascal or not. One must keep one's eyes open, that's all. A good person is good, a bad one bad; where's the difficulty? To eradicate an evil, if it's not too deep, is only a question of energy and circumspection. But it seems to me, it does seem to me, the teacher continued to meditate silently within himself, as though there were some quite different things hidden here; the gentlemen are not speaking their minds.

And in this reflection he had probably hit upon the truth, as was soon apparent. He began to develop for the benefit of the politely listening lord his attitude toward morality, toward intercourse in human society, how to deal with pupils, the necessity for attention, the worth of censure, all diffusely and with circumlocution, but everything simple, astonishingly simple; only his worried expression gave him an appearance of difficulty and philosophy. Lord Stanhope nodded his head several times while Hickel gave decided signs of impatience. Then, as they were leaving, while Stanhope was saying good-by to Quandt's wife, Hickel drew the teacher aside and whispered to him: "Don't let yourself be intimidated by the Count's speeches, my dear Quandt. The good Count is deceiving himself and would like not to recognize what is as clear as day. This devilish story affects him curiously. You will do him a great service if you expose the swindler."

That was the catchword and the keynote. It contained the kernel of the plot. Now Caspar, you are to go into a small town, into a small house; you are to live hidden away, and the walls of the world are to press in upon you until they again become a prison. Force and cunning have joined; the judge will pronounce a sentence upon what he sees and will not know what he feels. You are to become insignificant in order that your friends may change into foes, and your loneliness may make you the more easily fall a victim to the pursuer. Blood is to bear witness against itself, light will fail, fruit will cease to grow, the voice of heaven will become silent and the night—for night will come—shall have no morrow.

15. A Chapter In Letters

Freiherr von Tucker to Lord Stanhope

For a considerable time I have been without news of Your Excellency. The uncertain situation in which I find myself toward Caspar causes me to intrude myself more upon you, Gracious Sir, than you may care to have me, in order to beg you to put a speedy end to the suspense with regard to his affairs. All the more, since my interest in the foundling is not what it formerly was, and he himself must regard his forced residence in my house more in the light of an imprisonment than as a guest and member of the household. A definite status would be most desirable for the boy, for his excited hopes prevent his mind from being in any way at rest, and from day to day he glows with such feverish expectation that continuous study cannot be thought of, and even the stupidest eye could not fail to perceive the state of unrest he is in. He spends his evenings in useless scribbling and his chief pleasure is to trace with a lead pencil on a large map the roads which he soon hopes to travel with Your Lordship, certainly a practical, though perhaps one-sided way of learning geography. He speaks, thinks and dreams of nothing but the trips which he is about to take with you, my lord, and if you retain the slightest interest in the welfare of the unfortunate boy I can make no stronger appeal to your kindness than to beg you to end this intense and fruitless disquiet as quickly as possible. You are the only person in the world whose word still has weight in his ears, and his measureless trust in you must move the heart even of one who, on account of the moods, the unreliability and the hybrid nature of this puzzling personality has been robbed of his former pronounced attachment.

Daumer to President Feuerbach

Your Excellency has paid me the honor to ask me for information as to Caspar's present condition. I must confess that this has to a certain extent embarrassed me. In the last year and a half I have purposely avoided approaching the boy, who has been so carefully segregated, since here in this part of the world Everyone is anxious to preserve his smallest privilege from the intervention of strangers, and thus an interest which concerns humanity, and must call forth pity from every free spirit, is inadvertently made a party cause. May Your Excellency pardon this insinuation and regard it solely as a proof of my inalterable interest in the fate of the foundling, which now gives his friends less reason than ever for exaggerated hopes. Your Excellency's confidential letter has conquered my scruples; I have recently visited Caspar at the Tucher house and he has also been at my house for the first time in a long while, and I will give you some information about him which, although of a general nature, will reveal the peculiarities of his present situation.

Caspar has become a tall young man who now makes the general impression of a boy of twenty-two. If he, who must now be counted among those accustomed to human society and manners, were to enter unknown among a group of people he would certainly cause surprise by his strange appearance: his walk has something of the anxious hesitation and carefulness of a cat's, his features are neither masculine nor childlike, neither young nor old (they are old and young at the same time); and particularly on his forehead a few slight wrinkles betray a premature ageing. A light down grows on his lips; this often seems to embarrass him, nor does it accord with the gentle girlishness of his face and the brown curls which still hang down to his shoulders. His friendliness is most winning, his seriousness deliberate, and over both there hangs a constant veil of melancholy. His behavior is precocious, but it has, however, a distinguished and quite spontaneous gravity. Some of his gestures are still clumsy and awkward, and his speech, too, is harsh, as he does not always find the right word. He enjoys looking serious, saying things presumptuously which would sound nonsensical if someone else said them, but which coming from him compel a pained and pitying smile. For example, it is highly absurd to hear him talk of his plans for the future, of the way in which he will establish himself when he has really learned something and how he will live with his wife. He regards a wife as a necessary article of furniture, as a sort of superior maid whom one keeps so long as she is useful and sends away if she puts too much salt in the soup or does not mend one's shirts properly.

    The constant calm quiet of his spirits resembles the peace of a lake, smooth as a mirror in the moonlight. He is incapable of offending; he cannot hurt any animal; he is tenderhearted toward the very worm, which he fears to tread upon. He loves mankind, the face of every human is to him the countenance of a god and he seeks all of heaven in it. There is no longer anything extraordinary about him except his extraordinary fate. He is now a mature boy who had no childhood, who lost his first youth without knowing how; a young man without a country, without a home, without parents, without relations, without contemporaries, without friends: the only creature of his kind, as it were. Every moment reminds him of his loneliness in the midst of the throng swarming around him, of his helplessness and his dependence on the pleasure and displeasure of others. And so his whole behavior is only a defense, defense his gift of observation, defense the circumspect clear-sightedness with which he sees every peculiarity and weakness of other people, defense the intelligence with which he executes his desires and knows how to utilize the good will of his patrons.

    Yes, Your Excellency, he is without friends. For we who wish him well, who have saved him from experiencing crass want, we are only the observers of the monstrous mystery of his existence. And that much talked of man, Lord Stanhope, can he really be called Caspar's friend? What shall we think? Where is there any fact to allay our well-grounded suspicion? I anticipate terrible things when I think of the boy's expectations with regard to the Count, who would have to be a saint without a peer, if all of the promises were to be fulfilled which his appearance connoted for Caspar. And if they be not fulfilled, or if only a one hundredth part of them be not fulfilled, I prophesy a bad end; for such a heart, lifted from the depths into the life of the world, which has been exposed after the most complete serenity to the most extravagant enticements, wants everything and demands the whole measure of happiness or, if cheated only of a little, must succumb to a measureless desolation.

I confess that my pessimistic temperament leads me to such bold considerations rather than the talk of the people here, which is becoming very frank indeed; how dare I express my distrust toward a man so highly situated? But today people are beginning to say that Caspar is to go to a tutor in Ansbach. Frau Behold, Caspar's old enemy, is spreading the rumor abroad, and announces everywhere with malicious pleasure that nothing has come of the English trip and of the Count's air castles. My sister tells me that the Magistrate's wife has had indirect news from Quandt's wife; the two women are childhood friends and grew up in the same house. God forbid that Caspar should discover this gossip. I should be most grateful to Your Excellency if you would have direct information sent me, so that I can contradict this absurd gossip, m accordance with the best interests of our protégé.

Feuerbach to Herr von Tucker

In response to Your Honor's request, as well as to the necessity of the situation, I hereby inform you that you are from today relieved of your position as tutor to Caspar Hauser. The local and city judiciary will simultaneously inform you of this officially, as well as of the fact that Caspar Hauser is to be given over to Lord Stanhope, of course, only as a matter of form, for the time being, for, until the present complicated and difficult conditions may admit a change, Caspar is to be taken care of in the house of Quandt, the teacher. Lord Stanhope will, during this time, provide for his regular education and care, while I myself, in the absence of his foster-father, will watch over the boy's welfare. On the seventh of this month, Police Lieutenant Hickel, an energetic officer, who has been appointed by a decree in council as special guardian for the period of Caspar's transfer to Ansbach, will appear at your house. His Grace, Lord Stanhope, at the last moment decided to absent himself from this formal step which in the eyes of the public is to have a completely official character, and his determination has my complete approval. I see no difficulty in informing Caspar of the changed condition of affairs and regard the anxiety concerning this as exaggerated. I myself expect within the next few days to make a long-planned visit to the capital. I hope during my stay to take the opportunity to bring about a definite and favorable change in Caspar's condition of life.

Baron Tucker to President Feuerback

I most humbly beg to inform Your Excellency that the sudden death of my uncle compels me to leave the city and to go to Ansbach. I have left the responsibility for Caspar, since he is still in my home, to Mayor Binder and Professor Daumer, leaving it to their discretion to have Caspar remain here or to take him to one of their homes. I have not yet communicated, nor even hinted to the boy what is to take place, and I must frankly confess that a certain unconquerable fear holds me back. Caspar still believes firmly and obstinately that he is to go either to England or to Italy with his distinguished patron, and an even temporary separation from the Count seems to him an utter impossibility. The person who would bring him such information would have to have godlike powers of persuasion to reconcile him with these new circumstances. With all due deference, it seems to me a mistake to put the boy back again into humble circumstances which will never satisfy him nor quench his thirst for life and activity. The trend of his ideas has become disastrously pretentious, he has grown away from the circle of peaceful bourgeois life, his interest in his studies in the last months has been equal to zero; all his thoughts and strivings were fixed upon Lord Stanhope, and if the latter leaves him now I am sure the boy will be left unhappy, useless and pitiful, a member of human society that has been severed from every social connection. If it were the essential characteristic of the children of princes to be useless and helpless in private life, certainly Caspar would be an elect among princes. Perhaps, however, fate is still molding him and he will become a man able to win a crown, even though it may not be a royal one. For me the Caspar Hauser incident is now at an end, and whatever the bitterness and disappointment I may have gotten out of it, it has given me an insight into human affairs and human delusions which for the sake of my later years I should not like to have missed. Thus Everyone has to pay in his own manner.

Daumer to President Feuerbach

I feel myself obligated to give Your Excellency an honest picture of the events of the last few days in so far as truth may be drawn from the evidence of one pair of eyes. Perhaps much of what I have to report sounds so unusual that I must ask myself whether a man who has the bad reputation of not being entirely dispassionate is the most suitable person to describe such occurrences. But I have no fear of Your Excellency's severe scrutiny; if I am objective the cause will speak for itself, and my only task is to state the facts in their proper sequence, which, of course, may not always be quite easy.

Four days ago Herr von Tucher called upon me and told me that he was obliged to leave town on account of a death in his family. He had previously asked Herr Binder and myself to assume the supervision of Caspar for as long as the boy would still have to remain in Nurnberg. Since this seemed curious to me, Herr von Tucher allowed me to perceive that the customary disregarding of his official station by those in high places imperatively obliged him to resort to this course. He meant the letter of Your Excellency through which I was, half against my will, moved to seek out Caspar again and to interest myself in him once more. This, Herr von Tucher had taken very badly. I did not give myself the trouble to alter the proud man's point of view; also I am inclined to think to his honor that his behavior was prompted by more serious and human impulses, for when I asked him whether he had given Caspar any hint to expect the arrival of Police Lieutenant Hickel he withdrew into his shell, replying quickly that he wanted to leave this to me since I had a more persuasive manner and Caspar had more confidence in me.

That afternoon I decided to visit Caspar. When I entered his room he was reading the Christian devotions of the day. He looked up cheerfully from his book, gazed into my face and—nothing more curious can be imagined — in an instant his face turned deathly white. I felt a weight on my chest, sat down on a chair and remained silent and anxious. I entirely forgot the role I had assumed, I only felt with him, for I perceived that he had read from my eyes everything that I had to say and why I had come. The unconscious fear must have been slumbering in him, for I cannot explain it in any other natural way; I felt that suddenly the roots of his heart were torn open. He got up and staggered; I tried to hold him up; he was scarcely aware of my presence; he seemed completely stunned. I followed him over to the bed, he threw himself on it, doubled his body up, and began to cry in such a way that it froze the marrow of my bones.

Nothing had yet happened; everything could still go right, so at least I imagined, and uttered a lot of consolations. His weeping lasted for about half an hour. Then he got up, crept into a corner, cowered down and covered his face with his hands. I talked to him incessantly; I don't know any more exactly all I said. Toward six o'clock in the evening I left him and, although up to then he had not once opened his mouth, I thought that he would get over the thing. I told the servant to look after Caspar occasionally and made a tacit resolve to return a few hours later, but it was impossible; my professional work kept me occupied far into the night. When I had left Caspar he was sitting on a bench between the stove and the closet; the next morning I entered his room again at half-past eight, and who can describe my painful astonishment when I saw him in just the same place, in an unchanged position, his hands still pressed against his face, just as I had left him fourteen hours before. The bed was still in the same condition, somewhat disordered from the way he had sunk down upon it; no object had been touched; on the table stood his porridge covered with a thick skin of milk, his evening meal, and next to it a cold cup of breakfast coffee. The atmosphere of the room was sticky and heavy. The servant came and answered my silent inquiry with a shrug of the shoulders. I turned to Caspar himself, I shook him by the shoulder, I seized his ice-cold hands— nothing, no answer, no sound—he continued lifeless, his eyes hardly moved. Another quarter of an hour passed, then, the situation becoming uncanny, I resolved to send for the doctor, perhaps I even murmured something about doing so, in any case Caspar understood what I intended to do, for now he moved, lifted his head as if out of an excavation and looked at me. Oh, what a glance! If I grow as old as Abraham I shall never forget it. He was a different person. Unfortunately, it is not my nature to seize the whole meaning of a situation in a moment. Instead of remaining silent, I began again with my attempts at consolation, but I felt at once that it would be better not to evoke a last glow of hope for this stricken soul. My excuse is that I scarcely knew clearly myself what was going on, and that the crushing effect of something entirely unspoken, which I was the witness of, was more paralyzing and shocking than the knowledge of it. But I will not confuse Your Excellency by observations and shall tell everything correctly in its sequence.

I had already lost too much time. I had to go. After a great deal of trouble I had succeeded in persuading Caspar to lie down a little and he had promised to eat luncheon with us. That was more than I had dared to hope, so, somewhat reassured, I went about my business and got home as usual about half past twelve; we waited some time but Caspar did not come. I supposed that he had fallen asleep, for I had seen that he had not closed his eyes the whole night, and without thinking anything was wrong I returned to the gymnasium at two o'clock, intending to look in at the Hirschelgasse on my way home. I did this; it was half past four and beginning to get dark, when I got to the Tucher House, but how did I feel when the porter told me that Caspar had left the house at twelve o'clock and said he was going to my house. I felt as though I had been struck on the head. In addition to all the responsibility I felt the most well-founded alarm for the boy. I ran home; Caspar had not been seen; I sent my sister to the Mayor, even my old mother went out to inquire among some of the neighbors. During this time I consulted Kandidat Regulein and, as my sister Anna came back quickly and we saw at once from her face that she had not found out anything, it seemed that we should at once inform the police, who in the case of an accident, were also responsible, since they had shown striking negligence in watching the boy of late. I hastily gave a few more instructions and was getting ready to leave when the door opened and Caspar stood on the threshold.

But was it really he? We thought that we beheld a ghost. I am not guilty of exaggeration when I assure you that we were all nearly in tears. Without looking about, without speaking, and with a curious slowness he walked through the room to the table, seated himself on a wooden bench, leaned his chin in his hand and gazed steadfastly and silently into the light of the lamp. We were all three as if bewitched, and my sister as well as the Kandidat confessed to me later that they felt chilled to the heart. Meantime my mother returned; she was the first to walk up to the table and to ask Caspar where he had been. He gave no answer. My sister Anna thought that she could more likely get him to speak; she took his hat from his head, stroked his hair with her hand, and tried in a low voice to draw him out of his brooding. It was all in vain; he gazed constantly at the light, right into the light, his hands spread across his cheek, his chin over his thumb. I approached him quietly and looked at him more closely, but his face betrayed nothing but an immovable, not even painful, but a numb, almost stupid seriousness. My mother continued to urge him to tell us where he had been and how he had come. Then he looked at us all in turn, shook his head and folded his hands imploringly.

We decided among ourselves that Caspar should remain in our house and spend the night there. In order to quiet the excitement about Caspar's disappearance, we at once sent the maid back to the Mayor and to the other people whom we had already disturbed, and my mother went into the kitchen to see about supper, when the Tuchers' servant appeared to inquire whether Caspar was with us, and when we replied in the affirmative, he said that Caspar must go home at once, as Policeman Hickel had come from Ansbach and Caspar must leave with him that night. Such a message was not unexpected, but I was to a certain extent upset that it should come so quickly, and I was thoughtless enough to give the man a sharp answer. If I remember correctly I sent word to the Police Lieutenant to wait a bit; he was not transporting a sack of potatoes, which one could load helter-skelter. My excitement must be comprehensible to anyone who gives fair consideration to the preceding events; but when I thought it over I was angry at my heedlessness and asked Kandidat Regulein to go to the Tucher house and talk to the gentleman from Ansbach and explain matters as diplomatically as possible. That would have been all right, only fate would have it that the Kandidat, who is rather fond of talking and who was glad to have anything with which to entertain the stranger, made haste to tell the Lieutenant the story of Caspar's disappearance, which was the cause later on of a most painful scene.

It was already seven o'clock when supper was placed on the table; the Kandidat had not yet come back; we all took our seats and were once again, as we had been formerly, quite alone with Caspar. But how different were the circumstances and how changed was Caspar! I could not keep my eyes from the boy as he sat there with downcast eyes and toyed listlessly with his porridge. His glance was restless and at times a shudder passed over his frame. I could not spend much time in these considerations, for about quarter past seven the doorbell was pulled with peculiar violence. Anna ran down to open the door and there at once appeared an officer in policeman's uniform, and before he could utter his name I knew who it was. Caspar had been much startled at the loud sound of the bell. I must add that the above mentioned discussion with the servant, as well as the conversation with the Kandidat, had taken place in front of the stairs in the hall and that Caspar had not heard any of it. He got up now and gave a penetrating glance toward the door, and when the police lieutenant came into sight his cheeks again become as deathly pale as on the day before when I had entered his room. When I consider the facts in their connection one with another, I can think of no other explanation than that Caspar from within himself, as if from some inner vision, had guessed what had been going on for the last twenty-four hours and needed no evidence from external events, for he fell into a state of such absorption that I can compare it only with the frightful calm of a sleep-walker. I was by this time so much affected that I am afraid I received Herr Hickel with unfriendly coldness. Fortunately the latter seemed to take no notice of this, and after he had bowed to the ladies, he turned to Caspar and said in a tone of surprise, which, of course, did not sound quite straightforward, "So this is Hauser. Why, he is quite a grown-up person, who can be talked to sensibly." Caspar stared at the man with a dark penetrating glance in which there was not the least trace of melancholy or complaint. There was now a general silence. I considered how I could arrange to have Caspar remain in my house for the night, for to entrust him to a stranger in such a condition seemed inadvisable. I explained the situation frankly to Herr Hickel, he listened quietly, but said that he had definite orders to take Caspar with him at once, there was no time to be lost, his things must be packed, the carriage was already waiting. My sister Anna, who is very impulsive, exclaimed that I should not pay any attention to the man and simultaneously walked up to Caspar as if to protect him. Herr Hickel smiled and said that if we cared so much about postponing matters and we still had something to say to Caspar — and his voice at this point became so insinuating that I became suspicious—that he did not want to be a killjoy but I must promise to bring Caspar to Baron Tucher's house promptly at nine o'clock. Now I lost control of myself and asked whether in heaven's name the matter were so urgent that he must travel at night. Herr Hickel shrugged his shoulders, looked at his watch and answered coldly that

I must decide. Now Caspar began to speak, and, in a voice whose clearness and decision were quite new to me, he said that he wished to go at once. We all saw, however, that he trembled with exhaustion and that his legs could scarcely support him. My mother and sister implored him to remain, Herr Hickel, who had smiled at Caspar's words—oh, I know that smile, how often has it caused me to turn scarlet with shame! —turned to me and said: "Well, then, Professor, at nine o'clock," and turning to Caspar he shook his finger at him and said with a jesting threat: "See that you are prompt, Hauser! And I must know where you loafed about this afternoon. And whatever you do, don't think of lying to me or there will be trouble. I won't stand any nonsense."

Hickel bowed and went out, leaving us in a condition of indignation, doubt and anxiety. The whole thing now looked much worse than our worst fears had led us to anticipate. The last words of the Lieutenant particularly had frightened me and my family. What could we think of Caspar's future, what could we hope for his happiness if threats of such a brutal nature could be made openly? My heart had grown heavy. But there was no time for brooding. I determined to go to the Mayor and consult him. Anna had quickly prepared a bed on the sofa, she led Caspar to it, he sank down; his head had hardly touched the pillow before he was asleep. While I was getting ready to go the bell rang and Herr Binder himself came. I quickly told him what had happened; he was greatly astonished at the procedure of the gentleman from Ansbach, and felt it advisable to speak to him himself, for which purpose he asked me to accompany him. We left Caspar in charge of the women and went to the Hirschelgasse. In spite of the late hour a number of people, principally of the lower classes, who had heard, I don't know how, of Caspar's impending departure, had gathered in front of the Tucher House and expressed their disapproval, some in murmurs, others aloud.

When we opened the door of Caspar's room a remarkable sight met our eyes. The drawers and closets had been completely emptied: underwear, clothes, books, papers, and toys, everything was lying in disorder on the floor and chairs, and Herr Hickel ordered the servant, who had begun to pack, to get the things in any order into a little traveling trunk and chest. When he saw us and read the displeasure in our glances he said smilingly, as if to say something flattering to us, that from now on a new regime would begin for the foundling; now everything would come to light. With a frowning face Herr Binder asked him what he meant, what actually was to come to light, at the same time informing him who he was. Herr Hickel became embarrassed; he uttered some meaningless words to evade making a reply; he said that he was fond of Caspar, that he only cared about saving the young man from false illusions. This made me very angry and I asked who had created and nourished such illusions, if it were not a certain gentleman, who seemed now to be making himself scarce, and who had first dressed up the unsuspecting lad in festive clothes, and when he dared to walk about in them, regarded his action as a dangerous presumption. Take it as one would, such a game was damnable. That was hasty and careless, I admit, but I must add that the policeman's ironic calm irritated me. All the more was I astonished when he agreed with me in every point, but declined to enter into any further discussion and turned again to the servant, urging him to hurry, since he did not want to leave too late at night. Hereupon Herr Binder remarked that the departure might well be postponed until the next day, as Caspar needed rest, and he was prepared to assume the responsibility. Herr Hickel replied that this was impossible; he had strict orders and must insist on his request. We were helpless.

The lieutenant had seated himself on the edge of the table and looked at us in silent sarcastic expectation. Then we heard steps, and when we turned around—the door was open—there stood Caspar and back of him my sister. Anna whispered to me that Caspar had awakened shortly after our departure and had declared that he would go with the strange man and could not be deterred by any objection; so she had accompanied him.

Caspar looked penetratingly about and then, turning to Herr Hickel, he said: "Take me with you, officer; I know where you mean to take me, and I am not afraid." There was in these words, although they were in themselves not peculiar, a remarkable spontaneity and that which one calls "bearing"; and I cannot conceal that they moved me profoundly. I would have given a great deal if I could have had Caspar alone to myself for an hour. The lieutenant did not refrain from showing his pleasure at the unexpected change and answered laughingly: "Come, come, afraid, Hauser, why be afraid! We are not going to Siberia V* Then he walked up to the boy, laid both hands on his shoulders and said: "Now be frank with me, Caspar, and tell me honestly where you kept yourself this afternoon?" Caspar remained silent, then collected himself and replied dully: "I can't tell you." "Why, what does this mean? Come, out with it!" exclaimed the lieutenant, whereupon Caspar said: "I was looking for something!" "Why, what were you looking for?" "A road." "Damn it," exclaimed Hickel, "no play-acting with me and don't try any of your humbugging, or I'll show you where you're at. We, in Ansbach, are not going to be taken in by any of your monkey-shines, let me tell you that."

Herr Binder and I were naturally much incensed at this provocative language. But Herr Hickel did not show any desire to justify himself; he briefly ordered Caspar to get ready, as he was to leave in half an hour. Meantime Baron Scheuerl, Herr Enderlin and other acquaintances of Caspar's, who had heard of his departure, had come to bid him farewell; I had no opportunity to say even three words to him; in a short time we were all gathered in the downstairs hall of the house. The crowd in the street had increased; in the darkness it looked as if all of Nurnberg were assembled. Those standing near uttered threats, and Herr Hickel demanded of the Mayor that he call out the guards, but the latter declared such a procedure to be unnecessary, and, as a matter of fact, his mere appearance was sufficient to restore order.

When Caspar walked up to the steps of the carriage Everyone crowded around him, Everyone wanted to see him once more. The windows of the houses opposite were illuminated and women waved their handkerchiefs. The luggage was strapped on, the coachman cracked his whip—and he was gone.

Convinced that Your Excellency is one of the boy's few honest well-wishers, I felt constrained to inform you accurately of these incidents. It is only a few hours since these events occurred; it is far past midnight; my pen is about to fall from my hand; but I did not dare to allow any time to elapse before writing, in order not to be guilty of misrepresentation owing to an error of memory. Where slander is so tirelessly at work, well-disposed persons must not shun night vigils if they fear that even slumber may cheat them of so much as a single trait in the accuracy of their narrations of their own observations. Perhaps Your Excellency may think that I interpret matters incorrectly, or overestimate their importance. It may be so, but I have in any case discharged my duty and am not conscious of any omission. I am deeply concerned about Caspar, without being able to say exactly why, but I have always been one who sees ghosts and spirits, and my eye perceives the shadows before it takes in the light.

I must not forget to tell you in closing that Herr Tucher, on his last visit, gave me the hundred gold florins which Caspar received as a present from Count Stanhope. I shall send the money to Your Excellency by the next post.

Frau Behold to Frau Quandt

Excuse me, dear Madame, for addressing you in writing, which may seem un peu extraordinaire to you, since I am quite a stranger to you, although you spent your childhood in my parents' house. It is a great *etonnement* to me to hear that Caspar Hauser is to live in your house from now on, and I feel myself impelled to tell you something about the curious fellow. You know of course that Hauser was the wonder child of Nurnberg. Spoiling and coddling came within a hair of making a fool of the boy, for the people here are simply crazy. In this misguided state we took him into our home, out of pure Christian charity, and I swear that this was our sole motive. The rest of the people were still crazy enough to be afraid of the masked man with the ax; we, however, were not afraid, and Caspar was loved and regarded as our own child in our house. We were badly repaid; no gratitude from Hauser and, moreover, the unpleasant talk of his champions. No one has a word to say about the many hours of irritation, and all the trouble which his horrible lying made for us. Afterwards, of course, he would at times promise to improve, and we would take him to our hearts again, but all in vain; the spirit of lying would not be vanquished, and he sank lower and lower into his horrible vice. There has been much talk about his purity of mind and his innocence in all such matters. About this, too, I have something to tell, for I witnessed with my own eyes at the time, how he approached my thirteen-year-old daughter—she is now in Switzerland, in a boarding school — in an improper manner, which could not be misunderstood. When he was taken to task he would not admit it; and in revenge he killed the poor blackbird which I had given him. God grant that you may not have similar experiences with him; he is chuck full of vanity, my dear, full of vanity, and when he pretends to be kind-hearted, the knave is in hiding; and if one crosses him there is an end to his cat-like friendliness. No matter how much ingratitude and calumny we had to bear because of his detestable behavior, no word of complaint passed our lips, and what would have been the use, you could not have believed him then, even if he had told the truth; and he is not a liar, only a poor devil, a poor, miserable devil. I believe that I am doing you and your husband a favor if I lift the cover under which he carries on his mischief. Count Stanhope, who is so kindly disposed towards him, will soon make the discovery that he has nourished a viper on his bosom. If only the Count had come to me, this however that sly boots Hauser prevented and with good reason. Be thoroughly on the alert, my good woman; he has all kinds of ways of being secretive, first here, then there, he hides something in a corner, which does not point to anything good. And now won't you or your husband after a time send me news of how your pupil gets on and what you think of him, for, in spite of all that has happened, he has a little bit of my heart and I only wish that he would work diligently at self-improvement before he enters the great world where he will need far more endurance and strength than in our little world.

Of myself I can't send good news: I am ill, one doctor says it is a growth on the spleen, another calls it *maladie du coeur*. The high cost of living is not calculated to improve one's humor either; however, business is on the whole, good.

Hickel Reports His Execution of the Order of the Transportation of Caspar Hauser

I arrived, as instructed, in Nurnberg on the seventh and went at once to Baron Tucher's house, but did not find the ward at home, being told to .my astonishment that he had wandered around the whole afternoon, no one knew where and why, which is, of course, against the rules. At that time he was at Professor Daumer's, probably intending thereby to delay his departure and obtain the aid of his friends in this effort. For when I spoke to Herr Daumer all kinds of excuses were advanced with this purpose in view. Hauser, too, indulged in some idiotic but quite transparent attempts to flimflam me, which did not prevent me, however, from adhering to the letter of my instructions. A vigorous inquiry as to where he had spent the afternoon remained fruitless; the boy gave the silliest answers in the world. My decisive behavior resulted in their ceasing to talk of a delay; at nine o'clock the carriage was at the house; there was great commotion in the streets, the people, probably secretly instigated, showed signs of insubordination, but were quickly subdued by my threats of calling out the militia. I ordered the coachman to hurry and in a quarter of an hour we were out of the precincts of the city. For three hours, until we reached the village of Grosshaslach, my ward did not utter a syllable, but stared uninterruptedly out into the dark. Certainly he may have been in low spirits, since he must have realized that the end of his illusions of grandeur was at hand. I had ordered the sergeant to meet us in Grosshaslach and while the horses were being fed and watered we went into the room of the post-inn. Hauser lay down at once on the bench by the fire and fell asleep. I could not, however, free myself from the suspicion that he was only pretending to sleep in order to deceive the sergeant and me, and to overhear our conversation. This suspicion was strengthened by the trembling of his eyelids every time I mentioned something not exactly complimentary about his person. In order to get to the bottom of things and to find out the truth with regard to the generally circulated fairy tale about his petrified sleep I resorted to a little ruse. After a while, I gave the sergeant a hint and we got up gently, as if about to leave, and behold! —hardly had we touched the door-handle, than my friend Hauser hurried after us as if stung by a tarantula, behaved as if he were a little confused and disturbed and followed us; we could hardly keep from laughing. In the carriage, Hauser suddenly asked me whether the Count was still in Ansbach; I answered in the affirmative, but added that his lordship would travel into France in a few days, whereupon Hauser uttered a deep sigh. He leaned back, closed his eyes and now really fell asleep, as I could perceive from his deep breathing. The rest of the journey was without noteworthy incident; it was quarter past three and a driving snow when we reached the Star-Inn. This time I had a great deal of trouble in rousing Caspar out of his sleep, and it was only after some energetic shouting on my part that he decided to get out of the carriage. Since only the porter was up, and I did not want to have the Count wakened, we accommodated the young man in a room under the roof. I ordered him to go to bed, and for the sake of safety locked the door from the outside and told my sergeant to remain on guard till the break of day. If, in conclusion, I should give my opinion about the personality and behavior of the ward, I must admit that the young man called forth but little sympathy or pity in me. His reserved, obstinate and secretive personality indicates if not a perverse at least a lazy and obnoxious character. I did not observe any remarkable characteristics about him, except his really remarkable gift of acting, which is putting it mildly. I fear that he will cause some disappointments hereabouts.

Binder to Feuerbach

In order to anticipate all the superfluous gossip and theories which may already have reached Your Excellency on this subject, I am writing to inform you that I already have sufficient disclosures concerning Caspar Hauser's puzzling absence for four or five hours on the last afternoon of his stay in this city. Of course this is not really a disclosure, for the various incidents of his behavior, as already known to me, explain the boy's actions just as little as what he was willing to tell us.

I will state matters briefly. On the morning after Caspar's departure, Hill, the prison warden, came to me and said that Hauser had appeared yesterday afternoon, after one o'clock, and had asked to be shown the room where he had once been imprisoned. It happened that there was no prisoner that day on the Luginsland, and Hill, after some surprised questions and interrogations, had allowed Caspar to enter. After he had stood there sunk in thought for a time, he went into the self-same corner in which his straw bed had once stood and cowered down on the floor and brooded silently. This seemed strange to Hill and since all his attempts to raise the boy from his lethargy were fruitless he returned to his house and told his wife what had happened. She was just considering what to do, when Caspar himself came down the steps and into the little room which was also well known to him from former days, but which he nevertheless scrutinized with a penetrating, thoughtful glance just as he had done above in the cell. Hill and his wife thought that the poor soul had nothing less than lost his wits. The latter approached him and asked him some questions, but did not receive any reply. Then his roving glance fell upon the warden's two children, who were playing together on a step by the window, and suddenly he smiled curiously, approached them, and sat down on the window-step which protruded over the floor.

Hill did the most sensible thing he could have done, he let him be, and waited to see what would happen. After Caspar had seated himself thus he began to stare at the two children in such a way as if he had never seen children in all his life. He bent forward, he literally studied their fingers and their lips; his hungry glance devoured, as it were, their every gesture. The woman became anxious and afraid; it was with difficulty that Hill prevented her from interfering, for he did not fear any harm from the lad. "Why, I know how gentle Caspar is," was how he put it to me. Suddenly Caspar jumped up, stretched out his arms in the air, groaned, stared straight ahead as if he beheld a ghost, then he turned around and ran with surprising quickness to the door and down the steps and out into the square. Hill followed him promptly for he concluded correctly that Caspar was in a dangerous state and should not be left to himself. As he ran down Castle Hill toward Full Street, Hill managed to catch sight of him, and could keep his eye on him.

Caspar now hurried quite senselessly through several streets which ran this way and that, then over the glacis towards the suburb of St. John's on the other side. Hill followed at a distance of about fifty yards and closely watched Everyone of Caspar's movements. Although the boy's course appeared to be purposeless, his steps were as quick, indeed as impatient, as if he were snatching at something that was eluding him. He now went through the Miihlgasse; at the end of this street there is a flat field and the street changes into a path running along the wall of St. John's Cemetery to the Pegnitz and leading to the woods. At the wall of the cemetery, which is so low that a medium sized person can easily look over the top, Caspar suddenly stood still, snatched his hat from his head and pressed his hand against his forehead. Your Excellency will know that once before it was observed that approaching a graveyard had an extraordinary effect upon him. He seemed to tremble, he breathed with his mouth open, his features expressed horror, his skin turned white, it looked as if he could not tear himself away; suddenly, however, he dashed ahead so quickly that his observer had difficulty in keeping up with him, also Hill thought that Caspar must fall into the water, for on the bank of the river he began to stagger in an alarming manner.

    Fortunately, he then turned towards the woods, which were near at hand, and at once disappeared among the branches. Hill was afraid that he might get away; he noticed some workmen who were shoveling sand in a pit and asked them to help him; three or four joined in the hunt and they went separately into the woods, but it was Hill himself, who, after searching for a long time, and having already begun to fear the worst, first caught sight of him again. He perceived him kneeling at the foot of a huge oak, and saw him raise his hands, and heard him exclaim in a voice of passionate entreaty: "Oh, tree, oh, you tree!" Nothing besides these words, but uttered with the feeling with which one says a prayer when one's soul is in direst need. Hill said that he could not bring himself to call to him; altogether the simple man showed a humanity and a delicacy of feeling during the whole procedure to which I feel bound to pay tribute. The workmen whom he had taken with him called to him; he made a sign and they came up; Caspar meantime had started, frightened, he looked at the men one after the other and did not seem to recognize Hill. The latter thanked the men and gave them to understand that he no longer needed them. Hill put his arm around Caspar, who allowed himself to be led out of the woods without resistance, and in contrast to his former behavior he showed complete composure. Hill asked him where he wanted to go and he replied that he must go to lunch at Herr Daumer's. Hill laughed and reminded him that lunch was over long ago. When they reached the city walls it was already getting dark; Caspar now walked with extraordinary slowness, and although Hill should have been at the police station at four o'clock, he accompanied the boy to Professor Daumer's house and did not leave the spot until the door had closed behind his protégé.

    This, Your Excellency, is an accurate record of what the man told me. There is no cause to suspect the trustworthiness of his account, and I have had it entered on the records. As I have said, I don't know what to make of the events themselves, but it is not for me to anticipate Your Excellency's conclusions. Yesterday I had Hill take me to the place where he found Caspar kneeling, for I thought that perhaps there might have been something peculiar about it. It is unusual to find so peaceful a place so near the city; the forest is thick and the silence and loneliness are conducive to a contemplative mood. Hill recognized the place with certainty and as evidence showed the footprints and the moss which had been trodden upon. Beyond this I remarked nothing noteworthy.

The police-soldier whose carelessness in guarding Caspar is responsible for all this has been duly punished.

Lord Stanhope to the Gray One

I am still here in this remote nest, although I wanted to be in Paris at Christmas. I long for free conversation, masked balls, Italian operas and a walk along the boulevards. Here all eyes are fixed upon me; Everyone wants to associate with me. It is said of a certain councilor's family, who are not in the best of circumstances, that they pawned a golden clock, a handsome heirloom, in order to give a soiree in honor of the lord. A lady, Frau von Imhoff — of the old patrician aristocracy—is suspected of intimate relations with me, perhaps only because the poor woman is unhappily married, a situation about which gossip has been thriving for years. Stupid nonsense! I regret to say the lady is perfectly chaste. The rest of the people are scarcely worth talking about. The good Germans are servile to the point of nausea. The portly bureau-heads, who take off their hats to me with slavish respect, would gladly polish my boots if I should order them to do so. Nothing prevents me from playing a kind of Caligula here. To come to business. There is no longer any external reason for my staying here. I have executed that part of my task which has been prescribed up to now. What more is required of me? Of what further acts am I still considered capable? If Your Lordship, or your superior officers, still have confidential wishes, it would be well to express them soon, for the humble writer is "full up." The repast has stuffed him to the gorge, and now he must consider his digestion. I am considering becoming a prelate in Rome, or locking myself up behind the walls of a monastery; I must, however, collect the necessary sum beforehand for an indulgence. If the pope will not hear me, I shall return to the bosom of the Puritan Church, and will at least be saved the trouble and disgust of having to let my beard grow. There are masks in my country, too, and certainly a more dignified costume. Has the retired minister H. in S. been informed of all this and protected against a sudden attack? At what bank can I get my next stipend? Thirty pieces of silver; how often may I multiply the sum? Multiplication, you see, is my law of life. Herr von F. went to Nurnberg a few days ago; for your information. A conscientious raven has fastened his eye upon the document as on a rancid piece of flesh, but it is still inaccessible for the present. How high is the price set and if, in case of war, bolder measures should become necessary, what is to be the emolument of him who would enrich hell with a new vassal? I must know this, for at present even the most puny servants of Satan make their demands. If Herr von F. goes so far as to take up matters with the Queen, as he intends, a suitable representative must be found to put out the fire which he would kindle; of course, in that case the rancid piece of meat would begin to spread its stench. A propos of this, a penetrating passage of Your Honor in your last letter occurs to me; how does it go? "You are beginning, my dear Count, to assign too much worth to what is corrupt and infamous, as soon as it offers even the slightest promise of utility and expediency." Removing unnecessary embellishments, I read as follows: "It is incredible what a rascal you are." Do you know the pretty reply of old Prince M. when the American ambassador called him a liar to his face? "My dear friend," replied the prince, "you simply cannot learn to be moderate in your expressions." Yes, let us be moderate, if not in action then at least in speech. Why such funny language? A scamp is born just as much as a nobleman. Anyone who has the arrogance to meddle in the life and fate of another is a philistine or a fool, or both. Who knows me? Who can judge or shape my character? Does not every breath betray me? Related stars shone over your cradle and mine. You are a faithful servant. That's a very fine excuse. Throw away everything which binds you and fly in solitude to the sea, to the desert, to the North Pole, or to another planet and find out whether you are still able to enjoy the splendor of the sky and the sun's light, and, if that is the case, we will discuss the subject further. Let us take refuge in the night like wolves and collect our strength, for our victim might become able to defend himself.

The person we are ordered to watch has recently given me some cause for anxiety, and I must admit that it is he who still keeps me in this god-forsaken spot. Of course, this is without his knowing it, and he seems quite suspicious to me now; and I seem to myself at times like a deaf musician who is obliged to play on a stopped flute.

However, not only this holds me, but something else besides, with which I do not want to importune your ear, which is not well-disposed toward sentimentality of any sort. In any case, and this is in all seriousness, dismiss me from the arena: I am dazed, I am tired, my nerves no longer obey me, I am becoming old, I am beginning to lose my taste for battles. My opposition is aroused when the frightened rabbit runs of his own accord into the teeth of the fiercest dog; I am too fastidious to find this sort of thing amusing and I could hardly undertake not to cut a breach in the chain of drivers at the last moment, which might help the hunted creature to escape. Then a remarkable metamorphosis might take place, the hare might become a lion and turn on his pursuers, and the blood-thirsty pack would have to retire trembling to their ambush. But do not be afraid, these are the last convulsive twitches and vagaries of a senile conscience. I, too, am a faithful servant—of myself. My job is my master. Our passions are the constables of our souls. Only the thief who has no philosophy in his carcass deserves to be hanged. In my youth I found tears when I looked at the boy playing the guitar in Carpaccio's picture, in Venice; now I should be unmoved to see a baby snatched from its mother's breast and its skull smashed against the curb-stone. This is what philosophy does for one; if it paid better, it might be happier. I must take this opportunity to tell you an amusing dream which I had recently, a real Gorgon of a dream. Both of us, you and I, were bargaining for a certain article, when suddenly you interrupted me with the words: "Take what I offer you, for when you wake up you won't get anything"; this seemed to me a divine argument and so impossible to oppose that, as a matter of fact, I woke up in terror, covered with perspiration.

 Enough, more than enough. My game-keeper will bring you this letter, which will annoy you by its lack of content. The enclosed draft, which I am asking you to sign, will conciliate you even less. I have paid the teacher a half year in advance. He is a man who can be used, as uncorruptible as Brutus and as docile as a gentle horse. Like all Germans, he has principles, which nurse his self-confidence. Greetings to you; night demands its sleep.

16.   Worship Of The Sun

On the morning after Caspar's arrival Stanhope remained in his room longer than usual. He still put off sending for Caspar, taking his daily walk first. When he returned, Caspar was walking up and down outside the drawing-room, he seemed to ignore Stanhope's gesture proffering embrace; he looked stiffly at the floor. They went into the room, his lordship took off his snow-covered fur-coat and asked as nonchalant questions as possible, how Caspar had been, his parting with his friends, and how the trip had proceeded, and more of the same sort. Caspar answered readily, although without going into detail; he was friendly, and not at all oppressed or reproachful. This made Stanhope thoughtful and it required a certain amount of concentration on his part to continue this curiously cold conversation. He could not even suppress a slight terror when he saw that Caspar now observed him constantly, like a stranger, with his wine-colored eyes.

It was a relief when the police-lieutenant was announced. Stanhope received him in the adjoining room; they talked there together in low tones for more than half an hour. After the count had gone out Caspar walked up to the writing-table, took the diamond ring off his finger and laid it with a deliberate gesture on a letter which had been begun; the letter was in English. Then he walked to the window and looked out into the snow.

Stanhope came back alone. He asked whether Caspar knew where he was going to live. Caspar replied that he did. 'We had better go at once to the teacher's in order to look over your future lodgings," said the lord. Caspar nodded and repeated: "Yes, it will be best."

"The distance is not great," said Stanhope. "We can go on foot. But if you prefer, and if you fear the importunities of the people, which you must expect, I can order a carriage."

"No," replied Caspar in friendly tones, "I should rather walk. The people will console themselves when they see that I walk on two legs."

Then Stanhope's glance fell on the ring. Astonished he picked it up, looked at Caspar, looked at the ring again, thought a moment with contracted brows, smiled a quick, savage smile, then he silently put the jewel in a drawer, which he locked. As if nothing had happened, he put on his coat and said: "I am ready."

The commotion in the streets was not very troublesome; everything went off peacefully, the people here were good-natured and shy.

Over the gate of Quandt's house there was a wreath of evergreen, in the middle of which, on a piece of cardboard, was painted the word "Welcome." Quandt came to meet his guests in a roast-brown coat, in Sunday attire; his wife had hung a Scotch plaid shawl over her shoulders in order that her physical condition might be less noticeable.

First they looked at Caspar's little room which was in the upper story. There was an oblique mansard roof on one side, otherwise it looked nice. Over the old fashioned, bright colored sofa there hung a print framed in black. The picture represented an indescribably beautiful girl stretching her arms out with an expression of grief towards someone disappearing into the bushes, whose legs and coat-tails were still visible. On the other wall hung two little covers, on which mottoes were embroidered; on one were the words: "Get up early, go to bed late, what you've lost will be yours again," on the other "Hope is the staff of life from the cradle to the grave." On the window-ledge there were pots with winter plants and the glance traveling over the low roofs could enjoy the sight of a peaceful shut-in landscape, snow-white hills not too far away marking the beginning of the valley.

Caspar, as he looked about, felt very sorrowful. He thought of all his former anticipations now dead and gone, a journey with a far-away goal: the road stretches gayly ahead, clouds part as one nears them, hills move obligingly aside, the air is rich with the songs of foreign parts, woods, meadows, villages and cities glide by in a sun-warmed mist, and beneath the encircling frame of heaven world after world comes forth.

But of all this there was nothing left.

Below, in the living-room, the freshly washed floor-tiles still steamed with dampness. Quandt explained to his lordship the important points of his program. At times he looked at Caspar and his glance was penetrating like that of a marksman who sizes up his target before taking aim.

Stanhope said that he considered himself fortunate in that Caspar was now at last to be given a systematic education; everything up to now had been arbitrary and uncertain. If Herr Feuerbach had not insisted with such determination that Caspar should stay in Ansbach—this was evidently meant as an explanation to the silently listening boy—they would doubtless be in England already, or on the way there. "But since I know him to be in good hands, I am nevertheless glad; one can see from this that even a thing one is compelled to do against one's wishes often has the most fortunate consequences."

His words were dry; it was as if his hat or his stick were talking. The compliment they contained was commonplace, and trite as dishwater. But for Quandt they were heartwarming. He became visibly animated and said eagerly it would be best for Caspar to come that very day. Stanhope looked at Caspar questioningly; the latter sunk his head, whereupon his lordship forced himself to smile indulgently. "We won't rush things," he said. "I'll have the luggage sent over to-morrow morning. I'll still keep him with me today."

It had become dark when they both left the house. Quandt accompanied them to the street. When he came back he closed the door very quietly and slowly, as he always did, then he stood in the middle of the room, laid both hands flat against his breast and shook his head at least a quarter of a minute in silent astonishment.

"Why are you shaking your head so?" asked Frau Quandt.

"I don't understand, I don't understand," answered the teacher anxiously and wandering about as if he were looking for something on the floor.

"What don't you understand?" asked his wife, with irritation.

Quandt pulled up his chair and sat down next to his wife and looked at her steadily out of his pale eyes before he continued: "Did you perhaps notice anything remarkable about that person? Tell me frankly, dear Jette, did you notice anything, anything in the least extraordinary, anything which at all differentiates him from other people?"

Frau Quandt laughed. "I only noticed that he was not particularly polite and that he wears silk stockings like a marquis," she replied lightly.

"Yes, just so, not particularly polite and silk stockings, quite right," said Quandt with peculiar haste as if he were on the track of a discovery. "Well, we'll break him of the silk stockings and that smart little vest too. Such things are not appropriate in our modest home. But I ask you: do you understand people? do you understand the world? For years we have been hearing of him as such a wonder as has never been seen before. This is what intellectual men, men of taste, men of the world, scholars, have been getting excited about! Is it comprehensible? Isn't there anyone who can see with the eyes God has given us to see with? Can it be understood?"

Meantime Caspar and Stanhope had returned to the inn. Stanhope was not exactly in good spirits. The silence of his companion angered him; he felt as if a pistol were being aimed at him from behind a curtain.

He was troubled; he felt driven into a corner. There is a point where individual destinies meet on a narrow plank spanning an abyss and where a settlement must be made; then words suddenly break forth, the demons wake from their slumber.

Stanhope rang for the butler, ordered the candles lit and wood put on the fire. Immediately afterwards, Hofrat Hofmann was announced; his lordship said that he could not receive him and gave orders that no one was to be admitted. He began to straighten his papers and while doing so asked Caspar: "How did you like the teacher and his wife?"

Caspar did not quite know and gave an uncertain answer. As a matter of fact he no longer knew what Herr Quandt and his wife looked like. He only remembered that Frau Quandt had drunk her coffee from a saucer and had bitten off her sugar, which had seemed stupid to him.

Suddenly Stanhope turned around and asked with the manner of a person who is becoming impatient: "Well, what about the ring? What did you mean by that?"

Caspar did not reply; with disconsolate obstinacy he stared into vacant space. Stanhope walked up to him, put a finger on his shoulder and said sharply: "Speak, or you'll be sorry!"

"I am sorry enough as it is," replied Caspar monotonously; and his glance descended from the figure of the Count, as from some slippery object, to the dark red carpet upon which the fire in the chimney was painting shadows.

What could he have said? For his feeling was almost unchanged towards him who had shown him the way, who had for the first time talked to him like a human being. Should he tell of the frightful night in the Tucher House, when he had sat with his fists against his breast, his heart torn, lonely and robbed of a world? How he had begun to look and look, how he had dug up time, as one digs up earth in a garden, how day had come and he had slipped away, how he had seen children, how he had seen the river, and had knelt down before a tree, everything as it had never been before, everything different, himself changed, having new eyes, freed from uncertainty — Impossible to tell such things; there were no words for them.

He continued to stare into space while Stanhope, his hands on his back, walked up and down and began to talk hastily, against his will, in sudden gusts. "Do you perhaps wish to complain? Shall I justify myself? God damn it, I have fought for you like my own flesh and blood, pawned my fortune and my honor, have shunned no humiliation, struggled with pedants and the common herd, what more? Anyone who asks the impossible of me is not my friend. There are still many days to come; the thread has not yet run out. I am still ready to do my share, but I cannot allow you to take me by the letter of the law like an underwriter of a bill of exchange and place my happy generosity under moral pressure. If you make demands upon me instead of being grateful for what has been done, then we must part."

What a lot he is talking, thought Caspar, who was scarcely able to follow.

Stanhope's next thought was that Caspar had perhaps some secret connection whence he had received information and encouragement, for he saw clearly and recognized with anxiety that the boy before him was no longer the former creature, devoid of any will power. But Caspar met his roughly uttered question with such an astonished face that he dropped his suspicion at once. Caspar pressed his hands flat together and said, with an attempt to be clear, that he had not wanted to offend Stanhope in any way, not with the ring either, only something had happened in regard to all these stories; he had always been told stories, stories of himself; he had listened, but he had never clearly understood. It had been as in the case of the wooden horse, with which he had played in his prison, and which nevertheless had not been alive. "But now," he added hesitatingly, "now the little wooden horse has become alive."

Stanhope threw back his head. "How? What do you mean?" he asked quickly and fearfully; "speak plainly." He took his lorgnette and looked frowningly at Caspar through his glasses, a gesture intended to express haughtiness, but which was really only embarrassment.

"Yes, the little wooden horse has become alive," repeated Caspar portentously.

Doubtless he thought with this childlike symbol that he had explained all that the unveiling of the past had revealed to him. Perhaps he had a dim foreboding of the forces which had shaped his destiny; in any case he understood the reality, the reality of his long imprisonment with its dark and heavy causes, which had placed him outside the pale, which had condemned him to remain half an animal till well into his youth. Perhaps it had become clear to him that it was a question of something which had in the eyes of the world a higher, indeed the highest, value, that his claim to this something continued unimpaired and that if he only went and showed that he was alive and said that he knew, all resistance and choice would be at an end and he might possess that of which he had been criminally deprived.

That was approximately the situation, but there was something more. And it was fitting that his lordship, anxious for himself and for those under whose orders he stood, anxious for the future and for the whole structure which he had helped to erect, and which if it collapsed would necessarily plunge him, perhaps with broken limbs, into a deep abyss, that he himself should find and utter the words which would illuminate this other, greater, unutterable thing for Caspar, fearfully, and with malignant magic.

Stanhope almost felt himself undone; he had little desire left to struggle against a power which seemed to have grown out of nothing and which like Ifrid emerging from Solomon's magic flask overcast the whole sky. I was too generous, thought he, I was too half-hearted. One pays for indecision with one's own skin; if one lets dreamers grow up they snatch at the reins and frighten the horses; sweets no longer taste good, now I must put salt into the porridge.

He sat down at the table opposite Caspar and, speaking through scarcely opened teeth, with a somber and vacant smile, he said: "I think I understand you. One cannot take it amiss if you drew certain inferences from the stories which I told you, I confess, somewhat indiscreetly. I shall now, however, go further and not leave you anything more to desire in point of clearness. I will put the bit and bridle on the wooden horse which has become alive, and if you like, so far as I am concerned, you may ride it. I did not deceive you: by right of inheritance you are the equal of the mightiest princes; you are the victim of the most infernal plot which Satan's deviltry ever conceived. If you had no other judgment to fear but that of virtue and moral right, you would not be sitting here and I would not be forced to warn you as I am doing. Just in the same measure as your demands and hopes are well founded, just so dangerous must they become if you take the slightest step toward the goal in question. The first act, the first word seals your death irrevocably. You will be destroyed before you have stretched out your finger to take what belongs to you. Perhaps a time will come, to-morrow, or in a month, or in a year, when you may doubt the honesty of what I am saying to you, but I beseech you, believe me. Let your lips be seven times sealed. Fear the air and fear sleep lest they betray you. It is possible that a day may come when you may be that which you are, but until then keep still, if life is dear to you, and keep your little wooden horse in its stable."

Caspar had slowly gotten up. An overpowering fright thundered about him like the bellowing of a waterfall. In order to distract his thoughts he stared with an attention bordering upon insanity at lifeless objects—the table, the closet, the chairs, the chandelier, the plaster figures on the chimney, the crooked poker. Was all this new to him or only unexpected? Not at all. Like an atmosphere envenomed it had been circulating around him for a long time. But it was one thing to suspect and sense a thing, and another to know with grinding certainty.

Stanhope, too, had gotten up. He walked up close to Caspar and continued with a curious nasal voice: "There is no help for it; you were born under this star, your mother bore you under this star.

It is in the blood. It judges you and justifies you; it is your guide and your seducer."

And after a while he said: "Now let us go to bed; it is late. To-morrow morning we will go to church and pray. Perhaps God will send us some light."

Caspar seemed not to hear. Blood! That was the word. That was the strength which penetrated all the pores of his being. Did not his blood cry out and was not the cry answered from afar? Blood was the foundation of all creation, hidden as it was in veins and in rocks, in leaves and in the light. Did he not love himself in his blood, was he not aware of his own soul as a mirror of blood in which he could rest and contemplate himself? How many people in the world so near to one another, so rich in movement, so strange and silent and all wandering through a stream of blood, and yet his own blood sounding differently, a peculiar thing, flowing in a lonely channel, full of secrets and full of an unknown destiny?

When he turned his eyes again towards the count it seemed as if the latter were walking in blood, a conception which was of course favored, or perhaps caused, by the scarlet color of the rug. When the candles are put out, thought Caspar, everything will be dead, blood and words, he and I; I shall not sleep to-night, not die. Yes, Caspar would gladly have swallowed again the words his mouth had uttered, he would gladly have locked them again in the prison of his body which enjoined silence. To be obedient, to be uncertain, to be unhappy, to bear shame and opprobrium, to stifle the voice of his blood, only not to have to die, to live, live, live! Oh, he will be afraid, he will be as cowardly as a mouse, he will bolt doors and windows, he will forget his dreams, he will forget his friend, and he will become insignificant, and bury the wooden horse, but only live, live, live—

His lordship wanted Caspar to sleep downstairs instead of in his mansard room in the teacher's house. He ordered the attendant to make a bed on the sofa. While Caspar was undressing he went out, but came back after a time, convinced himself that the boy was quiet and put out the lights. He left the door communicating with his room open.

Heedless of his resolution Caspar quickly fell asleep with all of his stirred up emotions. After he had slept four or five hours his leaden rest changed into a restless tossing about. Suddenly he woke up with a deep sigh, and stared into the darkness with burning eyes. There was a crackling and a fumbling at the window-pane which proceeded from the snow beating against it, and which resembled the light tapping of a hand. From the next room he heard Stanhope breathing evenly in his sleep; the breathing of another person in the night sounded most strange, like a threatening whisper: take care, take care!

He could no longer bear to lie in bed. He felt as if his body were bound with a thousand threads, and when he got up it was only to assure himself that he could still move freely. He wrapped the woolen blanket around his shoulders, and walked barefoot to the window.

The whole great world was full of the words which had been spoken, and which hung like red berries in the dark. Everywhere danger; merely to think was dangerous.

He began to tremble, his knees were loose in their sockets; he felt simultaneously light and oppressed. His thinking had another and closer consequence; all other objects were nearer, and the whole of the earth, and of heaven, clouds and wind and night, had lost something, something incomprehensibly temporary and changeable. Caspar holds the broken bits of a beautiful vase in his hand, and his fantasy will not even recreate the beautiful form as it once was.

Below, in the street, the night-watchman walks silently. The moving shimmer of his lantern gilds the snow. Caspar's glances follow him, for it seems as if the man was in some incomprehensible way connected with his destiny. They wander together over the snow-covered fields. The former asks Caspar whether he is cold and throws a part of his coat over his shoulders, so that they both are walking under the same covering. Suddenly Caspar is aware that it is not the face of a man which is turned towards his with such a mild and pitying expression, but the beautiful sad face of a woman. This sadness and this beauty have an articulate quality, and that they should walk thus under the same coat has the very deepest significance, something that is at once joy and pain, and which springs from the beginning of things.

Then the tremendous words of the count sounded in the night with a new meaning. "Under this star your mother bore you." Bore you! What a sound! What was not contained in that word! Caspar placed his two hands over his face. He was dizzy.

Then he heard the sound of steps. He turned around; suddenly, as if emerging from dark waters, the count stood before him in a dressing gown. Probably Caspar's being awake had roused him, for he was a light sleeper. "What are you doing?" asked Stanhope irritably.

Caspar came a step nearer to him and said urgently, breathlessly, at the same time threatening and entreating: "Take me to her, Heinrich! Let me see my mother once, not now, perhaps later; once, only once, only let me see her once."

Stanhope drew back. This cry had something unearthly in it. ""Patience," he murmured, "patience."

"Patience? How much longer? I have been patient a long time."

"I promise you— "

"You promise, but shall I believe you?"

"Let us set the period of a year."

"A year is long." "Long and short. One little, short year and then— "

"Then?"

"Then I will return—"

"And fetch me?" "And fetch you."

"Do you swear to?" Caspar fastened a searching glance like a slowly dying fire on the count. The reflection of the snow illuminated the night so that each could see the other's features clearly.

"I swear it."

"You swear it, but how can I know?"

Stanhope became peculiarly embarrassed. This face-to face discussion at such an hour, the constantly increasingly masterful and violent questioning of the boy worked upon his imagination like ghastly apparitions. "Cast me out of your heart if I don't come," he murmured in hollow tones; at this moment he was suddenly forced to think of the man who was thrown alive by the devil into the fiery crater of Vesuvius.

And Caspar hereupon: "How can that help me? Tell me the name, tell me her name, tell me my name."

"No, never, never, but only believe me. There is a God who watches over you, Caspar. Nothing can be denied to you, for you have paid the purchase-money for your happiness in advance, which we others are obliged to pay piecemeal day by day. And we must pay, pay for everything; that is the meaning of life."

"So you promise to be back in a year?"

"In a year."

Caspar dug his fingers into Stanhope's hand and fixed a deep, extraordinarily soulful, extraordinarily proud glance on Stanhope, who slowly lowered his eyes, while his face looked old and stone like. When he returned to his room he suddenly began to repeat the Lord's prayer in low tones.

It was morning before he fell asleep again. When he got up at noon, Caspar had been up a long time; he was sitting at the window, apparently studying the frost-flowers.

At one o'clock he left the hotel with him. Arm in arm, a spectacle for the inhabitants, they walked through the deep snow, through the Herrieder Gate to the market place. There was a big gathering of peasants and traders. Before the entrance to the Gumbertus Church, Stanhope stopped and suggested to Caspar that they go in. The latter hesitated, but nevertheless followed the count into the high, plain building with its dark raftered ceiling.

With quick steps Stanhope hurried to the altar, threw himself upon his knees on the stone steps, bent his head and remained so, completely motionless.

Caspar, painfully moved, looked involuntarily around to see whether there was any witness to this abject behavior. But the church was empty. Why does he crouch together so, he thought, much upset, God cannot be in the floor. Gradually he became fearful; the silence of the immense room penetrated into his breast. And as he looked up, he saw the sun through an open vaulted window, trying hard to conquer the wintry fogs. Then his pale face blushed with timid joy and the silence in his heart changed into an uplifting worship.

"Oh, Sun," he said half aloud, and with innocent intensity, "do see that everything shall not be as it is. Make things different, Sun. You know how things are; you know who I am. Do shine constantly, Sun, so that I may see you all the time, my eyes want to see you always."

While he was talking thus a golden wave of light streamed over the chalk-white flagging, and Caspar was content, for he thought that the sun had thus answered him in its own way.

17.   Some Points About Herr Quandt As Well As About A Lady As Yet Unknown

Caspar's removal to the teacher's house was effected without incident.

"Well now, Hauser," said Quandt, during their first meal together, while the soup was being served, "a new life is beginning for you. I hope it will be an industrious one and full of the fear of God. If we occupy ourselves worthily and think of our Saviour at all times, our earthly endeavors will always be crowned with success."

After lunch Quandt was obliged to go to school, and when he returned at four o'clock he inquired eagerly what Caspar had done in the meantime. His wife could only give him an insufficient reply, and he scolded her for this. "We must be watchful, dear Jette, we must keep our eyes open."

And actually Quandt did keep his eyes open. Like an indefatigable bookkeeper he established an account in his memory in which he noted every word and action of his pupil. In this assiduous business it soon became evident that debit and credit did not balance and that the scale of indebtedness gradually outweighed the credit scale to an alarming extent. This honestly distressed the teacher, but there was a secret little corner in his heart where he rejoiced.

For this man was so constituted that he lived a peculiar double existence. One part of him was for the public: the citizen who paid his taxes, the colleague, the head of a family, the patriot; the other part was, as it were, Quandt himself. The former was a pattern of virtue, an exhibition gallery of all the finer qualities; the latter lay in hiding in a quiet corner and watched God's beautiful world slyly. The public person, the citizen, the patriot took a warm interest in matters concerning the general welfare, whereas Quandt himself rubbed his hands with pleasure when something went wrong

Some Points About Herr Quandt As Well As About A Lady As Yet Unknown

somewhere: whether it were an unexpected death, or a broken leg, or the compromising of a worthy employee, or some theft from a society's funds, the damaged wheel of a post-carriage, some small fire on the property of any rich farmer, or the scandalous marriage of Countess Blank with her stable-boy. No matter how scrupulously the taxpayer, the head of the family, the colleague performed his duties, Quandt himself had something of the revolutionary about him, and was always on the spot to pick flaws in the way the world was run, and always careful that no one should obtain more honor than an accurate balancing of his merits and shortcomings, his virtues and his vices, could demand. The citizen Quandt seemed content with his lot; the man Quandt felt himself constantly imposed upon, offended, slapped in the face, deprived of his inviolable rights.

One would suppose that it would be difficult to keep house with two such different lodgers under the same roof. Nevertheless the two Quandts got along excellently together. Of course, jealousy is a dangerous animal, and it sometimes penetrated the wall separating the two souls. Just as sometimes the strongest dam is not sufficient to prevent a devastating flood, so envy at times broke into the orderly and well-cultivated fields of the God-fearing, philanthropic Quandt.

And what a lot there was in the world for the sly monster to batten upon! Now someone had received a decoration who all his life had sat loafing by the fire, then someone inherited ten thousand thalers who could afford to eat patties and drink Moselle twice a week without this new bequest; again someone was praised in the newspapers without anyone's being able to ascertain why he should deserve such recognition. Or someone or other had made a discovery which one could easily have made oneself if one had merely happened to interest oneself in the same subject. Why he? Why not I? brooded Quandt in secret revolt. There was a constant and invisible struggle with fate, the slogan of which was: Why he, why not I?

Perhaps poor Quandt suffered from his heredity; his father had been a clergyman, on his mother's side he sprang from peasants. He had in him much of the peasant and much of the clergyman. His thoroughly earthy desires were steeped in theology. At the same time the peasant was constantly troubling the clergyman, for where had one ever heard of a religious and peaceful disposition which was revengeful, envious and ambitious? Quandt loved truth above all things, he stated so, he protested that it was so and so indeed so it was. Evidently nothing was sufficient for him; the account was never correct; the sums never tallied; everywhere people had added falsely or altered the tense. He said and maintained that he had never in his life lied. A thing to be marveled at; and actually it was a fact which could be proved that he had quarreled for good with an intimate friend, the only one he had ever had, a young school teacher in Tauberbischofsheim, because he had caught him in a lie.

How helpless must Caspar be in the face of such a combination of extraordinary and excellent qualities as the better nature of the teacher presented! For us, for the reader and me, it is an easy game and we cannot be deceived, for us the raiment has been cast aside and the skin over the heart is transparent; we are on a watch-tower, we are observers and humorists. We follow Herr Quandt when he enters a grocery-store and with polite gravity orders half a pound of cheese, at the same time observing and jotting down in his memory the purchases of his fellow human beings with eager restless eye, whether they be cooks or generals. We hear him talking with Herr Kakelberg, the inspector of schools, and expressing regret over the increasing demoralization of the school children; we see him every Sunday morning washed, brushed and combed, hurrying to church and modestly opening his prayer-book; we know that he is respectful towards his superiors, and severe towards his inferiors, for his consciousness of what is due to both suffers from no doubts. But we know, too, that every night before retiring he sits in his shirt on the edge of his bed, remembering with somber mien that Hofrat Hermann greeted him very casually today, and with regret we recognize the fact that he punishes his pupils severely —of course, only the lazy and obstinate ones—with a carefully dried Spanish rattan. Unfortunately, too, we must add that he does not always treat his good-natured wife with the same consideration and delicacy which he shows to straners who, according to their observations, are forthwith of the opinion that this marriage is a shining example of an excellent understanding between man and wife.

So for Caspar, who has naturally not the advantage of our omniscience and omnipresence, Herr Quandt was a dark and joyless, but nevertheless a thoroughly imposing figure. He did feel a little overpowered every time that Quandt spoke to him in remarkably searching tones, with his eyes constantly upon him. At first he felt oppressed in this narrow domesticity, in which one could scarcely be alone with one's own thoughts, and the only consolation was that the count, who should have left early in December, was still in the city. Stanhope stated that he had to wait for important letters; as a matter of fact he was waiting for President Feuerbach's return, for he was as anxious about the man's doings, and the reasons for his absence, as a traveler about a threatening storm.

Caspar, too, kept him, and that in his own way. He was in the habit of calling for the boy every afternoon and of taking him to walk for an hour or an hour and a half; they usually went along the road to the Schlossberg, and towards the Bernadotte Valley, which lay in fair seclusion like a beautiful portal to the surrounding dark and far-reaching woods. Caspar derived much benefit from the exercise in the cold, usually clear and frosty air.

Their conversations always turned from some irrelevant personal matter to more general topics, where speech was without danger; and nevertheless both the didactic and the narrative elements had the charm of gracious intimacy. This seemed to be the result of an agreement, a declaration of peace with regard to a dimly felt change which would necessarily destroy the past beauty of their relationship entirely. So they walked along, viewing matters like friends in a region which was unfamiliar to their destinies, honestly attached to one another, compensating for the difference in their years by the willingness of one to give and the equal readiness of the other to receive.

Lord Stanhope found himself greatly attracted, indeed literally captivated, by this form of intercourse. He could feel himself once again at ease, without any yoke, not urged on to a preconcerted goal; he could rest within himself, watching and seeing, not without sorrow, how life had lodged within his breast and what had been left of it for the random play of the spirit, which is the true quality by which man recognizes man. He passed over the depths of his being as over a frail bridge which the slightest puff of wind may hurl into the abyss below.

He liked best to talk about human destiny and human affairs; he told how one person had begun life and how another had ended it, what had made trouble for one man and had helped another to recognition, how he had seen one person at the height of his fortunes, feasting at a king's board, and how two years later the same man had died miserably in an attic. Conditions on this earth were uneven; flowers bloomed on heights difficult to scale, nothing was certain, nothing dependable. Certain rules which the individual had to comply with in his acts must not go unobserved. Stanhope mentioned the book of Lord Chesterfield, an ancestor and distant connection, who had given excellent advice in his famous letters to his son. He could repeat whole pages of these by heart. The same Chesterfield, in order to deride the pride of ancestry, had hung two pictures in his castle, a naked man and a naked woman, and had written underneath them: Adam Stanhope, Eva Stanhope.

The count often expressed great surprise at discovering how clever Caspar was, in spite of his silence and simplicity; his replies were always to the point, and worldly in spirit; his questions and answers were always at first hand; he readily grasped opposing details and united them with delicate imagination.

A change came suddenly. An unimportant incident brought it about.

One day, on their return towards the city, Stanhope was calling attention to the great profit that might accrue to a man's inner development if he did not permit events to flow by lightly, but tried to utilize them for his moral training by enriching his memory as he set them down in writing or stated them verbally. Caspar asked just what he meant. Instead of an answer the count, who had long been uneasy on this subject, replied with the watchful counter-question of whether Caspar still kept a diary.

Caspar replied in the affirmative.

"And will you not some time read me some of it?"

Caspar became frightened, thought for a moment, and answered hesitatingly that he would do so.

"Well, let us take advantage of the hour and set about it at once." said Stanhope. "I only want a general idea and am curious how you go about such a thing."

When they reached the house, Stanhope accompanied Caspar to his room and, expecting that the promise would be carried out, seated himself on the sofa. The fire was crackling in the stove, outside there had been a strong wind since noon, dusk was falling, the hills were covered with purple.

Caspar busied himself with his books, but minute after minute passed without his showing any sign of doing what Stanhope expected.

"Well, Caspar," the count finally exclaimed with impatience, "I am ready."

Then Caspar shook himself and said he could not do it.

Stanhope stared at him; Caspar's eyes dropped. His diary was hidden among a lot of other things; it was inconvenient to get at it, he murmured hesitatingly!

"Ah, so," replied the lord and laughed almost soundlessly through his nose. "How quick you are in finding excuses, I should not have thought that you were so quick in finding—pretexts. What a shame!"

At this moment there was a knocking and scraping at the door, the count answered and Quandt's figure sidled slowly into the room. He behaved as if he were astonished to find the count still there and asked whether he would care for some light refreshment. His lordship silently declined and kept his eyes on Caspar.

Quandt noticed at once that something was going on. He inquired whether his grace had reason to be dissatisfied with Caspar. Stanhope replied that he certainly had cause to be angry and in a few words he told the teacher what it was all about. Then he turned to Caspar saying loudly and pointedly: "If you did not intend from the beginning to take me into your confidence you should not have promised to do so. And if you regretted your promise you might properly have asked to be released from it. But instead of that to take refuge in such a"—after an eloquent little pause —"subterfuge, that seems to me to be unworthy of both of us."

He got up and left the room. Quandt followed him; downstairs in the hall he remained standing and asked the teacher brusquely whether in the time that had elapsed he had been able to form an opinion of Caspar's abilities and good will.

"I was most respectfully just about to request your lordship to grant me a quarter of an hour to discuss this question." replied Quandt. He took a little oil lamp from a nail, and bowed his lordship into his study. While Stanhope seated himself in a leather chair, with one leg crossed over the other, gazing boredly into space, Quandt collected his note books and said that from the first day he had gone about matters thoroughly with Caspar; he had dictated to him, he had had him read and do arithmetic, had asked him many questions in German and Latin grammar, in the most cursory manner, just for the sake of getting a general impression.

"And the result?" asked Stanhope, his nostrils expanding with *ennui*.

"The result? Unfortunately pretty unfavorable, unfortunately."

It must have been painful for Herr Quandt, for this "unfortunately" was uttered with deep feeling. It must have been painful to him that Caspar's handwriting left so much to be desired: "There is nothing free and flowing in his handwriting, and with spelling he is not on the best of terms," he said. It must have been painful for Herr Quandt that a person should not in all cases know the dative from the accusative: "He has not the slightest conception of the functional significance of the subjunctive," said Quandt, and he continued: "He is not unskillful in the use of language, indeed in this point he surpasses his general level of education. He is sufficiently familiar with sentences and sentence structure to know how to use the period, the colon, quotation marks, question and exclamation points correctly, and he even is sometimes right in his usage of the semicolon, which linguistic specialists use so diversely."

Certainly a ray of light! On the other hand, arithmetic, woe is me: He had not yet fully mastered the four fundamental operations with ordinary integers. "A zero now and again becomes for him an unconquerable obstacle," said Quandt. "The theory of fractions and the rule of three, as well as simple and compound proportions, are a hopeless muddle. Curiously enough he works hardest at just these things," said Quandt.

"How do you explain that?" asked his lordship with the curiosity of a sleeper whose feet are being tickled.

"I explain it thus: every example represents for him a unit by itself. He always enjoys and wishes to create such a unit, and it gives him pleasure to see it in finished form. What takes a long time, however, arouses his dislike and can even drive him to all sorts of untruthful excuses. He also shows irritation to the point of fury if he has calculated wrong in a simple example and cannot find the errors due to his own carelessness."

On and on: History, geography, painting, drawing. So far as history is concerned, Quandt has never seen such a degree of indifference in any person, either in regard to the history of his own country, or towards the facts of general history, towards monarchs, towards statesmen, towards battles, revolutions, heroes and explorers. "Only an anecdote charms him, a little story, and you can win him. Sad! Geography! He does not feel at all at home on this globe," said Quandt. "He is often wool gathering. He does not pay attention. The Nurnberg enthusiasm about his marvelous memory is a puzzle to me, my lord, a complete puzzle."

My lord had had enough. About painting and drawing my lord did not care to hear. He interrupted the teacher, who wanted to show him some specimens, remarking that instruction in these subsidiary branches seemed to him desirable indeed, but that he did not attach great importance to it.

"Desirable, certainly," replied Quandt, "and the desirable should certainly be cultivated. The soul of a man is like a cultivated garden in which the beautiful and the useful may flourish side by side. I believe the strongest spur for Hauser is his vanity. If one knows how to satisfy his vanity one can induce him to do anything. One more question, my lord, have you any particular wishes about his religious instruction? I have already talked to the clergyman, Herr Fuhrmann, who has offered to give Caspar a lesson twice a week. I have already started going through the Bible with him."

Stanhope had no objection, he wanted to get away; but stammering with embarrassment, Quandt now brought up the question of the cost of Caspar's maintenance; his wife was worrying him about the increasing cost of living. Stanhope, like a grand seigneur, briefly granted an increase; it was agreed that Caspar should have lunch for twelve and supper for eight cents.

In order to erase the unpleasant impression of this discussion, which shamed and humiliated him, Quandt expressed the wish to send his lordship, after his departure, periodic reports on Caspar's progress. Stanhope, already completely submissive, left this to Quandt's discretion. "It would be advisable," suggested Quandt, "to regard Caspar's letters to you also in the light of exercises in style. I could without changing the thought correct the chief mistakes and write my criticisms underneath in red ink. In this way you would constantly have a picture of what he was doing at the time."

This idea seemed incomparable to Stanhope. They walked into the hall; Quandt again preceded, with the oil lamp. Suddenly he stepped back and lifted the lamp high. On the staircase stood a dark figure. It was Caspar.

Aha, he has been listening to us, went through Quandt's head. He turned around and looked meaningly at Stanhope.

Caspar walked up to Stanhope and in a voice full of emotion asked him to come up to his room again. The count answered coldly that he had little time, Caspar should express his request here. Caspar shook his head. Stanhope thought that Caspar had changed his mind for the better, he pretended that it cost him some overcoming of himself to grant Caspar's wish; then he went up the staircase with small steps as if counting them. Quandt, without being asked, followed and remained standing, a silent witness, at the door.

Caspar said that he would gladly show Stanhope his diary, but he would please promise not to read any of it. His lordship folded his arms across his chest. This was becoming too much for him. But he answered with the calm of complete self-control. "You will certainly believe that I will not interfere with your private affairs without your permission."

Caspar opened the drawer of a bureau and lifted the corner of a silk cloth under which the blue copybook lay. The count approached and looked in silent astonishment first at the book, then at Caspar. "What a childish ceremony," he said gloomily. "I had not expressed the slightest desire to see your paper treasure. I understood that you wanted to read to me from it. Please spare me any fooling."

Quandt too had walked up and measured the mysterious book with doubtful glances. Caspar meanwhile, while his lordship silently left the room, looked straight ahead with a wry, thoughtful Chinese glance, a look of absorption and of something beyond this world, like certain heads on very old pictures.

"If I may with due deference express my opinion," said Quandt, who had accompanied the count to the gate, "I must admit that I do not believe in the diary. I don't think that a character like Hauser would find the inspiration within himself to write a diary. I can't help it, my lord, I don't believe in it."

"You think that he was showing us blank paper?" replied Stanhope brusquely.

"Not that, but—"

"What then?"

"Why, one must look into the matter, one must pay some attention to it, one must see what is behind it."

Stanhope shrugged his shoulders and left. He had hoped to hear something about himself from the boy's writing. This was enticing; he knew that there he stood on a high pinnacle, and that he had been adored. It is a fine feeling to be adored, no matter how little resemblance to a god one may have, and even though the picture of god-head had fallen from its pedestal, a charming romance might still cling to the fragments. This was enticing. With regard to what might betray him in the book he did not think, he did not care to think; let the constables settle that.

Nevertheless the next afternoon he called at the teacher's house, went up to Caspar's room and briefly and sharply told the boy to give him the letters which he had written to him at Nurnberg during their separation. Caspar obeyed without questioning. There were only three letters, one being the dangerous, gossiping one which the count had reason to be afraid of; they lay in gold paper in a case of their own. Stanhope counted them, put them into his breast-pocket and then said in a somewhat gentler voice: "Call for me this evening at eight at the hotel. We are invited to Frau von Imhoff's pavilion. Dress well."

Caspar nodded.

Stanhope walked to the door. His hand on the handle of the door, he turned around once more. "I leave to-morrow." In the twitching of his mouth there was satiety and disgust. He was suddenly disgusted with this city, disgusted at its people, disgusted at something which seemed to him like a hostile demoniacal face which he saw hanging above him in the air and which he hoped to escape from by the speed of his horses. He had given up waiting for the President, for Feuerbach had written his acting substitute that he would not come until after New Year's Day.

"Tomorrow already," murmured Caspar sadly; and after a pause he added shyly: "but what we have agreed upon holds?"

"What we have agreed upon holds." The party at the Imhoff' was at the same time a party in honor of the count's departure. The guests were President Mieg, Hofrat Hofmann, Director Wurm, General-Kommissionar Stichaner with his wife and daughters, and several other society notables; all came in gala array. There was great interest in Caspar's first appearance in their society.

His bearing did not disappoint them. He was feted and surrounded. They paid him compliments, the most ridiculous compliments, praised his small ears and narrow hands, were of the opinion that the scar on his forehead, from the wound the masked man had inflicted, made his face interesting. They expressed astonishment at his conversation and at his silence, and thought that all this would delight Stanhope who did not feel himself bound to observe more than a cold politeness and met the extreme enthusiasm of the ladies with his most sarcastic compliments.

After supper was over, Stanhope's valet appeared and brought a package containing about a dozen copies of a copper-print portrait of his lordship in the court dress of an English peer with an earl's coronet. He distributed these pictures among "his dear Ansbach friends," as he said with a bewitching smile.

The work of art was loudly praised, both in regard to resemblance and execution; after Everyone had expressed his thanks, the talk turned upon pictures in general and differences of opinion were expressed as to whether one could tell the characteristics of a person from a picture. Hofrat Hofmann, as the negative spirit which he generally was, disputed this with great eagerness and with a quantity of objections. Every picture, he said, gave really only the essence of the best, or most flattering, or the most accessible qualities of a person; the painter or the engraver cared only about exaggerating a particular trait for the sake of his art, so that very little was left of the real nature of the individual in question. This was hotly denied: it depended above all on the genius of the artist, was the retort; and Lord Stanhope, who, of course, felt these remarks of the Hofrat's as a lack of delicacy, much against his usual habits, was eager in expressing the contrary. He, for his part, was confident that he could guess the mental make-up of anyone portrayed in any picture, no matter whom it represented and from whose hand it proceeded.

At these words the hostess smiled with a peculiar meaning. She disappeared into an adjoining room and returned at once with an oval oil-painting in a gold frame, which, still smiling, she placed upright on the table near the count. The guests pressed around and from almost all their lips there was an exclamation of admiration.

It was an extremely lively and naturally painted picture representing a young woman of astonishing beauty: a face white as alabaster, flushed with pale pink, clear, regular features, an expression which was rendered somewhat poetical and shy by an obvious myopia, and the whole face illuminated with heavenly warmth.

"Well, my lord?" asked Frau von Imhoff teasingly.

Stanhope assumed an expression of extreme wisdom and uttered his estimate of the painter's subject:

"Really, this being combines an oriental warmth with the grace of Andalusia."

Frau von Imhoff nodded as if she thought what had been said was excellent. "Very good, my lord," she remarked, "but we want to hear something about the lady's character."

"Oh, you are trying to catch me," said Stanhope gayly. "Very well. I think that she is a woman who can bear tribulations of any kind with extraordinary long-suffering. She is gentle, she is God-fearing, she loves the idyllic peace of country life, her tastes are all for the fine arts."

Frau von Imhoff could not contain herself any longer and broke into merry laughter. "I am certain, count, that you have only interpreted her so falsely in order to tease me," she said.

Herr Hofmann looked his scorn, and Stanhope blushed. "If I am mistaken, please correct me, madam," he replied gallantly.

"To do that would require more patience on your part than is desirable," replied Frau von Imhoff, suddenly serious. "I should have to tell you of the extraordinary fate of this woman, who is my best friend, and I should have to risk disturbing the good humor you are all in."

But no one was satisfied with this and Frau von Imhoff was finally obliged to yield to the general pressure.

"My friend arrived as a girl of eighteen at the court of a capital in central Germany," she began with a charming embarrassment. "She had neither father nor mother and was entirely dependent upon her brother. This brother, whom for the sake of brevity I will call the Baronet, in spite of his youth—he was only ten years older than his beautiful sister—was regarded as a man of extraordinary talents. The Prince, although weak and dissolute, thoroughly appreciated his abilities and gave him one of the highest positions in the country, overwhelming him with honors and favors. However, the Baronet only took part in the pleasures of the court on the occasions when he introduced his sister into the drawing-rooms and gatherings of the aristocracy, and he had the satisfaction of seeing her the center of every circle in which she appeared, not only on account of her beauty, but also on account of her intellect, her charm and her natural vivacity.

"One day the quiet life of these two people was disturbed in a horrible manner. Almost accidentally, the Baronet discovered that tremendous embezzlements of the state funds had taken place; it was a question of many hundreds of thousands of thalers; and that the prince himself, in difficulties on account of his ill-considered concessions to mistresses and favorites, was involved in this fraudulent business at the expense of his people. The Baron did not know what to do. He confided the matter to his sister. The latter said: 'In such a matter there cannot be any indecision; go to the Prince and tell him frankly of what a crime he is making himself guilty.' He did so. The Prince became furious, he showed the young man the door and told him to get out. When the Baronet told his sister of the unexpected result of his undertaking she urged him to tell the story to an assembly of the delegates of the cities. This also the Baronet declared himself prepared to do, but beforehand he confided the matter to a friend who seemed to approve of his decision. The same friend wrote him a little note the next evening in which he urged him strongly to come at once, for an important consultation, to a little country-seat near the city. Without hesitation the Baron accepted, although it was already late and dark, ordered a horse to be saddled, and rode off.

"That was the last that was seen of him. Several people asserted that towards midnight they had heard shots in the vicinity of the pavilion, but whatever may have happened the Baron disappeared and what became of him remained an unsolved mystery. One can easily imagine his sister's grief. But from the first day she disdained to give way to it and developed the most astonishing activity. Since she was gradually forced to believe in her brother's death, her one endeavor became at least to find his body. She employed workmen, who for weeks dug up the earth around the pavilion. With kindness, with cunning and with threats she implored the assumed friend of her brother to tell what he knew of the affair. It was in vain, the man maintained that he knew nothing. No one would admit knowing anything. She threw herself at the feet of the Prince, who, listening graciously and apparently moved, promised to do everything in order to trace the mysterious disappearance. It was in vain. A few days later she became ill, without doubt poisoned. The attempt: was repeated. Suddenly, however, the Prince died of a stroke; she could no longer remain in this terrible spot. She began to travel and tried in all the courts of Germany, big and little, and later on even in London and Paris, to interest ministers, monarchs, and men in public life in the task of securing retribution or at least enlightenment. Think of the life," Frau von Imhoff continued, "that my friend thus led for more than three years, constantly traveling, constantly in haste, constantly struggling with vexations. Her fruitless efforts were gradually bringing about the loss of a considerable part of her fortune. When she was finally obliged to realize that her work would lead her nowhere, that the collusion between the wicked and the indifferent was too strong, she gave up all further attempts with the same resoluteness which she had shown up to this time, retired to a small university town and threw herself with remarkable zeal into the study of politics, law and economy. Not as if she were thus shutting out the world, on the contrary: she had exchanged her private affairs for a public cause. Her glowing soul, enflamed with a desire for freedom and human rights, sought occupation. Two years ago she married an unimportant man, whom she did not love. She did so because this man, whom she had once before refused, had attempted to commit suicide in his bath out of passion for her; he was saved and she accepted him. However, the marriage was dissolved peacefully a few months later; the man went to America and became a farmer. My friend recommenced her remarkable life of wandering. I have letters from her now from Russia, then from Vienna, or from Athens. For several months now she has been in Hungary. She studies the situation of the peasants and the needs of the working people everywhere, not merely superficially and emotionally, but with scientific thoroughness. Her profundity, her knowledge of law, of national constitutions and public administration has compelled the admiration of many a learned man. She is today twenty-five years old and still looks almost as she did in that picture, which was painted six years ago. After all this, my lord, you will readily believe that one can't well speak of her oriental softness and gentleness of spirit. Yes, gentle she is, but gentle in quite a different way from the usual conception. Her gentleness has something joyous and active about it, for she has a keen mind and a lofty confidence in everything that is human. The present is always the most important thing for her."

A profound silence convinced Frau von Imhoff of the deep impression she had produced. What a splendid and interesting sensation and how pleasantly gruesome to listen to such tales in a well-heated, brilliantly illuminated room! The man in front of the fireplace rubs his hands comfortably when the weather storms and rages outside. It gives him a pleasant prickling sensation to realize that outside there are people walking about without gloves or overcoats. He, seated in front of his chimney, is even able to express the liveliest sympathy with such unfortunates.

When Frau von Imhoff had begun to speak, Caspar had been seated somewhat outside of the circle of listeners, then he had gotten up slowly and had come nearer until he stood at her side looking, as if enchanted, at her mouth while she spoke. Now that she had finished, he suddenly laughed. His features in motion became extraordinarily attractive. Frau von Imhoff confessed later that she had never before seen such an expression of childlike joy; it did indeed resemble the laughter of a little child, only there was a higher, clearer strength of consciousness in it and it pictured clearly his inner feelings. Those sitting about were curious as to what he would say, but he only asked timidly: "What is the woman's name?"

Frau von Imhoff put an arm on his shoulder and answered, smiling in a kindly manner, that she was unable to betray that at present; perhaps later on he would find out. For him, too, the unknown lady felt the deepest sympathy.

He remained thoughtful. Even when the party became more noisy again, and the youngest Fraulein von Stichaner sang some songs at the piano, he retained his distrait thoughtful expression. The vividly described fate of the unknown woman caused him to project his feelings curiously into the outer world, and, as if in response to a signal from an invisible spirit, for the first time his heart opened to the suffering of another I, of another existence. "Women can't be the way I thought they were," he reflected.

This gave him food for thought. At a certain point the structure of the universal was beginning to tremble, and its creatures showed him a double face, one to which he was well accustomed and which he did not love, the other, as intangible as a shadow, distant as the moon, almost related to the mother he had never seen.

Life moves over the bridge between evening and evening; what it gives today becomes a possession to-morrow. Except for this hour an incident of the following night, which he briefly witnessed almost without being noticed, would not have weighed so tremendously on his imagination that for days thereafter he was in a state of the most painful disturbance.

18. Joseph And His Brethren

As a parting gift Caspar received from Stanhope two pairs of shoes, a box with some Brussels lace and six yards of fine stuff for a suit. After he had already spent the whole morning with him, Stanhope came to Quandt's house after lunch to bid Caspar farewell. At half past three the carriage drove up. Caspar accompanied the count into the street. He was white even to his eyes; three times he embraced the departing man, gritting his teeth in order not to cry out, for it was a piece of his innermost self which was being cruelly wrenched from him—forever. This he felt to be the case, whether he should ever again see the man who had become so dear to him or not. In him he was bidding farewell to the innocence of blissful confidence and the sweetness of beautiful longings and illusions.

His lordship, too, was moved to tears. It was characteristic of his sensitive nature to permit himself to be profoundly touched and moved on such occasions. His last word sounded like a defense against self-reproach, as if he wished to interpose a last obstacle to the wheels of fate and turn them back; the carriage was already in motion when with eyebrows solemnly raised he called to Quandt and Police-Lieutenant Hickel, who were standing at the gate: "Preserve my son."

Quandt pressed his hand protectingly against his breast. The carriage rolled off towards Rrailsheimer Street.

Five minutes later, Herr von Imhoff and Hofrat Hofmann appeared; they were grieved to find that they had come too late. To console Caspar, they invited him to walk with them in the court garden, a proposal which the teacher eagerly accepted. Heckel asked to be allowed to join them.

Scarcely had these four turned the nearest corner, when Quandt hurried back into the house. He beckoned to his wife, who followed him without asking into the upper hall —for the matter had been prearranged—and took her place as a sentinel. Quandt for his part now set to work to look for the diary. For this purpose he had had a second pair of keys made, with which he could open the bureaus and closets. He found nothing in the drawers. The blue copy book was no longer there. He also rummaged through the closet in vain, as well as through the clothes, the books, the sofa. He searched fruitlessly in every nook and cranny but he found nothing.

Exhausted, he dried the perspiration from his forehead and called to his wife through the open door: "Now, Jette, haven't I always said so! That boy is a sly fox."

"Yes, yes, he's as false as can be," replied his wife, "and puts us to a lot of trouble." She only scolded to please her husband, for as a matter of fact she liked the boy, for no one had ever treated her so nicely and politely before.

Quandt remained depressed for the rest of the day, like one who has been cheated of some noble accomplishment. And was it not indeed so? Was it not his mission on earth to separate the bran from the chaff and as an alchemist of souls to show his fellow human beings the pure unalloyed elements of good and evil? He could not be calm or forbearing so long as the breath of a lie existed.

Moved by such considerations, he gave his wife a long talk that same evening, in which he expressed himself as follows: "Now consider, Jette, hasn't his straight and upright posture at the table struck you? Can one believe that such a person vegetated for years in a hole under the ground? Can one think such a thing if one has possession of one's five senses? I frankly confess I can't discover anything of his famous childishness and innocence. He is good-natured, yes, but what does that prove? And how he fawns and cringes before fine people like the excellent hypocrite that he is! As to that, your friend Frau Behold has hit the nail on the head. And then think, often when I enter his room unexpectedly—I naturally make a point of surprising him—there he is, hunched up on the floor; it is an extraordinary sight. I don't know whether his thoughts are wandering, or whether he is only pretending, but as soon as he sees me, like lightning his face assumes that hypocritical grimace of friendliness which unfortunately disarms one. Once I found him in broad daylight with the window shades down. What does that mean? There is something back of that."

"What could there be back of it?" asked his wife.

Quandt shrugged his shoulders and sighed. "Heaven knows," said he. "For all that I like him," he continued with an anxious expression. "He is a keen and responsive boy. But I must find out what is back of it. There is something uncanny about him."

Frau Quandt, who was combing her hair for the night, was tired of this chatter. Her pretty face had the expression of a stupid sleepy bird and her eyes, which were strikingly close together, glanced dully into the light of the candle. Suddenly she put down the comb and said: "Listen, Quandt."

Quandt remained still and listened. Caspar's room was above the couple's bedroom and in the silence which now reigned they heard their puzzling household companion walking incessantly up and down the room.

"I wonder what he's up to," said the wife, puzzled.

"Yes, I wonder what he's doing," repeated Quandt, staring darkly at the ceiling. "I don't know, I was always told that he went to sleep with the chickens; I haven't noticed it. There you see, how's one to know? In any case I'll break him of the habit of walking at night." Quandt gently opened the door and slipped out cautiously in his slippers. Carefully he moved up the stairs and when he reached Caspar's door he tried to peek through the keyhole, but when he found that he could see nothing, in the same bent posture he placed his ear against the lock. Yes, there he was, walking up and down, the inscrutable creature, walking and shaping his dark plans.

Quandt pressed the door handle. The door was locked. Then he raised his voice and energetically demanded quiet. At once everything inside was as still as a mouse.

When the teacher returned to his wife he found that her difficult hour had come with unexpected suddenness. She already lay moaning on the bed and asked for the midwife. Quandt wanted to send the maid but his wife said, "No, that won't do; she is stupid and will lose her way." Whether he liked it or not, Quandt had to decide to go, unpleasant as the errand was, for in the first place he had been looking forward to his bed, also he was a little afraid of walking through the dark streets, for only last Lent a tax assessor had been attacked and half murdered back of St. Charles' Church.

With irritation he put on his clothes; then he summoned the maid from her feather bed and ordered her to call a friendly neighbor in case of need; he slipped in again and ransacked the chest for his pistols, in doing which he threw over the night table which disturbed him so that he seized his head in his hands and cursed his unlucky stars. His wife, whose pains had already disturbed her faculties, took courage from her condition and hurled at his head all manner of reproach, which she generally kept to herself from cowardice, with regard to himself and to men in general. This had the best effect, and after he had carried his little boy, who slept in the adjoining room and who had awakened from the noise, into the maid's room, he finally set out.

Caspar, as he was getting into bed, suddenly heard with a shudder the agonized voice of the woman beneath. The sounds became constantly more frightful, they penetrated with increasing loudness. Then there was silence for a time, then the house door creaked, steps came and went and now the screaming began worse than ever. Caspar thought some great misfortune must have occurred; his first instinct was to save himself. He ran to the door, unlocked it, and hurried down the steps. The door of the living room was open and an over-heated atmosphere proceeded from it. The maid and the neighbor stood busily at work over Frau Quandt's bed; the latter was screaming for her husband, calling to God, and writhing in agony.

Ah, what did Caspar see? What were his sensations! He saw a tiny little head, a little white body, a tiny little human being now raised aloft, which had correspondingly tiny hands. Caspar's whole body began to tremble; he turned around, without having been seen by anyone, and fleeing up the stairs sank down breathless on the top step, where he remained sitting.

Again the front door sounded; Quandt appeared with the midwife, but already the neighbor rushed to greet him exultingly! "A little daughter, Herr Quandt."

"Well, think of that," exclaimed Quandt in a voice of pride, as if he had made a contribution worth mentioning.

A piping little cry corroborated the presence of a new citizen in the world. After a time the maid came out humming, and Caspar saw that she carried a dish full of blood.

In all probably not more than an hour had passed before Caspar finally got up and stumbled back into his room. As if drunk, he undressed, tumbled into bed and dug his face into the bedclothes.

He could see nothing before his eyes but this: out of the darkness like a purple disk there appeared a dish full of blood.

He could see nothing but this; out of a bleeding gap young animals crept forth and were called human beings. Naked and tiny, lonely and helpless, while their mothers suffered unspeakable torments, they crept painfully forth out of an incomparable prison and were born, yes, born, as his mother had given birth to him.

So that's it, thought Caspar: He felt the tie, he grasped the connection, he felt his roots deep in the bloody earth, life hitherto motionless began to quiver, the secret was revealed, the meaning evident. But pity and revulsion, yearning and fear were now one, life and death were fused in one name. He wanted not to sleep, yet he did fall asleep, but the nearer sleep came the more distressing became the fear of death, so that he yielded reluctantly; it was a fearsome little death in life.

When he did not appear at the usual hour next morning, Quandt wondered why, went upstairs and knocked at his door. Although he knew that the room had been locked the night before, he pressed the handle and found to his surprise that the door was unlocked. Walking up to Caspar's bed, he shook him and said angrily: "Well, Hauser, are you becoming one of the seven sleepers? What's the matter?"

Caspar sat up and the teacher saw that his pillow was quite wet; he pointed to it and asked what that meant. Caspar thought a moment and said it came from crying; he had cried in his sleep.

What, cried! thought Quandt suspiciously, why did he cry and how does he know so quickly that he has been crying in his sleep, and why did he wait until I should have decided to call him?

There is some trick back of that, thought Quandt, he wants to put me in a good-natured mood. He looked around keenly and his glance fell upon the glass of water which stood on the night table. He took the glass, lifted it up observingly; it was half empty. "Did you drink any water, Hauser?" he asked severely.

Caspar looked at him without understanding. The glance of the teacher—extending from the glass to the pillow — became reproachful. "Did you not accidentally spill the water?" he further inquired. "I said accidentally and don't mean anything else; you can speak to me quite openly, Hauser."

Caspar slowly shook his head. He did not understand what the man was driving at.

Obdurate, obdurate, thought Quandt, giving up his inquiry.

When Caspar came into the living-room for his lesson, Quandt informed him with suitable dignity that a little daughter had been given to him.

"How given?" asked Caspar naively.

Quandt frowned. The indifference with which the boy accepted such an event irritated him greatly. His bearing was cold and formal when he said, "We will begin as usual with the Bible. Read your lesson."

It was the story of Joseph.

There is an old man who has many sons, but he loves the youngest of them best and gives him a coat of many colors in order to distinguish him. For this reason his brothers hate him and do not wish to speak pleasantly to him any longer. And Joseph tells them the dream of the sheaves. "Think, we were binding sheaves in the field," said he, "and my sheaf stood up and remained standing whereas your sheaves, which were roundabout, bent down before my sheaf." Then the brothers answer: "Do you wish to become a king over us, do you wish to rule us?" And they hate him the more because of his dreams. But Joseph is quite unsuspecting; the reason for their dislike does not seem to dawn upon him and he soon tells them a second dream, namely, how the sun and the moon and eleven stars bent down before him. A dream easy to interpret, for eleven is the number of the brothers. Even his father scolds him because of this dream. "What are you thinking of, Joseph?" he says reproachfully, "shall your mother and I and your brothers come and bow down before you?" And soon after this the brothers, who are all shepherds, go out into the fields to tend the sheep and Joseph is sent to them by his father. And when the brothers see him from afar they talk to one another, saying: "Look, the dreamer is coming!" And they decide that they will strangle him and that they will throw him into a pit and pretend that a wild animal has devoured him. "Then we'll see what becomes of his dreams," said they jeeringly. But there is one of the brothers who is merciful and warns the others. He advises them to throw him into the pit but not to kill him. And this they do; they take off his coat, his coat of many colors, which he wears, and they throw the boy into the pit. And when all this has been accomplished, there appears a caravan of merchants from a distant country, and the brothers agree to sell Joseph, and they sell him for money. Then they take Joseph's coat, dip it in the blood of a slaughtered animal and say to their father: "We have found this bloody coat, see if it is not the coat of your youngest son." The old man rends his clothes and exclaims: "In mourning I will descend into the lower world to my son."

When Caspar had gotten so far his voice failed him. He got up, put his book aside and his breast heaved with sighs. He pressed his hand before his mouth and with difficulty choked down the rising sobs.

Quandt was suspicious. He looked at the boy closely. His glance was a sidelong one, like that of a goat tied to a post. "Listen to me, Hauser," he said finally. "You can't pretend that you are so moved by this simple story, which moreover you must know very well. To my knowledge you already went through this part of the Old Testament at Professor Daumer's. You must therefore be aware that Joseph later fared very well, for he was a pure and good man. Save yourself the trouble, I beg you. If you are conscientious, honest and obedient, you will get ten times more from me than by an untimely exhibition of such far-fetched emotions. I simply don't believe in your tears; I think that I have already clearly enough indicated as much this very day. By this means you are only obtaining the contrary of what you may be aiming at. For I don't like outbreaks of emotion, not in general, and particularly not such ill-founded ones. It is high time for you to become accustomed to the seriousness of life. And since we are already talking so frankly with one another I should like to warn you seriously against regarding all the people you come into contact with as stupid. That is a mistake of yours which may lead to the most unfortunate consequences. I am well disposed towards you, Hauser, I really mean well by you, perhaps you have no better friend than myself, which, of course, you will only recognize too late. But beware of deceiving me. And now let us continue. I am ready to regard this incident as not having happened."

In the course of this impressive speech, the teacher's voice had become soft and kindly, and it almost looked as if he wanted to take Caspar and press him to his breast. But Caspar stood there in front of him with a silly face, smiling helplessly. What's the matter, he thought, what does the man mean?

Afterwards, when he thought the matter over, it was not in the least clear to him what the teacher was driving at, and he came to the conclusion that Quandt was the most puzzling person who had ever crossed his path.

19. Castle Falkenhaus

The President did not get back to the city until Epiphany, after an absence of almost four weeks. Persons closely associated with him thought that they noticed a great change in his behavior; he seemed somber and silent, and his participation in his professional duties seemed at times indifferent.

It was striking that he let several days go by without inquiring about Caspar. When Hofrat Hofmann, as they were walking home together, frankly asked him whether he had already seen the boy, Feuerbach did not answer. The next day the Police-Lieutenant came to see him. Hickel appeared to be worried about Hauser's safety and was of the opinion that a guard should be set; the President did not go into the matter; he merely said that he would consider it. The same afternoon he sent for the teacher and questioned him about the boy's behavior and condition. Quandt said this and said that, it was neither black nor white. In the end he pulled a letter out of his pocket; it was what Frau Behold had written; he had decided to give it to the President.

Feuerbach read the letter and a cloud of displeasure gathered on his brow. "You must not pay any attention to such stuff, my dear Quandt," he said sharply. "What would become of us if we listened to the gossip of such a fool? Caspar's past is no concern of yours; that's not your business. I have employed you to make a useful man of him. If you have any complaint to make in this connection I will gladly listen, but as for other matters, please spare me."

One can well imagine how deeply such a sharp snub offended the teacher's sensitiveness. He went home full of bitterness, and although the President had told him to send Caspar to see him on Sunday morning he did not tell the boy of this until Saturday night, two days later.

When Caspar arrived at Feuerbach's house at the hour set, he was obliged to wait in the hall for a considerable time, then

Henriette, the President's daughter, appeared and led him into the living room. "I don't know whether father will receive you today," she said, and proceeded to tell him of a robbery which had taken place the night before in the President's work-room. The unknown perpetrators had had duplicate keys and had ransacked all the papers in the desk. It was assumed that the criminals had been looking particularly for certain letters and documents, for they had stolen nothing, nor had they gotten hold of their booty, since her father kept his most important papers carefully concealed; their presence had been shown by the tremendous disorder and the broken window only.

While relating this, the young lady had walked up and down in masculine fashion, her arms crossed over her breast, anger and rancor in voice and expression. She said that her father was of course beside himself over the incident; while she spoke, the door opened and the President, accompanied by a rather slender man of perhaps thirty, stood on the threshold. "Ah, that's Caspar Hauser, Anselm," said the president. The person addressed stopped short and looked thoughtfully and absent-mindedly into Caspar's face. Caspar was struck by the extraordinary beauty of the man; as he found out later, he was Feuerbach's second son, who, pursued by a malign fate, had fled to the paternal house for a few days in order to get help and advice from his father. Caspar loved beautiful faces, especially when they were full of soul and melancholy, particularly in men; but this was only a brief apparition, he never saw Anselm again.

The President showed Caspar into the large reception-room and only came back after a considerable lapse of time. Caspar's eye at once fell upon the picture of Napoleon on the wall. How wonderful it was; such a resemblance, between the expression of haughty majesty and the dark sorrow about the gracefully curved lips, to the man he had just seen. There were, moreover, the gorgeous insignia, the crown, the jewels and the purple mantle. Caspar was moved, a higher world opened up before him. He would have liked to go and seize in his hands what seemed to him embodied in the picture, in order to transfer that which addressed him so majestically, into a spoken dialogue. Unintentionally he drew himself up as if the royal presence compelled him to imitation; he took a few steps up and down the room and was pleasantly frightened at realizing that the eyes followed him, glowing darkly.

Occupied thus, the President found him and remained standing in surprise at the door. Was it accident, or was it one of the inexplicable links in which this unusual destiny revealed itself? Feuerbach saw in the almost enchanted relationship between the picture and the boy something like an ordeal, a corroboration from above. For Caspar's mother —in so far as the whole structure of frightful assumptions and half-certainties had any validity at all in the light of reality—was connected by the bonds of relationship with the great Napoleon.

"Do you know who that is, Caspar?" asked Feuerbach in a loud voice.

Caspar shook his head.

"Then I will tell you. That is a man who convinced the world that a strong will can accomplish everything. Have you never heard anything of the Emperor Napoleon? I knew him, Caspar, I saw him, I spoke to him. I was the intermediary between him and our King Max. It was a great era, and there is not much left of it."

With a melancholy, thoughtful glance Feuerbach broke off. He felt the weight of years, he had struggled long enough in their claws. His eye glided almost with fear over the figure of the still silently standing boy, as if the latter expected him to deliver that judgment, which Feuerbach's impotence—which he could no longer conceal—must soon announce to the world. His recent experiences in consultation with the powerful ones down there filled his heart with shame; a flame of resentment and hatred towards all mankind suddenly blazed within him,, and grinding his teeth he ran up and down between the door and the windows half a dozen times, and only the sight of Caspar, who had turned white with fear, recalled him in some measure to himself, and he sullenly asked the boy whether he got enough to eat at Quandt's.

"On that point there is no ground for complaint," replied Caspar.

Feuerbach seemed not to hear the equivocal tone. "And what about Lord Stanhope?" he inquired further, with a rigid and threatening glance. "Have you news of him? Have you yourself written to him?"

"I write to him once a week," replied Caspar.

"Where is he?"

"He intends to go to Spain."

"To Spain; well, well, to Spain. That's far away, my dear boy."

"Yes, it appears to be far."

This monotonous conversation was interrupted by the entrance of a police official who brought a written report on the nocturnal burglary. Caspar said good-by.

"Where have you been all this time?" were the angry words with which Quandt received him.

"I was with the President. You know that," replied Caspar.

"Very good; but it does not betoken much knowledge of how to behave if you can't cut a visit short when supper is waiting for you at home."

Indeed eating was an important affair at the Quandts'. The teacher always sat down to his meals with a certain emotion, and his penetrating glance seemed to examine all of the participants of the meal as to the degree of their respect. When Frau Quandt announced what good things were to be expected the teacher accompanied her recitation either with a nod of the head or a questioning frown. If a dish pleased him his good humor grew, if it did not meet with his approval he ate every bite with the ironical expression of a man who is superior to the world. For certain things he had a particular predilection as, for example, sour pickles, or warmed-up potato salad; and while he was enjoying these he seldom ceased emphasizing the simplicity of his wants. Frau Quandt was a good cook, and when she had been successful with a favorite dish of her husband's she was not unsusceptible to his praise, although it was sometimes expressed in too learned a form. Thus, Quandt used to say jokingly that if he had not taken her to wife the deceased Trimalchio would have risen from the dead to marry her. After supper came the comfortable hour with slippers, dressing-gown, arm-chair and the perusal of the papers. Into restaurants Quandt almost never went, partly on account of the expense and then because he found no one to talk to. He preferred the comfortable corner by the stove.

But since Caspar had been with them, this idyllic evening mood had lost its charm. Quandt was worried and sometimes he did not know exactly why. Let us think of a dog, an intelligent, nervous, alert dog; suppose this dog in ferreting about in a district familiar to him has somewhere picked up a bit of poison and. that he carries about this destructive poison in his body, unconsciously seeking darkness, running, panting, into every damp corner, leaping after a shadow, growling at a fly, attributing everything around him and about him to this one mad urge, regarding the whole world as poisoned, whereas it is only his own poor stomach, and you will have a true picture of the condition of the unfortunate teacher. His demon chained him to the boy; beyond everything else it was important to him "to get back of things"; he would have given several years of his life if in this way he could quickly have come to the knowledge of what was "behind the affair."

At eight o'clock the Police-Lieutenant came for a visit, he was in a bad humor, for he had played faro in the Casino the night before, and had lost twenty-five florins, which he still owed. Towards Caspar he Was strikingly friendly; he asked him what he had talked to the President about, but he received the boy's literal report with suspicion, as it seemed too unimportant.

"Yes, our good friend is very reserved," complained Quandt. "I did not know anything of the robbery at the President's, and it was with difficulty that I got him to talk about it at all. Do you know anything about it, lieutenant? Have they any traces?"

Hickel replied indifferently that a suspicious tramp had been arrested near Altenmuhr.

"What things do happen!" exclaimed Quandt. "What impertinence it takes to make the head of the government the victim of such an attack." Secretly, however, he reasoned: that's right, that will strike at his Excellency's delusion of inviolability; big men can now and again learn something useful from rogues.

"It would not surprise me," said Hickel, keeping his lips closed in a distinguished manner, a finesse which he had copied from Lord Stanhope, "if this story were not again in some way connected with our friend Hauser."

Quandt stared, then he looked slantingly at Caspar, whose frightened glance avoided his. "I have grounds for such an assumption," continued Hickel, staring at the cleanly scoured nails of his red peasant hands. These hands always filled Caspar with a nameless disgust.

"I have grounds, and perhaps I shall come forth with them in due time. The President himself has sense enough to know that the clock has struck. But he does not want to talk about it. He does not feel quite right about it."

"Not quite right? You don't say so I" replied Quandt, and a pleasant thrill ran down his back. Frau Quandt too stopped darning her stockings, and gazed curiously from one to the other.

"Yes, indeed," continued Hickel, smiling through his yellow teeth, "they gave it to him hot and heavy down there in Münchro, and he carries his head considerably less high. Don't you think so too, Hauser?" he asked looking first at Quandt and then at his wife.

"I think it is not proper that you should speak so of the President," replied Caspar boldly.

Hickel turned white and bit his lips. "Just think of that, just think of it!" he remarked gloomily. "Did you hear that, Herr Quandt? The toads are croaking; spring is coming."

"A very unsuitable remark, Hauser," Quandt exclaimed angrily. "You ought to be respectful and modest towards the lieutenant as well as towards me. Towards Baron Imhoff or the General Commissioner you would not dare to behave so, I am certain of that. And double-faced is false faced, it is said. I shall write that to the count."

"Don't get excited, Herr Quandt," interrupted Hickel. It's not worth while; we must ascribe it to his lack of understanding. Moreover, I had a letter from the count yesterday." He put his hand in his breast pocket and pulled out a folded paper. "You would like to know what he writes, Hauser? Well, it is not exactly complimentary to you. The good count is worried, as usual, and recommends us to use great severity in case you don't obey."

Caspar looked incredulous. "He wrote that?" he asked hesitatingly.

Hickel nodded.

"He was very angry too, that time, at your secrecy about the diary," said Quandt.

"I shall explain all that to him when he returns," replied Caspar.

Hickel rubbed his back against a corner of the stove and laughed. "When he returns! When! But who knows whether he will return? It seems to me that he has no great desire to return. Do you think, you silly boy, that such a man has nothing better to do than to pass away the time here?"

"He will return, lieutenant," replied Caspar with a triumphant smile.

"Oh, ho," exclaimed Hickel. "That certainly sounds final. How does one know that so exactly?"

"Because he promised," replied Caspar with steadfast honesty. "He gave me a sacred promise to return in a year. He promised on the eighth of December, so there are ten months and sixteen days up to that time."

Hickel looked at Quandt, Quandt looked at his wife and all three broke out laughing. "He seems well versed in arithmetic," remarked Hickel dryly. Then he put his hand on Caspar's head and asked, "Who cut off his beautiful curls?"

Quandt replied that Caspar had wished it done himself since he had imagined that it was not suitable for a grown up man to go about with such a quantity of hair. "You may go to bed, Caspar," he then said.

Caspar shook hands with Everyone and left. When he had gone, Quandt opened the door softly and listened. "Look here, lieutenant," he whispered anxiously to Hickel, "if he knows, or assumes, that anyone is listening to him he walks upstairs slowly and thoughtfully, but if he thinks he's unobserved he can jump like a hare, three steps at a time. Isn't it so, wife?"

His wife corroborated the remark, and how much trouble he gave! She added irritably that he had now been in the house for six weeks and had had fourteen shirts in the laundry; he always had to be dressed up like a doll, and at the crack of dawn was already brushing his clothes.

She placed a glass of brandy in front of the lieutenant, and went into the next room to nurse the baby who was crying.

"Yes, it's the very devil with him," Quandt continued his wife's lamentations. "The other day I was reading from the Bavarian Chamber of Deputies. Hauser walked up back of me and when I had finished he read the title half aloud to himself as if the name astonished him. Now, the Bavarian Chamber of Deputies is read in every decent house, is it not? Besides, he has had the opportunity day after day to see the paper on our table and the name could not possibly be new to him. So I asked him whether he did not know what a chamber of deputies was. Whereupon he replied with his most innocent expression that it was probably a room in which one locked people up. Now I ask you if that doesn't beat the Dutch? An angel would have to come down from heaven for me to believe, and be taken in by such nonsense, and even then I think I should doubt whether it were a real angel or only an assumed one."

"What do you expect, it's all a swindle," answered the Police-Lieutenant. "The whole thing is a swindle." And as he swayed affectedly to and fro an indefinable dull hatred glowed in his eyes.

Everything a swindle. This was a judgment relating not only to the anecdote just narrated, but to all of the activities of mankind, to which he was indifferent to the verge of nausea, in so far as they were unrelated to his own wellbeing. Let them hack off each other's heads, let them quarrel about heaven and hell, king and country, build their houses, bear their children, let them murder and steal and rob, betray and cheat or labor honestly and perform noble deeds, everything to him in the final analysis was a swindle, except the underwriting of a carefree existence, which society in his own eyes owed him.

Baron von Lang, who liked Hickel because of his flattering ways, enjoyed telling how Hickel had met the baron's son, a young doctor of philosophy, walking over the Landstrasse one evening, and how the young man pointing towards the stars in the sky had begun to speak of the countless worlds up above, whereupon Hickel, with his most sarcastic expression, had said: "Do you really, seriously believe, Doctor, that those pretty little lights up there are anything but . . . lights?"

This was not merely ignorance, but the expression of that superiority which culminated in the words: "everything a swindle."

It was known all over town that Hickel lived above his means. It was his ideal to be a cavalier, his passion to be elegant, and he had a tremendous flair for the genuineness and legitimacy of everything connected with these desires. Some time ago when his application for membership in a distinguished club for officials had been under discussion there had been a long period of hesitation, for he was not at all popular and was, moreover, of low birth, his parents being humble cottagers in Dombiihl. Finally he had been able to put through his wishes by frightening certain persons with the disclosure of family secrets. Hofrat Hofmann expressed the predominant feeling in regard to him when he said: "He does not reveal himself, this Hickel, he does not reveal himself." As a matter of fact it always seemed as if Hickel were lying in ambush with something dangerous up his sleeve.

He understood excellently what role to play with the President. He could even permit himself to express certain truths to the otherwise so unapproachable man, which sounded friendly or interested, but which, as a matter of fact, were nothing but sugar-coated malice. He had a certain undeniable skill in telling amusing little stories and bits of current city gossip. This amused Feuerbach and made him lenient towards many other things. "Curious," said people, "that the President should be so fond of this fellow Hickel." In any case, the lieutenant always found a ready listener in Feuerbach and slyly took pleasure when the President would attack him in his bearlike manner, censuring his frivolous mode of life and exposing his bad instincts at their very root with astonishing keenness. Is it not likely that precisely this thing misled and attracted the President? Perhaps he had perceived too clearly the emptiness and sullenness of Hickel's soul and had become too familiar with it to be able to cast him aside.

Hickel finally managed to convince the President that Caspar should not be allowed to go about as freely as heretofore, and a guard was appointed, an old veteran, with a wooden leg and one arm. This good man took his new obligations very conscientiously, and followed Caspar's every step, accompanied by the laughter of the street urchins. The policeman had speculated correctly, if the regulation, which looked as if it were the outgrowth of a great solicitude, was intended to restrict the boy's freedom as much as possible. There was complaint after complaint now from Quandt, then from Caspar, again from the invalid, whom Caspar not infrequently outwitted by stealing away secretly.

He complained of his troubles to Herr Fuhrmann, the clergyman, who gave him religious instruction; the latter, who was well disposed toward him, urged him to be patient. "Of what use is patience," exclaimed Caspar obstinately, "things get worse all the time!"

"Of what use," replied the clergyman mildly, "what use is it to God to watch our senseless behavior! By patience he directs us towards good. Patience brings roses."

Nevertheless the clergyman appealed to the President who promised help without, for the time, doing anything. His annual visit of inspection through the circuit took him away from the city for three weeks; when he returned he sent one day for Hickel to come to his study. "Listen to me, Hickel," he said, "you know this neighborhood pretty well? Good. Have you ever heard of the Falkenhaus?"

Certainly, Your Excellency," replied Hickel. "The so-called Falkenhaus is a very old hunting castle of our margraves in the Triesdorf Forest."

"That's it. It has interested me for some time. I have made inquiries and I have discovered the following. The Falkenhaus until about four years ago served as a ranger's lodge, and the last ranger lived there entirely alone for many years. The man never associated with anyone, was never seen at any inn, and made his purchases in the neighboring villages himself. One day he was suddenly found to have disappeared, and a discharged policeman is said to have seen him in Suabia as the proprietor or the manager of an estate farm. I followed these traces and it appears not only that they are correct, but that in October, 1830, the man was found one night murdered in his bed."

"Of that I know nothing. I only know that the Falkenhaus is old and uninhabited, and that all kinds of spooky stories are told about the uncanny hermitage."

"In any case put your mind on the matter," said the President. "You had better send someone familiar with the place to make a careful investigation."

"Your orders will be carried out, Your Excellency. May I ask what case is in question?"

"It's connected with Caspar Hauser and his imprisonment."

"Ah," Hickel cleared his throat and made a bow, heaven knows why.

"I believe that I can assume with certainty that Falkenhaus was the place of his cruel imprisonment. From Caspar's first stories about his mode of travel with the unknown man I was certain that the place itself must be sought in Franconia, not too far from Nurnberg or Ansbach; now the traces have led me to the Falkenhaus."

"Probably Your Excellency needs this evidence for your monograph on Caspar Hauser," remarked Hickel flatteringly.

"Yes, that's it."

"And will the work still appear this year? Your Excellency will forgive the question, but I am deeply interested in the affair."

"You ask too much, Hickel. Never mind. There is a note for Hofrat Hofmann, give it to someone outside to be delivered. I want to drive with the Hofrat and Caspar to the Falkenhaus to-morrow. Inform Caspar to be ready, but on no account mention the purpose of the trip."

Caspar arrived at the appointed hour and soon found himself to his astonishment seated opposite the President and Herr Hofmann in the former's comfortable carriage. They drove in silence, which was seldom interrupted, through the sunny spring landscape.

They arrived. A walk through the deserted forest lodge and a thorough examination of its surroundings did not reveal anything. If a room underground had formerly existed and been used for this frightful purpose the former inhabitant had certainly filled it up, and time had covered all traces.

Then the eye of the President, looking sharply about in the open, discovered in a tract to the right of the building a curiously formed earth-pit. The trace seemed to indicate that formerly a wooden shed of some sort had been built over it, for all around there still lay rotting boards and beams and torn shingles. Seven steps, hewn in the soil and already decayed, led down into the cavern where the curiously smooth earth was covered with yellow moss.

On seeing this Feuerbach turned white. After standing a long time sunk in thought he descended the steps, touched several spots on the walls and in one corner bent down on to the ground, all the while somber and silent. When he came up again he looked penetratingly at Caspar, who stood quietly there, and let his unconscious glance sink into the depths of the forest. Does he not divine anything, thought Feuerbach, has he no foreboding of where his feet are resting? Does no breath from the past stir within him? Do the trees not speak to him? Does the air not reveal anything? And since it does not appear so, may I venture to terminate the ending of this horrible uncertainty with a definite yes or no?

The carriage remained standing on the Heerstrasse outside. On their way back through the woods, Caspar, who had suddenly been seized by an unconquerable fit of depression, which compelled him to walk slowly, remained quite a distance behind the two men.

Hofrat Hofmann seized this opportunity to communicate a few of his rational doubts to the President. "There is only one thing I should like to know," he said with a face full of doubt, "I should like to know why, if the boy languished so long in prison, he was suddenly set free; and not only that, but also why he was brought to a big city, where he would create the greatest excitement and necessarily betray his tormentor? Such logic is incomprehensible to me."

"Ah, well, one could think of several explanations," replied the President, quietly, "either one was tired of him; to keep him longer meant difficulties, even danger; or his jailor may have been ordered to kill him, but seized by some comprehensible emotion of pity or affection or fear decided to have him disappear in a different manner, and where could this be accomplished with greater hopes of success than just in a big city? They reflected thus: Herr Wessenig would, in accordance with the letter, put him into the army. There are lots of illiterates and half-idiots and he won't be noticeable, thought the criminal, with an optimism which, of course, merely proves his own want of knowledge. When, however, affairs turned out differently, he was seized with fear and told, was obliged to tell, those people who held the thread of the matter in their hands from the beginning, and these were obliged to search for a means of rendering harmless this most fearful witness to their guilt who, now protected by the world, appeared to them like one resurrected."

"Very clever, very clever," murmured Herr Hofmann approvingly, without permitting the President to notice that he was still unconvinced.

Late that afternoon they got back to the city. Caspar separated himself from the gentlemen and went homeward. On his walk he met Frau von Imhoff. She greeted him and asked him why he had not been to see her for so long.

"Haven't any time, have lots of work." replied Caspar, but with such an embarrassed face that the intelligent woman noticed that this could not be the real reason. She did not pursue the matter, however, and changing the subject, asked whether he was thoroughly enjoying the spring.

Caspar looked up into the sky and at the tops of the elms, as if he had overlooked the spring up to then, and shook his head. Gladly he would have said much, his heart was full to overflowing, but his tongue seemed weighted with lead; furthermore, he did not have the feeling that this woman, however friendly she might appear, was really interested in him. And what would be the use? he thought.

"I am to deliver greetings to you," she said as she was leaving after having invited him to dinner on Sunday. "Do you still remember the story of my friend which I told the evening that Lord Stanhope was at the house? She sends her greetings. And greetings from her mean a great deal."

"What is the woman's name?" asked Caspar, as he had asked it the time of the incident, only not smiling and happy, but rather detachedly.

Frau von Imhoff smiled. This curiosity about names seemed funny to her. "Kannawurf is her name, Clara von Kannawurf," she answered kindly.

Very nice of her to send greetings, thought Caspar as he continued on his way, but what is the use? How can it be of any use to me?

20. Quandt Treads On Delicate Ground

Caspar had scarcely gotten back to the house and entered the living room before he noticed that something unusual was afoot. Quandt sat at the table correcting copy books with a somber face, his wife was rocking the baby on her knees and, following the example of her husband, did not return Caspar's greeting. The lamp was not yet lighted, a scarlet evening sky flamed through the window, and when Caspar had hung up his hat he went out again into the yard. There the teacher's four-year-old boy was playing with marbles, Caspar sat down next to him on the stone bench; after a while Quandt appeared and he had scarcely seen the two side by side than he hurried over, seized the boy by the hand, and quickly led him away as if from the proximity of someone suffering from a contagious illness.

Caspar at once followed the teacher into the house. But Quandt was not in the room and he found the wife alone. "What is the matter here, Frau Quandt?" he asked.

"Why, don't you know?" replied the woman with embarrassment. "Haven't you heard that Frau Behold has thrown herself out of the window? It's in the newspaper today."

"Threw herself out of the window!" whispered Caspar with excitement.

"Yes, she threw herself from the garret into the court and crushed her skull. For some time already she is said to have been behaving like a crazy woman."

Caspar did not know what to say, his eyes grew large and he sighed.

"It doesn't seem to touch you greatly, Hauser," Quandt, who had come in silently when he heard the two talking, said suddenly.

Caspar turned around and said sadly: "She was a bad woman, Herr Quandt."

Quandt walked up to him and exclaimed cuttingly: "Unfortunate boy, to have the effrontery to desecrate the memory of a dead woman. You will never be forgiven for that. Now you have revealed your black soul. Shame, shame, and shame upon you! Get out of my sight! Does it not stir your soul that the departed may perhaps have been driven to such a deed by worry over your ingratitude? Does that not dawn upon you? Of course, a self-seeking boy like you does not worry about the sufferings of other people, only his own welfare is important to him."

"Husband, husband, calm yourself," the wife broke in after casting a shy glance at Caspar, who had turned deathly pale, and stood with his eyes completely closed, pressing the fingertips of his hands against one another!

"You are right, wife," replied Quandt, "I am wasting my indignation upon deaf ears. How can one hope to improve a person who has no humility and veneration in the face of death itself? It's simply throwing away time and trouble."

When Caspar reached his room the last rays of the setting sun were still glowing over the hills. He sat down by the window, took up a flower-pot, and looked down at it. The stem of the calix shook and it seemed to him as if he heard distant sounds. He wished to have the countenance of a flower in order not to have to return the glance of a human eye. Or he wished at least to hide himself in a flower until the year from whose ending he hoped so much was over. There one could be still and wait.

During the following days no mention of Frau Behold was made, and Quandt carefully avoided her name. He was all the more surprised when Caspar returned to the subject of his own accord. On Saturday at lunch he suddenly said that he regretted what he had said of the dead woman, he realized it was wrong to complain of a dead woman.

Quandt at once became attention. Aha, thought he, his conscience is beginning to stir, but he did not reply at all and only looked askance as if he wanted to say: let that drop, I know what I know. But his spleen was stirred and, while they were all three silently eating their soup, he could not refrain from saying: "You ought to be ashamed down to the very ground, Hauser, when you think of your behavior towards Frau Behold's innocent daughter."

"Why?" replied Caspar, surprised. "What in the world did I do?"

"Oh, now you want to play the little lamb," replied the teacher, contemptuously. "Thank heaven, I have everything in Frau Behold's own handwriting, so denial won't help you."

Caspar looked uneasy and puzzled. He questioned once more, then Quandt went to his desk and took Frau Behold's letter out of a drawer and standing beside Caspar read in a low voice: "There is much talk about his chastity and innocence in all such matters. About this, too, I have something to tell, for I witnessed with my own eyes at the time, how he approached my thirteen-year-old daughter. . . ."

Gradually Caspar understood. Slowly he laid down his spoon and his bread; his food stuck in his throat. His eyes grew very dark, he got up and exclaimed in a voice full of misery, "Oh, these people, these people!" and dashed out of the room.

The couple looked at one another. The wife put her hand flat down on the table cloth and said firmly: "No, Quandt, I can't believe it. Mrs. Behold must have been mistaken. He does not even know what a woman is."

Quandt, too, was touched. "That remains to be seen, that would have to be proved," he said, shaking his head. "You are very credulous, my dear. I remember at the birth of our daughter that to my surprise he talked of the matter like a mature man. That seemed very suspicious to me at once. Nevertheless, I admit that Frau Behold may have gone too far in the letter, and that consequently I may have been premature in my judgment. But I must get behind the matter and find out how far his knowledge goes, for as to his childishness, you know, I simply don't believe in it."

"You must conciliate him, Quandt, this thing was a little too strong!" said his wife.

Quandt looked thoughtful. "Conciliate him, yes, indeed, I'll do it gladly. But then he's always so clinging and affectionate that I find him hard to resist, and thus my objective opinion is colored. Tomorrow I'll talk to the clergyman about the matter."

No sooner said than done. Unfortunately Quandt on this occasion showed the fussiness of an old maid, and was as full of circumlocutions and flowery figures of speech as if the relations between men and women were only of an ethereal nature, which were at times sullied and defiled by offensive incidents which could not be eradicated.

The clergyman could not but smile. After some surprise and reflection he replied that he had never observed anything in the least objectionable in Hauser's character in this regard; Caspar seemed to him, as far as the relations between the sexes were concerned, to be a complete child as yet. As a proof of this he told the teacher how, about a month ago, when he was explaining to Caspar as well as he could a passage in the Bible which had struck him, the boy with charming hesitation had spoken of certain recurring periods of uneasiness, a condition which had certainly often oppressed him and for the interpretation of which he had never found anyone to confide in. The old man assured him that he could never forget the way in which Caspar had brought up the matter, it had sounded like an unsuspecting reproach against nature, which was doing things to him against which he could not defend himself.

No word of this escaped Quandt. He saw the matter with different eyes. He looked upon this as the indication of a perverted fantasy. However he did not say anything in the presence of the clergyman, but went home with his silent premeditation, and lay in ambush eagerly awaiting his opportunity.

The next day Caspar was to lunch at the Imhoffs', but came back again, for the Baroness was sick in bed. At supper the conversation turned upon this, and when Quandt expressed his regret Caspar said: "Ah, perhaps she will never get quite well again."

"What are you saying, Caspar?" the teacher's wife broke in, "such a young woman, so rich and so beautiful."

"Ah," replied Caspar sadly, "riches and beauty don't help. She has already worn herself out too much with grief."

"Has she perhaps confided her grief in you?" inquired Quandt incredulously.

Caspar did not reply to this question and continued, as if speaking to himself: "There is nothing in the world the matter with her, except that her husband is not as he ought to be; he prefers other women. Why? Otherwise he is so intelligent. But even if the woman grieves herself to death, it won't help matters. And people take back everything to her. I told her that those are not your friends who tell you such rubbish, they are not real friends."

"Hm," remarked Quandt and looked down at his plate smiling curiously. He overcame his feeling of shame and asked with forced lightness whether Herr von Imhoff had recently given his wife fresh cause for worry; to his knowledge a reconciliation had taken place only in March.

"Why, of course, he has given her cause," replied Caspar simply. "He has again become the father of a child!"

Quandt was frightened. Now, we've got it, he thought. And hard as it was for him, he decided to get to the bottom of the matter at once. He exchanged a glance of comprehension with his wife and told her she should see what the children were about. When she had left the room the teacher, white and excited by the difficulty of his undertaking, turned to Caspar and asked him whether he had as yet had anything to do with a woman; various conjectures had been advanced, and Caspar was to speak only to him, as to a father.

Caspar was grateful for these words. He regarded them as a sign of sympathy, although he did not understand their meaning or purpose, but only had a timorous foreboding of the murky element from which they emanated. He considered. "With a woman, what do you mean?" he murmured.

"My question is clear, Hauser, don't pretend to be so childish."

"Yes, I understand," replied Caspar quickly, in order not to dissipate the teacher's good humor, "and there has been something."

"Well, come out with it! Take courage!"

And harmlessly Caspar began to narrate: "About six weeks ago I took my Sunday suit to the cleaner's in Qzensgasse. You know, Herr Quandt, it is the little house next to the baker's. When I got there the store was locked and I knocked at the door. A young girl opened and was in her night-gown, that was all that she had on her body, one could see her whole breast, it was horrible. She took the things from me and said that she would tell the cleaner. I was still in front of the door. 'Just come in,' she said. Then I went in and asked her what she wanted. Then she began to dance about in front of me, laughed and talked a lot of rot, and asked me whether I wanted to be her bridegroom and finally—" he hesitated, smilingly.

"Finally, what finally?" asked Quandt, bending his head forward.

"Finally she asked me to give her a kiss."

"Well, and?"

"I told her to look for someone else, I did not care about smacking lips."

"And further?"

"And further, further there was nothing. I went away and she looked out of the window after me."

"How could you notice that?"

"Because I turned around." "Ah, so; you turned around. What's the woman's name?"

"I don't know it."

"You don't know it. Hm. . . . And. . . . Were you there a second time?"

Caspar said "No."

"A fine tale," murmured Quandt, getting up and casting his eyes towards heaven.

He made careful inquiries. He found out that a woman of doubtful reputation really did lodge at the cleaner's. Consideration for his reputation prevented him from going to the root of the matter, and anyway he had gotten the impression that the boy could not be as innocent in the whole affair as he pretended to be. For, so he argued, only a person whose brow bears the stamp of a certain moral deficiency could offer the opportunity for such low behavior as that of this female creature.

Yes, if he did not lie, thought Quandt, then everything would be different, but he lies, that's the frightful thing, he lies. Had he not said that the Archduchess of Kurland gave him a dozen embroidered handkerchiefs? No word of truth in it. Had he not stated that he knew the minister, Herr von Spiess, and had spoken to him at the theater? Lies. Had he not given himself the air with the musician Schiiler of having read the Gessner Idylls, and when the latter asked him about them had he not been unable to say a word about them? He did not even know what an idyll was. Does he not always pretend to have pressing errands first with the President, then with the Hofrat, and later it turns out that he has merely loafed about in order to go walking in a new cravat? Is not all this a fact, or am I so stupid and so unjust that I put an interpretation on these matters which would not occur to anyone else?

Quandt went to Herr Fuhrmann and presented to him these damnable transgressions point by point.

"Do you not see, my dear Quandt," replied the clergyman, "that these are a lot of pitiful little lies which hardly deserve such a name? It is more a desire to win favor, or an attempt, pitiful because of its inadequacy, to break bonds, or perhaps it is only a harmless pleasure in words, a form of speech. Perhaps he is merely playing with words, as other people play with them, only much more awkwardly."

"So," replied Quandt eagerly, "then I will tell your reverence a story which affords decisive evidence to the contrary. Just listen. Last week our maid one morning found the handle of his candlestick broken; she showed it to my wife, who brought the matter to my attention, and I found that the handle was not broken but melted off; the hollow part was burned black right down to the bottom from the heat of the candle, and the outside a reddish blue from the flame; in the saucer one could clearly see how high the melted wax had reached, and how in several spots it was scratched away. There was no trace left of the whole candle which Hauser had received the night before. Now you must know that I had strictly forbidden him to read or to study by candle-light; nevertheless I wanted to spare him and only had my wife warn him. But then he suddenly denied everything, assured her that he had neither knowingly let the candle burn, nor fallen asleep with it burning, and finally was bold enough to state that it was not his candlestick at all but that of the maid, for both looked alike. What do you say to that?"

The clergyman shrugged his shoulders. "We must not forget in spite of everything that he is a curiously constituted being," he replied thoughtfully. "I have convinced myself of it. I own a little electrical machine with which I sometimes experiment. Recently I took the thing out while Caspar was present, produced some sparks and charged the Leyden jar. Whereupon the poor soul turned white and whiter before my eyes, commenced to tremble, spread his fingers out stiffly in front of him, his body quivering like a live pike thrown on the sand. I was greatly frightened and put away my apparatus, whereupon he returned to his usual state. However, his head ached for days later, as he confessed to me, when he was in bed he had cold sweats and the things which he touched pricked him as if with tiny needles. Characteristically enough, he declared that during storms it was always the same; his blood burned and tickled so that he constantly wanted to scream. "And you believe in that?" exclaimed Quandt, striking his hands one upon the other.

"Yes, why indeed not?"

Well, if you believe in that I find myself at a great disadvantage among other people, that I must admit," said Quandt. "That I must admit," he repeated miserably.

It's always so, thought the teacher on his way home. First things are excused and embellished and when one brings cogent reasons people shrug their shoulders and present you with little stories which are highfalutin and improbable, and no iota of which can be proved. What a Satan there is in that boy that everywhere, wherever he goes, he knows how to call forth liking and sympathy. Curious that no one wants to see his faults, that perfect strangers are bent upon meeting him and express the shallowest enthusiasm as if they were bewitched, or as if he had given them a love potion.

This embittered Quandt. He said to himself: let us assume that I suddenly should appear among people who did not know me and give out that I was the Holy Ghost or his Apostle or pretended to be able to work miracles and it happened that this or that person demanded a real miracle, and I should then confess to complete dissimulation—what would happen? I should either be shut up in an asylum or given a flogging. Yes, they would do that to me, even if I assumed an angel's face, that's what they would do and they would do right; people would not load me down with presents and regard me as a saint and admire my beautiful eyes and white hands, and cut off locks of my hair as a souvenir as I have, I confess to God, been obliged to witness misguided people about me doing.

From self-communion of this sort one can clearly see that his association with his pupil was a source of worry and of serious internal conflicts for the teacher.

And what about the boy's past? Quandt racked his brains. Where does he really come from? One ought to be able to get to the bottom of that. How has he devised all these combinations with which he fools the esoteric? Yes, that's just the secret, the obscurants say. Secret? There is no secret; I repudiate secrets. The world from top to bottom is a clear structure and when the sun shines owls hide. If only God would give me some hint on how to cope with this diabolically artful deception. One ought sometime to see what this diary business means and what there is back of that. The diary seems to exist, that seems to be a real fact, in spite of all the nagging; perhaps it is a kind of confessional for him; one must get to the bottom of this.

Events helped Quandt to get to the bottom of it more quickly than he had hoped.

21. A Voice Calls

One afternoon in the middle of the summer Hickel appeared and gave Caspar a letter addressed to him, the lieutenant, but intended as a matter of fact for Caspar. It was from Count Stanhope and specifically directed the young man to hand over his diary to Hickel.

Caspar read the writing through three times before he finally found any words, then he refused to obey.

"Then, my good boy," said Hickel, "if kindly means won't do, I shall have to resort to force."

Caspar recollected himself, then he said sadly that the only person to whom he could give the diary was the President, and he would take it to him to-morrow morning if it was insisted upon.

"All right," replied the lieutenant, "I'll call for you tomorrow morning and then we will go to the President with the diary."

Hickel wanted to gain time. He had naturally no desire to have the diary get into Feuerbach's hands; it was just this that he had orders to prevent and he pondered what he should do. As regards Caspar, toward noon be stole out of the house and ran to the President's residence in order to complain. Feuerbach was in the Senate. Caspar confided his trouble to the President's daughter and she promised to tell her father.

In the afternoon the bell rang at the Quandts' and the President entered the room. Meantime Caspar, in order not to be obliged to hand over his cherished treasure even to this man whom he revered, had thought of an excuse, and when the President in Quandt's presence asked for the diary and whether it was true that he did not want to show it, Caspar replied that he had burned it.

Then the teacher gave a start and could not restrain an exclamation of anger.

"When did you burn it?" asked Feuerbach quietly.

"Today."

"And why?"

"In order not to be obliged to give it up."

"Why do you not want to give it up?"

Caspar remained silent and stared at the ground.

"That's a lie, he has not burned it, Your Excellency," cried Quandt, shaking with anger. "And even if he did keep a diary he must have done away with it long ago. Since Christmas I have been looking for it everywhere, I have searched in every corner of his room and never anywhere have I found a trace of it."

The President, silent and astonished, looked at Quandt with large eyes; it was a glance that contained fatigue and grief.

"Where was the diary kept, Caspar?" he then continued to inquire.

Caspar replied hesitatingly he had hidden it first here, then there, now among his books, then in a closet, finally on a nail on the back of his writing desk. Quandt meantime shook his head constantly and smiled an evil smile. "Did you put in the nail yourself?" he inquired.

"Yes."

"Who gave you permission?"

"Go now, Caspar," the President commandingly interrupted the conversation between the two. "I do not understand," he turned to the teacher when Caspar had left, "why Lord Stanhope suddenly places such importance upon the diary. He probably overestimates the doubtless innocent records. Moreover, with kindness and persuasion one would have gotten on better than by a categorical order."

"Kindness, persuasion?" replied Quandt, wringing his hands. "Then Your Excellency has a poor understanding of this person. Through kindness one only unleashes his self-seeking, and persuasion increases his obstinacy. Yes, he already regards himself as a somebody, gets up on his hind legs, opposes one and is capable of giving me an answer which leaves me standing as if slapped in the face. I beg Your Excellency's pardon, but I am of the opinion that even you will not make any progress with him through kindness and persuasion."

"Come now," said the President, and walking to the window, he looked gloomily at the dripping branches of the pear-tree which grew by the wall of the yard.

"I venture to assure Your Excellency with certainty that he has not burned the diary," Quandt finished, with an imploring voice.

The President did not reply. How repulsive it was to him to be obliged to put up with all these petty squabbles which they brought to him. He longed for peace. The one piece of work, that must be completed—then .... peace.

Feuerbach had scarcely left when Quandt hurried to Caspar's room, pushed the writing desk away from the wall and looked to see whether there was a nail there. Actually a nail had been hammered into the wall. Quandt called the maid up. "Has Hauser had a hammer recently and have you heard him hammering?" he asked. The maid replied, yes; last week he had fetched a hammer and nails from the kitchen and she had heard him knocking.

Suddenly Quandt had an inspiration. It is summer, he thought, and if he has really burned the diary, the ashes must still be in the stove. He went to the stove, knelt down and with greedy hands emptied all the charred and burned contents of the cavernous opening out upon the floor.

The ashes of much paper came out. Quandt took care that the big pieces should not break, for one can read writing even upon ashes. He pushed the fragments apart with care. He feared to touch this or that piece with his fingers and blew it aside with the breath of his mouth; when there was writing upon it he tried to read the words, but could not make out any connection.

Then steps approached and Caspar entered, not a little astonished at the posture in which he saw the teacher, whose hands and face were black with soot while the sweat poured down from his forehead.

Quandt did not permit himself to be deterred. "Such a quantity of ashes cannot possibly come from your diary alone," he said.

"I burned old letters and papers with it," replied Caspar.

The cool, matter-of-fact answer made Quandt's face turn red with rage. He got up hastily, murmured something through his teeth and left the room, banging the door after him. "You shall not come with us to the Dance this evening," he screamed on the steps.

In the Ressource there was a garden party, organized by the Rifle Club. Quandt as a matter of fact had no desire to go; such things always cost money. But his wife wanted amusement like other people for once, was sick of this tiresome hanging about at home. She had already made herself a chintz dress for this purpose a week before, and so the teacher was obliged to yield, and "pay his tribute to folly," as he put it, especially since the weather had become fine toward evening.

Caspar remained sitting at the open window until nightfall and enjoyed the silence. Then he struck a light and a smile played about his lips as he went to the wall, took down the steel engraving over the sofa, loosened the wooden board that backed the frame, and drew forth the diary which was hidden under it. He sat down with it at the table, thoughtfully turned some of the pages of the book and read through several passages.

Here a whole generation, the entire period of development of a human being, had been condensed into the course of not more than four years, one stage pressing upon another with weird rapidity. That which it contained scarcely uttered or pictured the innocent outpouring of early pleasures and griefs: the first fearful understanding of the world, boyish philosophy and obstinate struggles with mundane and super mundane nature, which he ominously felt to be hostile, all this would have bitterly disappointed these huntsmen intent on their prey. But it was not meant for them, it was meant for his mother; to her it was dedicated once and for all, and with the eccentricity so characteristic of him the thought that any other eye than hers should even rest upon these pages was quite inconceivable to Caspar. It may also have been that gradually in his imagination this copy-book had become his only real possession, the only thing that fully belonged to him and which possessed his whole confidence.

On one of the first pages stood: "Recently I sowed my name with garden cresses, it grew very nicely and gave me great pleasure. Someone came into the garden and stole pears and trod on my name and then I cried. Herr Daumer told me I should make it again and I did make it again and the next day the cats trod on it."

Then followed in the same helpless style some attempts to describe his imprisonment somewhat as follows: "The Story of Caspar Hauser: I want to tell, myself, how badly things went with me. But then when I was locked up in prison it seemed all right to me, because I knew nothing of the world, and never saw a human being."

In this tone it continued; later on there were some attempts at fine writing, one of which began with the sentence: "What adult would not think with sorrowful emotion of the undeserved imprisonment in which I spent the most blooming period of my life; and at a time when many youths live in golden pleasures my nature was not yet in the least awake."

Dreams, hopes, images of longing, reports of little outings, of conversations with strangers, here and there an encouraging word found in a book or scratched down out of a wilderness of talk without content, and gradually sentences which contained something like a personal polish and a curious concealed melancholy in their style. A grief was never expressed plainly, or a judgment or an opinion stated; he was, as Quandt described this characteristic, sly as a fox. Of an important day he frequently noted only the date and next to that a little star; sometimes an event was only indicated by shy circumlocutions, nor was his spirit lacking in laconicisms; of the attempted murder in Daumer's house he stated briefly: "The harvest moon was almost the moon of my death."

Little incidents of daily life: "Yesterday a bee stung me, Fraulein von Stichaner sucked the wound, she said 'Whomever a bee stings is lucky/ " Or: "Yesterday there was a raging fire, the woods at Dautenwinden burned; I sat half the night through at the window, and thought the world was coming to an end."

The delicacy of his senses was incisively expressed: "Herr Quandt smells like stale air, his wife like wool, the Hofrat like paper, the President like tobacco, the lieutenant like oil, the clergyman like a wardrobe. Almost Everyone smells badly, only the count smelled like a body which consisted of nothing but fair air."

Several pages were dedicated to the count; here the tone became poetical and not infrequently entreating, after the manner of a prayer. Stanhope and the sun became pictures of related forces. Since his departure from Nurnberg this had ceased, his lordship's name was no longer mentioned; only the solemn promise of the eighth of December was written down.

In the last few days a drawing had been made which filled half of a whole page; it was the outline of a masculine head sketched with a strikingly skillful hand. It was a strange face, not like any mortal's, rather resembling that of a statue—as if snatched from some frightful vision and painfully rigid. Underneath was written:

> Oh! Great One! Say! What wouldst thou have of me?
> Thou followest me, and followest a blind track.
> Beneath thy gaze my aspect is transformed:
> The dungeon doors are opened, and the child
> That lay there long imprisoned issues forth.
> Gone are the mantle and the sword and crown:
> And riderless the white horse rides afield.

The drawing had been made one night; starting up from a dream Caspar had seen the face before him; he had jumped out of bed and had drawn it by moonlight. The verses he had found ready on his lips when he awoke the next morning. He had not puzzled himself further about their meaning; only now he became perplexed and whispered them to himself several times.

Meantime darkness had come, Caspar was just about to get up from the table when he heard the front door creak, quick steps approached, there was a knock at the door and Quandt's voice ordered him to open it. Frightened, Caspar blew out the light. In the darkness he felt his way to the sofa, put the diary back in its hiding place, and while Quandt knocked louder and louder he succeeded in hanging the picture back on its nail.

Quandt, walking along the Spitalweg, had already noticed at a distance the light in Caspar's room. He seized his wife by the arm and exclaimed: "Look, wife, just look." "What's the matter again?" complained his wife, who was angry because Quandt had spoiled the whole evening for her with his ill-humor.

"Now you have proof that he's sitting up by candlelight," said Quandt.

The house also had an entrance in the rear, through a little garden-gate. Quandt chose this and as he stood in the yard with his wife he wondered whether he could not eavesdrop in some way and see what the boy was doing. The pear tree along the wall was just the thing for the purpose. Quandt was strong and athletic; without trouble he climbed the wall and then reached a broad branch, whence he could look into Caspar's room. What he saw was sufficient. After a short time he came down much excited, rushed to his wife and said: "I have caught him, Jette," and rushed into the house and up the steps.

When no stirring inside resulted from his knocking he fell into a rage. He began to pound on the door, first with his fists, then with his heels and when this did not help the pitiful man decided in his rage to get a hammer and to break in the door. But he first ran down quickly into the yard again and saw that meanwhile Caspar's room had become dark, a circumstance which only increased his rage.

The children and the maid had awakened from the noise, his wife met him with a wail of lamentation when he ran out from the kitchen with an ax. He pushed her aside, frothing, "I'll just show him," and rushed up again.

At the first stroke of the ax the door opened and Caspar in his shirt stood on the threshold. The sight of his calm figure was so unexpected and sobering in its effect on the teacher that he simply collapsed and was not able to say or do anything but grind his teeth curiously. "Make a light," he murmured after a long pause. But his wife had already come up the stairs with a light, crying quietly. Caspar saw the ax in the teacher's relaxed hand and began to tremble violently. At this sign of fear, Quandt completely lost his self-possession. He became ashamed of himself, and sighing deeply, he said: "Hauser, you worry me very much." Hereupon he turned around and went slowly down the steps.

Caspar did not fall asleep until the day broke. At breakfast, before the usual hour for his lessons, he found out that Quandt had already gone out. Noon came and during luncheon the teacher was completely silent; at the last bite he got up and said: "Be in your room at five o'clock, Hauser. The lieutenant wishes to speak to you."

Caspar lay down upstairs on the sofa. It was a hot August afternoon, swallows flew by the open windows with a frightened chirping; the hot, heavy air buzzed and sang in the narrow room. Still tired from the night Caspar soon dozed and only woke when his shoulder was strongly shaken. Hickel and the teacher stood by him; he sat up, rubbed his eyes and looked silently at the two men. Hickel, with a vocational gesture, buttoned his uniform tightly and said: "I hereby order you, Hauser, to give me your diary."

Caspar got up breathing deeply and answered with a decision proceeding more from inner compulsion than from courage: "Lieutenant, I shall not give you my diary."

Quandt struck his hands together and exclaimed complainingly: "Hauser, Hauser, you are carrying your unfilial obstinacy too far."

Caspar looked about despairingly and replied with a trembling mouth: "Am I another man's chattel? Am I like an animal? What do you still want? Haven't I already said that I have burned the book?"

"Do you perhaps wish to deny, Hauser, that last night you wrote by candlelight?" asked Quandt pressingly. "You did not have any letters to write and you were through with your exercises."

Caspar remained silent, he could not find his way in nor out.

"A virtuous man needs not to object at all to having his diary seen," continued Quandt, "on the contrary he must wish it, since his stainless record is thus shown. You, least of anyone, my dear Hauser, have reason to keep a secret diary."

"How much longer are you going to keep us waiting?" asked Hickel with cold politeness.

"I would rather die than bear all this," exclaimed Caspar, raising his arm in order to hide his face in it.

"Come, come," said Quandt, who was uncomfortable, "we mean well with you; the lieutenant, too, only wants what is best for you."

"Of course," corroborated Hickel dryly, "moreover, I can tell you that to die just now would not be an especially good idea for you. One might under certain circumstances read upon your gravestone: Here lies the deceiver, Caspar Hauser"

"Quite aside from the fact that such an exclamation expresses a sentiment that is highly reprehensible," added Quandt reproachfully, "it is a cowardly and immoral idea."

"I don't care about life if I am always to be plagued with such matters and people don't believe," replied Caspar sadly. "I did not live formerly either, and did not know for a long time that I was alive."

Meantime, Hickel went along the wall, tapping with his knuckles, as if in play, at certain places on the wall; suddenly his attention seemed to turn toward the picture over the sofa. He took it down smilingly, looked at it on all sides and finally opened the hinge in order to remove the board.

Caspar turned chalk-white and shook like an aspen.

But when Hickel, simpering with satisfaction, took the blue copy-book in his hand, a curious transformation came over Caspar. He looked as if he were suddenly growing and had become a head taller. With two long strides he stood close in front of the lieutenant His face was fairly quivering. In his expression there was an exalted resolution. His glance glowed with a passionate and commanding force. Hickel, with the dull sense of being torn to pieces and trodden under foot, stepped back slowly against the door, fascinated. Cold sweat broke out over his skin as Caspar followed him slowly step by step, stretched out his arm, snatched the book from his fingers, tore it through the middle, then tore it again and again, until finally the whole thing lay in tatters on the ground.

Who knows what more would have happened if the entrance of a fourth person at this instant had not altered the situation? It was the clergyman, Herr Fuhrmann, who as he went by had wished to call on Caspar to ask him why he had stayed away from his lesson today. As he entered, some perception of what had occurred must have forced itself upon him; he glanced silently from one to the other. Quandt, who had followed the whole process with horrified eyes, only regained his composure with difficulty and said in an embarrassed voice: "What a lot of scraps you have made there, Hauser."

Hickel walked through the room with a few long strides, then he gave the clergyman a military salute and left with a cold and sinister face. At the door he turned around, pointed to the heap of papers and made an imperative motion of the head toward Quandt. The latter understood. He bent down in order to collect the scraps of paper. Caspar, however, perceived his intention, placed both feet on the pile and said: "That goes into the fire, Herr Quandt."

He knelt down, collected the scraps with both his hands, carried them to the stove, opened the little door with his foot and threw everything into it. Then he struck a fire and a minute later the whole heap was blazing brightly.

Herr Fuhrmann was merely a silent witness of the scene, Hickel had left and the teacher, with a reiterated slight cough, walked up and down in front of the stove with the regular tread of a policeman, while Caspar tremblingly watched until the last spark had burned out; then he took the poker and beat the ashes into dust.

The clergyman later had a conversation with Caspar, which in spite of the boy's depressed mood and a really sick distaste for talking, nevertheless led to some disclosures which moved the clerical gentleman to write to President Feuerbach on the subject of this occurrence.

"It is curious that this teacher," he said, in the course of his communications to Feuerbach, "an otherwise so excellent man, should seem veritably bewitched in all matters concerning Hauser. The calm of Hauser makes him irritable, his gentleness rough, his silence talkative, his melancholy sarcastic; and the boy's awkwardness seems the most crafty cunning. From everything that Hauser does and says he quietly deduces the contrary, even the multiplication table seems a lie in Caspar's mouth. I really believe he would prefer to cut open the boy's breast to determine what goes on within it. That is, God knows, no charitable thought of mine, but I cannot help seeing how he regards everything with suspicion. He is suspicious if something seems new to Caspar, and suspicious if he already knows it; suspicious if he sleeps long, suspicious if he gets up early. That he loves the theater and does not care for music is suspicious, suspicious that he swallows things without resistance when he is scolded; however, that he tries to settle quarrels between others, between Quandt and his wife, for example, is suspicious. Everything is suspicious. How is this to end!"

But as the pertinent saying goes: one word led to another and in the end nothing came of it.

The President, curiously distrait, promised to take Lieutenant Hickel to task. He sent for Hickel and screamed at him as soon as he came in so that the disconcerted man was dumfounded. Unfortunately, the scolding served the purpose badly, for when the President's anger had evaporated Hickel's superior calm and calculated submissiveness carried the day. Nothing came of the matter. Everything remained as it was. Only, the lieutenant, whose vanity had been deeply wounded, went his way twice as calmly and coldly.

"One must certainly regard our efforts to arrange a pleasant existence for Hauser as unsuccessful," said Feuerbach one day to his daughter. "The boy suffers in his present surroundings and the way in which he is treated seems to be against all sense and justice."

"Perhaps, but how can we change it?" replied Henriette, shrugging her shoulders.

"I am only relieved because a decision must be given when once the report is published," said the President aloud to himself.

"How will it hurt the young man if the waves of life do clash together over his head!" continued Henriette.

"Perhaps it will teach him to swim. It is not your place, father, to be his tutor." "Perhaps he will thus learn to swim. Excellently expressed, my daughter. Later he may think with gratitude of the trials he has undergone. A crowned head who has undergone such a fate, who has risen from the lowest depths to the most exalted eminence—that would give one hopes. If the great ones of this earth were not lacking in a knowledge of life, the broad masses would mean something more and something different to them than a milch cow. Let us allow the steel to temper so that it may remain hard. Have any proof-sheets come today?"

Henriette said no, and left the room sighing.

There is an inner voice which speaks more strongly than all the wisdom of maxims; Feuerbach constantly felt the strength of this voice anew whenever he found himself face to face with Caspar. He was not capable of finding subterfuges to deny the appeal of a higher instance than reason and experience. Age had not chilled but rather consolidated a frank sense of responsibility which he felt toward his own heart; he had to confess that what troubled him was simply his own bad conscience.

What a dilemma for such a man! On the one hand, he had fulfilled his intellectual mission to the point of extreme self-denial; on the other hand, there was the reproachful eye of him whom the mission concerned and to whom he could not and dare not give himself, for fear of too much partisanship, for fear of beclouding his judgment, for apprehension lest the angel of justice would have to fly from his chosen path if inclination, consideration and affectionate sympathy should enter into the matter.

The President sent Stanhope, who was at that time in Rome, as well as his own closest friends, advance-sheets of his book on Caspar Hauser. The count did not thank him, nor send as much as a word in reply.

Feuerbach did not need a worse sign. How had the great words sounded which formerly, in a living hour, he had addressed to that man. "If this face lies, my lord, with which you stand before me, then— "

Yes, then, what then? Childish arrogance! Would the world go under because a Feuerbach had made a mistake? How many-sided is man, how many faces, how many words he finds for his pitiful advantage! For a bite of bread every beggar becomes a prince of words, and what carriages of state, what peerages, what gracious manners and persuasive feelings if he, to whom the word is only a pretense, thus saves his own leprous skin. For this, then, had he dissected hearts, burrowed in the depths of souls, measured justice and crime according to the needs of mankind, with legal science and humane feeling, in order that a foppish scamp should come from England to play a sardonic game with him, and smilingly reduce everything to the absurd.

The old man was disgusted, but his conception of the power and strength of the enemies with whom he had become engaged in an unequal struggle gradually became tremendous, and, although his conduct was not in the least influenced and he did not waver even for an instant, a dark unrest nevertheless took possession of him. Since the nocturnal raid, whose perpetrators remained undiscovered in spite of all efforts, his sleep had not been sound. At times he got out of bed and wandered with a light through the rooms, down the steps and along the corridors; he shook the windows and tried the soundness of the locks and not infrequently became frightened at his own shadow. It was a shocking spectacle for his children to see a man of such passionate and deep-rooted courage enmeshed in such a world of apparitions. Once, in the early morning, on the outer side of the house door, the following words were found written in chalk:

> Anslem of Feuerbach, Knight, beware!
> Quench the fire in your own lair!
> False is the friend who sits beside thee!
> Hew him in twain, or woe betide thee!

One evening toward the end of October, Quandt came and asked to speak to the President. Feuerbach bade him come in and observed at once that he was embarrassed and disconcerted; the teacher did not present his usual circumlocutions, but came to the point at once. He stated that Caspar had received a letter from the count the day before yesterday, since when he had been completely changed, could His Excellency not spare an hour to talk to the boy, he himself could not get a word out of him.

The President asked wherein the change consisted.

"It is as if he had become deaf and dumb." replied Quandt. "At the table he leaves the dishes untouched; at his lessons he is excessively inattentive; indeed, his mind wanders, he does not prepare his work, he does not answer questions, and he wanders about like one deathly sick, staring into space. Last night my wife and I listened and we heard him whimpering to himself for a long time, then suddenly he uttered a dreadful scream."

"Do you perhaps know the contents of the count's letter?" inquired the President.

"Oh, yes, of course," replied the teacher naively, "it is my habit to open all letters before he gets them."

Feuerbach looked up sharply and stared at the teacher with dark curiosity. "Well, what?" he asked.

"I can't reconcile the contents of the letter with such an effect in the least," replied Quandt suspiciously.

The President stamped impatiently with his foot. "All right, all right," he exclaimed abruptly, "but what was in the letter, since you already know it?"

Quandt was scared. "The letter said that the count could not come to Ansbach again this year, unexpected events having compelled him to postpone this plan indefinitely. Now, of course, I know that Hauser counted greatly upon his lordship's coming; he even spoke of a definite date and regarded it as a sacrilege if one tried to dissuade him from it. He actually seemed to regard it as the count's duty, for in his childish head he still believed that the count would take him to England to his castle and he has no idea that the count has long since ceased to care for him."

"How do you know that, man?" the President roared, as he jumped up with such violence that the chair back of him fell over.

"I beg Your Excellency's pardon," stammered Quandt, frightened, "but that is as clear as day." He went over, picked the chair up with a polite grimace, and while the President walked up and down with his short stiff steps, he said shyly: "In spite of everything, the effect of this refusal, which is couched in the most urbane forms, is to me inexplicable and worries me. There must be something back of it, perhaps Your Excellency will be able to find out what."

"I shall look into the matter," the President interrupted curtly. Quandt made his bow and retired. He did not go home, but turned toward the Herrieder suburbs, for he wanted to call for his wife at her mother's house. There was a heavy storm, leaves and branches whirled through the air, Quandt's coat was blown up about him and he was obliged to hold the rim of his slouch hat with both hands.

Caspar had secretly left the house shortly after the teacher without any real object. When he was on the street it occurred to him that he might go to see Frau von Imhoff, and regardless of the darkness and the bad weather, and although the Imhoffs* little summer-house was a quarter of an hour's walk out of the city, he decided to go. But when he had gotten there, and stood at the gate looking up at the lighted windows, all his desire disappeared and he was afraid of the illuminated rooms. He already saw himself upstairs, he already heard the words which were nothing to him and meant nothing, he knew them all and could have repeated them by heart on the threshold. Yes, he was now familiar with people's words, he learned nothing new from them, they fell into the immeasurable ocean of his sadness like dismal little drops whose sound was quickly consumed in the depths.

A shadow glided by the windows, another followed. So they dwelt in their houses, silently and diligently, and lighted their lamps and did not know who stood outside at the gate.

In the midst of the roaring of the wind, Caspar heard tones which seemed to proceed from a stringed instrument hanging up under the clouds. There was an Aeolian harp on the roof of the summer-house, but Caspar did not know this and regarded it as a ghostly music. As he turned back the organ-like chords continued to sound in his ears from time to time.

He still did not wish to go home. The same dull urge which had driven him to the Imhoffs' pavilion led him on to the general commissioner's house, then to the residence of the Regierungsprasident, then to the Feuerbachs', and finally in front of an unoccupied building whose closed shutters, moss-covered ledges, and high arched door, over which an eye was carved in the stone, and above this the words "The Eye of God" had already stirred his curiosity long ago. At the time of the Margraves a jeweler was said to have lived there. He felt as if he had been a guest in all these houses, as if he had walked about unseen among all their inhabitants or had wandered through their empty rooms, and as though he had thus acquired a remarkable knowledge of the past and present lives of these people.

Fairly tired, and at the same time profoundly excited, he got to the teacher's house. Quandt and his wife were not yet home, the children were asleep, the maid was nowhere to be seen, a tremendous silence reigned; only the wind howled about the walls, and the little lamp in the hall flickered as if from fear. Then, as Caspar walked to the steps, he heard a long-drawn delicate voice, like the chirping of a cricket, and the voice called:

"Stephan!"

Puzzled, he remained standing and looked about. Since everything was silent, he thought that he was mistaken and that it was a voice outside on the street. But hardly had he taken three steps than the voice sounded again, only incomparably louder, as if very nearby:

"Stephan!"

There was something endlessly moving in the tone; it sounded like someone who calls from the water, fearing that he will drown. Unmistakably it was a masculine voice which now for the third time, as if strangled with sobs, called:

"Stephan!"

There was no doubt that the call was for him, Caspar. He stretched out his arms and asked, "Where, where are you; where are you?"

Then he saw above the door a face, illuminated with a livid glow, floating without a body. It was Stanhope's face; the eyes staring open, the mouth wide open, as if in a state of the utmost terror; the whole was ugly, incredibly ugly.

Caspar stood as if nailed to the spot, his limbs, his eyes even, seemed turned to stone. When he looked a second time the head had disappeared and the voice, too, could no longer be heard. There were lights on corridor and steps; all the doors were shut; no one was visible; no sound could be heard.

22.   A Journey Is Decided Upon

One afternoon in December the surprised neighbors saw Herr Quandt storm out of his house like one possessed and run towards the more modern part of the city, where the police-lieutenant lived. He walked into the room, and without giving himself time to take his hat off, he put his hand in his coat pocket and silently handed a small pamphlet to Hickel.

It was Feuerbach's brochure on Caspar Hauser, which had just recently appeared. Quandt had just gotten the little book today and had read it through in great haste. Hickel took the book, looked it over, and said calmly: "Well, what about it? Do you think that's anything new for me? You are not getting excited about it? The old boy writes because it's his natural weakness. You can more readily break a hen of laying eggs than a born scribbler of writing."

Quandt breathed deeply. "Writing, well and good, I admit all that," he replied, "but this thing nevertheless goes too far. Permit me," he seized the pamphlet, opened to the title page and read aloud, Caspar Hauser: An Example of a Crime Against the Soul of a Human Being. That sounds like something," he remarked bitterly. "It throws sand in people's eyes from the very beginning. But the whole thing is a romance and not even one of the best sort."

He turned the pages and pointed with his finger to a passage, simultaneously reading aloud with ironic intonations: "Caspar Hauser, a rare specimen of mankind!—I am at the end of my wits. I feel as if the notoriously worst among my pupils were declared to be great scholars before a large assembly of people. A rare specimen! In this regard I know more, I am thankful to say, than Your Excellency. On this score I could open the eyes of the respected public in quite a different way! A rare specimen indeed, but one must read the alphabet from the beginning and not from the end. So this is the great criminologist, the omniscient one whom all admire. That's what fame is like when looked at close at hand. And, then, that whole back-stairs romance of dynastic intrigue. It would be laughable if it were not so sad. Dear God, what times and what a world!"

The lieutenant listened to the teacher's outbreak with a scarcely noticeable smile. When Quandt had finished, he said indifferently: "What would you have? As faithful servants we cannot help it that we are condemned to watch the silly pranks of our superiors. Moreover, I can reassure you in one respect—the President himself is not overjoyed with his book. He complains of lapses of memory which mar it, and that it has cost him more work than a whole Corpus juris. And now he must submit to being hard put to it in the hands of other German officials. They say that the Federal Commission in Frankfort will confiscate the pamphlet."

"That would be well," exclaimed Quandt. "And the princes, too, should do something against it."

"Just leave that to the princes," replied Hickel, whose face had suddenly grown angry and worried. "Hang it all, my dear Quandt, you are getting as excited as if your neck were at stake. I'd love to know if you would show as much courage if his Excellency were here in the room."

Quandt looked distrustfully about. Then he shrugged his shoulders and replied: "You are fond of joking, lieutenant. It's bad enough that we must keep our real opinions under cover. We have all forgotten how a man should carry his head. We have all learned thoroughly how to lick boots. But I don't want to lick boots any longer."

"Hush," interrupted Hickel peevishly. "Drop that! It sounds like demagoguery. Tell me, my friend, does Hauser know of the pamphlet?"

"Not so far as I know." replied Quandt. "But it will not be possible to prevent his hearing of it. There are enough senseless people who will take pleasure in seeing that he does. Haven't you also heard, lieutenant, of the book of a certain Gamier?"

At the mention of this name Hickel started and looked darkly at the teacher. It took quite some time before he decided to answer. "Gamier? Yes, that's the fellow who has fled the country. In his pamphlet he brings forward the same nonsensical stuff as the

President, but embroidered with the silliest court gossip. The asinine book is not worth mentioning."

"How shall I behave if Hauser somehow comes into possession of either of these products?" asked Quandt.

Hickel walked up and down with his long strides and bit at his underlip nervously with his teeth.

"Take care," he replied coldly. "Don't let him out of your sight. However, the matter does not concern me; it's all the same to me. The young man will be told how to behave!"

Quandt sighed and was oppressed. "Lieutenant," he said, "I can't tell you how I feel. I would give the half of my salvation if it were granted me to move that boy to a frank admission."

"You may pay less than that," replied Hickel darkly.

"Do you know the latest?" continued Quandt. "The President wants to employ Hauser as a clerk in the Appellate Court. He is to start work to-morrow."

"And what will the count say to that?"

"He wanted to write it to him, but does not know where he is. In the last month only one letter came from the count and Hauser didn't even look at it. From my point of view, the count ought to be glad of this measure. For a trade, in the narrower sense of the word, Hauser is useless; unfortunately he has enjoyed the association of the more cultivated and higher classes too long not to become rebellious if he were obliged to exchange it suddenly for the surroundings of a workshop. On the other hand, he is not suited either for any calling requiring a more thorough instruction, for he has neither the understanding nor the concentration for serious study. The President has accordingly found the best solution and one which also frees me from a part of my responsibility. By means of this activity, Hauser can not only fit himself for a clerkship in the lower service, but if he is industrious he can get a position in the registry or accounting department."

Hickel scarcely listened to these long-winded remarks. They left together; in front of the Court Drug Store, Hickel took his leave, in order, as he said, to get a powder for sleeplessness.

On the way home Quandt was greeted very cordially by Hofrat Hofmann, a fact which was sufficient to raise his depressed spirits considerably. At lunch there was roast veal and ox tongue salad, and he even became gay and condescended to joke with his wife. But as is apt to be the case with serious natures, his joviality was rather heavy. Among other things, he seized a knife and waved it violently just in front of her nose, laughing all the time. Caspar turned white, got up and said, "For God's sake, Herr Quandt, do put that knife away; I can't stand it!"

Quandt, at once out of humor again, grumbled: "Come, now, Caspar, such behavior smacks strongly of affectation."

"You're a fine Jack," said Frau Quandt. "What will you do if there is a war some time? Then one must die like a man."

"Die? No thanks! I don't care to die," replied Caspar hastily.

"And yet that time in the presence of the lieutenant you expressed yourself in a most objectionable way about the same point," came from Quandt.

"Oh, such a coward," continued the teacher's wife. "You were just as cowardly, too, with Cadet Hugenpoet of the dragoons last summer."

"What was that about?" inquired Quandt. "I don't" know anything about it."

"He was often together with the cadet. The latter constantly raved to Hauser about becoming a soldier; in a few years he would easily become an officer. Would not be such a bad idea; cadets have an easy time of it and get on quickly. Our Hauser was enthusiastic about the idea, but suddenly the friendship was over."

"Ah, and for what reason?" "It was thus: One evening in September he went walking with the cadet along the banks of the Rezat and they came to a place where many boys and young men were bathing, for it was frightfully hot that day. The cadet says, 'Let's do that, too/ gets undressed and wants to persuade Caspar to bathe also. He, however, was scared to death at the suggestion and said that he would not go into the water. The others heard this, they got out of the water, surrounded him, jeered at him and wanted to force him into the water. Whereupon he breaks loose, before anyone is aware of it, and in his devilish fear, runs off over the fields with the naked boys jeering after him. This was too much for the cadet and he hasn't been to see Hauser any more since then. Is that true or not, Caspar?"

Caspar nodded. The teacher shook with laughter.

A few days later Frau von Imhoff and Fraulein von Stichaner came to see Caspar. The teacher's wife, proud at having such distinguished guests, did not move from the spot. For the sake of entertainment, and because nothing more sensible occurred to her, she again told, in Caspar's presence, the story of the cadet and the boy's refusal to bathe; however, this time the tale was received less favorably than by her husband. The two ladies listened in silence.

"Such cowardice really isn't nice," remarked Fraulein von Stichaner later, in the street, to Frau von Imhoff.

"One can't really call it cowardice," replied the latter; "he loves life too dearly, that's it. He loves life like a madman, the way an animal loves it, the way a miser loves gold. He confessed to me himself that every time before going to sleep he was afraid that his sleep might turn into death without his knowing it, and he prayed to God not to fail to have him wake up again the next morning. No, it is not cowardice, it is perhaps the foreboding of a great danger, and the instinct to make up for much that he has lost. One ought to see at times how pleased he can be, even over some trifle which Everyone else passes over with indifference. His pleasure has something magnificent about it, something aloof from the world, just as his fear and sadness have a certain weird quality."

At home, Frau von Imhoff was surprised by a letter from her friend Frau von Kannawurf, surprised in a doubly agreeable way, since Frau von Kannawurf wrote—she was at that time in Vienna—that she wanted to come to Ansbach in March. In the letter there was, besides this, much talk of Caspar Hauser: "I have recently read Feuerbach's book," she wrote among other things, "and must confess to you that no book has ever before stirred me to the depths to such an extent. I can't think of anything else since then and I cannot sleep. Does Caspar Hauser himself know of the book, and what is his attitude towards it? What does he say about it?"

Frau von Imhoff failed to reply to this; it was difficult to ask Caspar. If he has not read the book, she thought, it is painful and strange to see him ignorant of it; it is still more painful and curious if he has read it; painful and curious his remaining here, his copying at the court, all of his pursuits; and how is it possible to bring the subject up for discussion? Any frank remark might be irremediable.

Nevertheless Frau von Imhoff undertook to sound Caspar out carefully to learn whether he knew anything at all about the matter, or whether he had heard it spoken of. And he did know about it. He did not, however, have the slightest wish to find out anything clearly concerning what was written. Firstly from fear: fear made him recoil from any change in his situation, from anything which might turn his thoughts away from the present, to which he clung tenaciously; and besides, because he probably assumed that the President's book dealt only with the groundless gossip which he already knew inside out and which, as he used to put it, merely gave him a headache and heartache and stupid afterthoughts. He had experienced all this so often that from sheer irritation he had finally become so little curious that a single hint in the course of a conversation was sufficient to cover his face with an expression of insipid boredom.

It was a curious turn of affairs that finally brought him to the knowledge of the work which had been written for him and for his sake.

It was on a rough March morning when suddenly the news spread through the Appellate Court Building, and soon after through the whole city, that the President had fallen in a swoon from his chair in the big court room, while he was conducting the hearings of a case. All the clerks at once ran out of their rooms and stood about on the steps and in the halls. Caspar, too, had left his desk and joined the rest. He, however, crept away purposely in order not to be obliged to witness the President being carried down from the upper story.

When he returned to the room in which he wrote every morning from eight to twelve, in the company of an old clerk, a certain Dillmann, his companion had not yet returned. Caspar, very sad and frightened, went to the window and, as he was in painful thoughts, painted the name of Feuerbach with his finger on the misty coating of the window-pane.

Meantime Dillmann came back and took his place, wringing his hands.

Up to this day the old clerk—and Caspar had now been in the office for nine weeks—had not yet exchanged a dozen superfluous words with his new colleague; he had not paid the slightest attention to him and had shown a peevish indifference to him. During the course of the thirty years during which this man had been copying documents, decrees, ordinances and judgments, he had attained a peculiar skill in sleeping, and it was amusing to see, when he had rested the quill of his pen on the paper, snoring gently while taking his siesta, how his hand at once resumed its calligraphic progress if the step of one of his superiors was heard outside, for he had studied the walk of every man and carried it, so to speak, in his head.

Caspar was therefore all the more surprised when Dillmann walked up to him and said in trembling voice: "The incomparable man! If only something does not happen to him! If only some human ill does not overtake him!"

Caspar turned around, but did not reply.

"And for you, Hauser, it would be an irreparable loss," continued the old man in a curiously chiding and disapproving voice; "where in this wretched old world does one find a person who so takes up another person's cause? It would not surprise me if the thing came to a bad end. Yes, it will end badly, it will turn out badly."

Caspar listened silently. His eyes glistened.

"Such a man!" exclaimed Dillmann. "I have, since I have been here, Hauser, accompanied seven presidents and twenty-two members of the board of council to the grave, but there was not one like him among them. A titan, Hauser, a titan! He could snatch the stars from the sky for the sake of justice. One has only to look at him—have you ever looked at him carefully?—that arch over his nose: that indicates genius, it is said; and that brow of Jupiter. And that book, Hauser, that he wrote for you! That is a book! It is his own funeral pyre! One must grind one's teeth and clench one's fists when one reads it!"

Caspar looked sullen. "I haven't read it," he said briefly.

The old man gave a start. His mouth opened and snapped. "Not read it?" he stammered. "You—not read it? How is that possible? May the devil take me alive!" Hurriedly he tripped to his table, pulled open a drawer, looked about in it and pulled forth the pamphlet. He reached it over to Caspar, actually stuck it into his hand and snarled: "The devil take you; now go and read it!"

Caspar behaved almost as Hickel had toward Quandt. He turned the book over and looked undecided. Then he finally opened the book and read the title, turning visibly pale. However, even this was not enough to make him curious or impatient. He put the book in his pocket and said dryly: "I will read it at home."

At the stroke of twelve he left the office as usual, sat down at the table at home as if nothing had happened and listened silently to the conversation, which turned solely upon the incident which had befallen the President.

"Last Sunday before church," the teacher's wife chattered, "I saw the President just as he met four corpse-washerwomen. The President was quite frightened and remained standing, looking after them. I thought at once that that can't mean anything good."

"If only you women would not presume to peek into the Almighty's cards every now and then," remarked Quandt peevishly. "One preaches and preaches the whole live-long year and thinks how wonderful it is to walk on the pinnacles of enlightenment, and then one's own family are the worst marplots of all."

Caspar laughed at these words, which caused the teacher's wife to glance at him angrily.

Then he went to his room.

At two o'clock he was to come for his lesson, as he did not have to be back at the office until four. When ten minutes past the hour had gone by Quandt walked into the hall and called. There was no answer. He went up and convinced himself that Caspar was not there. His displeasure changed into fright when his spying glances encountered Feuerbach's pamphlet lying on Caspar's table.

"So he's got it, anyway," he murmured bitterly.

He took the book and went in search of his wife downstairs and said in a toneless voice: "Jette, I have made a frightful discovery. Hauser had the President's pamphlet upstairs in his room. Oh, what unscrupulous people. I wonder who is responsible for this new trick!"

Frau Quandt showed little understanding for the incident. "Let him alone," or "tell him so," or "just give it to him," was mostly all that she was able to reply when Quandt was angry at Caspar.

"When did Hauser go away?" Quandt inquired of the maid. She did not know anything about it. Then Caspar came into the room and excused himself politely.

"Where have you been?" inquired the teacher.

"I went to the Feuerbachs' to inquire after the President's health."

Quandt swallowed his displeasure and contented himself with reproaching Caspar for having gone away without permission. When he was alone with the boy he wandered up and down for a time perplexed. Finally he began: "I was in your room just now, Hauser. While there I made a discovery which filled me with anxiety, to put it mildly. I don't want to express myself at length about the President's pamphlet, although all sensible people are of the same opinion about it. I don't consider myself entitled to belittle so distinguished a man in your eyes. Nor do I wish to ascertain who put the book into your hands, since I should thereby only incur the danger of your lying to me. But it has disturbed me that you think you must be secretive even in such a matter. Why don't you come to me, as is proper, and talk the matter out? Do you think that I would have robbed you of the pleasure of reading a pretty fable written by a once great and famous man, though he is now sick and mentally fatigued? Don't I know also how you must feel inwardly when someone improvises such a fairy tale about your past? A past which is probably better known to you than to the poor President? But why, for heaven's sake, this perpetual hide-and seek? Have I deserved this of you? Have I not been like a father to you? You live in my house, you eat at my table, you enjoy my confidence, you share our weal and our woe; can nothing in the world move you, you secretive boy, to be open and unreserved for once?"

And then how strange! The teacher's eyes riled with tears. He pulled the President's pamphlet out of his pocket, went to the table, and laid the little book with emotion before Caspar.

Caspar looked at the teacher as if he were far away. There was something vacant in his glance and his thoughts were completely absent. His brow seemed wrapped in ghostlike clouds and his lips were open and trembled.

How angry he looks, thought Quandt, and commenced to be afraid. "Do say something," he screamed at him hoarsely.

Caspar slowly shook his head. "One must have patience," he said as if in a dream. "Something will happen, Herr Quandt; just wait and see. Believe me, something will happen soon!" Unintentionally he stretched out his hand towards the teacher.

Quandt turned away with disgust. "Spare me your usual rubbish," he said coldly. "You are an incorrigible actor."

With this the conversation was at an end, and Quandt left the room.

Through the director of archives, Herr Wurm, Quandt found out that Caspar had as a matter of fact been at Feuerbach's house at noon, but that he had not only inquired about the President's condition but had asked with striking urgency to speak to him. Naturally they had not been able to permit this. He had remained standing half an hour longer immovably at the gate and had walked around the whole house, looking up at the windows while his face appeared quite different from usual, wild and disturbed.

However, he came again the next day and again on the third and fourth day, each time with the same urgent request, and each time he was refused. He was told that the President needed rest; his condition, which in the beginning had given cause for anxiety, was improving constantly.

Director Wurm finally told the President about it. Feuerbach ordered Caspar to be brought to him the next time he came and insisted on having his way in spite of Henrietta's persuasion to the contrary. A whole week passed, however, before Caspar was seen again.

He appeared one afternoon fairly late and was received by Henriette, not very graciously, who conducted him to her father's room. The President sat in an easy chair and had a little mountain of documents piled up before him. He looked much older; a white stubble dotted his chin and cheeks, his eyes glanced quietly, but had an anxious gleam, like those of one who has been nearer a much feared death than he is ready to admit.

"Well, what do you want of me, Hauser?" he said, turning to Caspar, who remained standing near the door.

Caspar walked up to him, stumbled over a stool, fell suddenly on his knee and bent his head with the devout humility of a page. His arms, too, depended limply and he remained with an humble and overcast expression in the same position.

Feuerbach lost his color. He seized Caspar by the hair and bent his head back, but Caspar's eyes remained closed. "What's the matter, young man?" exclaimed the President harshly.

Now Caspar raised his eloquent eyes. "I have read it," he said.

The President bit his lips and his eyes disappeared beneath his eyebrows. A long silence ensued.

"Get up," the President finally ordered Caspar, who obeyed.

The President seized him by his wrist and said half threateningly, half imploringly: "Don't let on, Hauser, don't let on! Keep still, keep silent. Wait. For the present there is nothing more to be done."

Caspar's face, in silent commotion, like that of a fever patient, became tenser.

"You shudder, of course," continued the President, "and I shudder, too, and there the matter must rest. Our arm cannot reach to all heights and all distances. We have neither Joshua's battle trumpet nor Oberon's horn. The great and mighty are armed with flails and their blows fall as thick as hail, so that no ray of light can force its way between stroke and stroke. Patience, Caspar, and don't make a sound; don't make a sound! One can't promise anything, but nevertheless some hope remains; but for that I need health. Enough for now."

He made a gesture of goodbye. Caspar looked at the old man for the first time clearly and steadily. His firm glance surprised the President. The deuce take it, though he, the boy has blood in him and not sugar-water. As he was already leaving, Caspar turned around once again and said: "Excellency, I have a great favor to ask."

"A request? Out with it!"

"It is such a nuisance to have to wait for the invalid every time I go out. He often comes so late that it's no longer worth going away. I certainly can go alone to the Court, and to my acquaintances, too."

"H'm," said Feuerbach, "I will consider it; I will arrange it."

As Caspar left the room, a female figure slipped along the corridor like an eavesdropper caught listening. It was Henriette who, in perpetual anxiety about her father, feared nothing so much as the danger which threatened him from his passionate interest in Caspar's fate. A letter which she wrote her brother Anselm, who was living in the Palatinate, showed this and suggested in every single line the ominous atmosphere that weighed on the President's environment.

"Father's condition," thus the letter began, "has, thank God, changed for the better. He is able to walk in his room leaning on a cane, and again enjoys a good roast, although his appetite is not what it used to be, and he now and again complains of pains in his stomach. As for his mood in general, however, it is worse than ever; and this chiefly because of the unfortunate Caspar Hauser pamphlet. You know what a tremendous sensation the brochure has caused all over the country. Thousands of voices were raised for and against it, but it seems that gradually those against it have gained the upper hand. The newspapers that are most widely read printed articles which were strikingly similar and which dismissed the work sarcastically as the product of an overheated brain. That back of this there is spite work, all proceeding from one and the same source, cannot be concealed; and I could bite my lips raw when I think of the times we are compelled to live in, when even such a man as our father cannot find a willing ear, let alone active help, for a cause which cries to heaven. Certainly human beings are lazy, dull, stupid animals, or there would be more indignation in the world. Now just think of father, his bitter depression, his pain, his contempt, and all kept back, all locked up in his breast. What did he not feel when even from his most intimate friends there was no sign of approval, of gratitude, or of love. Certainly persons in high places did not conceal their anger, and here in this horrid provincial hole little attention was paid to the whole story, comprehensibly enough, for Christ may win Rome, but in Jerusalem He will remain a dirty rabbi. I am in great anxiety about father. I know him well enough to realize that his present external calm only conceals an inner storm. Sometimes he sits for hours and stares at a single spot on the wall, and if you disturb him he looks at you with big eyes and laughs silently and painfully. Recently he said to me quite suddenly, with a gloomy expression: 'The right thing would be for a man to give himself entirely to such a cause; he ought to sacrifice his skin, and the hair of his head, as in the olden days, and not hide behind a wall of printed paper. He is turning over plans in his mind; the news that a revolution has broken out in Baden has stirred him greatly, and, as a matter of fact, this catastrophe seems to be closely connected with the Caspar Hauser affair. He believes that he has reason to regard a pensioned minister, living somewhere on the Main, as one of the chief instigators of the crime committed against the foundling and—my pen will scarcely write the words—he intends to look up the man and to compel him to confess. Police Lieutenant Hickel, that sinister fellow whom I don't trust across the street, comes daily to the house, and has long conferences with father and, as far as I have been able to make out from father's hints up to now, Hickel is to accompany him on his trip in a few weeks. If I could only prevent just this! He will give up the last piece of his old age on account of this miserable story, and he will not accomplish anything, nothing, nothing, not if he were an Isaiah in persuasion, a Sampson in strength or a Maccabeus in courage. Ah, we Feuerbachs are a marked race! Cain's mark of restlessness is stamped on our brow. We play havoc with our strength and our fortune, and if we have just enough left to reach the grave we are fortunate. We are not able to take a harmless walk; we must always have an immediate goal before our eyes; we cannot breathe without recalling an important mission, and in the expectation of the next day we lose sight of every beauty in the present. He is so, you are so, I am so, we are all so. I have never yet smelled a rose without grieving that to-morrow it would be faded, never yet seen a beautiful child begging without meditating about the inequalities of human fate. Farewell, brother; heaven grant that my pessimistic forebodings be wrong."

Thus was the letter. The mistrust expressed in it towards Lieutenant Hickel finally assumed such dimensions that Henriette exerted herself in every way to separate her father from Hickel. It was of no avail, but Hickel scented danger and at once showed an inscrutable, sweet and gracious attitude towards the President's daughter. When Quandt came to him and complained bitterly that the President had allowed himself to be won over by Hauser, and had permitted him to go about unwatched and unhindered in the city, Hickel said that that did not suit him; he would put other ideas into the President's head.

He had himself announced at Feuerbach's and told him of his doubts about this undesirable measure. "Your Excellency has probably not considered what a responsibility you are thus putting upon me," he said. "If I have no control over where the boy spends his time how can I guarantee his safety?"

"Stuff and nonsense," growled Feuerbach; "I can't lock up a grown person in order that you may spend your afternoons in the Casino with a quiet conscience."

Hickel cast an evil glance at his hands, but answered, with not ill-assumed ingenuousness: "I am conscious of the fault which Your Excellency condemns so severely. Nevertheless a man must have one spot where he can warm himself, particularly if he is a confirmed old bachelor. If you were in my place, Excellency, and I in yours, I should be milder towards a poor harassed officer."

Feuerbach laughed. "What has gotten hold of you?" he asked good naturedly. "Have you love-troubles?" He regarded the lieutenant as a great masher.

"In that regard, Your Excellency, I am unfortunately too hard-boiled," replied Hickel, "although a cause for interest does exist; our city has had for several days the honor of harboring a great beauty."

"So?" asked the President curiously. "Tell me about it." He had, it could not be denied, a little naive weakness for the ladies.

"The lady is visiting Frau von Imhoff."

"Yes, just so; the Baroness mentioned it," interrupted Feuerbach.

"At first she lived at the Stern," continued Hickel. "I went past a few times and saw her sitting thoughtfully at the window, her glance raised to heaven like a saint; I always stood still and looked up, but she scarcely noticed me before she stepped back frightened." "Now that's excellent; that's good observation," the President teased him; "so there's already a sort of understanding between you."

"No, unfortunately, Your Excellency, frankly, the times are too serious for gallant adventures."

"I should say so," corroborated Feuerbach, and the smile died from his face. He got up and said energetically: "But the time, too, is ripe. I intend to leave on the twenty-eighth of April. You will get leave of absence from your duties and place yourself at my disposal."

Hickel bowed. He looked at the President expectantly and the latter understood the glance. "I must confess, to be sure, that there is something unsuitable about leaving Hauser entirely to himself. On the other hand, it's not easy to shut off the entire world before his nose. He has had enough of that. The restriction of free activity is just as hard on a person's will to live as chains and handcuffs." He could not become at peace with himself, as always, when he found himself opposed to the lieutenant, he found himself checked in his resolves; there was an impact of strength, youth, coldness and unscrupulousness which always defeated him.

"But Your Excellency knows the dangers—" Hickel put in.

"So long as I have my eyes on this city no one will dare to touch a hair of his head, you may be sure of that."

Hickel raised his eyebrows and stared again at the outstretched fingers of his hand. "And if some day he makes off altogether?" he asked darkly. "He is capable of a good deal. I suggest that he should be watched at least at night and on his walks.

On errands in the city he can, if necessary, go alone. We can get rid of the old invalid and I will put my boy in his place. He will appear at the teacher's house every afternoon at five o'clock."

"That would be a solution." said Feuerbach; "is the man reliable?"

"As true as steel."

"What's his name?"

"Schildknecht, the son of a Baden baker." "Settled; let it go at that."

When Hickel was already at the door the President called him back and emphatically told him he must keep entirely quiet about the trip which they were about to take together. Hickel replied that he did not need such a warning.

"I could in no case undertake the journey alone," said the President. "I need the help of a circumspect man. The opportunity must be carefully sought out. Care must be taken. Never forget that I am giving you a great proof of confidence in this matter."

He looked penetratingly at the lieutenant. Hickel nodded mechanically. A cloud of foreboding anxiety settled suddenly on Feuerbach's brow. "You may go," he ordered curtly.

23. The Journey Is Undertaken

That same evening Hickel called on the teacher and told him that from now on the soldier Schildknecht was to have charge of Hauser. Caspar was not at home and when questioned about him Quandt replied that he had gone to the theater.

"At the theater again," exclaimed Hickel. "That's the third time in two weeks, if I am not mistaken."

"He has acquired a great love for it," replied Quandt; "he spends almost all his pocket money buying tickets."

"His pocket money is not going to be quite so liberal, incidentally," said the lieutenant. "The count has only sent me half of the prearranged sum this month. Obviously, the thing is getting too expensive for him."

Stanhope from the beginning had sent Hickel the money which was to be used for Caspar.

"Expensive? for a lord? A peer of the British crown! Such a trifle, expensive?" Quandt opened his eyes with astonishment.

"You had better not tell that to anyone else, or people will think you are making fun of the count," said Frau Quandt. She looked curiously and penetratingly at the lieutenant. This smooth, slippery, smartly dressed man had always seemed unusual and attractive to her. He stimulated her scant patrimony of imagination.

"Can't help it," Hickel closed the conversation peevishly; "so it is. The post-office money order is at your service for inspection. The count knows what he's about."

When Caspar came home, Quandt asked him how he had enjoyed himself. "Not at all; there was so much about love in the play," he answered with irritation. "I simply can't stand that sort of stuff. They talk and complain until one loses one's wits, and what's the end of it? They marry. I would rather give my money to a beggar."

"The lieutenant was here just now and told us that the count has considerably diminished your allowance," said Quandt. "You will therefore have to cut down all your expenses and give up going to the theater entirely, I fear."

Caspar sat down at the table and ate his supper; for a long time he said nothing. "That's a pity," he said finally; "week after next they are giving Schiller's Don Carlos. That is said to be a magnificent play; I should like still to see that."

"Who told you that it was a magnificent play?" asked Quandt with the indulgent, superior expression of the specialist.

"I met Frau von Imhoff and Frau von Kannawurf in the theater," explained Caspar; "they both said so."

The teacher's wife raised her head: "Frau von Kannawurf? Now who is that, pray tell me?"

"A friend of Frau von Imhoff," replied Caspar.

Quandt discussed with his wife until midnight how they might adjust themselves to the count's financial innovations. It was agreed that Caspar should from now on have lunch for ten and supper for eight cents. "If it's as the lieutenant says, I must in any case bear a slight loss," was Frau Quandt's opinion.

"We must not forget that in matters of food and drink Hauser is really extraordinarily moderate," replied Quandt, whose honesty struggled against an unjust niggardliness.

"That doesn't matter," insisted the wife. "It will oblige me to supply so much in the kitchen as will feed one more mouth. And no one gives it to me."

The next afternoon Hickel brought the money for the month. He and Quandt had just entered the hall when Caspar came down from his room ready to leave the house. When the teacher asked him where he was going he answered with embarrassment that he wanted to go to the watchmaker, his watch was not in order and he wanted to have it repaired. Quandt asked to see the watch, Caspar handed it to him, the teacher held it to his ear, tapped the case, tried to wind it and finally said: "There is not the least thing wrong with the watch."

Caspar blushed and said that he had only wanted to have his name engraved in the lid, but he would have had to be a much more skillful pretender to free his words from the stamp of dissimulation.

Quandt and Hickel looked at each other. "If you have a particle of honesty about you now, confess openly where you meant to go," said Quandt, earnestly.

Caspar considered and then said hesitatingly that he had had the intention of going to the orange-grove.

"To the orange-grove? Why, for what purpose?"

"On account of the flowers. There are such beautiful flowers there in the spring."

Hickel cleared his throat significantly. He glanced sharply at Caspar and said ironically: "A poet. Among flowers — let me sigh." Then he assumed a military expression and stated curtly that he had persuaded the President to retract the permission which he had thoughtlessly given him to go out alone. A boy would arrive daily at five o'clock; Caspar could do as he pleased in his company.

Caspar looked silently out into the street where the spring sun shone. "It seems," he murmured, hesitated however, and looked humbly down.

"What seems?" asked the teacher. "Come, out with it. Half-said things burn one's tongue."

Caspar fixed his eyes penetratingly upon him. "It seems," he finished his sentence, "that the person who comes last is the person the President agrees with." When he saw the effect of these bitter words, he would have been glad if he could have recalled them. The teacher shook his head with horror and Hickel whistled through his pursed lips. Then he took out his notebook which was stuck between two buttons of his coat and wrote something down. Caspar watched him with a shy glance; there was a flash as of lightning over his brow.

"Naturally, I shall tell the President of your improper remark," said Hickel, in professional tones.

When the lieutenant had left, Caspar asked the teacher to let him go out today, as an exception, because the weather was so fine.

"I am sorry," said Quandt; "I must act according to my instructions."

Hickel's boy did not appear until half-past five. Caspar then went with him along the road to the court garden, but when they got to the orange-grove it was already shut. Schildknecht suggested walking along the Onolzbach, but Caspar shook his head. He stationed himself at one of the open windows of the greenhouses and looked in.

"Are you looking for someone?" asked Schildknecht.

"Yes, a woman was to have met me here," replied Caspar.

"It does not matter; let's go home again."

They turned around; when they came to the Schlossplatz, Caspar saw Frau von Kannawurf standing in the middle of the square scattering bread crumbs to a lot of sparrows. Caspar remained standing outside of the group of sparrows; he watched and entirely forgot to say how do you do. The feeding was soon over, Frau von Kannawurf put her hat on again, which she had hung on a ribbon over her arm, and said she had waited an hour and a half in the greenhouse.

"I am not a free agent and can't do as I promise," replied Caspar.

They went along the Promenade and then to the left, towards the gardens in the suburbs. Schildknecht walked back of them; the red-cheeked little man in the green uniform had a comic look. The biggest of the three was Caspar, for Frau von Kannawurf, too, had a child-like figure.

After they had walked silently next to one another for a long time, the young woman said: "It was really on your account that I came to this city, Hauser." Her voice, which had a slight sing-song, had also a strange accent, and while she spoke she was in the habit of blinking her eyelids occasionally, as do those whose eyes are tired.

"Yes, and what do you wish of me?" replied Caspar, more helplessly than roughly. "You already told me yesterday in the theater that you had come on my account."

"That's not new to you, you're thinking. But I don't want anything from you, on the contrary. But it is hard to talk about it while walking. Let us sit down up there in the grass." They climbed up the side of the hill and sat in front of a hedge on the grass. Opposite them the sun sank into the treetops of the Swabian hills. Caspar gazed meditatively; Frau von Kannawurf leaned her elbow in the grass and looked into the violet air. Schildknecht, as if he understood that his presence was not desired, had seated himself far beneath them, on a fallen tree.

"I own a little place in Switzerland," began Frau von Kannawurf. "I bought it two years ago in order to have a refuge and a place of rest in a free country. I propose that you go there with me. You can live there entirely according to your wishes, without danger or annoyance. Not even myself will disturb you, for I cannot stay anywhere; something constantly drives me to other places. The house is completely isolated in a valley between high hills and on a lake. You cannot conceive of anything grander than the view of perpetual snow that one may enjoy seated in the garden under the apple-trees. Since it would be very difficult and take much time if I wanted to carry out my purpose and take you there in the eyes of all the world, I think the best thing would be for you to flee with me. You have only to say 'yes' and everything is ready."

She had moved so that her face turned straight on Caspar, who shifted his somewhat dazed glance from the red sun-disc and looked at her. He would have had to be of wood to remain insensible towards this beautiful countenance, and quite of his own accord, as if he had not listened to her at all, the words, "But you are very beautiful," fell from his amazed lips.

Frau von Kannawurf blushed. She did not succeed in concealing an expression of pain behind her ironic smile. Her mouth, which had something childishly sweet about it, trembled constantly when she was silent. Caspar became embarrassed at her surprised glance and looked again at the sun.

"You are not answering me?" asked Frau von Kannawurf gently and with disappointment.

Caspar shook his head. "It is impossible for me to do what you want me to," he said.

"Impossible? Why?" Frau von Kannawurf sat up suddenly.

"Because I do not belong there," said Caspar firmly.

The young woman looked at him. Her face had the expression of an attentive child and became gradually as white as the sky above them. "Do you wish to sacrifice yourself?" she asked, stunned.

"Because I must go there where I belong," continued Caspar unswervingly, as he gazed steadily at the spot where the sun had now sunk.

It is vain to try to convert him to my plan, thought Frau von Kannawurf at once. Good heavens, how true, how simple everything seems to him—yes, no—beautiful, ugly; he looks at things only from above. And how his face unites a boundless goodness with a naive and delicate sadness; one is confounded with astonishment when one looks at him.

"But what do you want to do?" she asked hesitatingly.

"I don't yet know," he replied as if in a dream, and with his eyes followed a cloud which had the shape of a dog running.

So what I was told is wrong, thought the young woman; he is not at all afraid. She got up, walked impetuously ahead down the hill, past Schildknecht, who seemed asleep. One must protect him, she thought further; he is capable of action and of running into his ruin. Naturally he does not know what he will do; he is probably not capable of making a plan, but he will act. He is brooding over some plan and will not be daunted by anything anymore. It is not difficult to read him, although he looks like silence itself.

She remained standing and waited for Caspar. "How well you can run," he said admiringly when he had reached her side.

"The fresh air makes me a little wild," she replied, and breathed deeply.

As Frau von Kannawurf and Caspar walked through the gate of the Herrieder Tower, they suddenly saw the police lieutenant near an empty guard-house. And both involuntarily stood still, for his aspect was somehow terrifying. Hickel was leaning with his shoulders against the booth and looked as if he had been turned into a statue. In spite of the darkness they could see that his face was an ashen gray, and a leaden gloom lay over his features. Back of him stood his dog. a large gray mastiff. The animal was as motionless as his master and gazed steadily up at him.

Caspar removed his hat to greet him; Hickel did not notice this. Frau von Kannawurf looked back again and whispered shiveringly: "How terrible; what a man he is. I wonder what's worrying him?"

Was it conceivable that the lieutenant, rendered desperate by some new loss at cards, could so far forget himself that even though protected by the darkness and a corner in the wall, he should present the spectacle of a man overcome by a convulsion? That is generally not a characteristic of gamblers; they sleep oil their depression and again surrender themselves coolly to the clutches of inconstant fortune. But gamblers are generally unscrupulous; when their money is not staked on cards they put it on souls, and thus it may well happen that the devil presents them with a frightful reckoning, which they must sign with their blood.

When Hickel had reached home that afternoon an unknown man had walked up to him in front of the door, handed him a sealed letter and disappeared without having spoken. The lieutenant's experienced glance could not fail to detect that the man wore false hair and a false beard. The letter, which Hickel at once opened, was in cipher, and although he was familiar with the key, it took the rest of the afternoon to read the letter. The contents were connected with the trip which Hickel was to take in the President's company. Hickel read and read, and read again. He had already understood the first time, but he read in order not to be obliged to think.

Promptly at seven o'clock he got up from his desk and walked for ten minutes up and down the room, whistling. Then he opened a little glass cupboard, took out a bottle of whiskey which he had received as a present from Lord Stanhope, filled a nice little silver goblet and drank it down in a single gulp. Then he snatched at a whisk broom, brushed his coat off and at half-past seven left his flat with his dog. He seemed in a good humor, for he whistled and hummed, and sometimes snapped his fingers. But under the arch of the Herrieder Tower he suddenly stood still and looked earnestly at the ground. A handcart going by struck him on the hip and therefore he walked a few steps further to the guard-house around the corner. There the pair on their way home saw him.

The assumption that this depression of the lieutenant's spirits lasted longer than a temporary lack of blood in the head generally does would indicate an insufficient insight into his character. At eight o'clock he was already eating fish with several colleagues at the "Golden Fork" and at nine he was at the Casino. In case this accurate indication of time should be in any way annoying, let us add that from nine till four he was no longer aware of the stroke of a bell, but solely of the monotonous flutter of cards over the gambling table. He won. On the way home, through the gray dawn, it was worthy of note that he stopped in the middle of the street in front of the Star Inn, pressed his sword against his leg and cast a long absorbed glance towards the window back of which he had once seen the beautiful stranger.

The next morning he slept late and when the boy came to make his report he scarcely listened. It was Schildknecht's duty to report every morning where he had been with Caspar the day before. From now on almost every day it was: We called for Frau von Kannawurf, or Frau von Kannawurf met us and we went walking, or, in rainy weather: We sat in the summer-house in the Imhoffs' garden. This "we" in Schildknecht's mouth sounded very modest; he always spoke of Caspar with respectful reserve. Since he perceived that his master was restless at the report on Caspar's and Frau von Kannawurf's being together so regularly, he knew how to put some assurance of harmlessness into his tone; for example, he would add: "They talked a lot about the weather," or, "They talked a lot about intellectual matters." He invented these details, for actually he, kept at a tactful distance from the two.

Hickel began to distrust the young man.

One evening he caught him sitting in a corner of the kitchen with a candle in front of him with his finger spelling out the words of a book. When he saw himself disturbed he seemed devitalized; his red cheeks had lost their color. Hickel took the book and his face turned as black as night when he saw that it was Feuerbach's pamphlet. "Where did you get that?" he screamed at Schildknecht. The boy replied that he had found it on the lieutenant's bookcase. "It was an illegal act to take it and I will have you disciplined and fired if such a thing ever happens again, just note that," thundered Hickel.

Probably the first pirate's yarn that he got hold of would have exalted the lout's curiosity equally, said Hickel to himself later on, and judged his outburst to have been unnecessary. Nevertheless he sensed danger; the boy was not to his taste, and he decided to get rid of him. An occasion soon presented itself.

When Schildknecht called for Caspar the next day he noticed that the latter was depressed. He tried to cheer him up by telling him some amusing stories of his life in the barracks. Caspar became interested in the conversation; he asked the confiding boy about his home and his parents, and Schildknecht tried to tell about these as good-humoredly as he could, although it was a sad chapter for him. He had had a step-mother, his father had placed him among strangers,*: scarcely was he away from the house when a lover of the woman had killed the father in a fight. Now the lover and the woman were in prison and his brothers had gone through all the money.

Schildknecht ventured to ask why Caspar was not meeting his friend that day.

"She is going to the theater," replied Caspar.

Why did he not go, Schildknecht inquired further.

He had no money.

"No money? How much is needed?"

"Six cents."

"I have just that with me," said Schildknecht.

"I'll lend it to you."

Caspar accepted the offer with pleasure. Don Carlos was just being given; he had looked forward to it for a long time.

The play, with the exception of the crazy woman who tries to seduce the prince, aroused his delight. And what were his sensations when the marquis said to the king:

> In vain
> Your bitter war with Nature, and in vain
> The royal life you sacrificed to further
> Destruction's irresponsible designs.
> Man is a creature greater than you thought:
> The fetters of long slumber he will break,
> And vindicate his hallowed right again.

He got up from his seat, stared eagerly with speaking eyes at the stage and only kept back a loud scream with difficulty. Fortunately the disturbance was not much noticed in the darkness; his neighbor, an ill-natured old bureaucrat, pulled him back to his seat.

His staying away during the evening at once caused the teacher to inquire where he had been. He confessed that he had been at the Court Theater. "Where did you get the money?" asked Quandt. Caspar replied that the ticket had been given to him. "By whom?" Thoughtlessly, still enthralled by the poetry, Caspar gave the first name which occurred to him. Quandt inquired the next day and found out, of course, that Caspar had lied to him and took him to task. Driven into a corner, Caspar confessed the truth and Quandt told the lieutenant.

At five o'clock in the afternoon the well-known whistle, two melodious thrills, with which Schildknecht was in the habit of announcing his arrival, were heard in the yard. Caspar went down.

"It's over between us two," Schildknecht said to him; "the lieutenant has discharged me because I lent you the money. I shall have to do barracks service again."

Caspar nodded sadly. "That's how it always goes with me," he murmured; "they can't stand it when anyone is kind to me." He shook hands with Schildknecht in farewell.

"Listen, Hauser," said Schildknecht eagerly, "two or three times a week, in fact whenever I am free, I'll come into the yard and whistle. Perhaps you will need me some time. Why not, it's quite possible?"

There lay a depth of kindness beyond all measure in these words. Caspar fastened an attentive glance upon Schildknecht's friendly, smiling face and replied slowly and thoughtfully: "It is possible, that is true."

"Fine, that's settled." exclaimed Schildknecht.

They went through the corridor into the street. In front of the gate stood an official messenger. When he saw Caspar, he said he had been looking for him, the President had sent him, Caspar was to come to him at once. Caspar asked what was doing. "The President is leaving this evening at six o'clock with the police lieutenant and wishes to speak to you before going," the man answered.

Caspar set out at once. A few hundred feet from the teacher's house he could get no further. The axle of a wheel had broken, upsetting a load of bricks in front of the gate, thus blocking the street. Caspar waited a while and was then obliged to go over Wurzburger Strasse and through the fields. As a result he came too late. When he got to the Feuerbachs' garden the President had already left. Henriette and Hofrat Hofmann stood at the garden gate and received Caspar's well-grounded excuses silently. Henriette's eyes showed that she had been crying. For a long time she looked down the street where the carriage had disappeared, then she turned silently and walked towards the house.

24. Schildknecht

May brought much rain. When the weather made it at all possible Caspar and Frau von Imhoff wandered for whole afternoons through the surrounding countryside. Caspar suddenly neglected his office work. When he was taken to task he replied: "I am tired of that silly writing." This the people concerned took very ill.

The new servant whom Hickel had engaged and with whom he left strict instructions for the period of his absence was at once so unpleasant that Frau von Kannawurf complained about him to Hofrat Hofmann. Less through real understanding than a desire to be obliging to the beautiful woman, the Hofrat permitted Caspar to go walking with her alone. "I hope you won't run away with Caspar," he said with a sly professional smile to the speechless woman.

Quandt, however, again made difficulties. "I insist upon keeping to my instructions," was his iron motto. One morning, therefore, Frau von Kannawurf appeared in the teacher's study and boldly took him to task. Quandt could not look her in the face. He was completely bewildered, and became red and white by turns. "I am entirely at your service, Madame," he said with the expression of a person who on the rack decides in favor of whatever is wanted of him.

Frau von Kannawurf looked with calm curiosity about the room. "What is your real attitude towards Caspar," she suddenly asked him. "Do you love him?" Quandt sighed. "I wish I could love him as his worthy friends believe that he deserves to be loved," he concluded with a masterly flourish.

Frau von Kannawurf started up. "How am I to understand that?" she broke out passionately; "how can one not love him, how can one not do everything for him?" Her face glowed, she walked up close to the frightened teacher and looked at him threateningly and sadly.

But she calmed herself quickly, and spoke of other matters in order the better to fathom this to her so astonishing creature. Every human being was a wonder to her and almost everything which they did was wonderful. For this reason she scarcely ever attained the goal which she sought. She forgot herself and overreached the bounds imposed by superficial intercourse.

Quandt was thoroughly angry afterwards at his indulgent attitude. I wonder what's back of that? he puzzled. Whenever little notes came for Caspar from Frau von Kannawurf he opened and read them before he gave them to the boy. He never made anything out of them; the contents were too innocent. Probably they communicate in some secret language, thought Quandt, and put certain recurring phrases together in the hope of thus finding the key. Caspar protested against this meddling, whereupon Quandt, with unusual loquaciousness, demonstrated to him the right of the tutor to peruse his pupil's correspondence.

Finally Caspar asked his friend not to write to him anymore. The teacher, had he been able to listen unseen to their conversations, would have found them equally innocent. Sometimes they walked for hours side by side without speaking; "Isn't it beautiful in the woods?" the young woman would then ask in the heartfelt tones of her sweet voice and a little twittering bird-like laugh. Or she would pluck a flower from the edge of a field and ask: "Is that not beautiful?"

"It is beautiful," Caspar would reply.

"So dry, so serious?"

"It is not for long that I have known it to be beautiful, remarked Caspar profoundly; "the beautiful comes last."

This time the spring made him happy. With every breath he felt himself favored to an unusual degree. The teeming world wound itself round him like a garland. So long as the sun stood high in the blue sky his eyes shone with surprised happiness. "He is like a child whom one takes into the garden for the first time after a long illness," said Frau von Kannawurf. Her kindly heart beat quickly at the thought that perhaps she was not without some share in this mood of his. Sometimes she would twine young forest leaves in his hat, which always made him look very proud. But he continued to be quite reserved, and with an abstraction that seemed to denote an inner struggle with some great decision.

One day they agreed that they should call each other Clara and Caspar. She was amused at the business-like precision with which he, on his side, observed their agreement. In fact, he often entertained her, particularly when he gave her little moral talks, or when he complained with irritation at something which he called womanish. He warned her, too, not to run about so much and to take care of her health. Indeed, it sometimes really looked as if she were trying to fatigue or exhaust herself. One of her passions was to climb towers. On the tower of St. John's Church there was an old watchman, a wise man after his fashion, who had become gentle and passive through long isolation. She did not shun the exertion of several hundred steps to be climbed, and often ran up twice a day, chatted with him as with a friend, or leaned over the iron railing of the narrow platform and gazed over the landscape into the distance. The watchman, too, had become so attached to her that at set hours in the evening he sent preconcerted signals with his lantern in the direction of the Imhoff's summer-house.

Every day she made new plans for traveling, for she did not like the little city. Caspar asked what it was that was driving her away, but she really was not able to say. "I can't take root," she had said; "I become unhappy if I am contented. I must go constantly on voyages of discovery; I must seek people." She looked at Caspar affectionately, while her little mouth trembled incessantly.

Once, and that was the only time that there was any talk of it at all, she mentioned Feuerbach's pamphlet. Caspar snatched her hand, which he pressed with a peculiar force, as if he were trying thus to strangle the word which he had heard. Frau von Kannawurf uttered a low scream.

It was already evening. They still walked along as far as the street crossing where they generally separated. Then Frau von Kannawurf said quickly and incisively, standing close to him and staring at his forehead: "So you are ready to assume the burden?"

"What?" he replied, visibly ill at ease.

"Everything—?"

"Yes, everything," he said dully; "but I don't know, for I am quite alone."

"Naturally alone, but you don't wish for anything else. Alone, as when you were in prison, only no longer below ground, but above " She could speak no further; he placed one hand on her mouth and the other on his, while his eyes gleamed almost with hate. Suddenly he wondered with a kind of joyful confusion whether his mother was like this woman? He had a thirsty burning sensation on his lips and at the same time he was aware of something in himself which was repellent to him. "I am going home now," he spurted forth, curiously vexed, and hurried away quickly.

Frau von Kannawurf looked after him, and long after the darkness had swallowed his figure she still fixed her big childlike eyes in the direction he had taken. She had a frightful sensation of fear about her heart. He is certainly the bravest of humans, she thought; he does not even conceive of how much courage he has. What is it that moves me so, whether I talk with him or am silent? Why am I so afraid when I know that he is left to himself?

She went homeward and took more than half an hour for a walk of a little more than a thousand steps. In the west, lightning shone like fiery veins. Caspar had gone to bed early. It may have been four o'clock in the morning when he was wakened by a loud call. It was from the street outside the yard, and the voice called "Quandt, Quandt!"

Caspar, still half asleep, thought that he recognized Hickel's voice. Somewhere a window was opened, the person on the street said something which Caspar could not understand, and soon afterwards a door in the house was banged. Then there was silence for a time. Caspar was turning over on his side to continue sleeping when there was a knock at his door.

"What is it?" asked Caspar.

"Open the door, Hauser," answered Quandt's voice.

Caspar sprang out of bed and pushed the bolt back. Quandt stood, completely dressed, on the threshold. His face looked a greenish white in the gray dawn.

"The President is dead," he said.

Overcome with dizziness, Caspar sat down on the edge of the bed.

"I am going there now. If you wish to go with me, hurry," Quandt continued in a mumble.

Caspar slipped into his clothes; he was as if drunk.

Ten minutes later he was walking next to Quandt on the way to Heiligenkreuz Street. In the garden in front of Feuerbach's house there stood groups of people looking half sleepy, half dumfounded.

A baker's boy sat on the steps, weeping into his white apron. "Do you think one may go up?" Quandt asked the clerk, Dillmann, who strode up and down with a wrathful face, with his hat deep down on his forehead. "The corpse is not yet in the city," said an old artillery officer, in whose beard raindrops were hanging.

"I know that," replied Quandt, and somewhat anxiously followed Caspar who had gone into the house. In the lower story all the doors were open. In the kitchen, two maids sat in front of a pile of wood which had been cut into logs. They seemed to listen fearfully. Caspar and Quandt became aware of the approach of a penetrating voice. At once they saw a female figure with arms flung up running through the rooms. She screamed to herself as if demented.

"The unhappy woman," said Quandt, disturbed.

It was Henriette. Her screams continued uninterruptedly until several ladies appeared, among them Frau von Stichaner. Quandt went with Caspar to the threshold of the state reception room. The women tried to soothe Henriette who, however, repulsed them with her fists. "I knew it," she screamed; "I knew it, they have poisoned him, they have poisoned him!" Her eyes were bloodshot and their glance was red. She stormed into another room, her loose nightgown fluttering back of her, and her screams sounding more and more piercingly: "They have poisoned him, poisoned him, poisoned him!"

Caspar could find no other place to rest his eyes than the picture of Napoleon opposite which he stood. It seemed to him that the emperor must already be tired of his immutable majestic turn of the head.

"Let us go, Hauser," said Quandt, "here there is too much grief."

In the hall stood Regierungsprasident Mieg, in conversation with Hickel. The lieutenant was recounting the details of the catastrophe. In Ochsenfurt-on-the-Main His Excellency had complained of being unwell and had gone to bed; during the night he had had a fever, the physician who was called had opened a vein and had said that the illness was unimportant. The next morning the end had suddenly come.

"And to what reason did the physician ascribe his death?" inquired Herr von Mieg, bowing at the same time, as Frau von

Imhoff and Frau von Kannawurf walked up to him. Frau von Imhoff was crying.

Hickel shrugged his shoulders. "He thought his heart was weak," he replied.

Regardless of the early hour, the whole city was already up. Over the roof of the Appellate Court two black flags were flying.

Caspar remained all day in his room. No one disturbed him. He lay on the sofa, his hands under his head, staring in the air. Late in the afternoon he became hungry and went into the living room. Quandt was not there. His wife said: "The corpse arrived at four o'clock; you should really go, Hauser, and see him once again, before he is buried."

Caspar choked over a piece of bread and nodded.

"Do you see how right I was that time about the corpse washer women?" continued the teacher's wife, talkatively, "But you men always think that everything goes as you have calculated."

The foyer of Feuerbach's house was filled with people. Caspar pressed his way into a corner and stood for a while unobserved. He shook from head to foot. The peculiar smell which pervaded the house stunned his senses. Then he felt his hand seized. Looking up, he recognized Frau von Imhoff. Signaling to him to follow her, she conducted him to a large room in the middle of which the corpse was laid out. Feuerbach's three sons sat at their father's head, Henriette lay motionless, stretched across the corpse. At the window stood Hofrat Hofmann and the Archive Director Wurm. There was no one else in the room.

The face of the dead man was as yellow as a lemon. Great knots of muscles had formed at the corners of the sharp, incisive mouth. The slate-gray hair resembled an animal's closely cropped coat. There was no longer anything of greatness in these features, only grinding pain and inhuman icy fear.

Caspar had never yet seen a corpse. His face assumed a tortured and curious expression, his eyes turned in their sockets and he clasped his mouth and chin with his ten fingers. His whole heart dissolved in tears.

Henriette Feuerbach lifted her head from the bier; perceiving the boy her features became frightfully convulsed. "It is on your account that he had to die," she screamed in a voice which made them all quiver.

Caspar opened his lips. Bending far forward he stared at the half-crazed woman. Twice he struck his breast with his hand—he seemed to laugh—suddenly he emitted a meaningless sound and fell senseless to the floor.

They were all dumfounded. The President's sons had gotten up and looked with anxiety at the boy lying on the floor. Director Wurm, when he had recovered himself, went to the door, probably to summon a physician. The coolheaded Hofrat held him back saying that one should not create any unnecessary excitement. Frau von Imhoff knelt by Caspar and moistened his temples with her eau de cologne. He recovered himself slowly, but it was a quarter of an hour before he was able to get up and walk. Frau von Imhoff accompanied him out. In order not to have to press their way through the crowd of visitors, she led him down the back-stairs into the garden and offered to accompany him home. "No," he said in unnaturally low tones, "I want to go alone." He stuck his nose into the air and sniffed unconsciously. His pulse beat so quickly that the veins in his neck seemed actually to be racing.

He turned away from the young woman's affectionate encouragement and went with heavy steps through the main walk of the garden. In front of the gate he ran into the lieutenant. "Well, Hauser?" Hickel said to him. Caspar stood still.

"You certainly have well-founded cause for grief," said Hickel in a dolorous voice. "Who will replace the precious support of a Feuerbach?"

Caspar did not reply, he seemed to look straight through the lieutenant as if he were made of glass.

"Good evening," said a bell-like voice which moved Caspar strangely. Frau von Kannawurf walked up to him. Hickel's face grew a shade paler. "Most gracious lady," he said with a gallantry which appeared forced, "may I take this opportunity to lay my unmeasured admiration at your feet?"

Frau von Kannawurf involuntarily took a step backwards and looked frightened.

The lieutenant had the expression of a person who is plunging into deep water. He bowed down and before Frau von Kannawurf could prevent it he seized her hand and pressed a kiss on it with his naked teeth; when he stood up his lips were still parted. Without uttering a syllable more he hurried away.

With wide eyes Frau von Kannawurf looked after him. "That man makes me shudder," she whispered. Caspar remained completely indifferent. Frau von Kannawurf accompanied him home in silence.

When he had reached his room his eyes assumed a weird expression and flamed in the darkness like two glow-worms. He placed himself in the middle of the room and, trembling from head to foot, he said the following in imploring tones:

"If I know you, thus I call to you. If you are my mother then hear me. I am going to you. I must come to you. If you are my mother, then I ask you: why wait so long? I have no longer any fear and the need is great. Caspar Hauser is what they call me, but you call me differently. To you I must go into the castle. The messenger is true: God will guide him and the sun will light his way. Speak to him, send me word through him."

Suddenly a curious peace came over him. He sat down at the table, took a sheet of paper and wrote down the same words unimpeded by the darkness. Then he folded the paper up and since he did not have any sealing wax he lit the candle, dropped some tallow on the paper and pressed upon it a seal representing a horse with the motto: Proud but gentle.

Half an hour passed. He sat silently with closed eyes. At times it seemed as if he were praying, for his lips moved seekingly. He thought of Schildknecht, and wished for him with the whole strength of his soul.

And as if this wish had contained the power to create reality the pleasant trill sounded suddenly in the yard. Caspar went to the window and opened it. It was Schildknecht. "I am coming down," Caspar called to him.

Downstairs, he seized Schildknecht by the sleeve of his coat and pulled him through the little gate into the lonely street. Then he silently ordered him to follow along further. They went by the house of the tax collector until they reached a field. On the edge stood a peasant's cart. Caspar sat down on the shaft and pulled Schildknecht down next to him. He approached his mouth to the soldier's ear and said: "Now, I need you."

Schildknecht nodded.

"Everything is at stake," Caspar continued.

Schildknecht nodded again.

"Here is a letter," said Caspar, "it must reach my mother."

Schildknecht nodded again, this time full of respect. "I know," he answered, "the Princess Stephanie— "

"How do you know?" whispered Caspar, amazed.

"I have read it, read it in the President's book."

"And you know, too, where you must go, Schildknecht?"

"I know, it's in our country."

"And you will deliver the letter?"

"I'll do it!"

"And you'll swear by your salvation that you'll give her the letter yourself? That you'll go to the castle? To the church, if she's there? Stop her carriage if she's driving along the street?"

"Swearing is not necessary. I'll do it and let onions rain!"

"If I should try to do it, Schildknecht, I should not get to the next village. They would catch me and lock me up."

"I know that." "How will you do it?"

"Put on peasant's clothes, sleep in the woods by day, travel by night."

"And where will you hide the letter?"

"Under my sole, in my stocking."

"And when can you leave?"

"Whenever you like. Tomorrow, today, at once, whenever you like. It's desertion of the colors, of course, but that does not matter."

"If you succeed, it doesn't matter. Have you money?"

"Not a dollar, but that does not matter."

"No, money is necessary. You need lots of money. Come with me, I'll get money."

Caspar jumped up and walked ahead in the direction of the Imhoffs' castle. At the gate he told the soldier to wait. He went in and said to the watchman that he must speak to Frau von Kannawurf. There was something in his appearance which made the old servant hurry. Frau von Kannawurf soon came toward him. She led him up the steps into a little room, which was not lighted. A mirror as tall as the wall glistened in the moonlight.

"Don't ask me anything," Caspar said with flying breath to his friend, who was unable to utter a word, "I need ten ducats, give me ten ducats."

She looked at him anxiously. "Wait," she answered and went out silently.

It seemed an eternity to Caspar before she came back. He stood at the window, constantly rubbing one hand over his cheek. Silently as she had left, Frau von Kannawurf came back and handed him a small roll. He took her hand and stammered something. Her face twitched again and again; her eyes swam as in a mist. Did she understand him? She must have had some conception, but she did not ask. A wan smile passed over her lips as she led Caspar to the door. At this moment she was strikingly beautiful.

Schildknecht was leaning against a pillar of the city gate and staring earnestly at the moon. They walked toward the city together; after a few hundred steps Caspar stood still and gave Schildknecht the letter and the money. Schildknecht did not utter a syllable. He puffed out his cheeks a little and looked harmless.

In front of Kronacher Buck, Schildknecht said it would be best for them not to be seen together. Then Schildknecht turned round once again and called, apparently cheerful: "Goodbye!"

Caspar remained much longer, on the same spot, as if bewitched. He wanted to throw himself into the grass, and to dig his arms in the earth for which he felt a sudden gratitude.

He got home late, but fortunately was not questioned, for Quandt had been ordered to call on Hofrat Hofmann on account of urgent business. He brought back news with him. "Just listen, Jette," he said, "the President during his last days, while he was with the policeman, entirely gave up the Caspar Hauser matter. He is even said to have thought of openly retracting his monograph as a mistake."

"Who said that?" asked his wife.

"The lieutenant. And it is so reported everywhere. The Hofrat is of the same opinion."

"It is also being reported everywhere that the President was poisoned!"

"Oh, what rot!" exclaimed Quandt hotly.

"Just be careful not to say anything of the sort. The lieutenant has threatened to arrest people who spread such dangerous talk and to make them answer for it without mercy. What's Hauser about?"

"I believe he has gone to bed. This afternoon he was in the kitchen and complained at the number of flies in his room."

"So, he has no other worries at present? Just like him."

"Yes. I told him to chase them out, but he replied that twenty more at once came in."

"Twenty?" said Quandt with displeasure. "Why twenty? That's an arbitrary number."

They went to bed.

On the day of Feuerbach's funeral, Daumer and Herr von Tucher arrived from Nurnberg and went to the Star Inn. Daumer at once sought out Caspar. Caspar was frank and open toward his first protector, nevertheless Daumer was tormented by the impression that Caspar did not see or hear him at all. He found him pale and grown, silent as always, and curiously joyous, yes, quite preoccupied and enmeshed in this curious gayety, which threw strange, dark shadows about him.

In a letter to his sister, Daumer wrote among other things: "I should have to lie if I said that it gave me pleasure to see the boy. No, it is painful for me to see him and if you ask me why, I am obliged to reply like a stupid schoolboy: 'I don't know.' Moreover, he lives here quite at peace and will probably, sad as it is to state, figure all his days as an obscure clerk or something of the sort."

Whereas Herr von Tucher left again on the same afternoon, and without having troubled himself about Caspar, Daumer remained in the city for three days, as he had business with the government. At the President's funeral he did not see Caspar; he discovered later that Frau von Imhoff had been able to prevent his presence. He soon made the painful discovery that Caspar was purposely avoiding him. An hour before his departure he spoke to Quandt about it.

"Can a man of your insight be at a loss to find an explanation for this behavior?" asked Quandt with astonishment.

"It is quite obvious that now, when he sees a constantly greater indifference growing up toward him and must feel the consequences of this fact daily, he must be embarrassed by the sight of his Nurnberg friends. For there he was in full fettle and thought what wonderful plums he might draw forth from his cake. We, however, respected professor, are close on his tracks; it won't be long before you will hear remarkable news."

Quandt looked worried, and his words had a fanatical sound. Whether Daumer could thereupon set forth on his journey homewards with high hopes may be doubted. He was tempted to shout as he had shouted the complaint over the summer fields in that silent night when he pressed Caspar in the spirit, and in the flesh, against his breast: "Man, oh man!" But that was not all. A grinding remorse seized upon the distraught man; his brain seethed like an evil conscience, and, slowly awakening the resolution to action and atonement—to action and atonement which came too late—produced the first dawning of the truth.

25. An Interrupted Performance

In the course of the following weeks there were all sorts of rumors in the drawing-rooms and burgher households of the city. Without assuming any definite form, gossip had it that the sudden death of the President was the fruit of a mysterious plot, and this was believed even by those only distantly concerned. This, of course, was not tangibly expressed; the whispers were careful. Very much in secret, they also murmured that Lord Stanhope was a party to this conspiracy, and gradually the definite rumor arose that Lord Stanhope had had a share in the plot and that his lordship was attempting to bring criminal action against Caspar Hauser and had already secured the assistance of a distinguished councillor-at-law. Suddenly, no one admitted having ever felt any enthusiasm for the count, the dashing impression that he had left behind him had been wiped out and in several influential families, where he had been regarded as a demi-god, his name was uttered only with timid concern.

Caspar's friends became anxious. Frau von Imhoff called on the lieutenant one day and asked what one was to think of all this mysterious talk. With cool regret, Hickel replied that public opinion was not mistaken in this point. "Times have changed," said he; "his lordship now sees in Caspar Hauser only a common swindler.,,

Whereupon Frau von Imhoff left the lieutenant without a word of reply, and without saying goodbye.

"Ah, the gentle souls," thought Hickel sarcastically to himself, "they are beginning to shudder."

Hickel had rented a new flat on the promenade and lived like a fine gentleman. Where can he have gotten the means, people asked? He has had luck at cards, said some; others declared, on the contrary, that he constantly lost large sums.

But this did not exhaust the subjects for gossip. Another curious incident: during the summer a soldier had disappeared from the infantry barracks in an unexplained manner. At other times such an event would perhaps have passed unnoticed. Now all kinds of fables attached themselves to the incident. It was said that the soldier who had guarded Caspar Hauser had obtained knowledge of certain secrets and had been done away with. People became afraid; they locked their front doors carefully at night. All was no longer easy in the quiet good city. Whoever was a stranger was regarded with suspicion.

Even Frau von Kannawurf was now looked at askance, although there was something inviolable about her which robbed the slanderous words of their strength. Nevertheless it resulted in her withdrawing from intercourse with her equals and in her frequently associating instead with persons of the lower classes. She spent many hours in insipid talk with peasant women and working women, ascended to her sexton in the church-spire, or joined the children coming home from school. Then, to the tremendous astonishment of the citizens whom they met, she often collected a noisy swarm of boys and girls about her and wandered through the streets, laughing in their midst.

Probably she is a demagogue, they said. Parents of sound principles forbade their children to take part in these scandalous parades. Doubtless the authorities, too, found these doings objectionable, for one evening it was noticed that the police-lieutenant took up his post in front of the Imhoff's summer-house; for two hours he had stood immovable in the darkness underneath a tree.

Frau von Kannawurf, it is true, was a striking person and behaved strikingly. But her curious actions had an appearance of lightness, even of carelessness. She had a way of smiling in which a self-forgetful devotion to something thought, or felt, was touchingly mixed with a despair of her own inadequacy. She lived in everything, she took part in everything and soared into super mundane space in every new pleasure.

One evening in August she entered her friend's room, breathless with running, threw herself on the sofa and was unable to speak for a long time.

"What have you been doing again, Clara?" said Frau von Imhoff reproachfully; "that's not living, that's burning up."

"Nothing is any use," murmured the young woman exhaustedly, "I must travel."

Frau von Imhoff shook her head in affectionate reproach. She had heard these words often during the last three months. "You will stay at least until our family party, Clara," she replied affectionately.

"How much strength of will it does sometimes take in order not to carry out a resolution," said Clara von Kannawurf to herself, and after a silent pause she turned her face to her friend and said: "Why, Bettine, can't you take Caspar here into your house? He may not and must not stay at Quandt's any longer. It is impossible for me to enter that house. His situation is frightful, Bettine. Why do I tell you this? You know why, all of you know it, but not one ever moves a finger. No one, no one has the courage to do what he will wish to have done when that which he silently fears will have happened."

Frau von Imhoff looked down with embarrassment at her embroidery. "I am not happy enough and not unhappy enough to sacrifice myself for the fate of a stranger," she replied at last.

Clara leaned her head in her hand. "You read a beautiful book, you see something moving on the stage and you are profoundly stirred by this merely imagined suffering," she continued with emphasis and emotion. "A sad song can move you to tears, Bettine, do you remember how you cried recently when Fraulein von Stichaner sang Schubert's Wandeter? At the words: There, where you are not, there is happiness, you cried. You could not sleep a whole night when you heard that a mother had let her own child starve over there in the vineyards. Why is it always on the unreal or the far-away that you waste your pity? Why always believe only the word, the sound, the picture, and not the living human being whose need is so tangible? I don't understand it; I don't understand it, it torments me, yes, it burns me up."

The low melodious voice ended in a sigh. Frau von Imhoff leaned her head in her hand and was silent a long time. Then she got up, seated herself by Clara and stroked her friend's forehead and said: "Talk to him about it. He shall come to us. I will see that it is done,"

Clara threw both arms about her friend and kissed her gratefully. But Frau von Imhoff had not come to this resolution with a free heart, and she drew an extraordinary sigh of relief when, the next day, Frau von Kannawurf announced to her that Caspar had with incomprehensible obstinacy fought the suggestion that he leave the teacher's house. At first he had not wished to give any reason for his refusal, but on realizing Clara's dismay, he had said: "There I was put and there I shall stay. I don't want it said that things at Quandt's were not good enough for him and therefore the Imhoffs took him out of pity. I have my bread and my bed, more I don't need, and the bed is the best thing that I have come to know in this world. Everything else is bad."

No further talk was of any avail. "Of course, you can do with me as you like," he added, "but I shall not consent to go willingly. And wherefore? It can't last much longer."

Thus the word had escaped him. Was that the reason for the deep gleam in his eyes? Was that why he glanced along the streets with silent tension when he went to the Appellate Court in the morning? Was that why he leaned out of the window for hours, staring at the highway? Why he listened eagerly whenever he saw two people talking quietly together anywhere? Was that why he had to be present daily when the mail coach arrived, and why he asked the postman whether he had anything for him?

Time did not alter this puzzling behavior. Frau von Kannawurf was eager to free him from this tension, which was bound to keep him from any intimate relations with the surrounding world and made any pleasant activity a hard compulsion. She was constantly thinking of some amusement for him, and the family festival which her friend Bettine had spoken of offered an opportunity of again dragging Caspar out of his own thoughts and surrounding him once more with a circle of sympathetic friends.

The celebration was planned by Herr von Imhoff in honor of the golden wedding of his parents, and was to take place on the twelfth of September. Young Dr. Lang, a friend of the family, had composed a clever little drama in verse which was to be performed by several ladies and gentlemen of the party. At the rehearsals, which took place in an upper room of the summer-house, it became evident that one of the young men, who was cast for the role of a silent shepherd, was unable, on account of his awkwardness, to produce the desired effect in the part. Then it occurred to Frau von Kannawurf, who was one of the actors, to offer the role to Caspar. The suggestion was approved.

Caspar agreed. Since he was to represent a person who did not have to speak he considered himself quite adequate for the task, which appealed to his old love for the theater. He went diligently to the rehearsals, and although the play was too grandiloquent and rhetorical to please him, he nevertheless enjoyed the rapid succession of incidents in a transaction of fixed outline.

The innocent drama had an intentional, and, for the audience, a readily perceived relation to a far distant event in the Imhoff family. One of the brothers of the Baron, at the beginning of the eighteen-twenties, had taken part in the subversive activities of the Burschenschaft, and pursued by his father's solemn curse, as well as by the political authorities, had fled to America. After an amnesty had been granted, he had returned home, had renounced all ideas of a freer life, in the presence of the head of the family, and from that time on the paternal good will had again beamed upon him.

This somewhat philistine incident had inspired the family poet in his composition. A king offers a meal to a friend and confrere in arms who is visiting him. A second Polycrates, he boasts on this occasion of his power, the peacefulness of his country, and the virtues of his subjects. The courtiers at the table strengthen his delusions of happiness with eager flattery, only his guest and friend ventures boldly to remark that he sees a spot on the royal purple. The king feels the truth of this, and berates his friend and prevents him from speaking further, since his queen shows signs of great emotional suffering. Meantime lads and lasses fresh from the fields fill the courtyard, laughter, gay talk and music accompany the harvest celebration. Suddenly there is a silence—the bagpipes, the gay voices and the laughter cease — and upon the king's asking the reason, he is told that the Black Shepherd who has not been seen in the country within the memory of man, has again appeared among the people. The friend inquiries about this shepherd and is told that the remarkable man possesses the gift, by his mere glance, of recalling to people the memory of their greatest wrongdoings, and of permitting the innocent to view the object of their dearest desire. As a corroboration of this, sounds of weeping and lamentation are heard to proceed from the midst of the people. The king orders the stranger to depart, but the queen, supported by the entreaties of their guest and the courtiers, implores her husband to let him enter into their presence. The king yields and the silent shepherd appears upon the scene. He looks at the king, who hides his face; he looks at the queen, and she, overcome with grief, breaks into a long soliloquy from which it is evident that her eldest son had been cast out by his father on account of a conspiracy in which he had engaged in thoughtless frivolity, and had since disappeared. With outstretched arms, drawn irresistibly to him, she walks up to the shepherd, who turns out to be the contrite prince, who has returned. He is recognized, he is embraced, the ice of the king's heart melts, and there is a general merrymaking and jubilation.

    Caspar did not play badly. In the course of the rehearsals he acquired as lively and spontaneous an interest in the role and felt his part as deeply as if he had become entirely detached from his everyday life. Frau von Kannawurf, who played the queen, was similarly affected; she, too, took her task with a seriousness which lent unseemly depth to the playful side of the episode and made the roles of her fellow actors appear merely subsidiary.

    It was a warm September day; toward six in the evening the invited guests appeared, altogether about fifty persons, the women in gala array dressed in their gayest, the men in frock coats and embroidered uniforms. The stage for the comedy occupied the whole of the narrow side of the room, movable scenes, properties and supernumeraries had been supplied by the director of the Court Theater. The table had been spread in an adjoining room, where the music was also accommodated, for there was to be dancing after the refreshments.

    At seven o'clock a bell sounded and all took their places. The curtain went up, and the king began his haughty tirade. The friend, acted by the author himself, made a respectful answer, then came the gay scene in the courtyard and the course of the action proceeded without mishap. Now Caspar appeared. The black suit became him well and intensified the whiteness of his face. His appearance on the stage had an immediate effect. The coughing and clearing of throats stopped; a deathlike silence ensued. The way in which he looked at the king and queen, the way he walked toward them, and his dreamlike smile—all were touching. Several people saw him tremble and observed that his fingers closed convulsively into his hands. Now the monologue of the queen—this, too, did not have the customary sound of an actor's delivery. She walks up to the boy, she places her arm around his neck

At this moment a man hurried forward from the back of the room to the footlights and called out loudly: "Halt!" The actors on the stage started with fright, the spectators arose, and a general commotion ensued. "Who is that? Who dares do that? What's the matter?" was exclaimed all at once. People pressed forward, women screamed with fright, chairs were thrown over and the host only succeeded in preventing a dangerous panic with great difficulty.

Meantime the originator of all this commotion still stood silently in front of the platform. It was Hickel. Pale and hostile, he stared at the stage and seemed to perceive only Caspar and Frau von Kannawurf, who, having moved close to each other, looked fearfully into the darkened room. The first who turned to Hickel was young Dr. Lang. In his fantastic "Friend's" costume he walked to the edge of the balcony and inquired furiously what was the reason for such irresponsible behavior.

The lieutenant breathed deeply and said, in a voice with a glassy sound: "I must beg the distinguished guests' pardon a thousand times, and since I am myself one of the invited you will believe me, I hope, when I assure you that this step was not easy for me. But I cannot permit Hauser to continue to take part in a childish trifling at a moment when I have had news of a terrible misfortune, which strikes him as it strikes no one else, and will be fraught with heavy consequences for his future career."

Angry, curious and disapproving eyes stared at the lieutenant. Dr. Lang replied angrily: "Nonsense, pure boorishness, that's all it amounts to. Whatever may have happened, neither I nor any of those present can admit your right to such a gross piece of despotism. If what you have to say is bad news, all the more reason for waiting; our play was over, as it was. It is a piece of folly, an abuse of hospitality."

"Yes, the doctor is right," several voices exclaimed. Hickel bowed his head and placed his hand over his forehead.

"May I know what is the matter?" Herr von Imhoff now interrupted.

Hickel pulled himself together and replied dully: "Count Stanhope has taken his own life."

There ensued a long silence. Almost everyone looked at Caspar, who leaned against the panel of a door and slowly closed his eyes.

"Did he shoot himself?" asked Herr von Imhoff.

"No," replied Hickel, "he hanged himself."

Rustling sounds of panic terror were heard. Herr von Imhoff bit his lips. "Is anything further known?" he continued to ask.

"No. That is to say, I have only the general information from his huntsman. He was visiting a friend, Count de Bellegarde, on the Norman coast. On the morning of the fourth of September he was found in the tower room of the castle, a corpse, hanging from a silken cord."

Herr von Imhoff looked down on the floor. "We are all heartily sorry. I believe that there is no one in this room who will not retain a living memory of the unfortunate man. Nevertheless, lieutenant, I shall call you to account for your extraordinary procedure."

Hickel bowed in silence.

The hostess and several other ladies sought to calm the assembly, but while the servant was lighting the candles of the big candelabrum, Frau von Imhoff received word that her mother-in-law, in whose honor the party was being held, was indisposed as a result of the agitation and had been obliged to retire to her room. She followed her at once. This was the signal for a general breaking up. The Regierungsprasident and the General Commissioner with their wives left the room first, and finally there remained only a few intimate friends who surrounded the Baron and, in an oppressed mood, seated themselves at the long banquet table.

"I always felt that the good Lord would some time give us some horrible surprise," said Herr von Imhoff.

"What will now become of poor Hauser?" asked one of the company.

All kinds of assumptions were expressed; conversation became animated, and, as is often the case, an unfortunate incident served to stimulate the fantasy of those who are only remotely concerned. A lively conversation ensued until after midnight.

Caspar during the quick departure of the guests had hidden himself in the little dressing-room of the actors. The young people eagerly laid aside their costumes and disappeared. After a while the servant came to put out the lights and he discovered Caspar. When Caspar went towards the stairs he heard footsteps behind him and Frau von Kannawurf walked up to him. She asked him whether he wanted to go home, and he said "Yes." "It's raining," said she, down by the entrance, as she held out her hand into the open air. She waited a little for the rain to pass, but it turned into a heavy downpour and the water spurted noisily upon the trees and the parched ground. A cold wet current of air encountered them and Frau von Kannawurf invited Caspar to go into her room with her; it might last too long. He followed silently.

Upstairs she struck a light; then she stood and looked thoughtfully into the flame. Her shoulders shook with cold. Caspar had seated himself upon the sofa. Gradually, he felt such a sensation of fatigue that it actually doubled him up and he was obliged to lie upon his back. Then Clara walked up to him and seized his hand which he, however, snatched away hastily. He closed his eyes, and for a moment his face was completely lifeless. Frau von Kannawurf uttered a dull cry of anxiety and fell upon her knees next to him. Then she called her maid and asked for water. She poured out a glass and handed it to him to drink. He drank a few gulps. "What is the matter with thee, Caspar?" she said, addressing him as "du" for the first time. He smiled gratefully. "Thou art like a sister," said he shyly, and with his fingers touched the hair of the head which she bent over him. This word "sister" in his mouth had a sound of its own; it was that of a word never uttered before.

Clara pressed against his side; she felt as if she had to warm him; he, however, moved anxiously away; then she wanted to get up again, but he slid his hand along her arm and looked at her with an imploring expression of grief and love. "Clara," he said, and she felt as if she must pass away, or wake up in another world, for the shy entreaty with which he uttered her name had something about it that was beyond this world.

And so it came that hour after hour passed and they continued to lie next to one another, silent, quite silent, and motionless, and both of them trembling all over. She stretched out her hand to him and the breath of his mouth melted into the air along with hers.

When the castle clock struck twelve Clara started. She got up and said with solemn protestation, aloud to herself: "Never, never, never!" Then she walked to the window and opened it. The rain had long since ceased, the sky was clear, the whole starry sky gleamed above her. Her overladen breast was drawn to the unknown worlds, for she was tired of this world in which she lived.

She told Caspar that he might spend the night in the castle, but he replied that he did not wish to. Then she went out to see whether Frau von Imhoff was still awake. She walked past the dining-room where the gentlemen still sat over their wine, talking. The Baroness had not yet retired either. Clara told her that Caspar had been with her until then. Frau von Imhoff nodded, but looked at her friend with some surprise and embarrassment. "I shall pack my trunks and leave to-morrow morning," said Qara in low tones, and with an expression of irrevocable determination, which sometimes was her wont, and made her child-like features look curiously hard and pained. Frau von Imhoff got up surprised and walked close up to her friend. Suddenly they fell into one another's arms and Clara sobbed.

They understood one another; speech was not necessary.

When Clara tore herself away, she said that she would accompany Caspar into the city on this last night. "You can't possibly do that," objected Frau von Imhoff, "or at least I will send a servant with you."

"Please don't," replied Clara, smiling. "You know that I have no fear. It irritates me, too, if anyone is anxious on my account. The night air does me good and I look forward to the lonely walk back."

A quarter of an hour later she was walking with Caspar over the still damp street towards the city. They did not speak now, either, and before the teacher's house they shook hands. "Now you will probably go away from me, Clara," said Caspar suddenly, and looked at her with a veiled look. She was as much astonished as moved over these words, for they betrayed a profound presentiment. How beautiful his eyes are, she thought; they are light brown like those of a deer; he resembles a deer in other respects, too, standing sad and surprised in a wood.

"Yes, I am going," she finally replied.

"And why? I liked being with you."

"I shall come again," she assured him with forced heartiness—behind which an exclamation was stifled. "I shall return. We will write one another. And at Christmas I'll come back."

"I'll come again! I have heard that before," said Caspar bitterly. "It's a long time till Christmas. And I don't like to write.

What does one get from writing? It's only paper. All right, go then. Farewell."

"It can't be otherwise," whispered Clara, and her glance sought the stars. "Look, Caspar, up there is the eternal; we won't forget it as all the others forget. We won't forget anything. Ah, forgetting, forgetting, therein lies all the evil of the world. The stars belong to us, Caspar, and when you look up at them I am near you."

Caspar shook his head. "Farewell," he said dully.

In the basement a window was opened and the teacher's head, crowned with a nightcap, became visible, disappearing again at once. It was a silent admonition.

I will ask Bettine to visit him daily, reflected Clara while walking alone through the deserted streets. I shall bring disaster upon him if I stay; an abyss yawns in front of me as frightful as anything one could conceive of. Sister! How I felt when he called me sister. Heavenly bliss knocked at my heart. Thus I should have found a lost brother, and still more: but just God, more may not be! To touch him. To disturb his sleep. Oh, criminal lips, for which a kiss has no meaning. Had I done it I should have been his murderess. What, can I do better than fly? A good genius will protect him. Presumptuous of me to think of protecting him by my poor presence. Such a noble creature cannot go under because two eyes turn away from him.

This disturbed and excited chain of thoughts reveals hopelessly entangled emotions which, in their exaltation, decide upon a sacrifice; dazed by the sight of so much tragedy, and in their sadness choosing the wrong path at the crossways of love.

Her glance fixed steadily on the heavens; gazing upon the beautiful constellation of Orion, shining like a jagged flash of lightning in the deep blue sky, Clara did not notice that someone was leaning against the gate of the castle. She only jumped back when the nocturnal figure barred the way. Oh God, that gruesome man, she thought.

Hickel, for it was he, bowed towards the dismayed woman.

"Forgiveness, Madame, forgiveness," he murmured, "and not only for this assault, but also for the other. You are too beautiful, Madame. If you would have the goodness to realize that your sublime beauty has turned my poor head the way a playful boy lashes his top, if you would consider that even in acting a comedy a point is reached where the fantasy runs wild and sullies the object of its wishes, and jealousy regards as a reality what is merely being enacted, you would perhaps favor your abject servant with a word of comfort."

All this sounded silly, unstrung, affected, ironical and desperate. He seemed to be lacerating the words between his teeth, and one could see that it was difficult for him to remain straight and calm.

Clara took a step backwards, crossed her arms and, pressing them tightly across her breast, said imperiously: "Let me pass."

"Madame, much depends upon your mouth at this hour," continued Hickel, as he lifted his arm with the stiff motion of a wax figure. "I have never been a beggar. I stand here now, begging. Do not disavow your face, which permits one to believe in angels!" He stepped to one side, Clara went by silently. She rang, and the watchman—who had been waiting for her return —opened the door at once. When she was inside she felt a horrible nausea. She felt as though something had been torn apart in her head. On the stairs she hesitated; it seemed to her as if she must turn around and say something once more to this dreadful man.

When Caspar arrived at the Imhoff the next afternoon he was told that Frau von Kannawurf had already left. He asked Frau von Imhoff to show him Clara's picture, which he had not seen since the evening of the first party he had attended in the castle. The Baroness conducted him to an alcove where the portrait hung on the wall between two ancestral pictures. He sat down in front of it and gazed at it a long time with silent attention. When he left, Frau von Imhoff promised to have a copy of the picture drawn for him. He was so absorbed that he did not even thank her.

26. Quandt Undertakes A Last Assault Upon The Mystery

Although there was some talk for a time about Hickel's being punished, nothing came of it and the affair finally was covered with oblivion. Doubtless there were all kinds of secret influences at work to assure the lieutenant's safety. "They can't get at the fellow," said the initiated, "he is too dangerous and knows too much." Of course, Hickel was useful in the service and greatly feared by those under him. At the same time, his way of living became more and more inscrutable. Except in the Casino and in the police station he spoke to no one. He sat half the night in the police station, but only in order to torment his subordinates.

Even Quandt had learned to fear him. One afternoon in October the teacher with his wife and Caspar were drinking coffee when Hickel walked into the room rattling his sword, and without any greeting walked up to Caspar and asked imperiously: "Tell me, Caspar, do you perhaps know anything about the whereabouts of the soldier Schildknecht?"

Caspar turned an ashen gray. The lieutenant fixed him with a glistening eye and thundered, impatient at his long silence: "Do you know anything, or don't you? Speak man, or by God I'll put you into prison at once!"

Caspar got up. A button of his jacket caught in the fringes of the tablecloth, and as he stepped back the coffeepot fell over and the black liquid spread over the linen. The teacher's wife screamed: Quandt, however, looked angry, for the lieutenant's overbearing manner irritated him; also he was all the more surprised at it because Hickel had observed a stiff and sinister reserve toward Caspar for several months. "What can he have to do with that deserter?" he asked unwillingly.

"Let that be my business," Hickel roared.

"Oho, lieutenant, let me request you to be politer to me in my own house," replied Quandt.

"Oh, come now, you're a weakling, Herr Quandt. What doesn't grow on your own dung-hill you don't see! Moreover, what's doing? For two years the boy has been living here and we know just as little as before. If this was all you were good for, I don't care a damn for your results."

The blow struck home. Quandt swallowed his anger in silence.

"But there will be an end to this business now," continued Hickel, "I shall talk to Herr Hofmann, and Hauser will come and live with me."

"That will only be doing me a favor," replied Quandt as he left the room, much excited.

Frau Quandt remained sitting with her eyes downcast. Hickel walked up and down, drying his forehead with his sleeve. "How I do feel, how I do feel," he murmured almost distracted. Then he turned towards Caspar, abusively: "You miserable boy, you damned miserable wretch! What the devil has got into you? Moreover," he walked up to Caspar and added in a low tone, "the soldier-servant has been caught and will be extradited. He will do time in Plassenburg, the rascal."

"That's not true," said Caspar, in equally low tones, drawling in a somewhat sing-song tone. He smiled, and then laughed and laughed again, while his face turned very white. Hickel became suspicious. He bit his lips and looked darkly into the air. Suddenly he snatched his hat, gave a quick angry glance at Caspar and left.

Quandt was not disposed to swallow the lieutenant's reproaches. He complained to Hofrat Hofmann; the latter, however, did not seem much inclined to interfere. The teacher took the opportunity to bring up another matter for discussion.

Since Feuerbach's death the Hofrat had had the supervision of Caspar's tutelage. One could no longer depend on such help as Count Stanhope's; Mayor Enders and the city authorities had been asked for support, but no decision had been reached. Meanwhile Caspar received a slight increase in wages from the court for his clerkship; this money he handed over promptly to the teacher. These limited funds did not permit him the slightest freedom in his expenditures. In the beginning of October he had been confirmed, and he was eagerly looking forward to the so-called "bounty allowance," which would be provided for him by the city on this occasion. Impatient at the delay, he appealed to Herr Fuhrmann; the latter advised him to ask the teacher to go to the office of the municipality in order to hasten the payment.

"I won't do such a thing, Herr Hofmann, I won't be a petitioner, my pride won't permit it," replied Quandt.

Herr Hofmann shrugged his shoulders. "Then give him these few dollars out of your own pocket in the meantime," he said, "you will certainly get them back soon."

In regard to Hauser, you never can tell," replied Quandt, I have expenses enough as it is and don't know whether I can provide for him much longer."

The Hofrat considered. "But he has well-to-do and rich friends," he then said, "they can help."

"Oh, heavens yes," replied Quandt, "but he is much too interesting to them for them to think of his little wants."

"I shall come here tomorrow morning to ask Hauser why he should need money so urgently," said the Hofrat in conclusion.

Late that evening Caspar again came to Quandt's room and begged him with uplifted hands not to send him out of the house, he would do whatever was asked of him, "Only don't send me to the lieutenant's, anything, only not that," he said.

The teacher calmed him as best he could and said there could be no question of that at present, the lieutenant had only wanted to frighten him. "No," replied Caspar, "the clerk Maier spoke of it in court today too."

"Now, Hauser, you are behaving like a little boy and after all you are a grown man," said Quandt complainingly. "I can't take that quite seriously; you love to exaggerate and behave childishly. The lieutenant would not bite off your head either, although I admit that at times his manners are somewhat coarse. But you have now become a Christian in the full meaning of the word and doubtless you have heard the saying: 'Do good to your enemy and thus you will heap coals of fire on his head.'"

Caspar nodded: "There is a maxim about it in Dittmar's Grains of Wheat," he replied.

"Just so, we went through it together," continued Quandt eagerly. "I'll tell you what, in order that you may remember the beautiful saying well, I suggest that you write down your own thoughts about it. I will, if you like, regard it as a set task, and you may take the whole of tomorrow afternoon for it."

Caspar seemed to agree.

The Hofrat did not come as he had promised the next day, but only the second day after that. As he came into the room the teacher was just talking to Caspar with angry gestures. Upon Herr Hofmann's asking what Caspar had done, Quandt replied: "I do have to get angry with him too often. The day before yesterday I gave him a theme for his German composition; he promised to do it and had the whole of yesterday afternoon for it. Just now I asked for his copybook and here—just convince yourself, Herr Hofmann —not a single line has been written. Such laziness cries to heaven."

Quandt handed the Hofrat the open copybook; at the top of the page there stood: "Do good to your enemy and thus you will heap coals of fire on his head." Then, however, there was nothing more; the page was empty. "Why did you not write it?" asked the Hofrat coldly.

"I can't." replied Caspar.

"You must be able to," exclaimed Quandt. "The day before yesterday you told me that the subject was treated in your reader; to find some thoughts about it could not have been difficult for you, if you had gone on from there."

"Do try it again, Hauser," the Hofrat interrupted, to smooth matters. "I will go to the adjoining room with Herr Quandt, and when we come back you must show us something in order to prove that at least you have good intentions."

Quandt nodded and went out with the Hofrat. When they were in the living-room, Herr Hofmann gave the teacher two golden ducats and said that they were from Frau von Imhoff. He had pictured Caspar's embarrassment to her, the good lady had even excused herself that it was so little, but she had so little money at her own disposal. "By the way, Caspar came to see me yesterday," continued the Hofrat, "he came to beg me to prevent his going to live with the police-lieutenant."

"It's the very devil; he bothers everybody with his childish miseries," complained Quandt. "He has approached me on the same subject already."

"He seems to be in a blue funk over Hickel."

"Yes, the lieutenant is very strict with him."

"I said to him that I, for my part, had no intention of the sort; if he only did the right thing, no one would trouble him."

"Very true."

"Then we talked over his money difficulties, but he would not make a clean breast of things. I promised to give him five thalers on his birthday and asked him when that was. Thereupon he replied sadly that he did not know, and there was something about him that touched me. But otherwise he seemed to me too fawning, and his pleasant batting and blinking was distasteful to me."

"Yes, unfortunately, he is fawning, you're right there, Herr Hofmann; particularly when he wants to put through some plan of his own."

After this exchange of opinions they returned to Caspar. He sat at the table, his head resting on his hand. "Well, what have you accomplished?" asked the Hofrat jovially. He took the copybook and was taken aback to find only one sentence written, and read aloud. "'If they have done harm to your body, do good to them for it' That is all, Hauser?"

"Curious," murmured Quandt.

The Hofrat placed himself before Caspar, turned Caspar's head in his hands and began directly: "Tell me, Hauser, of all the people you have known up to now, whom have you learned to love the best?" His face looked crafty; from his occupation as a lawyer he had retained the manner of expressing even harmless matters with a sour irony.

"Do standup when the Hofrat speaks to you," the teacher whispered to Caspar.

Caspar got up; he stared straight ahead much perplexed. He sensed a trap behind the question. Then he suddenly thought: Probably the teacher is so angry because he thinks I did not do the composition because I regard him as my enemy. He looked over towards Quandt and said conciliatingly: "I love my teacher best."

The Hofrat exchanged a glance of understanding with Quandt, and cleared his throat meaningly.

Aha, thought Quandt, he's trying to bribe me, and was proud at not being at all edified at the boy's answer.

Caspar's life now became constantly more monotonous and withdrawn from the world. He had no one with whom he could carry on any confidential intercourse. Frau von Kannawurf, too, did not write and this galled him, although he had told her that he did not care anything about letters. Moreover, where was she? Was she still alive? Often he did not care to go out, he hated all the walks, he was lukewarm towards every occupation. Furthermore, the weather was constantly bad, November brought bad storms, so that during his leisure hours he would sit in his room, his glance passing over the hills, or anxiously scanning the sky, brooding constantly. He waited and waited. Once he went to the barracks and inquired cautiously whether anything was known there about Schildknecht. They could not give him any information. This nourished the dying flame of hope, but during the following days he felt ill and could scarcely decide to get up in the morning. Strangers still sometimes came to see him; his deportment was obstinate and silent. When he was invited to go to social gatherings, he would say bitterly: "Oh, what use is all their talking to me?" One evening, when he was walking over the Schlossplatz and looked up at the great facade with the constantly closed windows he thought that he saw, in rooms which he had considered unoccupied, gigantic figures observing him inimically. They all seemed dressed in purple with gold chains about their necks. A tremendous prostrating grief bore down upon him and he felt tempted to throw himself down on the pavement and whine like a dog.

He felt so cold and so sad. One night he dreamed that he saw a boulder of green stone with a gold dish upon it on which there lay five curiously steaming hearts, not of a natural form, but shaped as pastry-cooks bake them. He stood in front of them and said aloud: "That is my father's heart, that is my mother's heart, that is my brother's heart, that is my sister's heart, that is my own heart." His own lay on top and had two sad, living eyes.

Not infrequently he had a definite sensation of the effect upon him of a dearly beloved person, operating from far away. This person acted, spoke and suffered for him, but a world lay between them and nothing that she undertook could lessen the distance between him and her. He felt these weird processes so clearly that he often stood listening as if to a conversation behind a thin wall. Then he would fold his hands under his chin and smile a timid smile.

The teacher would have had to be blind not to notice any of this. He gathered all his observations under one head, as it were, and this heading ran: a struggle against an evil conscience. "I have no more kindness in me for that creature," declared Quandt, "I have no more kindness towards him since seeing how indifferent he was toward Lord Stanhope's sad end. I myself felt as if I had lost a brother, and he did not even try to pretend to assume an appearance of sorrow. He has a heart of stone and shows the most vulgar ingratitude."

We see the teacher hidden, as it were, behind a hedge; we see him lying in wait and bringing together the information gathered about Caspar in former years: facts and circumstances which he ferrets out with the sagacity of a prosecuting attorney, which he interprets, and exposes to the limelight, and silently keeps ready for his purposes. We see him burning with hate towards the ever obstinate, obdurate boy, and we cannot avoid thinking that he resembles someone who has been so long provoked and lured on by a will o' the wisp that he finally succumbs to a state of raving intoxication.

In the beginning of December, it was a Thursday evening after supper, Quandt asked Caspar whether he had already finished his translation for the next day. Caspar in a serious mood but with insincere friendliness (as it seemed to Quandt) said yes, he was through with it. Quandt took the book, showed him how long the task was and asked him again whether he had really translated as far as all that.

Caspar said, "Yes, I even got one exercise further."

Quandt did not believe him; it seemed improbable, the lesson contained some constructions which Caspar could not have gotten through alone, and for which he would undoubtedly have been obliged to seek some assistance. However, he thought it best not to say anything further in the presence of his wife, but let the boy go quietly to his room.

About five minutes later, Quandt seized the Latin primer and followed Caspar upstairs. Caspar had already locked the door and before he opened it he asked the teacher whether he wished anything from him before retiring. "Open the door," ordered Quandt curtly.

When he was inside he selected several sentences aloud at random and asked Caspar how he had translated them. Caspar was silent for a time, then he replied that he had only prepared the work, he was about to do the translation now. Quandt looked at him quietly, then said meaningly, "So!" wished him goodnight and left.

Downstairs he told his wife what had occurred and they agreed that there was a perverted obstinacy back of it, nothing further. The next day he told the Hofrat about it and the latter wrote Caspar a little note which he gave the ceacher to take with him. Caspar read the letter in Quandt's presence and when he had finished he handed it to the teacher, visibly depressed. In the letter the Hofrat warned him tactfully against qualities which only vulgar natures gave way to, but which "unfortunately are not unknown to our Hauser."

The same evening, again after supper Quandt, produced a copybook of Caspar's and said: "A page has been cut out of this book, Hauser. You know that I have already forbidden you to do that countless times."

"I made a spot on the page and I did not want to have that in my exercise," replied Caspar.

Instead of any answer Quandt ordered the boy to come with him to his study. He asked his wife to light the candles, took the lamp and walked ahead. When he had reached the other room he carefully closed both doors, told Caspar to be seated and began.

"You don't really expect me to take your excuse for the truth, do you?"

"What excuse?" asked Caspar dully.

"Why, that tale of an ink spot. I don't believe in that spot."

"Why don't you want to believe me?"

"You know the proverb, 'Who lies once is not believed, no matter when the truth he tells.' You, my dear friend, have lied more than once."

"I don't lie," replied Caspar in equally dull and lifeless tones.

"You dare to say that to my face?" "I don't know that I lie." You wretched quibbler!" exclaimed Quandt bitterly. That I don't discuss your frequent lies every time is because I have gradually come to think that I cannot cure you of the evil. Why should I distress myself in vain? You are in the habit of saying no, until you have been found guilty so flagrantly that you cannot say no any longer, and even then you don't say yes."

"Shall I say yes when it is no? Prove to me that I have lied." Caspar looked at the teacher with one of the glances which the former was accustomed to call crafty.

"Ah, Hauser, how it pains me to see your attitude towards me," replied Quandt; "I am not at a loss for proofs and have so many that I don't know where to begin. Don't you remember the story about the candlestick? You stated that the handle was broken and it was irrefutably proved that it was melted off."

"It was as I said."

"I won't let myself be put off with that. You may moreover be assured that I have noted these incidents carefully, indeed in writing, so as to be able in case of need to give a complete account of you."

Caspar looked exceedingly confused and was silent.

"And furthermore, let us look at a recent case," continued Quandt. "It was all the same whether you had finished the exercise the day before yesterday or whether you wished to do it later in your room. Since you had been busy all day you were entitled to do the work at night. Why did you say that you had finished it when you had not done any of it?"

"I thought that you had asked whether I had prepared it."

"Nonsense. This is not the first time you have had the impertinence to twist my words about. I asked clearly: Have you finished your translation? My wife was present and witnessed it."

"When you spoke, I simply understood differently."

"The usual excuses. You had not even prepared it. You can palm that off on someone who does not know you so well as I. I wish I had never known you, in the end you will deprive me of the reputation of being an honest man. But you are being seen through, not only by me, but also by other people. There are only a few families left who regard you as honest and friendly. Most of them realize that you have a vulgar conceit and a low kind of pride, that you are indifferent and presumptuous towards simpler people when you have the entree to more distinguished houses. And as regards your lying I am ready to tell you to your face, in every single instance, whether you stuck by the truth, what things are included in and what things lie beyond your horizon, and what can hold your attention and what not. I can give you a good example from the recent past. At lunch there was some talk about Regierungsrat Fliessen. My wife thought that it was unpleasant for the good old man that he could not be with his people in Worms. Whereupon I remarked that Herr Fliessen had many relations in the Rhine district and had so and so many grandchildren. Upon that you said: He has eleven grandchildren; I heard so at the General Commissioner's. I replied that I had heard of nineteen; you assured me, however, that there were eleven. I was not able to contradict that, but I was sure that you had only snatched hastily at the number in order to impress us, and in order to speak of the General Commissioner, and to show us that you are familiar with the relations of people who visit at that house. Your hand upon your heart, isn't that so?"

"Someone at the table spoke of eleven, I am quite certain."

"I don't believe it."

"Yes, they did."

"Shame upon you, Hauser, to stick to a lie in such a serious moment. It's a miserable, not to say contemptible, thing to do. The matter itself is not so important, but your obstinate unabashed statement permits one to see far. It shows that you never want to take a fault upon yourself, that you never want to confess a weakness, and that you will go to the very limit. At the first leisure moment I shall ask Herr Fliessen how many grandchildren he has. If there are really eleven I shall give you full satisfaction, if it is not the case I shall humiliate you so that you'll think of me!"

Caspar bowed his head humbly.

"But the thing I really want to remonstrate with you about is still coming, my dear friend," began Quandt after a pause, during which the wind could be heard beating against the windows and howling down the chimney. "It is now time that you should finally tell the truth to a man like myself who has a genuine sympathy with your misfortune. You still seem to be of the opinion that the whole world believes in the fancy tale of your secret imprisonment or even that of your noble descent. You are frightfully mistaken, dear Hauser. At first, I grant, people were intrigued with it, as with an enigmatical situation, but gradually all sensible people have come to perceive that they have been victimized by activities which I do not like to designate by name. I can readily believe, Hauser, that at first you did not want to carry the trick so far. Last winter when the

President's pamphlet appeared you showed that you were frightened at the results of your deed, and you reminded me of a child that has played a little with fire and unexpectedly set the whole house in flames. You were afraid of losing the meal ticket which you had obtained by your craftiness and you feared discovery and a well-deserved punishment, just there where your infatuated friends looked for your happiness. Just examine yourself carefully and see whether I am not right."

Caspar looked the teacher in the face with a lifeless glance.

"All right! I won't compel you to answer," continued Quandt with somber satisfaction. "Now you have not so many friends, Hauser. They have become curiously silent. People don't seem to take a very hearty interest in you anymore. Things had quieted down similarly that time just before the alleged attack of the murderer in Professor Daumer's house. No one among all the thousands of people who live in Nurnberg observed anyone at the critical time, or later on, who could in the slightest degree be suspected of any connection with such a horrible deed. Your friends nevertheless believed in the masked monster just as they believed in the fantastic jailor, who was said to have taught you to read and write. Nevertheless Professor Daumer soon put you out of the house. He must certainly have known why. And today matters stand so that you must make a decision. Your most powerful protectors, President Feuerbach, Lord Stanhope and Frau Behold have all departed from this earth. Do you not regard this as a hint from heaven? There is no longer any reason for you to maintain the fiction. You are a man now and you want to become a useful member of human society. Speak to me, Hauser, open yourself to me! Speak with an honest mouth out of a true heart."

"Yes, but what shall I say?" asked Caspar dully and slowly, while his figure shrunk like that of an old man and his face too became worn like an old man's.

The teacher walked up to him and seized his stone-cold heavy hand. "The truth, speak the truth," he exclaimed imploringly. "Oh, Hauser, it is painful to see your bad conscience peeping like a phantom out of your every glance. Your spirit is oppressed. Open your tormented breast, Hauser! Let the sun finally shine in! Courage, courage, have confidence! The truth, the truth!" He seized Caspar by the collar of his coat as if he wished to snatch the secret away from him with his hands.

What now, what now, thought Caspar his glance wavering painfully.

"I will meet you half-way," said Quandt. "When you came to Nurnberg you produced a letter. You had several books in the pocket of your ill-cut coat, they were old monks' books, among them one with the title: *The Art of Making up for the Lost Years*. Who wrote the letter? Who gave you the books?"

"Who? The person with whom I was."

"Yes, that's clear," replied Quandt with an excited smile. "But you are to tell me the name of this person with whom you lived. You won't think me so stupid as to believe that you don't know. It was doubtless your father, or your uncle or your brother, or at least some playmate! Hauser! Assume that you were in the presence of God, and God should ask you: Where do you come from, where is your home, where the place where you were born? Who gave you your false name and what is your real name, which you received in your cradle? Who was your teacher and who taught you to deceive people? What would you in your agony of soul answer, what would you answer to almighty God if he demanded a justification, an atonement, for the deceit which you have practiced?"

Caspar stared breathlessly at the teacher. His blood stood still. The whole world seemed to turn upside down.

"What would you answer?" repeated Quandt in a tone between hope and fear; it seemed to him that he was on the point of penetrating into the closed citadel.

Caspar got up heavily and said with a quivering mouth: "I would answer, you are not God if you demand that of me."

Quandt jumped back and struck his hands together. "You blasphemer!" he exclaimed with a penetrating voice. Then he stretched out his right arm and exclaimed: "Get out of my way, you lecher, you cursed liar! Get out, you infamous boy! Don't sully the air here any longer!"

Caspar turned around, and while he was feeling for the door handle, the clock on the wall back of him hammered out ten strokes into the noise of the storm.

Sighing and sleepless Quandt tossed all night on his pillow. He probably regretted his impetuosity, for in the course of the next day he tried to make an approach to Caspar. The boy, however, remained cold and withdrawn. In the evening, Quandt began to talk about Herr Fliessen; he said that he had inquired and called out jokingly to Caspar: "Eighteen grandchildren, Caspar; there are eighteen. Now, do you see that I was right?"

Caspar remained silent.

"But, Hauser, you don't eat any more," said Frau Quandt with concern.

"I have no appetite," replied Caspar, "I have no sooner begun to eat before I already have enough."

On Wednesday, the eleventh of December, Quandt came home to lunch late and much excited. On the way home from school he had had an angry dispute with a driver who had shamefully beaten a horse in the steep Pfarrgasse, because it could not pull the heavily laden wagon up to the market. Quandt had reproached the rough churl and called several citizens to witness his inhuman brutality. For this the driver had gone at him with uplifted whip and had yelled to him to go to the devil and not to meddle in matters which did not concern him. "Thank God I remember the man's name, I shall report him to the police-lieutenant," concluded Quandt. He did not grow tired of describing how the poor jade had constantly strained in vain at the traces of the cart and how the dark blood had oozed from under his ribs. "The rascal," he said, "I'll teach him to abuse an animal thus."

Later on, after Caspar had left, his wife asked whether it had not struck him that Caspar had not uttered a word about this incident.

"Yes, he was quite silent, I noticed it," corroborated Quandt.

Half an hour later he went into Caspar's room and asked him to take the written complaint against the cart driver to Hickers lodgings. At three o'clock Caspar returned with the news that the lieutenant had taken a vacation of several days and had left on a trip.

27.   Aenigma Sui Temporis

It happened two days later, on Friday, as Caspar was about to leave the court, shortly after twelve, that he was addressed by a stranger in the hall in front of the lower stairs. The gentleman, apparently a very distinguished man, tall and slender, wearing a dark beard over his cheeks and chin, asked Caspar to grant him a few minutes' interview.

Caspar was startled, for the voice was one of great urgency and very respectful.

They went a few steps to one side of the staircase, where no one could come upon them. The stranger smiled encouragingly when he noticed Caspar's shy manner, and began at once in the same urgent and respectful way: "So you are Caspar Hauser? You have been he until today. Tomorrow you will lay aside this name. How the first glance at your face told me and moved me. Prince! My Prince! Allow me to kiss your hand."

He bent down quickly and respectfully kissed Caspar's hand.

Caspar had no words. He looked like someone whose heart had suddenly stood still.

"I come from the court, I come as the envoy of your mother, I have come to take you away," continued the stranger, not less quickly, not less respectfully. "I assume that you have been ready for this for a long time. Nevertheless we must be on our guard. We have great obstacles to circumvent. You must fly with me. Everything is ready. The question is only whether you are willing to trust yourself to me without reserve and whether I may depend upon your absolute silence?"

How could Caspar be in a condition to make any reply to this? He looked into the man's face, which seemed to him unusual, indeed romantic in every respect, and with stupid attention he fastened his gaze upon the countless little pockmarks which showed upon the stranger's nose and cheeks.

"Your silence is eloquent for me," said the stranger with a quick bow. "The plan is this: you are to be in the Court Garden tomorrow at four o'clock, next to the poplar grove when one comes from the Freiberg house. From there you will be conducted to a carriage which will be waiting. The oncoming darkness will favor our flight. Come without a coat just as you are; you will find clothes suitable to your position. At the first halt for rest, at the boundary—which we shall reach in three hours—you will change your clothes. I am unknown to you. You should not give your faith and trust to an unknown person. Before you get into the carriage I shall give you a token by which you will recognize with certainty that I have been given full power by your mother to execute this plan."

Caspar did not budge. But his whole body swayed a little as if he had become numb, and the wind was threatening to bowl him over.

"May I regard it all as settled?" inquired the stranger.

He was obliged to repeat the question. Then Caspar nodded—seriously, heavily—and suddenly he felt as if his throat were burning.

"Will you be at the set place at the set hour, my Prince?"

My Prince! Caspar turned pale as a corpse. He looked again at the pock-marks, with devouring attention. Then he nodded again with a gesture which had the appearance of coldness or of sleepiness.

The stranger lifted his hat with a gesture of humble politeness and then left, disappearing in the direction of the Schwanengasse.

During the whole incident, which had lasted eight or ten minutes, not a single word had passed Caspar's lips.

Was it joy that Caspar felt? Was joy of such a consistency that it froze one to the very marrow, that a constant shudder ran down one's back like cold water?

He walked only half a dozen steps at a time and then stood still because he felt the earth sinking under his feet. People, get out of my way, he thought; snow, don't blow upon me; wind, don't be so wild. He looked at his hand, and with the tip of his finger touched the place which the stranger had kissed, staring thoughtfully.

Why are the shoemakers still at work, it's noon, he thought, as he walked by a store. Shudders ran constantly down his spine from the nape of his neck.

It was fine to know that with every step, with every glance, with every thought time passed. That's the only thing which matters now—that time should pass.

When he got home he told the maid that he did not care to eat anything, and locked himself in his room. He went to the window and with the tears pouring down his cheeks he thought: "Ducatus has come."

His thoughts had something of the nocturnal flight of a wild bird. Up to today I was Caspar Hauser, he thought, tomorrow I shall be someone else, what am I now? Yesterday I was still a little scrivener and to-morrow I shall perhaps wear a blue coat with gold braid; and Ducatus shall bring me a sword also, long and narrow, and straight as a reed. But is it all true? Can it all be true? Certainly it can be, for it must.

Not until it was completely dark did Caspar make a light. The teacher's wife sent up to ask whether he did not want to eat something. He asked for a piece of bread and a glass of milk. This was brought. Then he began to clear out his drawers; he threw a whole bundle of papers and letters into the fire, his copybooks and library he put in punctilious order. He opened a chest, and from under a lot of odds and ends he pulled forth the little wooden horse, which he still retained from his imprisonment in the Vestner tower. He looked at it a long time: it was white lacquer with black spots, and had a tail which came down to the board on which it stood. Oh, little horse, he thought, you have accompanied me many years; what shall I do with you now? I will come back and get you and I will build you a silver stable. Then he placed the toy carefully on a little corner table near the window.

It may well surprise one that such a spirit as his—so endowed with presentiment, so filled with many experiences — should from the first instant of a supposed change in his fate have fallen into such blind confidence, that no spark of distrust, of fear, of doubt or even of surprised astonishment glimmered in him. A procedure so far removed from tangible reality, so adventurous in its suddenness, so simple and stark that a schoolboy, a child, an insane person would have found difficulty in accepting it—and he who had seen so many people's faces undisguised or with the mask removed by crime, he to whom the world was nothing but the nest disturbed by a boy's hand to which the swallow returns from the south, he with unflinching confidence seized the unknown hand stretched out to him from the unknown darkness, the stiff, cold, silent hand.

But he no longer had any other hope. Or, indeed, it was not a question of hope at all. Here was the matter-of-course ending, the future certainty, the unquestioned which no word of human speech, not even a thought, a conception, a vision could approach and which fulfills itself in the same predetermined way as the rising of the sun when day breaks. Oh, you weary driven limbs, you fetters on these limbs, you slothful minutes, you silent hours! The plaster still crackles in the wall, the dog still barks in the distance, the storm still blows the snow against the window, the light of the candle still flickers and all this is full of malice, because it seems so permanent and passes so slowly.

At nine o'clock he went to bed. He slept soundly; later in the night he heard the church clock strike every quarter of an hour. At times he raised himself and looked anxiously into the dark. Then came a dream, in which sleep and waking melted imperceptibly into one another. And he dreamed that he was standing in front of a mirror and he thought: how curious, I have such a certain sensation of the smooth surface of the mirror, and yet I am merely dreaming. He awoke, or thought that he awoke, left his bed, or thought that he did so, occupied himself in the room, lay down again, fell asleep, awoke once more and wondered: did I merely dream that about the mirror? Now he walked up to the mirror, saw his reflected picture, thought that there was something strange about it, which repelled him, and covered the mirror with a cloth which had blue and gold edges. When he had lain down and really awakened after a while he realized that it had all been a dream, for the mirror was in no way covered over.

It was a long night.

The next morning he went as usual to the court. He performed his task of copying, as if with veiled eyes. At eleven o'clock he shut up the ink well, put everything neatly in order, here too, and left silently.

Quandt was away at noon on account of a teachers' conference. Caspar sat down at the table with Frau Quandt. She talked constantly of the weather. "The storm blew the chimney from the roof," she said, "and tailor Wust next door was almost killed by the falling bricks."

Caspar looked out silently. He could hardly see the building opposite. Rain and snow, mixed, whirled through the darkened street.

Caspar ate only his soup; when the meat came, he got up and went into his room.

Promptly at three he came down again, wearing only his old brown suit and without an overcoat.

"Where are you going, Hauser?" called the teacher's wife from the kitchen.

"I must go to the General Commissioner's to call for something," he replied calmly.

"Without an overcoat? In such cold weather?" asked the woman with surprise, as she came to the threshold. He looked at her absent-mindedly and then said: "Goodbye, Frau Quandt," and left.

Before he closed the front door he threw a farewell glance into the hall, upon the curved balustrade of the steps, at the old brown cupboard with the brass hinges standing between the kitchen and the living-room, upon the ash-barrel in the corner which was filled with potato peelings, cheese rinds, bones, chips of wood and bits of broken glass, and at the cat, which constantly glided about here in search of tit-bits. In spite of the lightning-like speed with which he looked at these things it seemed to Caspar that he had never seen them more clearly and never so singularly before.

When the latch had caught on the closing door the quite unbearable pressure which had constricted his breast relaxed a little, and his lips moved in a shallow smile.

I will write to the teacher, he thought, or no, it will be better to come myself. When the winter is over, I will come and drive up in front of the house in the carriage; I'll arrange it for the afternoon when he is at home. When he walks up to the gate, I will not reach out my hand to him; in my handsome clothes he will, of course, not know me! He will make a deep bow. "Will Your Grace be so kind as to enter?" he will say. When I am in the room I'll place myself in front of him and ask: "Do you know me now?" He will fall on his knees, but I will give him my hand and say: "Do you realize now that you were unjust to me?" He will realize it. "There now," say I, "show me your children and send for the police-lieutenant." I will bring presents to the children and when the lieutenant comes to him I shan't speak, only stare at him, just stare.

In front of the Gumbertus Church the clock struck half past three. It was still much too early. On the lower market place Caspar walked all around the houses. In front of the rectory he remained standing thoughtfully a while. In consequence of his internal heat he scarcely felt the cold. He saw only a few people who passed quickly by, as if driven by the wind.

When in front of the Court Drug Store he turned to the right towards the passageway by the Castle; the clock struck quarter of four. Then someone called; he looked up, the stranger of yesterday stood next to him. He wore a coat with several collars and over these again a fur collar. He bowed and said a few polite words. Caspar did not understand him, for the wind was so strong that one would have had to scream in order to be heard. Therefore the stranger merely made a gesture, by which he begged Caspar to be allowed to go with him. Obviously he too was on his way to the appointed tryst.

It was only a few steps to the Court Garden. The stranger opened the little gate and allowed Caspar to pass first. Caspar walked ahead as if it must be thus. A mixture of ingenuous humility and quiet pride showed in his face, only to change with curious suddenness into an expression of horror, for the moment was too strong; he could not bear the force of it. In the space of time which he needed to walk from the little gate over the densely snow-covered square of the Orange Grove to the first lane of trees, he lived through, within himself, a series of quite unrelated scenes out of the distant past, a phenomenon which students of the psychic life can trace back to the same roots as the fact that someone falling from a tower, during the duration of his fall, sees his whole past glide by before him. He saw, for example, the blackbird with its wings spread out, lying on the table; then he saw with uncommon clearness the water-pitcher from which he had drunk in his dungeon; then he saw a beautiful gold chain which Stanhope had shown him among his treasures, and with this was connected the pleasant sensation which Stanhope's fine white hands had excited in him; then he saw himself in the hall of the Castle of Nurnberg, where Daumer had taken him; and his eye rested on the soft line of a curved Gothic window with a delight which he had certainly not felt at the time.

They came to a cross-road where the stranger hurried ahead, and with his arm raised made some kind of sign. Caspar saw two other persons behind the bushes, whose faces were completely hidden by their upturned coat collars.

"Who are they?" he asked, and hesitated, because he assumed that this was the place which had been agreed upon.

His glance sought the carriage. The snow storm, however, prevented his seeing more than ten yards ahead.

"Where is the carriage?" he asked. As the stranger did not answer either question, he looked helplessly over toward the two men back of the bushes. They came nearer, or at least it seemed so. They called something toward the pockmarked man, first the one, then the other. Then they both drew back again and stood on the other side of the road.

The stranger turned around, felt in the pocket of his coat, brought forth a little lavender-colored bag and said in a hoarse voice: "Open that; inside of it you will find the token which your mother gave us."

Caspar took the little bag. While he was trying to untie the thread by which it was bound, the stranger lifted a long shining object in his clenched hand and struck with it against Caspar's breast.

What is that, thought Caspar, dismayed. He felt something ice cold gliding deep into his flesh. Oh, God, that cuts, he thought, and at the same time swayed. He let the bag fall.

Oh, monstrous, monstrous consternation! He snatched toward the branch of a tree and attempted to scream, but he could not. Suddenly his knees gave way. Everything turned black before his eyes. He wanted to ask the stranger to help him, but the man's feet, which a second before he could still see, had disappeared. The blackness before his eyes left him again and he looked around; there was no longer anyone there, the two men behind the bush were no longer there either.

He crept along the shrubbery a little, on all fours, bending his head down in order to protect his face from the wet snow which the wind drove against him. He made a few motions with his body as if seeking a hole in the ground into which he could slip, but then could go no further and remained sitting. It seemed to him that something was gurgling inside of his body. He was now miserably cold.

I'd like to see what's in the bag, he thought, while his teeth were chattering. Oh, monstrous fright, which kept him from looking toward the place where the stranger had stood!

If I only knew a word which would make me feel easier, he thought, like a person accustomed to protect himself by magic formulas. And he said twice: "Ducatus."

What a miracle. Suddenly he felt well. He thought that he could get up and go home. He got up. He saw that he could walk. After he had taken a few stumbling steps he began to run. It seemed to him as if his body were without weight, it seemed to him as if he were flying. He ran, ran, ran. To the gate of the garden, across the Schlossplatz, over the market-place, past the church, to Kronacher Buck, to the hall of Quandt's house, ran, ran, ran.

Bathed in sweat he dashed into the hall. Further he could not go; gasping, he leaned against the wall. The maid was the first to see him. Horrified over his appearance, she uttered a piercing scream. Thereupon Quandt came out of the room, his wife followed him.

Caspar gazed toward him, but did not speak; he merely pointed to his breast! "What has happened?" asked Quandt roughly and curtly.

"Court Garden—stabbed," stammered Caspar.

And Quandt, we see him simper. Nothing else: we see him simper. And where the ages, festively arrayed in purple, as the angels of God, walk up to us face to face and implore us not to distort facts there is nothing to reply — but that Quandt simpered, simpered curiously.

"Where were you stabbed, my dear fellow?" he drawled.

Caspar again pointed to his breast.

Quandt opened his coat, vest and shirt to look at the wound. Certainly there was a stab, but not bigger than a hazel-nut. But not the slightest trace of blood could be noticed. A wound without blood does not happen, that's like a statement without a proof.

"So, stabbed," said Quandt. "Let us turn around at once and you will show me the place in the Court Garden where you say this occurred," he added energetically. "What did you have to do at this hour and in this weather in the Court Garden? Come along, now. The matter must be cleared up without delay."

Caspar did not contradict. He dragged himself on to the street again by the teacher's side. Quandt seized hold of him, Caspar slid along like a cripple.

After a long silence, Quandt said in a restrained voice: "This time you have played your stupidest trick, Hauser. This time the matter won't end so well as at Professor Daumer's, that I can give you in writing."

Caspar stood still, cast a quick glance toward heaven and said: "God—knows."

"Spare me your tricks," stormed Quandt, "I know what I know. No matter how much you may call upon God, that won't help you with me, for you are a godless creature from the bottom up. I can only advise you no longer to play the mute of Portici, but rather to confess at once. You want to frighten people a little, want to create a little unpleasant excitement. Stabbed? Who would have stabbed you? Perhaps to have taken a few pitiful coppers out of your pocket. Such nonsense! Don't walk so slowly, Hauser, my time is short."

"The bag—I want to get it," stammered Caspar in low tones.

"What kind of a bag?"

"The man—gave me."

"What man?"

"The man who stabbed me."

"But, Hauser, Hauser, the thing cries to heaven! Do you suppose that I in the least believe in this man? As little as I believe in Black Peter! Do you imagine that I am for a moment in doubt as to the real perpetrator? Do confess! Confess that you stabbed yourself a little. I will be silent about the matter once more; I will be lenient instead of just."

Caspar was crying.

Just before the Court Garden he suddenly collapsed. Quandt was perplexed. Some men came along the road, and he asked them to take the boy home, he himself would go to the police station. The men had to wait a considerable time before Caspar had recovered a little, and even then it was difficult to persuade him to walk.

The doctors later said that it was incomprehensible that Caspar, with the frightful wound in his breast, had been able to traverse the path from the Court Garden to the teacher's house, then from the teacher's house to the Schlossplatz and finally from the

Schlossplatz back to the house again, the first time running, the second time on Quandt's arm, the third time half dragged by the men, in all more than sixteen hundred paces.

When Quandt started for the town hall it had become dark. The man on duty explained that without a special order from the Mayor, who was at the Bath Restaurant, the report could not be accepted officially. The teacher gossiped with him for a while, then unwillingly and irritably he went to the Kleinschrott Bath House, which lay a quarter of an hour outside of the city, where he found the Mayor drinking beer with his cronies. Quandt presented the case. They were astonished, they doubted, they discussed, they went through much red tape, after which the formal report was allowed to be made. At six o'clock the interesting legal report was given over by the light of candles and lanterns to the city judiciary for further investigation.

Quandt returned home. In the street in front of his house he found many people, persons of every condition, who had turned out in spite of the bad weather and remained silent in a way that startled Quandt. He went at once to Caspar's room; he had been put to bed. Dr. Horlacher was there. He had already examined the wound.

"How is it?" asked Quandt.

The doctor replied that there was no ground for serious anxiety. "That's what I thought," replied Quandt.

Now Hofrat Hofmann appeared. A military policeman had given him the lavender-colored bag, which had been found at the spot of the crime.

"Do you know this bag?" asked the Hofrat.

With eyes shining with fever, Caspar looked at the bag which the Hofrat opened. There was a slip of paper in it which appeared at first to be covered with hieroglyphics.

Frau Quandt stood near and shook her head. She pulled her husband aside and said: "That is curious, Caspar always folds his letters just the way that paper in the bag is folded." Quandt nodded, then he walked up to the Hofrat, who first looked carefully at the note and then asked for a hand mirror.

"It is probably mirror-writing," said Quandt, smilingly.

"Yes," replied the Hofrat, "a curious piece of childishness."

He placed the mirror and the writing opposite one another and read aloud. "Caspar Hauser will be able to tell you exactly what

I look like and who I am. In order to save Hauser the trouble, for he might be unable to discuss the matter, I will tell you myself where I come from. I have come from the Bavarian frontier, by the river. I will even betray my name to you. M.L.O."

"That sounds almost contemptuous," said the Hofrat after a surprised silence.

Quandt nodded bitterly.

When Caspar heard these words read aloud, his head fell heavily into his pillow and boundless despair pictured itself in his features. He closed his mouth with an expression as though he never wanted to speak, again. And that he could have spoken, a fact which this "M.L.O." obviously had not calculated on, he regarded as a painful triumph well into his fever.

Quandt, with the note which the Hofrat had given him in his hands, wandered up and down excitedly. "These are pretty tricks," he exclaimed, "pretty tricks you are playing in vain for the pity of your generation, Hauser. You deserve a whipping, that's what you deserve."

The Hofrat frowned. "Calm yourself, Herr Quandt, that's enough," he said with an unusually serious voice. Before he left he promised to send the circuit doctor the next morning, from which it was evident that he thought there was no immediate danger.

Meantime the doctor—urged by Frau von Imhoff—came that same evening. It was Dr. Albert, the Medizinalrat. He examined Caspar with great care and looked grave when he had finished. Quandt, curiously irritated by this, said almost challengingly: "No blood is flowing from the wound."

"The blood is flowing on the inside," replied the Medizinalrat, casting a glance at the teacher. He placed a mustard plaster on the heart and recommended the greatest possible quiet.

Quandt struck his forehead. "Is it possible that the boy in his thoughtlessness should have injured himself seriously?" he said to his wife. Frau Quandt remained silent.

"I doubt it, I must doubt it," continued Quandt. "Just see yourself, the boy generally so given to complaining, doesn't utter a word about any pain."

"He does not answer if he's asked either." continued his wife.

At nine o'clock Caspar began to be delirious. Quandt was determined not to believe in this delirium. When Caspar wanted to jump out of bed he screamed at him: "Don't be such a repulsive impostor, Hauser! Get back into bed, quickly!"

Pfarrer Fuhrmann was just coming into the room and heard this. "Why, Quandt, Quandt!" he said, horrified. "Show some gentleness, Quandt, in the name of our religion!"

"Oh," replied Quandt, shaking his head, "gentleness is wasted here. In Nurnberg, where he played the same wretched comedy, he behaved the same way, and they tell me it took two men to hold him. As far as I am concerned, I won't put up with such a comedy."

Frau von Imhoff had sent a nurse from the hospital, who watched by Caspar's bed during the night. He dozed from two to three hours.

Early the next morning the legal authorities appeared: Caspar was clearly conscious. Upon the question of the investigating attorney he said that a strange gentleman had told him to meet him in the Court Garden by the artesian well.

"For what purpose?"

"I don't know."

"Didn't he say anything about it?"

"Yes, he said one could see the kinds of mineral in the well."

"And that was enough to make you go with him? What did he look like?"

Caspar gave a short, rough mumbling description and told how the stranger had stabbed him. That was all that could be gotten out of him.

They endeavored to find witnesses. Witnesses appeared. Too late to pursue the perpetrator. The first declaration had already been irresponsibly delayed by Quandt's complicity. When they wanted to examine the traces of blood on the spot of the crime, it turned out that too many people had been there in the meantime, and had tramped on the snow. So they had from the beginning to give up any hope of gaining anything from this important evidence.

There were witnesses enough. The landlady of the Zirkel in the Rosengasse said that about two o'clock a man had come to her house and inquired at what time there was a return coach to Nordlingen. The man was about thirty-four years old, of medium size, with a brown skin and pockmarked.

He had worn a blue coat with a fur collar, a round black hat, green trousers and boots with yellow screw spurs. He had carried a riding crop in his hand. He had only stayed five minutes and had spoken little; it was striking that he did not want to say where he was lodging.

Assessor Donner described in the same way a man whom he had seen in the Court Garden next to the lane of poplars at three o'clock and in the company of two other men whom the assessor had not observed.

A glazier named Leich, a little before four o'clock, went from his home along the New Road through the Poststrasse to the Promenade and from there across the Schlossplatz. From the Castle he saw two men leave the bridle-path on the left, and go to the Court Garden. He recognized Caspar Hauser as one of them. When the two came to the lantern post at the corner of the bridle-path, Caspar Hauser turned around, and looked up toward the Schlossplatz, so that the observer was able to see him once more clearly. At the fence the stranger stood still and permitted Hauser to go ahead with a polite gesture. The workman thought to himself: how can the gentlemen go walking in such a storm and snow.

"Three-quarters of an hour later," the man continued, "when I came back from an errand at Cooper Pfaffenberger's, a lot of people were standing on the Schlossplatz, who were lamenting and saying that Hauser had been stabbed in the Court Garden."

And so on. A gardener's assistant, busy in the orange house, hears voices towards four o'clock. He looks out and sees a man in an overcoat running by. The man is running at a brisk gait. The voices are perhaps a rifle shot distant from the hothouse, not so far away as the Uz Monument. There were two voices, a bass and a high voice.

Next to the Willow Mill there lived a seamstress. Her window opens upon the Court Garden, she can see as far as the two lanes which lead to the wooden temple. As dusk is beginning to fall she sees the man with the coat; he walks out of the new wrought-iron gate and descends the ravine toward the Rezat meadow. He is dismayed when he finds himself faced by a swollen stream. He turns around and goes toward the bridge along the Eiberstrasse and disappears. Of his face the woman was only able to discern the black crooked beard.

The clerk Dillmann, too, had something to say. It was an unalterable habit of the old clerk, no matter what the weather was, to walk every afternoon for two hours in the Court Garden. He saw Caspar and the stranger. He was certain, however, that Caspar had not preceded the stranger, but had walked behind him. "He followed him as a calf follows the butcher to the slaughter-house," he said.

Too late, too late was this zeal. Too late the publication of warrants, as well as descents by the police. It was no longer any use, even if they should have changed the course of the river Rezat in order that they might perhaps discover the murderous instrument which the unknown perpetrator might have thrown away in his flight.

What did the witnesses matter? What did the cross-examination matter? What did the evidence matter by which a dilatory justice sought to cover over its inefficiency with gestures of efficiency. It was said that the investigations were conducted planlessly and brainlessly. It was said that a mysterious hand was at work whose machinations culminated in gradually and intentionally obliterating the real traces, and purposely misleading the attention of the authorities. Who it was that said this, one could naturally not find out, for public opinion—a thing as cowardly as it is intangible^— only expresses itself in enigmas from behind safe entrenchments! And in this case it soon became silent; here where calumny, malice, lying, stupidity and hypocrisy ground a beautiful picture of humanity between mill-wheels, until nothing remained of it but a pitiful fairy-tale with which the inhabitants of this neighborhood entertain themselves before the fire on cold winter evenings.

On Sunday afternoon Quandt met young Feuerbach, the philosopher, on the street.

"How's Hauser?" he asked the teacher.

"Oh, he's quite out of danger, thank you for asking, doctor," answered Quandt, talkatively. "Jaundice has set in, but that is said to be the usual sequel to any great excitement. I am convinced that he will be able to leave his bed in a few days."

They talked a little while of other matters, principally of the recently planned steam railroad between Nurnberg and Furth, an undertaking against which Quandt uttered a volley of skepticism; then he bade good-by to the silent young man, with the gratitude of a gossip who has had an opportunity to talk, and hurried home, smiling constantly to himself. He was in a very benign frame of mind, in a frame of mind in which one is ready to be charitable to one's bitterest enemies. Why? The gods may know. Was it on account of the beautiful day? One must not forget that in Quandt, too, there was a kind of poet; or was it the approach of Christmas, which promises every good Christian a species of renewal of his soul? Or was it, after all, the fact that at present so many distinguished and unusual people visited his modest home, and that he, in his unpretentious surroundings, occupied a position of undreamed-of importance? Enough said, however, all that might be; he was content with himself, and consequently his smile proceeded from the very purest source.

In front of his house he met the police lieutenant. "Ah, you're back from your vacation." Thus he greeted him, with thoughtless friendliness. Immediately afterwards he said: "I still have a bone to pick with you."

Hickel pressed his eyes together and looked as if he wanted to laugh.

They went upstairs together.

Caspar was sitting up in bed, with the upper part of his body naked, and leaning against a mound of pillows, stiff as a clay figure, his face as gray as pumice stone, the skin of his body as radiantly white as a magnesium flame. The doctor had just taken off the bandage and was washing the wound. Besides him there was a court clerk present. He had seated himself at the table; a registry blank lay before him, on which were written the laconic words: "The wounded man persists in the deposition which he has made hitherto." One could not have expressed oneself better, or more elegantly, about a street thief who had been arrested.

Caspar had scarcely seen Hickel enter, than he raised his head, which had fallen to one side, like the broken calix of a flower, and with wide-open eyes, in which an unspeakable fright lay, stared into the face of the newcomer.

Without speaking, Hickel threateningly raised his finger. This gesture seemed to excite Caspar's fright to the utmost. He folded his hands and murmured with a groan: "Don't come near; I did not do it myself."

"But, Hauser, what are you thinking of," exclaimed Hickel with the kind of joviality which one might display in a tavern, while his yellow teeth gleamed between his full lips. "I only raised my finger at you because you went into the Court Garden without permission. Do you perhaps wish to deny that?"

"I must ask you to avoid any discussion," warned the doctor, not without anger. He had renewed the bandage and drew the teacher aside, and said in low and earnest tones: "I must inform you that Hauser will probably not live through the night." With open mouth Quandt stared at the physician. His knees became as soft as butter. "Why? What?" he murmured. "Is that possible?" He looked at all those in the room slowly, one after the other, while his face resembled that of a person who was about to sit down comfortably to eat, and from whom the dishes, plates, knife, fork—yes, even the whole table is suddenly snatched away by magic. "Come with me, Herr Quandt," said Hickel in a hoarse voice; he was standing by the tiled stove and rubbing his hands with meaningless assiduity against the tiles.

Quandt nodded and walked ahead mechanically.

"Is it possible?" he murmured again, as he stood upon the steps. He looked at the lieutenant, as if looking for aid. "Oh," he continued elegiacally, "we certainly did our part honestly. We really did not fail in faithful care."

"Just quit that nonsense, Quandt," answered the lieutenant roughly. "Tell me rather what Hauser has said in his delirium. "

"Nonsense, nothing but nonsense," replied Quandt, anxiously.

"Have a care, Herr Quandt, just look down there," exclaimed Hickel, bending over the railing.

Why, what's there?" was Quandt's frightened reply.

You don't see anything! The deuce take it; I don't either! We neither of us see anything, it appears." He laughed curiously, drew himself up again, erect as a candle, and coughed dryly. Then he left, while Quandt gazed after him with considerable surprise.

And indeed what is to become of the world if people like Hickel take to seeing ghosts. Upon their shoulders rest the principles of order, of obedience, and all the officially recognized virtues. And although possibly matters are so disposed in this peculiar case that this monster, endowed with a mixture of praiseworthy qualities, nevertheless felt his conscience stir, then it must be explained that this bad conscience was blessed with such a martial appearance that it developed an enviable appetite for all its meals, and that it formed the softest pillow for an incomparably healthy sleep which no fire alarm or Te Deum could have disturbed.

In Caspar's room, the registrar had begun his questioning again. Caspar was to tell him whether a third person had been present while he had spoken with the stranger in the Appellate Court.

Caspar answered limply that he had not noticed anyone, only in front of the gate there had been people. "Poor people always wait for me there," he said, "for example, a certain Feigelein woman, to whom I sometimes gave a copper, or the widow of the weaver Weigel."

The registrar wanted to question him further, but Caspar whispered: "Tired—very tired."

"How do you feel, Hauser?" inquired the nurse.

"Tired," he replied, "I'll soon leave this wretched world." For a while he screamed and talked aloud to himself, then he became quite still again.

He saw a light, which slowly went out. He heard sounds, which seemed to come from the inside of his ears; they sounded as if one were to strike upon a metal bell with a hammer. He perceived a wide lonely plain in the dusk. A human figure runs quickly over it. Oh, God! It is Schildknecht. Why are you running so, Schildknecht? he calls to him. "Am in a hurry, a great hurry," the latter replied. Suddenly Schildknecht shrivels up until he becomes a spider climbing on a glowing thread up to the branch of a huge tree. Tears of horror fall like rain from Caspar's eyes.

He saw a curious building. It resembled a colossal cupola, it had no gate, no door, no window. But Caspar could fly, and he flew up and looked through a circular opening into the interior, which was filled with a heavenly blue air. On sky-blue tiles there stood a woman. In front of this woman there appeared a person, scarcely more visible than a shadow, who told her that Caspar Hauser had died. The woman raised her arms and cried with grief until the rafters resounded. Then the floor opened up and a long procession of people appeared, all of whom were weeping. And Caspar saw that their hearts trembled and shook like live fish in the hands of fishermen. And one of them, who was armed, and carried a sword, stepped forward and uttered tremendous words which revealed the whole secret. And all of those who listened pressed their hands over their ears, closed their eyes, and fell upon the floor.

Then everything was changed. Caspar felt now full of a wonderful strength. He felt the metals in the earth—from deep below they drew him toward them—and he felt the stones, which had veins of bronze. Among these there were many kinds of seeds and the little roots sprouted, and the little roots spread, and the stalks quivered and grew. And wells sprang out of the earth like fountains, and the welcome sun shone upon their spray. And in the midst of creation there stood a tree with a wide top and countless branches; red berries grew from these branches, and at the top of the tree the berries formed a heart. Inside in the trunk blood flowed, and where the bark was broken, black-red drops oozed forth.

In the midst of this tumult of frenzied images and sick fantasies, it seemed to Caspar as if someone carried him into a room where there was no air left to breathe. Struggling and resisting were of no avail, something carried him thither, and a cool wind blew over his hair, and his fingers bent inwards as if he were seeking to seize hold of something. An unutterable exhaustion accompanied the vain struggle.

Out in the road the Nurnberg mail coach drove by, and the postillion blew his horn.

Many people came, until evening, to inquire how he was doing. Frau von Imhoff remained sitting a long time at his bed.

At eight o'clock the nurse sent for Herr Fuhrmann, who appeared very promptly. He laid his hand on Caspar's forehead. With big anxious eyes Caspar looked about; his shoulders shook. He made movements with his finger upon the bed cover as if he wanted to write. But that did not last long.

"You once told me, dear Hauser, that you trusted God and wanted to fight every battle with his help," said the clergyman.

"I don't know," whispered Caspar.

"Have you already prayed today and asked God for His succor?"

Caspar nodded.

"And how did you feel after that? Did you not feel strengthened?"

Caspar was silent. 'Do you not want to pray again?"

"I'm too weak; my thoughts leave me at once." And after a while he said to himself with a curious refrain: "The tired head begs for rest."

"Then I will pray," continued the clergyman, "pray with me silently."

"Father, not my—but thy will be done," concluded Caspar, breathing with difficulty.

"Who prayed thus?"

"The Saviour."

"And when?"

"Before—his—death."

At this word his body struggled up and his face quivered painfully. He gritted his teeth and screamed three times piercingly: "Where am I?"

"But, Hauser, you are in your bed," said Quandt, soothingly. "It often happens that sick people think that they are in a different place," he explained, turning to the clergyman.

"Give him something to drink," said the latter.

Frau Quandt brought a glass of fresh water.

When Caspar had drunk, Quandt wiped the cold sweat from his forehead. He himself was shaking in every limb. He bent over the boy and asked urgently, imploring him ceremoniously: "Hauser, Hauser, have you nothing more to say? Look at me once, quite honestly, Hauser! Have you nothing more to confess?"

Then Caspar in great agony of soul seized the teacher's hand. "Oh, God—oh, God—to have to pass on this way in shame and disgrace!" he exclaimed painfully.

These were his last words. He turned a little on his right side with his face to the wall. Every limb of his body died separately.

Two days later he was buried. It was afternoon and the sky was a cloudless blue. The whole city was in commotion. A famous contemporary, who called Caspar Hauser the child of Europe, tells that at that hour the sun and the moon were to be seen in the heavens at the same time, the one in the west and the other in the east, and that both their discs shone with the same leaden light.

About a week and a half later, three days after Christmas, it was evening, and Quandt and his wife were about to go to bed, when sharp knocks were heard against the front door. Greatly frightened,

Quandt hesitated a while; only when the pounding was repeated did he take a light and go to open the door.

Outside stood Frau von Kannawurf. "Take me to Caspar's room," she said to the teacher. '

"Now? At night?" the latter dared to object.

"Now, at night," the woman insisted.

Her manner intimidated Quandt so that he silently stepped aside, allowing her to pass, and followed with the light. In Caspar's room there was little that reminded one of the dead boy. Everything was changed and put away. Only the little wooden horse still stood on the corner table near the window.

"Leave me alone," commanded Frau von Kannawurf. Quandt set down the candlestick and went silently away; he waited below on the step with his wife. "It is very good-natured of me to allow such a thing in my house," he grumbled.

With arms crossed, Clara von Kannawurf walked up and down the room. Her glance fell upon the table, where a copy of the post-mortem examination lay; herein it was stated that, after Caspar's death, the side wall of his heart was found to have been pierced through. Clara took the paper in both hands and tore it in her fists.

Of what avail was all grief and repentance! One cannot recreate the departed out of air; one cannot force the earth to give back her victim. Tears are soothing, but this mourner had no tears left. For her there were no longer any stars and the sky had lost its radiance; for her the grass no longer grew, and flowers had no odor left; for her days and nights had lost their relish and all human activity, even the existence of the elements, had rolled itself into a dark cloud of never-to-be-expiated sin.

Perhaps half an hour had passed before Clara came down again. She stood quite close to the teacher and, looking at him with wide-open eyes, said quiveringly and coldly: "Murderer!"

This was for Quandt about as if one were to hold burning sulphuric acid under his nose. As one may readily imagine, the good man had not the dimmest notion of what was going on; he was waiting in his dressing-gown and embroidered house-cap and bedroom slippers for the uninvited guest to leave his house, and suddenly a word is spoken which he does not expect to hear even in an evil dream.

"The woman is mad! I shall call her to account," he still raged in bed.

Clara was living at the Imhoffs'. She found her friend still up. Frau von Imhoff said that tomorrow they would go to the cemetery, because then the cross was to be put upon Caspar Hauser's grave. Clara's silence rested like an incubus upon Frau von Imhoff and she talked and talked —much about Caspar and about those surrounding him. Quandt intended to write a book in which he expected to prove minutely that Caspar had been a swindler; Hickel had left the service and moved from Ansbach, no one knew whither; all attempts to get any information about the terrible crime had been in vain.

Clara remained as if of stone. When they separated for the night, she said in low tones and with uncanny gentleness: "You, too, are his murderer."

Frau von Imhoff started back, but Clara continued in equally low and gentle tones: "Don't you know it; don't you want to know it? Are you hiding from the truth like Cain from the voice of God? Do you not know who he was? Do you think that the world will always be silent about it as it is silent now? He will arise, Bettine, and call us to a reckoning and cover our names with shame; he will poison the conscience of generations to come; he will be as powerful in his death as he was impotent in his life. The sun will bring it to light."

Hereupon Clara left the room as quietly as a shadow.

The next morning she left the house early. She visited her bellman on the tower of St. John's and sat a long time on the stone bench of the narrow gallery, looking far out over the wintry plain. But she did not see the snow, she only saw the blood which had flowed. She did not see the landscape, she only saw a stabbed heart.

Then she took her way to the cemetery. The grave-digger took her to the grave. Two workmen had just come and leaned a wooden cross against the trunk of a weeping willow.

A few minutes later the clergyman appeared. He recognized Clara and greeted her seriously and politely. She, without replying, looked past him; her glance rested upon the mound of the grave, covered with, dirty snow, and upon the workmen who now planted the cross at the head of the grave. On a large heart-shaped shield, fastened in the middle of the cross, stood the following words in white letters:

> Hic Jacet
> Casparus Hauser
> Enigma
> Sui Temporis
> Ignota Nativitas
> Occulta Mors

She read it, pressed her hands before her face and broke into a painful, piercing laugh. Suddenly, however, she became quite still. She turned to the clergyman and called to him: "Murderer."

At this moment several people came along the main path, persons who had intended to be present at the ceremony of erecting the cross: Herr and Frau von Imhoff, Herr von Stichaner, Dr. Albert, Hofrat Hofmann, Quandt and his wife. They saw the clergyman white and excited, and Everyone had the impression that something unpleasant was going on. Frau von Imhoff, full of premonition, hurried up to her friend and put her arms about her. But with a wild gesture Clara shook herself free, rushed toward the approaching group, and with a penetrating voice screamed: "You are murderers, murderers; murderers!"

She then ran out upon the street, where a number of people at once surrounded her, continuing to scream. Finally she was surrounded by some men and prevented from running further.

Quandt had once more been right. She had become insane. On the same day she was taken to an institution. In time her raving subsided, but her mind remained clouded.

Herr Fuhrmann took the scene at the grave very much to heart. He could not be satisfied when told that it was an insane person who had behaved so. Before his death, which came soon afterwards, he said to Frau von Imhoff, who had gone to see him: "I can no longer enjoy the world. Why did she complain of me? Why just of me? I loved Hauser."

"The unfortunate woman," replied Frau von Imhoff in low tones, "love alone was not enough for her."

"I bear no blame," continued the old man, "or not more than is the lot of mortals in general. Guilty we all are—all of us who wander here on earth. Life springs from guilt, or our ancestor in paradise would not have been allowed to sin. Nor can I absolve our dead friend. Of what use was it to dream about his origin? Where betrayal emanates from Everyone's mouth, a real man must take refuge in a circle of useful activities. But madmen hear only their own voices. Guiltless, my dear, guiltless is only God. May He have mercy upon my soul and that of the noble Caspar Hauser."

THE END

Printed in Great Britain
by Amazon